# Inclusive Leadership
―― The Essential ――
Leader-Follower Relationship

# SERIES IN APPLIED PSYCHOLOGY

EDWIN A. FLEISHMAN, GEORGE MASON UNIVERSITY,
JEANETTE N. CLEVELAND, PENNSYLVANIA STATE UNIVERSITY
SERIES EDITORS

---

**Gregory Bedny and David Meister**
The Russian Theory of Activity: Current Applications to Design and Learning

**Winston Bennett, David Woehr, and Charles Lance**
Performance Measurement: Current Perspectives and Future Challenges

**Michael T. Brannick, Eduardo Salas, and Carolyn Prince**
Team Performance Assessment and Measurement: Theory, Research, and Applications

**Jeanette N. Cleveland, Margaret Stockdale, and Kevin R. Murphy**
Women and Men in Organizations: Sex and Gender Issues at Work

**Aaron Cohen**
Multiple Commitments in the Workplace: An Integrative Approach

**Russell Cropanzano**
Justice in the Workplace: Approaching Fairness in Human Resource Management, Volume 1

**Russell Cropanzano**
Justice in the Workplace: From Theory to Practice, Volume 2

**David V. Day, Stephen Zaccaro, and Stanley M. Halpin**
Leader Development for Transforming Organizations: Growing Leaders for Tomorrow's Teams and Organizations

**James E. Driskell and Eduardo Salas**
Stress and Human Performance

**Sidney A. Fine and Steven F. Cronshaw**
Functional Job Analysis: A Foundation for Human Resources Management

**Sidney A. Fine and Maury Getkate**
Benchmark Tasks for Job Analysis: A Guide for Functional Job Analysis (FJA) Scales

**J. Kevin Ford, Steve W. J. Kozlowski, Kurt Kraiger, Eduardo Salas, and Mark S. Teachout**
Improving Training Effectiveness in Work Organizations

**Jerald Greenberg**
Organizational Behavior: The State of the Science, Second Edition

**Edwin Hollander**
Inclusive Leadership: The Essential Leader-Follower Relationship

**Uwe E. Kleinbeck, Hans-Henning Quast, Henk Thierry, and Hartmut Häcker**
Work Motivation

**Laura L. Koppes**
Historical Perspectives in Industrial and Organizational Psychology

**Ellen Kossek and Susan Lambert**
Work and Life Integration: Organizational, Cultural, and Individual Perspectives

**Martin I. Kurke and Ellen M. Scrivner**
Police Psychology into the 21st Century

**Joel Lefkowitz**
Ethics and Values in Industrial and Organizational Psychology

**Manuel London**
Job Feedback: Giving, Seeking, and Using Feedback for Performance Improvement, Second Edition

**Manuel London**
How People Evaluate Others in Organizations

**Manuel London**
Leadership Development: Paths to Self-Insight and Professional Growth

**Robert F. Morrison and Jerome Adams**
Contemporary Career Development Issues

**Michael D. Mumford**
Pathways to Outstanding Leadership: A Comparative Analysis of Charismatic, Ideological, and Pragmatic Leaders

**Michael D. Mumford, Garnett Stokes, and William A. Owens**
Patterns of Life History: The Ecology of Human Individuality

**Kevin Murphy**
A Critique of Emotional Intelligence: What are the Problems and How Can They Be Fixed?

**Kevin R. Murphy**
Validity Generalization: A Critical Review

**Kevin R. Murphy and Frank E. Saal**
Psychology in Organizations: Integrating Science and Practice

**Susan E. Murphy and Ronald E. Riggio**
The Future of Leadership Development

**Margaret A. Neal and Leslie Brett Hammer**
Working Couples Caring for Children and Aging Parents: Effects on Work and Well-Being

**Steven A. Y. Poelmans**
Work and Family: An International Research Perspective

**Robert E. Ployhart, Benjamin Schneider, and Neal Schmitt**
Staffing Organizations: Contemporary Practice and Theory, Third Edition

**Erich P. Prien, Jeffery S. Schippmann, and Kristin O. Prien**
Individual Assessment: As Practiced in Industry and Consulting

**Ned Rosen**
Teamwork and the Bottom Line: Groups Make a Difference

**Heinz Schuler, James L. Farr, and Mike Smith**
Personnel Selection and Assessment: Individual and Organizational Perspectives

**John W. Senders and Neville P. Moray**
Human Error: Cause, Prediction, and Reduction

**Kenneth S. Shultz and Gary A. Adams**
Aging and Work in the 21st Century

**Frank J. Smith**
Organizational Surveys: The Diagnosis and Betterment of Organizations through Their Members

**Dianna Stone and Eugene F. Stone-Romero**
The Influence of Culture on Human Resource Processes and Practices

**Kecia M. Thomas**
Diversity Resistance in Organizations

**George C. Thornton III and Rose Mueller-Hanson**
Developing Organizational Simulations: A Guide for Practitioners and Students

**George C. Thornton III and Deborah Rupp**
Assessment Centers in Human Resource Management: Strategies for Prediction, Diagnosis, and Development

**Yoav Vardi and Ely Weitz**
Misbehavior in Organizations: Theory, Research, and Management

**Patricia Voydanoff**
Work, Family, and Community

# Inclusive Leadership
## —— The Essential ——
## Leader-Follower Relationship

Edwin P. Hollander

Taylor & Francis Group
www.routledge.com

Routledge  
Taylor & Francis Group  
270 Madison Avenue  
New York, NY 10016

Routledge  
Taylor & Francis Group  
2 Park Square  
Milton Park, Abingdon  
Oxon OX14 4RN

© 2009 by Taylor & Francis Group, LLC  
Routledge is an imprint of Taylor & Francis Group, an Informa business

Printed in the United States of America on acid-free paper  
10 9 8 7 6 5 4 3 2 1

International Standard Book Number-13: 978-0-8058-6439-7 (Hardcover)

Except as permitted under U.S. Copyright Law, no part of this book may be reprinted, reproduced, transmitted, or utilized in any form by any electronic, mechanical, or other means, now known or hereafter invented, including photocopying, microfilming, and recording, or in any information storage or retrieval system, without written permission from the publishers.

**Trademark Notice:** Product or corporate names may be trademarks or registered trademarks, and are used only for identification and explanation without intent to infringe.

**Visit the Taylor & Francis Web site at**  
http://www.taylorandfrancis.com

**and the Routledge Web site at**  
http://www.routledge.com

*To our delightful grandchildren,
Rachel, Sean, Beatrice, and William, and
their Mom and Dad, Kim and Peter*

# CONTENTS

Series Foreword ..... xix
EDWIN A. FLEISHMAN AND JEANETTE N. CLEVELAND

Preface ..... xxi

About the Author ..... xxv

## PART 1. INTRODUCTION

Chapter 1   Overview of Inclusive Leadership ..... 3

Chapter 2   Historical Background of Modern Leadership Study ..... 21

Chapter 3   Applications and Implications of Inclusive Leadership ..... 37

## PART 2. LEADERSHIP-FOLLOWERSHIP ISSUES

Chapter 4   What Is the Crisis of Leadership? ..... 47

Chapter 5   Contemporary Trends in the Analysis of Leadership Processes ..... 55
WITH JAMES W. JULIAN

Chapter 6   The Essential Interdependence of Leadership and Followership ..... 67

Chapter 7   Women and Leadership ..... 73

Chapter 8   Leadership, Followership, Self, and Others ..... 81

Chapter 9   College and University Leadership from a Social Psychological Perspective ..... 91

Chapter 10   Presidential Leadership ..... 103

Chapter 11   Power and Leadership in Organizations ..... 117
WITH LYNN R. OFFERMANN

Chapter 12   Organizational Leadership and Followership: The Role of Interpersonal Relations ..... 129

Chapter 13   Legitimacy, Power, and Influence: A Perspective on Relational Features of Leadership   139

Chapter 14   Ethical Challenges in the Leader-Follower Relationship   149

Chapter 15   The Balance of Leadership and Followership: An Introduction   157
WITH LYNN R. OFFERMANN

## PART 3. CONFORMITY-NONCONFORMITY AND INDEPENDENCE

Chapter 16   Conformity, Status, and Idiosyncrasy Credit   163

Chapter 17   Some Current Issues in the Psychology of Conformity and Nonconformity   171
WITH RICHARD H. WILLIS

Chapter 18   Independence, Conformity, and Civil Liberties: Some Implications from Social Psychological Research   185

## PART 4. CONCLUSIONS

Chapter 19   Summing Up: Lessons from Experience   195

Afterword   A Career in Leadership: A Life in Psychology   199

Appendix   Development of Inclusive Leadership Scale (ILS-16)   221
Bibliography   223
Name Index   247
Subject Index   257

# DETAILED CONTENTS

Series Foreword .................................................. xix
EDWIN A. FLEISHMAN AND JEANETTE N. CLEVELAND
Preface ........................................................... xxi
About the Author ................................................ xxv

## PART 1. INTRODUCTION

**Chapter 1  Overview of Inclusive Leadership** ........................ 3

*Introduction* ...................................................... 3

*Passivity, Compliance, and Independence* ........................... 4

*Listening Is Respectful* ........................................... 4

*Foundations of Inclusive Leadership and the Content of This Book* ... 5

*Decision Making and Power Sharing* ................................. 6

*Ethics and Morality* ............................................... 6

*The Context of Inclusive Leadership* ............................... 7

*The Leader-Follower Relationship in Transactional and Transforming Leadership* ... 9

*Power Distance* ................................................... 10

*Leaders and Followers Are Not So Sharply Distinctive, Nor Are Leadership and Followership* ... 12

*Legitimacy and Credit* ............................................ 13

*Idiosyncrasy Credit* .............................................. 14

*The Dynamics of Leader Legitimacy* ................................ 16

*"Critical Incidents" Research on Follower Perceptions of Leaders* ... 17

*Charismatic Leadership* ........................................... 17

| | |
|---|---|
| *Relationship to Transformational and Transactional Leadership* | 18 |
| *Critique of IC Model* | 19 |

## Chapter 2  Historical Background of Modern Leadership Study — 21

| | |
|---|---|
| *Introduction* | 21 |
| *Cooperative Action* | 22 |
| *"New" and "Old" Views* | 22 |
| *Trait Approaches* | 24 |
| *The Individual and the Situation* | 25 |
| The Situational Approach Emerges | 26 |
| Contingency Models | 27 |
| *Power and Influence* | 28 |
| *Perceptions of Performance* | 30 |
| *Style and Substance* | 30 |
| *Transactional and Social Exchange Models—VDL & LMX* | 32 |
| *Social Exchange and Non-Normativity* | 33 |
| *Higher Status, Influence, and Innovation Potential* | 33 |
| *Appointment-Election and Follower Responsiveness* | 34 |

## Chapter 3  Applications and Implications of Inclusive Leadership — 37

| | |
|---|---|
| *Introduction* | 37 |
| *Learning Inclusive Leadership Skills* | 37 |
| *Inclusive Leadership Connections with TF Leadership and the IC Model* | 38 |
| *Performance over Time* | 38 |
| *Multiple Features of the Leader Role with Followers* | 39 |
| *A "Fair Exchange"* | 39 |
| *Measuring Inclusive Leadership with a New Scale* | 42 |
| *Extending Inclusion: Resolving Conflicts* | 42 |
| *Use of the IL Scale* | 43 |

## PART 2. LEADERSHIP-FOLLOWERSHIP ISSUES

**Chapter 4   What Is the Crisis of Leadership?**     47

    *Commentary*     47

Leadership in Retrospect     49

Leadership as a Transaction     50

Leader Legitimacy and Authority     51

Credibility and Accountability     52

**Chapter 5   Contemporary Trends in the Analysis of Leadership Processes**     55
WITH JAMES W. JULIAN

    *Commentary*     55

An Overview     58

Legitimacy and Social Exchange in Leadership     60

The Perception of Leadership Functions within Group Structure     61

Source and Nature of Leader Authority     62

Effectiveness of the Leader     63

Identification with the Leader     64

Some Conclusions and Implications     65

**Chapter 6   The Essential Interdependence of Leadership and Followership**     67

    *Commentary*     67

Leadership and Followership as a Unity     68

Leader Traits and Follower Attributions     68

Relational Qualities of Leadership     69

Transactional Leadership and the Active Follower     70

Leader Responses to Followers     70

Transformational Leadership and Charisma     71

Bringing Followers into the Process     71

**Chapter 7   Women and Leadership**     73

    *Commentary*     73

Gender Differences in Social Behavior     75

Taking the Leader Role     77

Performance as a Leader     78

## Chapter 8  Leadership, Followership, Self, and Others    81

*Commentary*    81

Leader Qualities by Stages    82

Follower Perceptions and Expectations    83

Leader-Follower Relationships    83

Role of Follower Attributions about Leaders    84

Self and Other: Dominance and Identification Motifs    84

Legitimacy as a Basis of Authority    85

Transactional Models of Leadership    85

Idiosyncrasy Credit    86

Social Self, Social Perceptiveness, and Self-Monitoring    87

Self-Serving Biases    87

Charismatic and Transformational Leadership    88

Conclusions    88

## Chapter 9  College and University Leadership from a Social Psychological Perspective    91

*Introduction*    91

*Inclusive Leadership on Campus*    91

*The Presidential Role or Set of Roles*    92

*Expectations and Perceptions*    92

*The Department Chair as a Leader*    93

Building Consensus and a Common Mission    93

Promoting Cooperative Relations    94

Securing Resources    94

Managing the Department    94

Motivating Scholarship and an Educational Environment    94

*Decision Processes and Fund Raising*    94

*Interpersonal Relations and Selection of Administrators*    96

*Student Leadership*    96

*Defining Success*    98

*Conveying Structure and Style*    99

| | |
|---|---|
| *Leadership and Management* | 100 |
| *Some Implications and Conclusions* | 101 |

## Chapter 10   Presidential Leadership — 103

| | |
|---|---|
| *Introduction* | 103 |
| *Party, Popularity, Promise, Performance* | 104 |
| *A Social Psychological Perspective* | 105 |
| *Postelection Surveys of Effects of Presidential Identification* | 107 |
| International Issues | 107 |
| Economic Issues | 108 |
| Party Loyalty | 108 |
| *Identification with the President, Perception, and Voting Behavior* | 110 |
| Popularity | 112 |
| Promise and Performance | 112 |
| The "Mandate" | 113 |
| Policy Making | 114 |
| *Images versus Performance* | 115 |
| Crises Create Even More Power | 115 |
| *Conclusions* | 116 |

## Chapter 11   Power and Leadership in Organizations — 117
WITH LYNN R. OFFERMANN

| | |
|---|---|
| *Commentary* | 117 |
| From Traits to Attributions | 118 |
| Leader and Follower Roles | 118 |
| Transactional Approaches | 119 |
| Organizational Culture and Leader Style | 120 |
| Newer Developments and Orientations | 120 |
| The Role of Power | 121 |
| Barriers to Empowerment | 123 |
| Empowerment as Career Development through Modeling and Mentoring | 124 |
| Informal Influence | 125 |
| Challenges to Leadership Research | 126 |

## Chapter 12  Organizational Leadership and Followership: The Role of Interpersonal Relations — 129

*Commentary* — 129
Background and Definitions — 129
Early Work on Interpersonal and Group Processes — 131
The Situational Approach: Antecedents and Accompaniments — 131
Some Aspects of Power and Identification in the Leader-Follower Relationship — 133
Charismatic, Transformational, and Transactional Leadership — 135
Summary and Conclusions — 136

## Chapter 13  Legitimacy, Power, and Influence: A Perspective on Relational Features of Leadership — 139

*Commentary* — 139
Introduction — 140
The Relationship of Leadership and Followership — 140
Transactional Models of Leadership — 142
Idiosyncrasy Credit — 142
Features and Effects of Leader Legitimacy — 143
Attributions about Leader Qualities and Performance — 146
Some Implications and Conclusions — 146

## Chapter 14  Ethical Challenges in the Leader-Follower Relationship — 149

*Commentary* — 149
The Centrality of the Leader-Follower Relationship — 150
Historical Context — 151
Charisma and Its Effects — 151
The Contrast between Power and Identification — 152
Self-Serving Biases — 152
Mutual Identification — 153
Joining or Distancing Followers — 153
Leader Performance — 154
Conclusions — 155

## Chapter 15  The Balance of Leadership and Followership: An Introduction — 157
WITH LYNN R. OFFERMANN

*Commentary* — 157
Introduction — 157

# PART 3. CONFORMITY-NONCONFORMITY AND INDEPENDENCE

## Chapter 16  Conformity, Status, and Idiosyncrasy Credit — 163

*Commentary* — 163
Conformity, Status, and Idiosyncrasy Credit — 164
Some Questions on Conformity — 164
Norms, Roles, and Group Expectancies — 165
Idiosyncrasy Credit — 166
Some Points of Reinterpretation Regarding Social Conformity — 167
The Perceptual Element in Conformity — 168
Status and Conformity — 168
Conformity as a Process — 169
Summary — 170

## Chapter 17  Some Current Issues in the Psychology of Conformity and Nonconformity — 171
WITH RICHARD H. WILLIS

*Commentary* — 171
An Overview — 172
Levels of Analysis — 173
Descriptive Criteria — 174
Unidimensional Approaches — 174
A Two-Dimensional Approach — 175
Studies of Movement Conformity — 177
The Situation and Conformity — 178
Personality and Conformity — 179
Conformity-Nonconformity and Social Exchange — 181
Conclusions and Implications — 182

## Chapter 18  Independence, Conformity, and Civil Liberties: Some Implications from Social Psychological Research — 185

*Commentary* — 185
Dependability and Independence as Social Requirements — 186
Impediments to Independence — 189
Some Implications for Maintaining Civil Liberties — 191

## PART 4. CONCLUSIONS

**Chapter 19    Summing Up: Lessons from Experience** — 195

*Introduction* — 195

*Inclusion and Noninclusion* — 195

*Leader Awareness of Followers Needs* — 196

*Inclusive and Noninclusive Leadership* — 197

*Power Over* — 198

*Conclusion* — 198

**Afterword    A Career in Leadership: A Life in Psychology** — 199

Appendix: Development of Inclusive Leadership Scale (ILS-16) — **221**
Bibliography — 223
Name Index — 247
Subject Index — 257

# SERIES FOREWORD

Edwin A. Fleishman
George Mason University

Jeanette N. Cleveland
The Pennsylvania State University
Series Editors

The *Series in Applied Psychology* offers publications that emphasize research and its applications to important issues of human behavior in a variety of social settings. The objective is to bridge both academic and applied interests.

This book, *Inclusive Leadership: The Essential Leader-Follower Relationship*, is an important addition to our series and represents a valuable contribution to the ever-expanding field of leadership research and its application in organizations. It represents a capstone work by Professor Edwin Hollander, one of the major figures in social psychology and in leadership research, in particular. During his stellar academic career, over a 50-year period, Ed Hollander has made lasting contributions to the field of leadership. His work has provided a strong theoretical and empirical foundation for guiding leadership development. This book offers a compendium of new chapters, together with chapters that include many of his key original papers, combined with reflective commentary. This approach gives the reader a depth of understanding of the topic and provides a demonstration of how a field develops over time in relation to a researcher's career goals, opportunities, and the status of the field at particular times in the history of the discipline.

A notable feature of the book is its frankly autobiographical aspect. Ed Hollander has provided us with details about his evolution as a social psychologist, intrigued by the questions about effective leadership. The reader will get to know Ed Hollander as a person and to appreciate the network of professional, institutional, family, collegial, and social relationships, which shaped his career and influenced his research. In this sense, the book really lays out Hollander's rich research legacy with a Who's Who of the American and international community of intellectuals who were his teachers, peers, colleagues, and students.

The book focuses on what Hollander termed "Inclusive Leadership," which highlights the role of followers as a key to effective leadership. Leadership is seen as an interpersonal process that entails mutual relationships with shared goals and a common vision for the future. The characteristics of talented leaders are seen as very much the same as those of committed followers. The book identifies and integrates for us the key constructs that influence this relationship. Although these ideas have evolved over a long career, they are still fresh and pertinent. The new chapters integrate the material with up-to-date references and concepts that have developed as the field has emerged. Hollander writes from a broad perspective, with many examples of issues that take into account the interdependence of leaders and followers in a wide variety of organizational settings.

Hollander's persistent focus on understanding "followership" in the study of leadership makes this book distinctive and unique. Through the force of his programmatic work over these many years, he helped transform our view of leadership. The book should be a basic addition to anyone's library on leadership. The primary audiences include students of leadership, those in graduate courses on leadership and organizational psychology, and students in nonacademic leadership development programs. The book's audience should not be confined to required reading for those in the psychological study of leadership; students and faculty in business, sociology, education, and political science should also find this book very useful in their courses.

# PREFACE

*"Not another book about leadership!"* These were among the first words from a colleague when asked to comment on part of my manuscript. I rapidly made two points about why this book is unusual: *It emphasizes the role of followership far more than most previous leadership books,* and *it combines elements of the scientific and autobiographical nature of the career of one individual.*

Major portions of my body of work, spanning over 50 years, are represented in this book's nineteen representative chapters. Six chapters are newly written or largely recast to cover additional applications regarding such topics as "College and University Leadership" (Chapter 9) and "Presidential Leadership" (Chapter 10), as well as two introductory chapters that provide an extensive "Overview of Inclusive Leadership" (Chapter 1) and the "Historical Background of Modern Leadership Study" (Chapter 2).

Among these new chapters is "Applications and Implications of Inclusive Leadership" (Chapter 3), which concludes with the development and application of an Inclusive Leadership Scale (ILS-16) appropriate for evaluation and training purposes. Its technical analyses are presented in the Appendix. It was developed from the actual words of respondents in our critical incidents research on good and bad leadership. It has utility in group discussions for identifying and encouraging Inclusive Leadership behavior. In the concluding chapter more conceptual and applied issues about Inclusive Leadership are offered. In the other thirteen chapters works are reproduced here with a newly written commentary to update them as related to some current concerns.

A reasonable question is why the older material is worthwhile, since it is usually the newest that is sought. My view, shared by others, is that there is still persistence of interest, as revealed by the "old wine, in new bottles" phenomenon identified by Gordon Allport (1985), regarding the history of psychology. Many issues from the past, such as the role of "leader traits," still exemplify lively points of concern. That is so despite their reconsideration in light of the current cognitive/attributional view, which I favor. This approach sees follower perceptions of the leader as key, rather than traits "possessed" by the leader.

My two previous books about leadership (Hollander, 1964, 1978a) were designed to be relevant and applicable for their time. The first emphasized theory and methodology, and the second applications to leader-follower relations, though each had some of both. This book carries these intentions forward, but with new and reproduced material from a larger expanse of time, permitting comparisons that can be instructive within that perspective.

Added to this collection is an autobiographical Afterword on my research career in leadership, from my undergraduate days and early military service. Then, I was a soldier in an army hospital doing psychological testing and interviews of mental patients after World War II had ended. Later, as a naval aviation psychologist, I did psychological research with aviation cadets during the Korean War. In giving these accounts, I have tried to remain as objective as possible, while recognizing the potential for memory and "social desirability" effects, which I believe were limited. All in all, I consider it of potential interest and educational value to tell others, especially younger people, about different times and situations. These are important functions of written biographies.

I came into psychology with a desire to help improve the human condition, on a larger scale than I thought was possible, by aiding individuals one by one. Though I know and respect colleagues who do both, I chose not to become a clinician soon after my service in neuropsychiatry at an army hospital. It was not a good fit for me. In teaching for over 50 years, and after writing a textbook (Hollander, 1967) on social psychology, among others, I found major fulfillment. The textbook has gone through four editions and has been translated into other languages, including Chinese and Spanish. I more than attained my early hope of reaching a larger part of humanity, and perhaps making a difference, for which I am continually grateful.

As a leadership scholar, I remained open minded on most issues, but I still gave special attention to learn generally about "good" and "bad" leadership, from a follower's perspective. The focus of my work was on the primary importance of the leader-follower relationship as a two-way influence process. I called this the "transactional," then "relational," approach. Unfortunately, these terms were open to distortions, such as "tit-for-tat," and the mistaken view that I was only concerned with the social aspect of leadership, rather than the task demands and performance. That is not true, as I hoped to make clear in my writings about the importance in leadership of competence and ethical-moral behavior. This means taking seriously the task to be performed and goals to be attained through supportive group processes and coalition building.

I pursued this relational line of research and publications with three lectures at the New York Academy of Sciences (1996, 2000, 2004), which led to this book's "Inclusive Leadership" theme. I also presented this concept at a seminar discussion with colleagues at the Center for the Advanced Study of Leadership, of the Burns Academy of Leadership at the University of Maryland in 1999, and St. Francis College of Brooklyn in 2000 (see Hollander, 2006, 2007). A useful discussion also ensued after a lecture about the concept and its implications at the 2007 Eastern Psychological Association annual meeting held in Philadelphia.

Awareness of what followers know and need is of course essential to leadership, as this book emphasizes, starting in Chapter 1. However, it does not mean giving up judgment as a leader. In a representative government, though, being informed about the will of the electorate is basic to public service, in the best sense. A popular misconception is the belief that a leader "keeping a finger to the wind" is usually bad, which it can be, if taken to the extreme. Said disparagingly, it suggests always trying to do what the populace wants. However, the alternative is not to bother at all, but to do whatever the leader wants and asserts as "doing the *right thing*."

Committed as I am to the scientific method, with the need for testing hypotheses and revising ideas, I am not stuck with what I wrote more than 50 years ago. For instance, one of my professors from Columbia, Paul Lazarsfeld, told me that my Idiosyncrasy Credit (IC) Model, was a "Good concept, bad term." He said that in a friendly way among a group of colleagues, in about 1960 when I was an associate professor at Washington University in St. Louis, where he came to speak at a social science conference. I took little offense, given my high regard for him, and a sense that he was probably correct on the latter element. Indeed, I have heard misstatements and seen misprints of the term as "Idiosyn*cratic* Credit." But that is less a source of concern than a misconception about the model allegedly urging conformity.

In fact, the IC Model is non-normative, describing what seems to occur as people rise in their accorded status, or "esteem," in groups and larger entities. The term "conformity" was not the best way to describe sufficient displays of loyalty to the group, rather than a slavish adherence to a norm, called "conformism." What I meant is hopefully better understood by the *Sociological Review* excerpts in Chapter 16, much of 17, and especially 18. Indeed, Chapter 18 emphasizes the contribution of "independence" to freedom of thought and testing of ideas, vital to a free society. I also give an updated critique of the IC concept in Chapters 1 and 16.

Finally, special gratitude is extended to the many people who have helped me with this book, in various ways. I much appreciate the assistance of Benjamin Elman and Rachel Pascall, who greatly aided in the book's preparation, particularly with the voluminous bibliography. I am grateful also to Jacqueline Harris, who typed many of the early drafts of the manuscript, and for the further assistance of Keisha Peterson, Anthony Friend, and Linda Santana. My thanks to all of them.

There are many others to whom I am grateful, beginning with my wife Pat for her splendid support and forbearance, as I invested as much time as needed to complete this book on schedule. I also am appreciative of the strong encouragement of my Editor, Anne Duffy, Senior Editor at Routledge/Psychology Press/Taylor and Francis, and Series Editor, Edwin Fleishman, a long-time, steadfast friend. My colleagues at Baruch College of City University of New York (CUNY), who showed heartening interest and provided intellectual stimulation, are too numerous to name, but I want them to be aware of my great gratitude.

Among colleagues who read and commented on portions of the manuscript are these to whom I am indebted: David Birdsell, Jan Cleveland, Richard Couto, David Day, Edwin Fleishman, Gwendolyn Gerber, Al Goethals, Manuel London, Robert Lord, Charles McClintock, Wilbert McKeachie, Susan Murphy, Douglas Muzzio, Paul Nelson, Patricia O'Connor, Susan Opitow, Ronald Riggio, Ralph Rosnow, Georgia Sorenson, Janice Yoder, Steven Zaccaro, and John Zipp. They provided me with the basis for improvements to the work, but bear no responsibility for the outcome, which is my own.

EDWIN P. HOLLANDER<br>
*NEW YORK CITY*<br>
*MAY 2008*

# ABOUT THE AUTHOR

**Dr. Hollander** has been CUNY Distinguished Professor of Psychology at Baruch College and the Graduate Center since 1989. A longtime Professor at SUNY Buffalo, he also served there as Provost of Social Sciences and Administration, and was the founding director of the Doctoral Program in Social/Organizational Psychology. His BS in Psychology was earned at Case Western Reserve and his Ph.D. at Columbia University. Subsequently, he taught at Carnegie Mellon, Washington (St. Louis), and American University (Washington). He has held visiting appointments as a Fulbright Professor at Istanbul University, an NIMH Senior Fellow at the Tavistock Institute in London, and as a faculty member at Wisconsin, Harvard, Oxford, and the Institute of American Studies in Paris, among others. He also served as Study Director of the Committee on Ability Testing at the National Academy of Sciences. Dr. Hollander's major interests have focused on group and organizational leadership, innovation, and autonomy. His current research is directed toward understanding follower expectations and perceptions of leaders. His books include Leaders, Groups, and Influence (1964), Leadership Dynamics (1978), and Principles and Methods of Social Psychology (4 ed., 1981), and he co-edited the series Current Perspectives in Social Psychology (4 ed., 1976) with Raymond Hunt, and the companion volume Classic Contributions to Social Psychology (1972). He also is author of many chapters and papers on leadership. He has been honored by recent awards from the Center for Creative Leadership (CCL), the New York Academy of Sciences, and the International Association of Applied Psychology (IAAP).

# PART 1

# Introduction

CHAPTER 1

# Overview of Inclusive Leadership

Executives can be given subordinates, but a following must be earned.

John Gardner (1987, p. 4)

## INTRODUCTION

Inclusive Leadership (IL) is about relationships that can accomplish things for mutual benefit. Reaching leadership at this next level means "doing things with people, rather than to people," which is the essence of inclusion. Improving decision making and achieving desired ends are among its goals, without relying on one person's capabilities alone. It also provides an atmosphere that promotes fairness of input and output to all.

Inclusive Leadership respects competition and cooperation as part of a participative process. In the political sphere, it is serious about the "consent of the governed" and taking responsibility as well as being accountable to them. More leader-centric conceptions of leadership continue to emphasize traditional leader qualities such as character and charisma. These have their effects, but often neglect the essential relationship with followers.

The major point of this book is to show how followers can be included actively in leadership, with a role in a mutual process. The overarching goal is to improve the understanding and practice of effective leadership. Leaders usually do have greater initiative, but followers are vital to success, and they too can become leaders. Leadership benefits from active followers, in a unity, including "upward influence" on a two-way rather than a one-way street (Hollander, 1992a, 1992b, 2004a).

This two-way operation of leadership and followership depends upon Respect, Recognition, Responsiveness, and Responsibility, both ways. These are the four Rs of Inclusive Leadership that are vital to successful practice. A leader's "vision," or cognitive skill, alone will not do. A *Fortune* magazine article (Byrne, Symonds, & Siler, 1991) dubbed the phenomenon "CEO Disease" for failings associated with power and insularity. A headline "CEO Evolution Phase 3," in the Business Section in the *New York Times* (Schwartz, November 10, 2007, p. 1), recently proclaimed the need for CEOs to create a team sense. Enabling people to work well together was emphasized in the article, which the article considered lacking in the style of two recently deposed CEOs, Citigroup's Charles Prince and Merrill Lynch's Stanley O'Neal. Both of them reportedly received nine-figure departure payouts, despite disappointing performance, and the loss of top executives during their tenure, who might have been successors. Many CEOs do accomplish much for their organizations by a team effort and through their cognitive skills, drive, and stamina (see for example, Bennis & Nanus, 1985; DePree, 1989; Harman, 2003). They are inclusive leaders, with followers, even if not stated as such.

Followers can and do "play a more active role in constructing the leadership relationship, empowering the leader and influencing his or her behavior, and ultimately determining the consequences of the leadership relationship" (Howell & Shamir, 2005, p. 97). There is good reason to recognize that an active role for followers is essential for attaining group, organizational, and societal goals, not least because their inclusion usually improves the likelihood of achieving desired outcomes. Yet, followers often are mistakenly left aside when the attention focuses on the leader. The quote in the epigraph of this chapter from John Gardner recaptures an important early distinction between "headship," from imposed authority, and leadership that engages others in a program of action (Cowley, 1928). Freud (1921) similarly saw dominance as different from leadership (Hollander, 1985, p. 487). This does not mean that leaders need to indulge followers by "stroking" them, with the aim of gaining their compliance, or votes, but instead to include them in the tasks of leadership.

## PASSIVITY, COMPLIANCE, AND INDEPENDENCE

Nevertheless, passivity is often signaled to "subordinates" in organizations. They may be treated at best as silent partners. Individuals can in fact be made silent when discouraged by an autocratic leader and an unresponsive situation. Bad things can happen to those breaking out of this pattern of keeping silent, although a willingness to speak up has productive features. Solutions to problems do not come from the leader alone. As a wise saying put it, "Even the brightest among us can benefit from criticism."

This theme of showing initiative through free expression is another important facet in leader-follower relations, considered in this book as independence. It is dampened or limited severely by the exercise of power, which often rejects outspokenness. This norm is revealed in the bitter "advice" in some places to "Check your head at the door," and "Don't disagree at meetings." Two noted motivational psychologists have addressed such control by authority. In the extremity of slavery, which demands ultimate compliance, David McClelland said that it is "the most inefficient form of labor ever devised. ... If a leader wants to have a far-reaching influence, he must make his followers feel powerful and able to accomplish things on their own." Mattina Horner said authoritarian leadership encourages "apathy or resistance on the part of others, while in a situation of democratic leadership, one finds more originality, less aggression, and more productivity" (both cited in Viorst, 1998, p. 201).

## LISTENING IS RESPECTFUL

Within these pages, the judgments and activities in leader-follower relations are revealed to go beyond such obvious and less satisfactory features as creating images and using and abusing power. A desired goal is an "inclusive process" that others are truly involved in, as partners making inputs, with persuasion preferred over coercion, whenever possible. Its paramount values are respecting and involving others, with listening. An analogue has similarly been called an "inclusive culture," central to a training program for managers at the J.P. Morgan Chase Bank (Quinn, 2006). Peter Vaill (1996) has a sequence that starts with listening and puts the order like this: Listen, Learn, Help, Lead. Operationally, Inclusive Leadership refers to prompting activity by asking questions that require thought, such as, "Could we do this in a better way?" Whether in creating teams, treating crises, attending to inequities, reducing conformist pressures, or managing change, it starts with *Respect* for others, *Recognition* of their input, and *Responsiveness* to them. The necessary quality of *Responsibility* in both directions is also enduring as a basis for leader-follower relations, which engenders approval. The case often cited is that of President John F. Kennedy accepting responsibility for the failed invasion of Cuba, at the Bay of Pigs incident, which illustrates a leader's approval from followers by taking responsibility.

## FOUNDATIONS OF INCLUSIVE LEADERSHIP AND THE CONTENT OF THIS BOOK

Inclusive Leadership evolved as a major modern theme drawn from my debt to others' pioneer work. Among contributors to my development were John Hemphill, Fillmore Sanford, Alvin Gouldner, Ralph Stogdill, Kurt Lewin, Jacob Moreno, Helen Hall Jennings, Alex Bavelas, and George Homans. Their early influence became clearer as my own views evolved. For the present book, I brought together a selection of my previous research and theoretical papers. For each I wrote a new, accompanying commentary, with needed updates.

Over many decades, my own research and writing has sought balance in studying the way followership is interdependent with leadership. An early study I did with Webb researched "followership" and its relation to leadership and friendship. The term may have been used in the literature before, but it was new in psychological research. Our study was evidently a first, and it employed naval aviation cadets as our respondents (Hollander & Webb, 1955). We found a high overlap in desired qualities for those chosen by peer nominations as leaders or followers for a special unit. Other work has affirmed this symmetry of such qualities as dependability, responsiveness, and clear communication.

Furthermore, leader attention to the interests and needs of followers is essential to achieve effective leadership. In the political realm, Burns said that "only the followers themselves can ultimately define their own true needs ... [given] an informed choice" (1978, p. 36).

From the outset, followers perceive and respond to a leader's qualities, including his or her recognized legitimacy, as well as motivation, and performance. In this vein, Gary Wills stated that "Followers judge leaders. Only if the leaders pass that test do they have any impact" (1994, p. 21). Although his latter point may not prevail in the face of someone in a determining position of authority, Wills says in his conclusion that "so much of leadership is the projection of an image that will appeal to followers" (p. 274). Therefore, "reality" is projected by a leader through perceptual manipulation (Gray & Densten, 2007).

The aphorism "An ounce of image is worth a pound of performance" may not be taken literally, but such perceptions by followers can obscure their awareness of actual deficiencies in a leader's performance. However, perception guides behavior, influenced by motivation. Changes can occur in perception, when enriched by experience. The prospect for trust or mistrust may thereby grow. If positive, there will likely be loyalty and solidarity of purpose, and the reverse is also likely. Trust and loyalty are among those qualities needed to bind relationships. Two-way communication, including listening, is also significant for recognition and responsiveness. Listening also facilitates communication and influence and is therefore vital to effective leadership and critical when absent. These features are elements of the "consideration" dimension of leader behavior, identified in the earlier empirical research of Hemphill (1950) and Fleishman (1953).

Granted again that those identified as leaders usually have greater potential for action and influence, followers can and do exert upward influence, whether through their initiatives or by resistance. Therefore, the traditional dichotomy between leader and follower is wrong on at least three grounds. First, it overlooks this influence potential in interdependent roles. It also is the case that those who rise to leader positions may have shown such qualities as dependability and communication skills. As just mentioned, these are among qualities likely to be valued in followers, as well as in leaders, in most settings and institutions. Finally, especially in hierarchies, individuals are expected to be responsive to those in charge and directive to those who require it, even who are simply less senior.

This state of looking both ways is an obvious feature of middle management, although it clearly exists at upper levels, too. However, the dichotomy is artificial. Hackman and Wageman underscore this point in stating that "Leaders are also followers, and followers also exhibit leadership. ... Each boss also is a subordinate—even chief executives who lead entire organizations invariably report to some higher-standing person or group" (2007, p. 45). Hierarchy is not essential to leadership. Wheatley (1992), for example, adopts a systems approach and sees leadership as an interactive influence process. She proposes a view of leadership from a biological standpoint that is much more creative and adaptable than the more typical top-down model.

## DECISION MAKING AND POWER SHARING

Encouraging follower involvement in decision making and power sharing is evident in the team emphasis in such practices as group-based management. This is an important benefit to organizations presented in Hollander and Offermann (1990a), which is presented in Chapter 11 in this book. However, effectiveness of participation is not always found (e.g., Ciulla, 1998; Locke & Schweiger, 1979; Mulder, 1971; Schweiger & Leana, 1986). As Vroom and Jago assert, variability in the effectiveness of participation is dependent on specific situational variables (2007, p. 21). Hence, there is a need for a contingency approach that takes account of variables that may enhance or diminish participation, yielding successful outcomes. Although leaders and their qualities are a central focus in leadership study, it is in engaging followers that these qualities become especially relevant to good leaders and their willingness to involve followers authentically in such matters as decision making (see Hollander, 2007b).

At the other end of the scale, poor leaders make for a lack of success, as Hackman (1998) has pointed out. In leading groups, he specifies several factors that can operate to cause this. Prominent among these are: assigning a task to a group that could be done by an individual; failing to let the group function as one in terms of its judgments; managing by being dictatorial or laissez-fare; and depriving the group of needed resources and structure.

## ETHICS AND MORALITY

Also significant for leader-follower relations are ethical conduct and considerations of moral values. Chapter 14 in this book examines the ethical challenges in these relations. From a critical standpoint, Rost emphasizes that leadership is an influence relationship that reflects mutual purposes (1991, p. 102). His view extends to the avoidance of coercion to effect change. In most instances, Drucker says, change is not necessarily planned, but rather the result of a variety of factors: an unexpected success, failure, or sudden event; an incongruity between what is expected and what occurs; a process need that produces an invention; a market and industry condition; shifts in perceptions and meanings; and new knowledge (1985, pp. 34–35).

Chapter 8 in this book examines the way a leader's self-concept affects relations with followers. There also are cultural differences in the way that followers perceive leaders and respond to them, regarding follower expectations. In that regard, the Globe Research Program (House, Javidan, Hanges, & Dorfman, 2002) is an international study of leadership across many cultures. Its goal is to learn what is considered effective leadership, regarding criteria of psychological welfare and international competitiveness. How that may vary worldwide was determined by a study involving 17,000 respondents to questionnaires administered in over 900 organizations. The researchers found 21 leader attributes (e.g., integrity) that were universally positive and eight impediments (e.g., irritability) that were negative. Another 35 were found to vary in different cultures; sensitivity, for example, was seen as a positive leader attribute in the United States and a negative one in Russia. Some of the main propositions from the program's integrated theory resonate with this book's approach. Several significant ones are as follows:

Whether or not the leader is accepted depends on how well the leader's attributes and behaviors fit with the culturally endorsed implicit leadership theories. The better the fit, the more accepted the leader will be.

How effective a leader is depends on how well the leader's attributes and behaviors fit with the strategic organizational contingencies. The better the fit, the more effective the leader will be.

Leaders who are accepted by their followers are more effective than leaders who are not. An effective leader will, over time, be increasingly accepted because a leader's demonstration of competence improves follower's attitudes toward the leader, resulting in increased acceptance.

## THE CONTEXT OF INCLUSIVE LEADERSHIP

The IL approach departs from the long tradition of focusing largely on the leader as a means of understanding leadership. By contrast, IL looks at what is needed in the context to help in such ways as improving problem solving and attaining mutual goals. Exemplifying this is Chapter 9 on college and university leadership and the campus presidency, a multiple-role and multiple-constituency position. As an example, it requires dealing with competing issues and participants, shown in that chapter. Some of the concepts that represent an IL orientation are summarized here.

Leadership is vital to the well-being and maintenance of a group, organization, or society, and interacts to affect other processes such as conformity, independence, and cohesiveness, as shown in Figure 1.1.

Leadership occurs throughout society and is basic to many significant features of life. The quality of leadership can affect the successes or failures of a group, organization, or nation. It also affects "social health," in regard to the well-being of others.

8 | INCLUSIVE LEADERSHIP: THE ESSENTIAL LEADER-FOLLOWER RELATIONSHIP

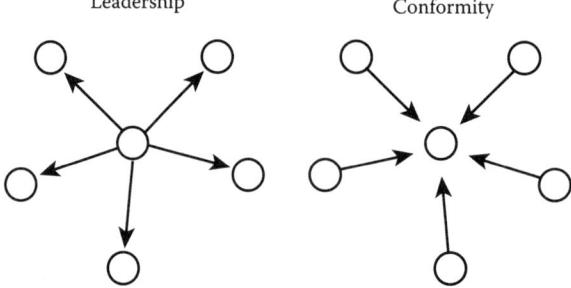

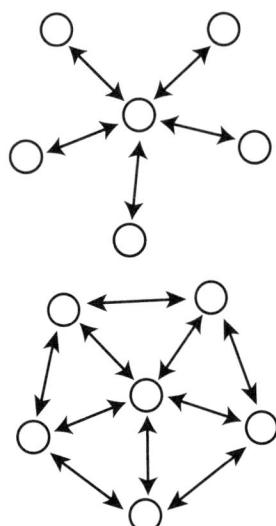

**Figure 1.1** Relationship of Leadership and Conformity

Leadership is not just about the leader, nor is studying leaders and their ability to exert influence and power all that understanding leadership involves.

Leadership is a process, not a person, as McGregor (1944) put it, although the leader is usually seen as central to the process.

Leadership does not exist without followership. More needs to be known about followers and their relationship with leaders, including their needs and expectations and how they may come to be leaders.

Leadership involves much more than direction of activity, but requires informing and supporting followers and their necessary activities, as well as representing and standing up fairly for their interests.

Followers feel they are entitled to good leadership, aimed at these ends, rather than bad, dysfunctional leadership. Trust and loyalty are two binding elements in the leader-follower relationship that spring from and nurture good leadership practices.

Leadership often refers to gaining direct action from individuals in an interdependent relationship. Whether that is achieved is seen to be central to a leader's role. However, active followers also are needed to achieve mutual goals.

Much of the literature on the study of leadership focuses on the leader, and his or her effects on followers, with far less attention given to follower effects on a leader's decisions and actions.

# THE LEADER-FOLLOWER RELATIONSHIP IN TRANSACTIONAL AND TRANSFORMING LEADERSHIP

Effective leaders build and bolster leadership practices that encourage bonding elements such as loyalty and trust. These help an enterprise by involving followers in shared processes. It is exemplified by having a role in decision making, which then can yield greater success of decisions and in their implementation. This illustrates a distinctive feature of IL: doing things *with* people rather than *to* people. It departs from the long-standing tradition of focusing on the leader's qualities, instead of giving attention to the followers and theirs, including perceptions, such as fairness regarding both tangible and intangible rewards. Significantly, IL is oriented more toward the involvement of followers rather than to the manipulation of followers by those in power.

James McGregor Burns, in his book on leadership, has put it starkly: "Leadership, unlike naked power-wielding is ... inseparable from followers' needs and goals" (1978, p. 19). Although I subscribe to it, this moral position may be overly optimistic when compared to practice. Furthermore, the dichotomy he presented between transforming (TF) and transactional (TA) leadership always seemed artificial given the different motives and tactics at work in relationships. Various possibilities can occur over time between a leader and those who are followers, and Burns has altered his view on this matter. Recently he wrote:

> I think my book [1978] is overly dichotomized. There is a stronger connection between transforming and transactional leadership than I led readers to believe. I think we have a spectrum. A few leaders operate wholly on the transforming side, but most work on both sides of that spectrum and combine transforming and transactional leadership. (2007, p. viii)

Illustrating this process is the research of Bensimon (1993). She studied new college presidents regarding their use of TA and TF leadership and with what effect. Those found to be successful showed adaptability in behaving as needed, usually building a constituency by a TA pattern, and only then when change was required using a TF pattern. Similarly, Wallace (1996) found, in her research with executives, that those perceived to be successful were more able to show a parallel pattern of flexibility in being neither TA nor TF. They used what was appropriate for the situation and their relationships there. No one leadership style is always "correct" and certain to be successful if it does not allow for flexibility.

In his insightful analysis, Yukl (1999) challenges the assumption that TF is beneficial for followers and their organization, regardless of situations, especially as it derives from charismatic leader qualities. Furthermore, he cites a "heroic leader bias" in the conception underlying this type of leadership and also sees rewards as often in TF as in TA leadership, although TF leadership is supposed to be less inclined in that direction. In concluding, Yukl says that TF leadership may be unnecessary and have negative consequences, in some situations, such as complying with the leader's request and making self-sacrifices in an extra effort to please the leader. In extreme cases, he says the follower's primary self-identity may come in serving the leader, rather than larger goals, and other parties, as considered in Chapters 8 and 14.

Bass and Riggio (2006) state that TF leadership has been criticized for being too positive as a portrayal of leadership by both Beyer (1999a, 1999b) and in the analysis by Yukl (1999). In providing an approving overview of the considerable volume of work on TF leadership, Bass and Riggio make their case, while acknowledging circumstances when TF leadership is less effective than other forms. Specifically, they treat negative occurrences with TF leadership as inauthentic and personalized (p. 235). This is a way to present TF leadership as a superior form of leader behavior. What about a leader who appears "authentic," in TF terms, in gaining a following, but later shows dictatorial behavior? In the political realm, the phenomenon is recognized in the supposed reformer who demands an election, which is likely to be the last one, once power is attained. Bass indicates that TF leadership can be effective, even if the situation requires autocratic behavior (1997, p. 132). Therefore, "attention to followers," appealing as it sounds, may mean their manipulation for the benefit of leaders who wish to control them, rather than to serve the broader good. The history of dictators, such as Hitler, Stalin, and Pol Pot, suggests that their charismatic/transformational qualities, initially with a few dedicated followers, led to disastrous consequences for the broader good.

Also, in treating TF leadership as the ultimate standard for good leader behavior, there is a commitment to change as a necessarily desirable end to be achieved. Circumstances may require that stability and continuity are better goals to seek. Moreover, Salas, DeRouin, and Gase (2007, p. 183) question the contention that TF leaders have attributes of confidence, dominance, and trust, which they say may result from an ongoing exchange that already exists. In addition, there remains the structural effect of the power differential that often exists between the leader and those who are led, with severely limited power, to which we turn now.

## POWER DISTANCE

The concern about the ethical and practical consequences of what Mulder (1971) called "power distance" is illustrated by the growth in CEO compensation relative to the average worker pay in their firms. Although largely unchecked, statements of concern about this massive gap have not abated. This is exemplified by the report of the heightened ratio in compensation of 350 to 1 in a *New York Times* (April 9, 2006, p. 1) Sunday Business Section article. Later in the week, many media outlets ran a story of the $400 million retirement package given to the departed CEO of Exxon Mobil. Other instances of record payouts involved pharmaceutical firm Pfizer's departing CEO Hank McKinnell receiving $200 million (*New York Times*, December 24, 2006, Sect. 3, p. 8), and retailer Home Depot's head Robert Nardelli getting at least that much, after being ousted by the board, following 6 years of disappointing performance. He most recently was appointed as the CEO of the Chrysler Corporation, which was purchased by an investment firm. As a private entity, it is without stockholders, who would otherwise need to be satisfied. The stockholders were a major source of discontent toward him when he served at Home Depot, most notably when he severely restricted their participation at a stockholders' meeting, resulting in some angry protests.

In a rare switch from Nardelli's standard, Home Depot's new CEO Frank Blake requested that his initial year compensation be set at a level comparable to that of the CEO of its main rival, Lowe's, reportedly $8.9 million (*New York Times*, February 8, 2007, p. C1). Although quite substantial, the story states that Nardelli was receiving an annual compensation of $39.7 million at Home Depot before his dismissal. The article says Blake also abolished Nardelli's "catered lunch for … top deputies, served daily on the 22nd floor of the company's headquarters in Atlanta … telling senior executives to take the elevator down to the first floor [to] eat with the company's rank and file in the cafeteria, according to an employee." What effect this will have is yet to be revealed, but its intent was to remove a particular "perk" that isolated top leaders from their employees.

Another problem of inequities in organizations resides in employee give-backs. These are sacrifices they must agree to accept for the firm to survive in a time of financial crisis. A recent report in the *New York Times* (Bailey, March 27, 2007, p. C1) publicized stock bonuses of $21 million to be given to American Airline's top executives. The largest bonus of $7.5 million was set for CEO Gerard J. Arpey. The pilots' and flight attendants' unions protested that their give-backs in salary and benefits, made to save the airline from bankruptcy in past years, had resulted in selective benefits paid only to already well-compensated managers. A spokesman for the pilots said, "When the ship was sinking, it was 'We're all in this together'," but now, he added, "the executives are benefiting while those flying the airplanes continue to get reduced wages." Thomas and Anderson (2007) report on the recent failure of Merrill Lynch's CEO Stanley O'Neal to inform the board of his activities, including the extent of substantial losses and secret dealings with Wachovia Bank regarding a merger/acquisition. His noninclusive operating style led to a push for his removal, but, nonetheless, with a departure sum reported in excess of $150 million.

Marvin Bower, a founder and longtime head of McKinsey, a major consulting firm, said regarding CEO compensation, "Excessive pay will make people in the company feel that the chief executive ... is not putting the business ahead of personal interests. These attitudes are demotivating to people in any company" (1997, p. 127). The thrust of his point concerns challenges to concepts of "team" and the "social contract" of playing fair, which can short-circuit successful leadership. However anticipated, the evidence for this is equivocal. One reason proposed is that of identification with those who succeed in making a great deal of money, in hopes that you will be able to get there, too. Another, on the pragmatic side, is that with corporate layoffs and generalized downsizing, a sense of threat to their job opportunities makes employees grateful for having a job at all. This may be so despite their dissatisfaction with working conditions, including pay. Eric Wanner (interviewed on Public Broadcasting Service's *Open Mind* program, in January 2007), head of the Russell Sage Foundation, a leading U.S. social science research organization, said the high value placed on individual initiative in U.S. society makes Americans less bothered by inequality than their European counterparts.

The question still remains why leader centrism prevails and is often imbued with a conception of dominance in directing others' actions and thoughts. At least part of the answer is associated with the matter of who is responsible, which is seen as fundamental to the nature of the role of leader. It is captured in a statement attributed to the French existential philosopher John Paul Sartre: "To be a leader, is to be responsible." A ready counter to this is that such responsibility requires awareness of "the territory," meaning access to information from those "in the know," on the working line, and in the boardroom (Murray, 2007). Letting these others "speak truth to power" is often needed for successful leadership.

My former colleague from State University of New York–Buffalo Warren Bennis put it succinctly in an op-ed piece in the *New York Times* in an article titled "Good Followers Make Leaders Look Good" (1989, Sec. 3, p. 3). As a major leadership scholar, he had interviewed and published about top leaders (Bennis & Nanus, 1985). One of his inferences is to learn from bad experiences. Failing to listen to those who know is often the cause of fatal outcomes.

Peter Vaill (1996) says that "Leadership is learning." The actuality of dangers from not attending to information from those on the working front is revealed in Karen Cerulo's (2006) recent book *Never Saw It Coming*. She makes the general point that American optimism tends to override warnings to be concerned about disasters that might befall us. In a related way, she recounts the case of the FBI leaders in Washington headquarters repeatedly disregarding warnings of the signs of a possible terrorist assault in the United States by air, including the significant alert in the noteworthy "Phoenix Memo" from FBI field agents before the September 11, 2001, attacks. She says that the institutional leader centrism that prevailed kept information, even such warnings, from being encouraged to flow from the field. The FBI's dominant pattern was to have information flow down from headquarters as directives, rather than to foster a two-way or even multiparty interchange of such material.

Ancient Chinese Taoist philosophy lays a strong claim to valuing a followership position. Exemplifying this emphasis is Lao Tzu's view that "The wise leader settles for good work and does not take all the credit for what happens. When the work is done, let them say with pride, we have done this together" (as cited in Heider, 1982, p. 34). That was in the sixth century B.C.

But even in the 20th century, Max Weber, who furthered the concept of the charismatic leader, stated that if the leader was "long unsuccessful, above all if his leadership fails to benefit followers, it is likely that his charisma will disappear" (1946, p. 360). In short, followers accord this quality, rather than having the leader possess it independently of them, as is more usually portrayed. There also is the downside of charisma in that it is associated with leader narcissism and self-serving behavior (Post, 1986). More on this topic is considered later in this book. For now, remember: Leadership is not just about the leader; and, studying leadership involves more than just leaders and their powers.

## LEADERS AND FOLLOWERS ARE NOT SO SHARPLY DISTINCTIVE, NOR ARE LEADERSHIP AND FOLLOWERSHIP

Traditionally, the leader is seen as the main actor in leadership. A newer emphasis has broken away from this "leader-centric" model and opened the way for participation by followers in such processes as shared decision making. Their increased participation has been justified on grounds of higher-order values, democratic process, and effectiveness, all of which are seen to improve the quality and success of the decision and its implementation.

A source of resistance to this development is the argument that there are "prerogatives" that belong to those in charge, the "formal leaders." This view overlooks the reality that organizations at every level require active followership, although credit, by tradition, goes to the leader. Further, the quality of being effective as an active follower will call attention to someone who then may gain a higher position as a leader. There also is the role played by informal leaders, which may be disregarded or obscured by the tendency to focus on the leader who is appointed, the so-called formal leader. A view of followership as both active and critical (Kelley, 1992) presents a considerable contrast to this more usual view of the leader as the center of attention and power, as with the sun in our solar system. Correspondingly, followers are too often seen as "sheep," which Kelley rejects in his analysis of the various ways they contribute to the goals achieved. Bennis (1998) conveys this point by asking, "Did Michelangelo paint the Sistine Chapel all by himself?" His answer is no because the master reportedly had 13 artists and a crew of 200 to help him.

Still, leader centrism continues to hold much allure. Even the old "Great Man" theory, better known as "Great Person," remains alive, seen for instance in the "corporate savior" who goes from one firm to another "slashing" jobs with his proverbial chain saw. The qualities of leaders are obviously important, but an equally important point is that "We need to honor our teams more, our aggressive leaders and maverick geniuses less" (Reich, 1987, p. 78). In particular, leaders need the skills to engage followers in productive and satisfying mutual pursuits. This view departs from the usual way of seeing leader qualities as possessions, rather than as interpersonal links to others involved in shared activities.

The relationship of leaders to followers has a small but enduring place in the study of leadership. Chester Barnard's (1938) "acceptance theory of authority" exemplified this process.

It centered on the follower's pivotal role in judging whether an order is authoritative. Followers, Barnard suggested, make this judgment according to whether they understood the order; believe it is not inconsistent with organizational or personal goals; have the ability to comply with it; and see more rewards than costs in complying and remaining with the organization or group (Hollander, 1978a, p. 47). Mary Parker Follett, in the 1920s and 1930s, has proposed similarly that attention be paid to who gives orders and how they are received by the persons to whom directed (see Graham, 1995).

Followers' needs are satisfied not only in tangible ways but also through such intangible rewards as support, fairness, and being heard. As part of good business practice, a founder of organizational studies in France, Henri Fayol (1916), long ago advocated attention to worker well-being, in addition to satisfying remuneration, bonuses, and profit sharing. Yet, the focus on just such tangible rewards left a significant gap in understanding the role of intangible rewards in leadership (Hollander, 2006). To enrich this conception, we need to turn to the actual experiences of followers with leaders.

A body of research shows how inattention to leader-follower relations can produce dysfunctional outcomes, or what Drucker (1988) has called "misleaders." For instance, Hogan, Raskin, and Fazzini (1990) found that organizational climate studies from the mid-1950s onward showed 60 to 75% of organizational respondents reported their immediate supervisor as the worst or most stressful aspect of their job. From a 10-year perspective, DeVries (1992) estimated the base rate for executive incompetence to be at least 50%. Marilyn Gowing, who was a director of personnel research in the U.S. Office of Personnel Management (OPM), reported that a similar figure was found in a survey conducted in the Federal Civil Service (personal communication, March 2006).

Lord and Maher (1990) say that these perceptions are checked against prototypes held by followers and their related expectations of how leaders should perform, called "implicit leadership theories" (ILTs). How leaders and followers mutually perceive and respond to each other's personal qualities and actions is crucial to their relationship. Argyle and Henderson (1985) stated their findings in these terms:

> [The] superior-subordinate relationship at work is seen by most people as full of conflict and as providing little satisfaction. On the other hand supervisors can have a considerable effect on health and satisfaction, if the right skills are used. Supervisors have power to reward and punish. (p. 262)

All of this has a redounding effect on a sense of purpose and well-being. This theme, regarding self-identity, is emphasized in the recent work of Lord and Brown (2004).

## LEGITIMACY AND CREDIT

A following can come about in various ways. The consideration here is on two primary ways. Legitimacy is the more usual way of signaling an acknowledged occupant of the leader role and how he or she attained that status. Credit is a less formal way of considering the leader-follower bond, in regard to positively disposed perceptions. By their role in accepting a leader, followers can affect the strength of a leader's influence, behavior, and the performance of the group or larger entity. In short, influence and power flow both from legitimacy and those extras affected by followers through their perceptions, attributions, and judgments. Neustadt (1960), similarly, considers follower perceptions of legitimacy as one of two main sources of presidential power, the other being sentiments of loyalty, which can be considered to be credits accorded by followers.

As already indicated, legitimacy plays a pivotal part in the leader-follower relationship because it is the base on which followers perceive and respond to the leader. Among its manifestations, legitimacy implicates such qualities as credibility, trust, loyalty, and the leader's ability to be effective in exercising power and influence.

Whatever power is imputed to a leader, actualizing it depends on its perception by followers. Power becomes real when others perceive it to be so and respond accordingly. But an emphasis on traditional "power over" others tends to dominate the field, at the expense of empowerment and resistance to unwanted power assertions, which have been called "power to" and "power from." They deal respectively with giving individuals opportunities to act more freely within some organizational realms, through "power sharing," and to fend off others' power demands (Hollander & Offermann, 1990a, p. 179). In that paper, we reviewed and assessed research on organizational leadership and power. Among other things we considered the benefits of, and sources of, resistance to delegation and empowerment of followers. On balance, we found that by sharing power and allowing followers to influence them, leaders foster leadership skills in others, as well as achieve other gains through their greater participation and involvement. But a major question posed is how a return to leader-centered approaches can be reconciled with this trend toward greater follower empowerment and influence.

Rather than be separate, leadership and followership exist in a reciprocal, interdependent system as a unity (Hollander, 1992a). Fundamental to this system is a relationship "in which the leader both gives something and gets something. The leader provides a resource in terms of adequate role behavior directed toward the group's goal attainment with status, recognition, and esteem [contributing to] 'legitimacy' in making influence assertions and in having them accepted" (Hollander & Julian, 1969, p. 388, appearing here in Chapter 5). To varying degrees, a leader's legitimacy can be altered by his or her approval by followers.

The usual expectation of the follower role as essentially passive is therefore misleading when considering followership as an accompaniment to leadership. Leaders do command greater attention and influence, but followers can affect a leader's activity significantly, not least because followers are usually the leader's most attentive strategic audience. Support is an essential element in the leader-follower bond. It can be considered as credit followers can accord or withhold from their leaders, as part of a personal bond that extends to loyalty and trust.

## IDIOSYNCRASY CREDIT

The idiosyncrasy credit (IC) model of innovative leadership deals with the latitude that followers provide a leader to render change beyond that accorded by legitimacy of authority (see e.g., Hollander, 1958, 1960, 1961, 1993, 2006). The model describes a dynamic process of interpersonal evaluation in which the effects of leader authority are not fixed but determined significantly by the support of followers. It is nonnormative since it does not tell how things ought to be, but reflects how they seem to operate in relatively noncoercive situations where power is not absolute but relative to the context and persons there.

Essentially, the model postulates credits to be positive perceptions of someone, earned by their showing competence in helping to achieve the group's task goals and conformity to the group's norms, as a sign of loyalty. Credits may then be drawn on to take innovative actions in line with expectations associated with the leader role. Therefore, it becomes possible that early signs of competence and conformity will permit later nonconformity to be better tolerated. This formulation was first verified in a set of experiments with groups involved in a joint decision task and has subsequently been supported in various ways (see for example, Estrada, Brown, & Lee, 1995), with some qualifications and refinements. Alvarez (1968), for instance, found that the credit loss, in terms of "esteem," was significantly less for a leader's nonconformity where the organization was successful rather than failing.

The idea of credit is embedded in everyday language in such general terms as "receiving credit," "taking credit," and "being discredited." On the "input" side of this refinement, the IC model illustrates how credits accumulate and then on the "output" side have operational significance in permitting innovations that would be perceived to be "deviations" if introduced by another person with less credit. Seniority can contribute to the accumulation of credits, but without uniform impact. A person may also benefit from having "derivative credit," as in a favorable reputation from another group, or from society, as in high socioeconomic status. Most usually, however, a new member of a group is in a poor position to assert influence, especially in the direction of change, unless he or she has a unique qualification. An example would be providing a solution to a major group problem or having needed knowledge or a skill. In these circumstances the new member's credit is gained by maximizing on the competence factor. However, credit may not accrue as readily to those who are perceived to be different, as in the case of a woman in an otherwise male group (see Wahrman & Pugh, 1974).

A new leader, whether appointed or elected, must still build credit by establishing a following. In the organizational sphere, as noted in Gardner's view in the epigraph of this chapter, there is the need to gain followers, not just subordinates. Katz and Kahn made the point that leadership is the "influence increment above compliance with organizational authority and directives" (1966, p. 304). This increment can be seen as representing credits that are part of a leader's informal following (Heifetz, 1994). In the realm of politics, this is especially evident where the legitimacy of one's authority is weak, as in a narrow election victory. This condition seemed obvious when President Bill Clinton had 43% of the vote when elected in 1992 in a three-way contest. There was clear difficulty in getting major parts of his program approved in 1993, attributed to that consideration, among others. Long before, the political scientist Verba (1961) offered the idea of "acceptance capital," built up through conformity to constituent expectations. However, such capital did not include inputs or outputs from the perception of a leader's competence, as the IC model does.

How credits are expended is of considerable importance. In Clinton's case, as in others', he took impulsive early actions that squandered the relatively little credit he had, even before he had begun to build a larger fund to work with. Furthermore, since failing to live up to followers' expectations for leader action can lose unused credits, the drainage was compounded by overpromising, and then apparent inaction in the face of stated need. Not least, the leader's self-serving and other negatively viewed behaviors can drain credits, as can perceptions of weak motivation, incompetence, and the responsibility for failure.

Underlying the IC model is the fundamental point that accepting influence involves a process in which attributions are made about the influence source. The same behavior seen to be nonconforming if shown by one person may not be so perceived when shown by another. Therefore, leaders may initiate change, even in seemingly nonconforming ways, as part of their accepted innovative role. Although there may be greater tolerance of nonconformity for the legitimated leader in some ways, there are restrictions regarding particular expectancies, which can be thought of as role behaviors expected by followers. At least two reasons explain why these restrictions may be imposed: first, higher status is usually perceived to carry with it greater self-determination for one's actions; second, such status usually means more possible influence on important outcomes for group members (Hollander, 1964, chap. 20). Because of these and other constraints, leaders are therefore still vulnerable to a loss of standing for evident infractions in their role, such as betrayal.

## THE DYNAMICS OF LEADER LEGITIMACY

As indicated, legitimacy depends on followers perceiving the leader's source of authority and then responding accordingly to that leader. The evidence indicates that a major difference exists in the realm of appointment or election as sources of a leader's authority (Hollander & Julian, 1970, 1978). In both cases, the possibility of being perceived to be, and acting as a leader, depends somewhat on those who are to be followers.

The election case is of course an obvious instance of emergence, which more closely approximates the IC model. Moreover, election usually creates a heightened psychological identification between followers and the leader, with followers having a greater sense of responsibility for and investment in the leader. One explanation is to view this as a social exchange in which the group gives the leader a "reward" in advance, by electing him or her, and then group members feel a claim on him or her to "pay back" by producing favorable outcomes (Jacobs, 1970).

Correspondingly, it is also true that the support of followers exacts a higher demand on the leader. Elected leaders who fail to perform well have been found to be more vulnerable to criticism than appointed leaders, particularly if they are seen to be competent in the first place (Hollander & Julian, 1970, 1978). Although election and appointment may create different psychological climates between leaders and followers, this leaves the prospect for even appointed organizational leaders to attain a "following" by doing more than exercising authority, as Katz and Kahn (1978) have observed. Nonetheless, the main thread running through results on leader legitimacy is the difference in support and involvement that have been found in comparing the two major sources of leader legitimacy: appointment and election.

Proponents of a perceptual/attributional perspective say that leaders also are credited or blamed for outcomes with which they may have had little input, such as the economy picking up with oil prices down under Ronald Reagan or faltering when they had been raised by Organization of Petroleum Exporting Countries under Jimmy Carter. This is seen to be a perceptual pattern that reflects the "romance of leadership," as Meindl and Ehrlich (1987) term it. They found that in perceiving group and organizational performance, positive or negative outcomes are more likely to be attributed to the leader than to other factors. Because leaders are symbols, Pfeffer (1977) says that if something goes wrong, the whole staff or entire team cannot be fired, but firing the manager can convey a sense of rooting out the basis for the problem. Obviously, it is less simple to dismiss an officeholder, especially in midterm, after formal election or appointment, although it can occur. Recent research by Gray and Densten (2007) studied the "idealized" images of leadership that leaders held of themselves.

One consequence of the attributional approach is to make more explicit the significance of followers' and others' perceptions of the leader, not least regarding expectations about leader competence and motivation. Imagery and self-presentation may still obscure the truth about the leader's intentions and dealings, yet there remains the basic question of the basis on which followers are able to evaluate the leader's performance.

## "CRITICAL INCIDENTS" RESEARCH ON FOLLOWER PERCEPTIONS OF LEADERS

Followers are the ones who experience the actuality of a leader's approach to leadership and are uniquely able to evaluate it and its effects. The research program my colleagues and I have conducted over a decade (see for example, Hollander, 2006) used critical incidents to study these relationships further. These were supplemented by open-ended questions and rating scales to study followers' perceptions of actual leader behavior in good or bad leadership situations, and followers' perceptions of ideal leader behavior. As with previous results, we found that such relational qualities as supportiveness and trustworthiness, along with effective communication, delegation/empowerment, and taking needed action, were emphasized in distinguishing good from bad leadership. We also found that characteristics reported for good leadership closely corresponded to those independently described for ideal leadership—honesty/trustworthiness and competence/confidence—irrespective of respondent gender.

These results are based on a total sample of 293 respondents, about half male and half female, drawn primarily from working master's degree students enrolled in evening courses on organizational behavior or leadership. Two-thirds held professional and/or administrative positions, and the great majority (80%) were employed full time. Although the findings are largely based on the work setting, they have wider implications for expectations of political leadership. This was revealed, for instance, in the weight attached to personal qualities of trustworthiness and fairness.

## CHARISMATIC LEADERSHIP

Charisma poses an intriguing case in evaluating a leader's performance. Recent decades have seen a revitalization of interest in the concept of the "charismatic leader." Max Weber (1946), the eminent sociologist of bureaucracy fame, promoted it from the Greek word *charisma* for divine gift. Such a leader, he said, has considerable emotional appeal to followers and great hold over them, especially in a time of crisis when there are strong needs for direction. Weber contrasted this mode of leadership with the traditional kind, which is handed down, and the legalistic kind, which can be considered constitutional. Charisma provides a "personal authority" that evokes awe in followers, less likely to be so in the other forms. It can be seen as a vast amount of idiosyncrasy credit at the leader's disposal.

Burns makes the point that charisma "is so overburdened as to collapse under close analysis" (1978, p. 243). In this vein, Corry (1995) reports on the acknowledged appeal of John Lindsay, republican mayor of New York City several decades ago. If anything, he raised excessively high expectations so that "there was no way he could meet them. Charisma," says Corry, "is the most attractive but least substantive of political qualities and is useless as a guide to predicting what a candidate will do after he is elected. By the end of Lindsay's first term as Mayor, New York was having second thoughts" (p. 111). His charisma seemed to have run out. Nonetheless, Lindsay managed reelection by expressing contrition for the things he said "had gone wrong" and by running as an independent after losing the Republican Party endorsement.

## RELATIONSHIP TO TRANSFORMATIONAL AND TRANSACTIONAL LEADERSHIP

Interest in charisma is now mostly associated with TF leadership (Bass, 1985; Burns, 1978) and reveals the importance of the followers' perspective in understanding such phenomena. Weber originally presented charismatic leaders as attracting others because of their strong appeal and extraordinary determination, especially in time of crisis. However, he also stated its dependence on follower affirmation and success, as in a quote from him that said charisma disappeared if the leader was long perceived as unsuccessful.

There is also a need to take account of the ethical distinction Burns (1978) made between the self-serving and socially responsible kinds of TF leaders. In the world of organizations, as well as in politics, charismatic leaders are still sought as saviors. But they also may present serious difficulties, such as tendencies toward narcissism (e.g., Post, 1986) and unethical behavior. For example, Howell and Avolio (1992) cite the dubious ethical standards associated with such business leaders as Robert Campeau, John DeLorean, and Michael Milken, all of whom were acknowledged to have charisma for many of their followers. Unethical leaders are more likely to use their charisma for power over followers, directed toward self-serving ends, usually in a calculated manipulative way. Ethical leaders are considered to use their charisma in a socially constructive way to serve others.

Charisma and TF leadership are frequently linked in the literature, as Yukl (1999) finds in his coverage and analysis. TA leadership refers to a fair exchange in which the leader gives something to followers and receives esteem and latitude for action in return, as noted earlier here by Jacobs (1970) and Homans (1961). Indeed, the TF leader may provide intrinsic rewards in heightened follower arousal and potentially elevated self-concept, which is reciprocated by greater esteem and influence accorded the leader. This process is an evident exchange, and now a "spectrum" linking the two has been proposed by Burns (2007, p. viii), instead of a dichotomy, as noted here. Earlier, Bass had said that "Since 1980, general findings have been assembled that the best of leaders are both transactional and transformational. Again, for many situations the circumstances may not make that much difference" (1997, p. 132). However, TF leadership centers in the leader, and not with active follower involvement, reciprocal influence, and rewards. All of these are central features of the IL conception. This difference is of major importance.

Although charisma need not be part of TF leadership, it is routinely imputed to the TF leader, for example, as in Bass's first aspect of TF and in House and Shamir's (1993) work. However, the research by Ehrlich, Meindl, and Viellieu suggests that "more transactionally oriented activities by a leader may also contribute to a leader's charismatic appeal" (1990, p. 242). At its heart charisma is attributed to a leader by followers, as indicated in the earlier cited Weber point. This is a clear parallel to the essence of idiosyncrasy credit theory, insofar as it emphasizes the pivotal role of how followers perceive and then respond to a leader.

Here we see that credits are inevitably transitory, inconstant, as in "what have you done for us lately," and therefore in need of replenishing. This is less so regarding legitimacy, which has more stability, usually signalized by a public rite. Yet, legitimacy may still need to be reaffirmed, as is obviously the case in the electoral process. As to the fundamental question of the relationship between legitimacy and credits, they can and do bolster each other. Those granted legitimacy may then exercise their authority to say and do things that gain credits for subsequent actions. Such actions, evaluated positively by enough constituents, then create the basis for relegitimation. This cycle is one way of seeing the ascent and decline of a political leader in a mainly open participatory process.

## CRITIQUE OF IC MODEL

As a critique of the IC's model relevance to the political process, I recognize three restrictions that have occurred in my thinking about it that do not include other points of criticism. There is, first, a "statute of limitations" that may limit a leader's latitude for influence and innovation after the passage of time from some approved action. Second, a leader may lack perceptiveness in being aware of the availability of credits and the need to use them for appropriate action. Third, followers may represent a variety of interests that are incongruent and even antagonistic to each other so that leader actions that earn credits from one subgroup or constituency may lose them from others. In short, there are mixed motives regarding desired leader behavior, in addition to what the leader may see as in his or her own self-interest. Also relevant is the basic assumption that these relationships exist in an "open system" that is not constrained by authority pressures, such as those found in top-down organizations. The scientific method means a commitment to testing hypotheses and revising ideas, including my own, written as a young person more than 50 years ago.

On balance, the IC model nonetheless does show a way that individuals may attain more independence, insofar as they gain credit to free themselves from some group pressures (Stone & Cooper, 2008, and Chapter 18 here). Nothing is perfect, and there is no "magic bullet" regarding leadership, in its many manifestations. Therefore, even within limits, the IC model has explanatory value as a basic heuristic. It tells about interpersonal evaluation and achieving influence, and resistance, as well. Also, it provides an understanding of how followers can affect a leader's standing and his or her potential for influence and innovation.

# CHAPTER 2

# Historical Background of Modern Leadership Study

## INTRODUCTION

The landscape for Inclusive Leadership includes many significant elements that helped shape it, historically and conceptually. This chapter is intended to provide some relevant landmarks that help explain its origins and place in the present. Basic research on leadership goes back to near the turn of the 20th century and to philosophical thought and observation from antiquity. A partial list of the latter would include Chinese and Greek thinkers such as Lao Tzu and Plato, and French and Italian ones like Montaigne and Machiavelli. There has been a long history of conjecturing about who became leaders and what effect they had on others who were followers. However, early thinking often left aside necessary distinctions between imposed and emergent leaders. There also was a failure to give attention to becoming a leader by appointment or election—or taking on a leader role by ancestry as opposed to election by vote, or both. Another lack, even in some empirical studies, was in not distinguishing "traits" related to who becomes a leader from those related to who performs well as a leader. This difference between *becoming* and *performing* is still required in discussions about leader qualities.

Trends in the study of leadership parallel those in psychology regarding the sources of behavior, which range from the biological to the social ends of the spectrum, with individual cognitive processes in between. Hereditary and instinct conceptions emphasized biological determinants. Trait approaches grew out of these notions but moved more toward recognition of personality adapted to the circumstances of leadership events. Situational approaches moved farther along the scale toward social determinants, almost to the exclusion of individual differences in personality. Today's interest in perceptual attributional conceptions reflects a fundamental point that permeates psychology. The effect of all events, and other so-called situational factors, depends on perceptions—and at times relatively transient ones. Therefore, it is not so novel to assert that leadership is an "attribution" or "inferred state" (see Meindl & Ehrlich, 1987). As is pointed out by philosophers, so are love and bravery.

The earliest psychological contribution to the study of leadership was largely testing of individual characteristics, done to identify leader traits. More on that shortly. Only later, however, did psychology provided a richer way to understand leadership through individual motivations and perceptions, under the heading of "cognition." Note also that these psychological processes also affect and provide understanding of such phenomena as group cohesiveness, conformity, independence, prejudice, and conflict, all of which are related to leadership. Indeed, one can see it playing a role as an influence process in many phenomena that are treated as separate from it, without any disrespect to their importance and the contributions of their investigators, such as "Groupthink" by Janis (1972) and the studies of obedience to authority by Milgram (1974).

Inclusive Leadership also involves modern insights into the reality world of power and politics in organizations. This includes such "values in action" as truth-telling and transparency versus deception; and respect for individuals versus abuse, as in the report from a respondent in our research that "He totally yelled at me." Concern for performance standards was also found to contrast with comments from respondents that "anything goes" or the boss "plays favorites." The success of the series that began with *The Dilbert Principle* (1996) by Scott Adams, a former organizationist, makes plain that the reality of the workplace is not always as described in texts on organizations. In fact, Mintzberg's (1973) observations on the actual behavior of managers and executives points up these differences dramatically. Keeley (2004) also provides a caution about the ready reliance on the presumed virtues or values that a leader will provide when the actuality is different. A conclusion from Emler and Hogan is instructive in stating that "There is no inbuilt tendency to use power responsibly. You cannot randomly allocate leadership responsibility and expect the interests of justice and or society to be well served" (1991, p. 86). This raises the question of how dysfunctional leaders, which Drucker (1994) aptly called "misleaders," continue to maintain a following. Such leaders frequently fail to show reasonable conduct, relying on coercion by their authority, and have poor outcomes. Even then, they gain grudging cooperation, which Barnard (1938), an organization executive and thinker, pointed out is a central organizational function.

## COOPERATIVE ACTION

Bearing in mind that a main, but by no means sole, function of leadership is to direct individuals toward cooperative action, there are severe problems in attaining its achievement. Leadership also has the function of dealing effectively with conflicting demands and constituencies. Although "image building" is a mainstay in the public display of political leadership, especially in election campaigns, the quieter, less evident mode of leadership is fundamental to maintaining institutions and providing for their success. As discussed in Chapter 1, those in leadership roles can and do affect the success and "social health" of a group, organization, or nation. A leader's action or inaction, and its informed or uniformed basis, can have multiple effects on others. It is no wonder that attention so often is focused on the leader.

Inclusive Leadership recognizes this tendency but takes a broader view of what a leader can do by way of distributing leader tasks such as monitoring, planning, scheduling, and the like. This mode of sharing is what Bower (2001) urges must be a part of a "leadership organization," as mentioned in the preceding chapter. Given what often will be a heavy agenda of matters to be addressed, it behooves a leader to find ways of involving others in these matters, and even further to bring them into decision making. This willingness to involve followers to this extent is another contrast between the "new" and "old" views of leadership.

## "NEW" AND "OLD" VIEWS

A basic feature of the "old" view of leadership is the unstated assumption that the "leader" and "leadership" are the same, and that it is the leader's action that achieves results. In the "newer" conception, of which Inclusive Leadership is a part, leadership is seen more as an interactive process that involves the leader and followers. It is not something just the leader possesses (e.g., Sanford, 1950; Hollander & Julian, 1969; Chapter 5 here). A leader is often the major directive agent, but not exclusively so; others can participate in taking initiatives. Furthermore, a leader is supposed to have a greater grasp of the "larger picture" and be able to communicate and share that with followers, by being "accessible" to those possibilities.

As shown in Figure 2.1, the "new" view recognizes that these are the situation, the leader, and the followers, shown as overlapping circles, in descending size order. The crosshatched area represents their intersection, which is the locus of leadership. The arrows indicate the social exchange which occurs there between the leaders and the followers, who are placed in the figure mainly within the situation, but not entirely so. This indicates their "partial inclusion," since they do have other roles and are open to effects from the outside world. Notice too that relevant attributes of the situation, leader, and followers are indicated, and that each contributes something and receives something in their relationship. In social exchange terms the leader is expected to live up to commitments and obligations to the group, which represents the responsibility element of the leader role. In turn followers are expected to be responsive to the leader's direction, which includes communicating, exerting upward influence, and taking part in decision-making and implementing decisions.

Another feature of the "old" view is suggested by two classic clichés. The first is that "leaders are born, not made," which expresses the belief that innate factors determine who becomes a leader. The second is the traditional concern in history with whether it is "the person or the times" that makes a leader. This either/or choice is a dichotomy that plainly leaves out the alternative of their interaction. Until the 1950s, the "old" view of who became a leader was often viewed in the stark and traditional terms of individual versus situational determinism. Psychologists typically worked at measuring the individual qualities of leaders, especially personality characteristics. Historians and sociologists were among those more inclined to impute leadership to situational factors. This earlier preoccupation with

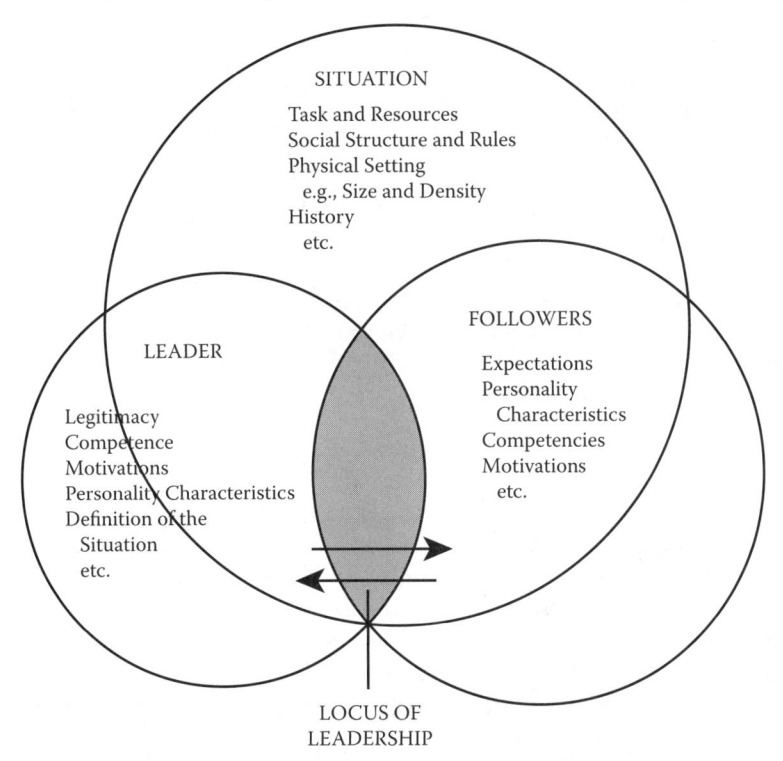

**Figure 2.1** Source: Leadership Dynamics: A Practical Guide to Effective Relationships by Edwin P. Hollander (Fig. 1, p. 8). Copyright © 1978 by the Free Press, a Division of Simon & Schuster Adult Publishing Group. Reprinted by permission of hte publisher. All rights reserved.

who emerged as a leader eventually yielded to an interest in how effective leaders differed from ineffective ones. But the concern with performance still required more development before the demands of differing situations were taken into account. Furthermore, in assessing leader behavior, its effects on followers and the counter-effects of followers on leaders were not yet given due weight. The emphasis still was on the leader, and the prevailing interest was usually his or her traits.

## TRAIT APPROACHES[*]

In the first half of the 20th century a great deal of attention in psychology was directed to the study of "traits" of leaders, but without considering these situational factors. Cowley was one of the investigators who put the case simply: "The approach to the study of leadership has usually been and must always be through the study of traits" (1928, p. 144). However, he recognized even then that there also were "situational traits" that required attention in understanding the context of leadership. At about the same time, in sociology, Thrasher (1927, pp. 245, 248) described leaders of Chicago youth gangs he had studied, thereby giving expression to a "trait-in-situation" model:

> Lacking the traits of a natural leader, a boy often manages to exert control in the gang through the possession of some special qualifications. ... The leader of the gang is what he is because in one way or another he is what the boys want ... the natural leader comes nearest fitting the requirements of his function: he "fills the bill."

In its pure form the trait approach grew out of the "great man" theory, which is probably the oldest conception about the basis for leadership. Whenever events are explained by recourse to the distinctive characteristics of prominent individuals, this theory is to some degree invoked. An extreme expression of it comes from the philosopher Sidney Hook, who wrote that "all factors in history, save great men, are inconsequential" (1955, p. 14). Alternatively, an evaluation of the validity of the great man theory led sociologist Gustav Spiller (1929, p. 218) to write:

> It is widely held that the man of genius is born, not made: that to him epoch-making ideas come in a flash and that he unfailingly imposes those on his social environment. If this view is correct, the secret of greatness lies just in being born great, but it is only fair to inquire how far particular individual, social, and historical circumstances possibly account for the phenomenon of greatness.

His more pointed conclusion was that "greatness, like littleness, is apparently determined by a combination of individual, social, and historical circumstances" (p. 231).

A hereditary basis for leader qualities was also a feature of the classic trait approach, as in the work of Sir Francis Galton with the success of members of eminent families. Galton saw these as genetic characteristics of a family. In his book *Hereditary Genius* (1869) he reported evidence of families where for generations male members followed a particular career line, such as the law, with evident distinction. However, this could be as much a sign of the "right" family ties as of genetic qualities. In a later time there was more possibility of getting ahead without such family ties. The prospect of greater social mobility meant that

---

[*] Material from the "trait approach" through "power and influence" is adapted in part from E. P. Hollander, "Leadership and Power," In G. Lindzey and E. Aronson, (Eds.) (1985). *The handbook of social psychology*, Third ed., New York: Random House, (pp. 485–537), with permiission of the McGraw-Hill Company.

becoming a leader was seen to be related more to individual capabilities, to what one could do, rather than to conditions of birth. The leader's own character and other personal qualities were then viewed as of greater importance.

Early in the 20th century trait research placed considerable stress on such factors as height, weight, appearance, intelligence, self-confidence, and any other variables that might be correlated positively with leadership. The broad aim was to determine what factor or factors made a person a leader. The results were summarized in an influential review by Stogdill (1948), which revealed a very mixed picture. The major finding was that, on the average, leaders tended to be slightly more intelligent than nonleaders. More will be said about this shortly.

Mann (1959) later reviewed 125 studies of leadership and personality characteristics representing over 700 findings. Once again intelligence stood out as the factor with the highest percentage of positive relationships with leader status. With lower percentages, general adjustment, extroversion, and dominance were found to be positively related to being a leader. However, Mann pointed out that the bulk of these studies involved a group organized around an assigned discussion task. Therefore, the "superiority" of the leader has to be viewed as likely to be affected by that kind of situation.

Stogdill (1974) concluded in his *Handbook of Leadership* that the typical leader is only slightly more intelligent than the group average. He said that there is nothing like a perfect relationship between intelligence and leader status. The most intelligent person in the group is not the one most likely to become the leader. Furthermore, measures of association between being the leader and level of intelligence indicate that other variables may intervene, especially when looking at the effective leader. For instance, a study of infantry squad leaders by Fiedler and Leister (1977) found that leader intelligence and group task performance were variously related as a function of situational "screens," allowing "openness" to the leader's intellectual output. In short, a leader's ability to use intelligence may be limited by the working circumstances, not the least by who is his or her superior.

An additional point about the relationship between intelligence and leading was made by Gibb (1968), who indicated that studies showed that nonleaders do not like to be led by those who are very much higher in intelligence than themselves. Although "the evidence suggests that every increment of intelligence means wiser government ... the crowd prefers to be ill-governed by people it can understand" (p. 218). Earlier he explained:

> Followers subordinate themselves, not to an individual whom they perceive as utterly different, but to a member of their group who has superiority at this time and whom they perceive to be fundamentally the same as they are, and who may, at other times, be prepared to follow. (Gibb, 1954, p. 915)

Today's emphasis shows a richer understanding of the benefits leaders provide in their interaction with followers. Intrinsic rewards, such as elevation of their self-concept, illustrate this development, as shown in the work of Lord and Brown (2004).

## THE INDIVIDUAL AND THE SITUATION

In the past 50 years, we have come at last to recognize that many situational elements can affect the process of leadership, apart from the characteristics of the leader and followers: the nature of the activity, its history and actors, the availability of human and material resources, as well as time and the quality of leader-follower relations. The latter, of course, are affected by the leader's attributes, including at least his or her perceived competence, motivation, and personality characteristics, as these relate to followers. Yet even within the situational approach, ideas about leadership were dominated for a long time by a view of the leader and followers in relatively fixed roles. The more *dynamic* realities of leadership—including features of change, the role of the leader as follower, maintaining legitimacy, and matters of succession—were given far less attention.

An important development, then, was the recognition that followership is vital to leadership. Furthermore, followership is an active role that has the potential to become a leadership role. Granting that there is an imbalance, influence can be exerted in both roles, given the relational nature of leadership. Effective leadership is achieved, after all, by the active involvement of responsive followers. Considering the reality that organizations require followership from leaders at all levels within a hierarchy, the subordinate who shows the quality of being responsive will call attention to his or her "leadership potential" and perhaps gain consideration for a higher position. Therefore, behaviors seen to represent effective leadership include attributes of good followership, although language differentiates sharply between the two. Whoever may bear a "leader label," leadership relies on mutual influence and responsiveness, which is the essence of an effective relationship (Hollander, 1978a).

A major breakthrough occurred in the 1940s and 1950s with the studies conducted by personnel psychologists at Ohio State University (OSU) of the actual behavior of leaders in their interactions with followers. Among the findings was the importance of how leader responsibilities and others' expectations of them were defined. A key development was the research by Fleishman (1953, 1973) on measuring leader behavior with the OSU scales that showed the particular importance of *consideration* and *initiation of structure* as two behaviors that accounted for the bulk of leader behaviors. Furthermore, these were variably predictive of the responses of followers in such measures as rate of grievance.

In that vein, Fleishman and Harris (1962) found in a study of foremen in an industrial firm that a lack of consideration took precedence over initiating structure in yielding grievances among workers. However, if foremen established a climate of mutual trust, rapport, and tolerance for two-way communication with their work groups, workers were more likely to accept higher levels of structure, which is attributable to a different interpretation of structure (Fleishman, 1998, p. 830). Interestingly, years later McCall, Lombardo, and Morrison (1988) did a study originating at the Center for Creative Leadership on "derailment" of managers who seemed to be on a fast track in their organization but did not make it to higher corporate levels. Their findings indicated that it was most often a failure in interpersonal skills, rather than technical proficiency, that led to this unsatisfactory outcome. In a different setting and different study population than that of Fleishman and Harris (1962), what was found seemingly is closely related, and the findings resonant with each other. Support and control are seen as two dimensions that affect the leader's ability to produce favorable performance and satisfaction among followers.

Although only a few people occupy the status of leader at a given time in a particular setting, they are not the only ones who have the qualities of a leader. In any group or organization, the range of leadership functions to be fulfilled are multiple—among others: director of activity, problem solver and planner, communicator, adjudicator of conflict, advocate of goals and values, and external liaison. Clearly the formal leader cannot do everything, but must gain assistance from others by a distribution of labor through delegation.

## THE SITUATIONAL APPROACH EMERGES

The shift from traits to interpersonal relations brought a new paradigm that was called the situational approach. It considered leadership as a process rather than something a leader possessed, and it took account of followers in a particular situation. Other features of the situation, including task demands, past history, and resources, were emphasized as important in the context in which the leader and followers functioned. John Hemphill (1949), Fillmore Sanford (1950), and Alvin Gouldner (1950) were among those whose writings led to the emergence of this approach. For example, Sanford (1950) wrote: "There is some justification for regarding the follower as the most crucial factor in any leadership event." (p. 4)

## CONTINGENCY MODELS

As the field of leadership study matured, new ways of reconciling the earlier trait-situation debate emerged through "contingency models." These addressed questions of how leaders actually function in varying situations with different contingencies, that is conditions such as leader-member relations, nature of the task, sharing of information, and time constraints, as examples. These were related to leader qualities and to those of followers and their responsiveness (Fiedler 1964, 1967; Vroom and Yetton, 1973). In determining leader effectiveness, as the major outcome, Fiedler's contingency model was a breakthrough that took account of several variables that interact with the leader's task or relationship orientation. These are leader-member relations, task structure, and leader position power. Fiedler considers task-oriented leaders to be more directive, more controlling, and less concerned with human relations. They perform better when the three situational factors are relatively certain, regarding favorability or unfavorability. He reports a variety of research showing this contrast. The oldest and best known contingency model, Fiedler's LPC, essentially differentiates two kinds of leader style, extending the contrast between consideration and initiation of structure.

The next contingency model, developed by Vroom and Yetton (1973), is specifically concerned with leader styles in decision making. These are the *autocractic*, *consultative*, and *group* styles, indicating heightened degrees of participation from followers. The quality of the decision, the time required to achieve it, and acceptance by group members constitute the standards or criteria for effectiveness.

Eight kinds of issues are considerations for the leader in determining the style, beginning with the importance of decision quality, the amount of information the leader has to arrive at a quality decision, and the amount of information possessed by group members to achieve such a decision. Others include the clarity of the problem, the acceptance needed for implementation of the decision, the likelihood that the leader's decision will be accepted by the group members, the degree of motivation of those members to attain the objectives of the problem and the amount of disagreement about preferred solutions. As a normative model, the emphasis is on participation and inclusion. No assumptions are made about the leader's personality, nor the motivations of the group. It is therefore highly situational, and requires some attention to the factors noted, which means training is desirable. Vroom and Jago (1988, 2007) have studied the validity of the model and find it to be more successful than others in predicting decision quality.

Greater emphasis is now given to the importance of followers' perceptions of and expectations about the leader's actions and the motives seen to underlie those actions. This element of the two-way perception or misperception of each other is considered a central feature of leader-follower relations in the transactional approach. An example of this process has come to prominence through attributional analysis, originating with Heider (1958). If a leader is perceived as able to achieve a favorable outcome but does not because of an apparent failure of will, this will cause a greater loss of following than the reverse, that is, an inability to achieve something desirable but an evident try nonetheless. How followers view the leader's source of authority, or "legitimacy," has a considerable effect not only in shaping followers' perceptions but on group performance. A classic experiment (Goldman & Fraas, 1965), for example, had leaders in male groups selected by three methods: (a) election by vote, (b) appointment by competence, and (c) appointment at random. There was also a leaderless control group. Groups with leaders appointed for their competence performed best, with those having elected leaders performing a close second. Poorest performance was found with groups that had randomly appointed leaders and no designated leader, which the investigators attributed to weak legitimacy in these instances. As a general proposition, it also seems clear that election creates a heightened psychological identification between followers and the leader, insofar as followers feel responsible and therefore more involved. They also have been found to have higher expectations about the leader.

The investment followers have in elected leaders also places higher demands on the leader's performance. Elected leaders who fail to perform well are more vulnerable to criticism than appointed leaders, particularly if they are seen to be competent in the first place and thereby create heightened expectations for performance (Hollander & Julian, 1970). When the group is said to be failing, the elected leader benefits initially by a "rallying around" effect, but if a "crisis" of this kind persists, followers are less willing to retain the elected leader than an appointed one (Hollander, Fallon, & Edwards, 1977). Therefore, election and appointment seem to create different psychological climates between leaders and followers, although the interactions involved may be complex (see Ben-Yoav, Hollander, & Carnevale, 1983).

The position of leadership is sought for a variety of motives. McClelland (1975) contends that explanations of this process may emphasize the motive of personal power, to dominate others, rather than recognize socialized power, oriented toward organizing activities and helping followers gain goals through their efforts. Furthermore, there are nonpower motives, such as achievement and affiliation, which he says may be involved in seeking the leader role. Obviously leaders gain the potential for "having an effect" and greater attention. In organizations leaders are among the best paid and generally are able to exercise greater control over their use of time (Jaques, 1961). Leaders also are likely to get "special handling" with respect to deferential behavior by others, not only by subordinates.

On the potentially negative side, leaders typically are perceived to be more responsible for outcomes in groups, and organizations, as well as in society, precisely because of the element of greater authority vested in the role (e.g., Homans, 1974; Jacobs, 1970). With authority comes responsibility. Since leaders are more visible, their failings as well as successes are apparent, especially to detractors who covet their role. The leader role often involves contention with others who are would-be successors or peers involved in "battles" for resources and territory. In this respect the availability of power and counter-power is vital in contending successfully for such benefits and in being able to fend off adversaries.

Leadership and the leader are embedded in a set of circumstances. For example, the historic political context plays an important part in the relationship of the royal leader and followers, especially regarding expectations of a fair exchange. During the pageantry associated with the wedding in 1981 of Britain's Prince Charles, a U.S. television interviewer asked passersby on a London street whether they thought the price of royalty was too high. Few said it was, with the comments shown distinctly favoring the monarchy. One woman put it succinctly, saying: "Yes, they do cost a lot, but a dictator would cost us a great deal more, and the people would get far less for it."

## POWER AND INFLUENCE

In common usage, power is the ability to exert a degree of control over persons, things, and events. Influence is used more to suggest the exercise of persuasion rather than control. As Pruitt observes: "influence and power are omnipresent in human affairs. Indeed, groups cannot possibly function unless their members can influence one another. Power can of course be used for the wrong purposes. But if so, it must be understood in order to protect oneself and others" (1971, p. 343).

A classic statement of the distinction between influence and power is by Bierstedt, who said: "Influence does not require power, and power may dispense with influence. Influence may convert a friend, but power coerces friend and foe alike" (1950, p. 731). Practically speaking, power relations have two features: the ability to exert power, in the sense of controlling others and events, and the capacity to defend against power. Cartwright (1959) has called the latter "counter-power."

Both elements are involved in studying the effects of power. As Weber wrote: "Power is the probability that one actor within a social relationship will be in a position to carry out his own will despite resistance" (1946, p. 152). Quite simply, having enough power means you can get your own way. A yearning for personal power will generate great efforts toward that end. Indeed the psychoanalytic thinker Alfred Adler (1925) considered the individual striving for personal power to be as central to psychodynamic functioning as sexual drive is to Freud's psychoanalytic theory.

The power construct is used in at least three major ways in social psychology (Ng, 1980). First, power is motivational, in the sense of striving for mastery or control (McClelland, 1975; Winter, 1973). Second, power is used in cognitive terms, as in perceived locus of control (Rotter, 1966) and the concepts of personal causation and self-efficacy (Bandura, 1977; deCharms, 1968). Third, power is behavioral, as in Heider's (1958) "can" factor in the analysis of actions of individuals and the distinction made between "behavior control" and "fate control" by Thibaut and Kelley (1959).

Most analyses of leadership and power begin with the basis on which one person, usually a leader, is able to exert power over others. In organizations the most fundamental sources of power are structural and personal (Wood, 1973). These refer to position or place and to individual qualities, respectively, including "resource dependency" on persons (Pfeffer, 1981; Pondy, 1977). A well-known formulation (French & Raven, 1959) elaborates several "bases of power," including legitimate power, reward power, coercive power, referent power, and expert power. The first of these is akin to the concept of the leader's legitimacy of authority, insofar as the leader's position is seen as validated by some acceptable mechanism, such as appointment or election. Reward and coercive power represent gains or losses for compliance or noncompliance with a person in authority. Referent power represents an extension of reward power through a process of identification with that person. Once such identification has occurred, it is no longer necessary for the person in authority to monitor the behavior of the less powerful person continuously. As the term suggests, expert power arises from specialized knowledge or distinctive competence that is valued.

Although power and influence constitute different processes, they are intertwined insofar as leaders may use both depending on the circumstances and the particular followers involved. Even appointed leaders, "put in charge" within an organization, must rely on influence, in the sense of persuasion, as much as or more than on power. The unfettered use of power can be highly dysfunctional in creating numerous points of resistance and lingering negative feelings. Therefore, both elected and appointed leaders are called upon to use persuasion in many instances, instead of the full power supposedly at their disposal.

The exercise of power has costs, both to the power-wielder and the person to whom it is directed. Among other things, there may be resentment when one person can exercise power over another, and the imbalance in their relative strength is thereby made explicit. Also the greater dependence of the less-powerful person on the more powerful one stands out as a feature of their relationship. Emerson (1962) says that such unequal dependence can promote the use of power, whereas a greater balance in dependence can discourage its use. In this regard Mulder (1981) has pointed out the effect of "power distance," which he sees as heightening the disparity between leader and followers, especially due to differences in information.

## PERCEPTIONS OF PERFORMANCE

Within the context of newer views of leadership, developments in attribution analysis remain important, beginning with analyses by Calder (1977) and Pfeffer (1977). Among other things they note is that in general a positive or negative outcome is more likely to be attributed to the leader, so that when things go awry he or she is more readily faulted and even removed. This effect is part of the "fundamental attribution error" (Jones & Nisbett, 1971). It also is associated with what Rush, Thomas, and Lord (1977) call "implicit leadership theories." If something goes wrong, the whole staff or entire team cannot be fired, but firing the leader can convey a sense of solving the problem. In the political realm, obviously, a term of office often limits the immediacy of this effect.

A major persisting question is: What earns a favorable judgment on a leader's performance? Obviously, one important answer has to do with success in achieving collective goals. But such goals may be set by the leader, who thereby defines—and redefines—the criteria for judgment within the system. The significance of followers' and others' perceptions of the leader, particularly their expectations about leader competence and motivation, is important. There also is the consequence of self-presentation: How does the leader come across personally in the process, especially in dealing with others, including followers, peers, superiors, and adversaries? Clearly, obvious instances of unfairness, self-seeking at others' expense, weakness, vacillation, and outright misconduct detract from the leader's image.

An older concept that serves as an overarching theme covering both leader performance and appeal is the notion of "charismatic leadership," mentioned earlier. Max Weber (1921, 1946) furthered this idea and based it on the Greek word "charisma," meaning "divine gift." A charismatic leader, said Weber, appeals to loyal followers and has considerable power over them, especially in a time of crisis when there are strong needs for direction. However, he said it would be lost if the leader were "long unsuccessful." Others have tried to update and refine the concept. Robert House (1977), for instance, proposed that the leader-follower bond is not so dependent on an emotional appeal but on a course of action: a goal and the path to achieve it.

James McGregor Burns (1978) developed a related concept in his idea of "transforming leadership." Such leaders engage followers and change their outlook and behavior. The term sounds similar to "transactional leadership," but it differs primarily in the heavy weight given to the leader's impact on followers, with attention less to the effect of followers on the leader. However, the transformational leader can be considered to be at an extremity of transactional leadership where he or she provides followers with a much-desired infusion of reality definition and a great sense of purpose. There need not, therefore, be such a sharp dichotomy between the two, as Burns (2007, p. viii) says, noted here earlier.

## STYLE AND SUBSTANCE

Applying Burn's notion of the leader as a transforming agent to the organizational leadership realm, Bass (1985) and Bennis and Nanus (1985) have sought to understand how it relates to exceptional performance. The essential point again is that the leader strives to go beyond the bounds of the usual to bring about a change in thinking that will redirect follower action. Although the purpose served is usually assumed by these writers to be for the good, that remains an open question since so much depends on the leader's motives. By contrast, this seems less problematic in the related ideas about achieving "excellence," exemplified in the popular book *In Search of Excellence* a couple of decades ago by Peters and Waterman (1983).

An expression of a new twist on the older situational approach is the idea of "organizational culture," where the founder and successor leaders set norms and values and a climate or tone in an organization that permeates its reach. Taking a leader role in this situation requires awareness of this culture, especially if changes are being sought (Kilmann et al., 1985; Schein, 1985). "Organizational climate" (Fleishman, 1953b) is a related concept in leadership study; Likert (1961) emphasized that an organizational leader cannot readily use a style (e.g., participative) that differs too drastically from that of one's superior (e.g., autocratic). Maccoby (1976) developed a psychological analysis of four managerial types: (a) the craftsman, (b) the company man, (c) the jungle fighter, and (d) the gamesman. He contended then that the gamesman dominated the top echelon of innovative organizations. That descriptive term "innovative" is an important qualifier insofar as it may limit wider generalizability beyond, for example, "high-tech" organizations. The highly popular books by corporate chiefs, like Harold Geneen (1984) and Lee Iaccoca (1984), present interesting countercases. The gamesman, says Maccoby, shows tendencies toward rashness, fantasy, manipulation, and lying—hardly a set of redeeming characteristics. Neither Geneen nor Iaccoca would seem to fit these descriptions.

Maccoby (1981) has presented a set of case histories about what he calls "new-style" leaders who are trying to make business and government more humane and effective. Contrary to the gamesman style, he says, they show greater concern for people functioning as independent teams. Certainly there is evidence of more attention now to group processes and teamwork, if only because of the interest in Japanese management practices, especially in manufacturing organizations, exemplified by such books as Ouchi's *Theory Z* (1981). This development originated with the "human relations" approach of the 1940s led by Likert (1961), McGregor (1960), and others; that approach "took" in Japan before it was reimported here.

Another approach to style considers it to be based on relatively stable cognitive qualities, an "outlook," such as open versus closed mindedness harking back to Rokeach (1960). In a related vein, Fiedler and Leister (1977) have presented data indicating that a leader's ability to use his or her cognitive capacity or "intelligence" is limited by what that leader's superior will allow. The more recent book by Fiedler and Garcia (1987) extends this research regarding the leader's cognitive capacity and effective group performance. Also, the work on "integrative complexity" in cognition by Suedfeld and Tetlock (1977) and Tetlock (1983) involves the content analysis of a leader's verbal material, particularly as it shows more "integrative complexity" (i.e., less categorical thinking). Leaders who have more integrative complexity generally are said to to be more successful.

Concerning the cognitive component of leadership, it also is instructive to look at the operating theory or conception with which leaders work. A key element is their idea of what makes things happen in organizations. March (1981) identified three such theories: the first attributes a large share of the variance to special characteristics of specific individuals; the second accepts the fact of loose coupling and a form of "organized anarchy"; the third acknowledges that leaders have an impact, but not so much as individuals as a class with a density of administrative competence—that is, a team of able individuals. March says that the first theory risks "false positive" errors, if efforts by the leader do not work out, while the second risks "false negative" errors, and yields self-conforming withdrawal from trying (pp. 28–29). The third is more balanced and less fraught with potential errors either way, according to March's analysis. One might surmise that there can be mixed or shifting types that occur, depending on the stage in the relationship of a leader and his or her institution, as in the case of a new president versus a long-standing incumbent.

Executive leadership has recently been studied by Fleishman, Zaccaro and their colleagues as part of a program under sponsorship of the Army Research Institute (ARI). This program is reported in a special issue of *Leadership Quarterly* by Yamarrino (2000). Their study of meta-cognitive processes among high-level army officers indicated that computer interactive measures of six meta-cognitive skills predicted performance of these officers. Zaccaro (1999) reported that these measures of cognitive, behavioral, and social complexities are necessary for leaders to be effective in drastically changing situations. It is noteworthy that the social component is prominent, supporting other findings about the importance of the relational factor in leadership-followership, which is basic to the IL approach presented here.

## TRANSACTIONAL AND SOCIAL EXCHANGE MODELS—VDL & LMX

When changes are needed in an organization, the expectations and perceptions of followers are significant for the leader's ability to achieve the desired outcome. The Idiosyncrasy Credit (IC) model presented in Chapter 1 is a major transactional approach to leadership that focuses on the two-way aspects of leader-follower relations involved in effecting change. Rather than look solely at the leader's actions and intentions, it considers the leader-follower relationship as central to understanding the ability of a leader to bring followers along in accomplishing innovative action through such elements as trust. The potential for two-way influence is also recognized in this relationship.

The original formulation (Hollander, 1958) was within a social exchange framework, furthered by such figures as Homans (1958, 1961). Other concepts that consider leader-follower exchange are represented by the work of Graen (1975) and his colleagues, who advanced the vertical dyadic linkage (VDL) model, which deals with "role-making" between a leader and particular followers. Graen considers that each leader has close and more distant circles of followers. While the first followers share a closer relationship with the leader, they do not necessarily have it easier as a result. Higher demands may be made on them to perform to the leader's standard and have an added cost associated with such closeness. That cost often is a stricter code of loyalty and obedience. Usually a follower who is close to a leader becomes more capable of making the leader appear effective or ineffective, especially because a leader generally is considered responsible for the acts of a subordinate given authority by the leader. Therefore, if the member fails, the leader may be perceived to have failed unless mitigating factors prevail.

Other costs occur to the followers because the leader can give only a limited part of his or her resources to do even critical tasks (Graen and Cashman, 1975, p. 154). The follower must do enough with these resources to avoid the high risks of failure that would hurt the leader. By contrast, success is more likely to be seen as the leader's. For those in the outer circle, the leader may make fewer personal demands. These followers are usually group members of relatively lower status of newcomers who are treated more as a bloc. However, they are still required to show performance helpful to attaining the group's goals. In the last two decades, the terminology has changed for this model to LMX, for Leader-Member-Exchange (Dienesch & Liden, 1986).

## SOCIAL EXCHANGE AND NON-NORMATIVITY

A social exchange perspective sees the leader in an implicit transaction giving followers benefits, such as a sense of direction and recognition of their needs and efforts. The followers in turn provide the leader with responsiveness to influence, greater status, and esteem (Hollander and Julian, 1969; see Chapter 5 here). Hence, the "transaction" offers the basis for mutual regard and two-way influence, including demands made on the leader by followers who may have a more active role than is usually acknowledged. Homans (1961) has summed up this process briefly in noting that "Influence over others is purchased at the price of allowing one's self to be influenced by others" (p. 286).

Two other points are noteworthy regarding the IC model's orientation. Though it applies most obviously to leadership as "accorded status," where followers have a determining role in giving legitimacy to the leader, it has important implications for appointive leadership situations as well, where a "loyal following" is essential. Second, the model is non-normative and descriptive, since it does not take a position on how things ought to be, but reflects how they appear to operate in relatively less power-oriented systems, as exemplified by colleges and universities (see Chapter 10 here).

In social exchange terms, conformity also has been treated as a reward that smoothes interaction (Homans 1961; Jones, 1964; Nord, 1969; Thibaut and Kelley 1959). The essential point in such a view is that conformity can be exchanged for acceptance and support from others. When extended over time, the IC model predicts the prospect that *early conformity may permit tolerance of later non-conformity, in the form of innovation.*

The perception of a person's conformity to group norms is based on observations that are matched against expectancies, including the competence displayed in helping the group attain favorable outcomes. A key consideration in the IC model is that behavior perceived to be nonconforming for one group member may not be perceived so for another. Associated with this consideration is that conformity and nonconformity are not fixed to a single norm applicable to everyone. Rather, nonconforming behavior can be seen to be variously defined by the group, depending on how the actor is perceived. Conformity is therefore assessed in light of that person's credits.

This feature of the IC model fits the everyday observation that individuals of higher status usually have more latitude to nonconform in regard to general norms. While this point has been substantiated in many research studies (see Hollander, 1985), there is the key proviso that the expectancies associated with the leader's role are more constrained and less able to be violated with impunity. Among these expectancies, for example, would be loyalty to the group and affirmation of its values.

## HIGHER STATUS, INFLUENCE, AND INNOVATION POTENTIAL

The IC model predicts that higher status in the eyes of others has a direct bearing on the ability to be influential. A person of rising status is subject eventually to new expectancies that allow the assertion of influence, making it appropriate there for others in the group to accept such influence. With a relatively high level of perceived competence, a group member should have increased influence to some maximum over time.

Accordingly, the consideration that the behavior of a person perceived to have higher status is evaluated differently from one of less status provides a bridge for understanding the innovation potential associated with leadership. Leaders may be initiators of change, perhaps in seemingly nonconforming ways, but they usually conform to group norms in establishing their position initially. Furthermore, as noted above, nonconformity can be viewed with regard to the distinction between common expectancies for group members, as well as those particularly restricted expectancies associated with the role of higher status. At least two reasons seem to explain why these restrictions may be imposed. First, because status is usually perceived to carry with it greater self-determination, those of higher status are assumed to be more responsible for their actions. Second, having greater status means having more visible potential for affecting important outcomes for the members of a group (Hollander, 1964, Chapter 20).

An experiment by Alvarez (1968) dealt with some of these issues and found that the high-status person loses esteem at a slower rate than the low-status one. But this was true only in "successful" organizations. If the organizations were "unsuccessful," the opposite was true. This dramatizes the point that the greater responsibility and visibility usually associated with higher status means that the outcome of any given act of nonconformity will be judged with respect to the rewards produced for the group or organization. With a history of past innovations, which have yielded success, the high-status group member's behavior is more likely to be perceived to provide good outcomes rather than bad outcomes. The reverse holds, too. A lack of success gives these deviations a negative coloration, which can rapidly drain credits. Again, the main point is that evidently nonconforming acts will be variously interpreted as a function of others' *perception of the actor* based on their past experience with and attributions about that person.

A benefit may also result from standing out in a figure-ground sense, if the outcome for the group is positive. This was verified in research by Sorrentino and Boutillier (1975) who found that initial *quantity* of participation in a group was viewed by others as a positive sign of a group member's motivation, while *later* participation was evaluated more for *quality*. Ridgeway (1981) has presented experimental evidence indicating that nonconformity may be a greater initial source of influence. Certainly, it is true that within a brief time a person may call attention to himself or herself by manifest nonconformity to prevailing norms, but this will be evaluated in due course by the task contribution made (Hollander, 1964, p. 227). This can be seen as a parallel to the influence generated by the sheer volume of early talking in discussion groups. However, both of these effects are doubtless nonlinear, and a point may be reached where rejection may result.

## APPOINTMENT-ELECTION AND FOLLOWER RESPONSIVENESS

One factor mentioned earlier is the leader's basis of legitimacy, which is how and by whom she or he is validated initially in that role. This factor has considerable primacy in shaping followers' perceptions. Leader legitimacy, as Read has stated, "involves a complex interaction of attitudes toward the leader and his source of authority, with the leader's actual behavior contributing substantially to his task influence and continuing legitimacy" (1974, p. 103).

Having authority is not the same as providing leadership, although it serves as a basis for it. A major difference exists in the realm of appointment or election as sources of a leader's authority. In both instances, the possibility of being perceived to be a leader, and acting as one, depends in practice on recognition from others who are to be followers. The election case is of course a more obvious instance of emergence with follower support. In that vein, Boyd (1972) found that elected representatives felt freer to act in negotiation than appointed ones, revealing their greater sense of having group support. Similarly, Lamm (1973) reviewed findings on negotiation behavior that showed appointed leaders to consult their group members in negotiation.

In general, there is a good deal of evidence for the proposition that election creates in followers more of a sense of responsibility and higher expectations for the leader's success (Hollander & Julian, 1970, 1978), as previously noted. One explanation is to view this as a social exchange in which the group gives the leader a "reward" in advance, by electing him or her, and then group members feel a claim on him or her to "pay back" by producing favorable outcomes (Jacobs, 1970).

In consequence, it is true also that the support of followers can produce higher demands on the leader. Elected leaders may well have a stronger basis for feeling follower support, but they also are more vulnerable to having higher expectations imposed on them. Also, this differential does not at all limit the very real possibility of institutional leaders attaining a "following" by doing more than merely exercising authority, as stated in the Gardner (1987) epigraph in Chapter 1, and Katz and Kahn (1978) have pointed out in speaking of leadership as "an increment of influence above compliance."

CHAPTER 3

# Applications and Implications of Inclusive Leadership

## INTRODUCTION

This chapter covers some of the major bases for Inclusive Leadership (IL) research and their relationship to applications. Three of these are *interpersonal evaluation, legitimacy as a source for leading,* and *social exchange,* especially the issue of fairness. They occur in the direct contact of individuals in groups, but can also be observed at the macro level in political processes, as presented in Chapter 10 here.

In general, studying leader-follower relations is important to better understand the operation of organizations and groups, and beyond. Increasingly, leadership is recognized as a system of relationships rather than being solely based on the leader's attributes and actions. A significant point in the IL approach is the *distinction between leadership processes and the leader.* Another point is the *two-way flow of influence that permits active followership.* Still further is the *role of "equity," or "justice," in the relationship of leader and followers and their organizational setting.* Illustrative of the latter is a recent summary by Komaki (2007) of progress over more than four decades in attempts to reduce employment discrimination in the workplace.

Although usually seen as involving direction and coordination activities, leadership affects many other processes, including maintaining the enterprise, with resource allocation, and its consequences in conformity, cohesiveness, morale, and satisfaction. In these and other aspects of organizational functioning, situational factors also impact leadership effectiveness (Vroom & Jago, 2007). The environment of leadership is also differentiated by the kinds of enterprise, such as a business or a public agency, its task demands, and setting. These are some of the key variables for attention and analysis (Fleishman & Zaccaro, 1992).

## LEARNING INCLUSIVE LEADERSHIP SKILLS

Executives and managers use interpersonal skills that make their relationships more effective and contribute to productivity. The need to acquire these skills is clear from some prominent instances of top-level corporate executives dismissed for performance failings based on interpersonal relations and communications, as noted in Chapter 1. Learning is basic to leading, as Vaill (1989, 1996) has consistently pointed out (see also Conger, 1993). Even if there are resistant cases, the investment in developing leadership skills through training programs can at a minimum address problems of poor leader performance that have costly individual and organizational consequences. In these cases, IL practices are likely to be successful, when appropriately applied. Problems of dysfunctional leader-follower relations can be reduced by using many of the seven guiding IL practices summarized here.

- Respecting members of the team and their individuality;
- Showing awareness of their contributions and giving recognition of those, with attention to fairness;
- Having group discussions about goals, and listening to what is said;
- Deciding what performance is needed to achieve those goals, and giving feedback on progress toward their achievement;
- Facilitating a forward-looking approach, rather than just reviewing the past;
- Living up to the responsibilities of fulfilling one's role, as it is depended upon by others;
- Being open as much as possible, with honest communications that foster trust and loyalty.

## INCLUSIVE LEADERSHIP CONNECTIONS WITH TF LEADERSHIP AND THE IC MODEL

A function of the leader role is often one of facilitating change, as in the Burns (1978) concept of transforming (TF) leadership, discussed earlier. The idiosyncrasy credit (IC) model also considers a leader to be a potential change agent, gaining accorded status within the group. The kind of esteem represented by "credits" provides a leader with some latitude in exercising influence toward change, which is underpinned by the IC concept of perceived legitimacy (Hollander, 1958, 1964). Comparing these two approaches, they vary especially in the degree to which the followers are seen as affecting a leader's ability to bring about change, with the cooperation of followers, including its implementation. This may also be a function of obvious sources of legitimacy, such as imposed authority. Bass (1997, p. 132) has made the explicit point that TF leadership can be autocratic and effective, in some situations. This differs from the way IL is based in a participative process that emphasizes "doing things with people, rather than to people."

## PERFORMANCE OVER TIME

There is also the group's success or failure in the task to be considered, with particular regard to the leader's perceived contribution to it, especially in immediate past memory (see e.g., Alvarez, 1968; Hackman, 1989). Appointing a successor in an organization may favor the inside person who will have amassed a record, but with perceived commitments, which can mean proponents and opponents. The outside person comes into a situation, perhaps as a new manager, having to learn about the terrain, the leadership structure, and its participants, perhaps stumbling along the way. He or she may have credits that are "derivative" from external status, as well as a reputation from past perceived performance.

Sometimes the lack of transferability from one setting to another is an issue, including the nature of the industry. A case in point is the commented upon appointment of a top Boeing Aircraft executive Alan Mulally to head the Ford Motor Company, a major automotive manufacturer. However, if a leader's successes are seen to depend on group performance and satisfaction, his or her relational skills with capable people may produce favorable outcomes. That was part of his reputation, and his background included knowledge he had acquired of Toyota's worldwide operation while at Boeing. All of which means that knowing about the primary function of a business helps, but so does building effective teams, to attain successful leadership (Katzenbach & Smith, 1993).

## MULTIPLE FEATURES OF THE LEADER ROLE WITH FOLLOWERS

More attention to those with whom a leader works should be part of a leader's role. A leader helps to develop followers' leadership skills by distributing tasks to them and evaluating their performance by giving them feedback. These functions are an important basis for assessing a leader's effectiveness, as Bower (1997) has emphasized. They are likely also to produce benefits in good leader-follower relations.

The role of leader involves a variety of functions, although managerial and supervisory conceptions of that role, especially those of the mass-production organization, still predominate. Greater specification seems needed in dealing with variations of the leadership setting, as well as for leadership style and related ideas, such as organizational climate. Participation, for example, can mean different things operationally. It can be structural or stylistic, in the sense that the organization may encourage it, but managers may not act on it, or in its spirit, due to their individual style.

More attention is needed for the leader's construction of his or her situation in attempting to woo followers (Gray & Densten, 2007), as well as to the perception of his or her own identity and legitimacy. The situational view, as covered in Chapter 2, was not intended to discard concern with individual leader attributes, including perceptions and behavioral tendencies. Rather it saw them as differentially appropriate to varying circumstances and the kind of decisions and outcomes sought. Individual differences still are a focus of attention in such issues as personal style, entrepreneurial zeal, and the ability to gain a following, with trust and loyalty.

## A "FAIR EXCHANGE"

Related to the process of gaining credits is another concept based on a social exchange framework, which helps in understanding leader-follower relations. That is the idea of a "fair exchange" in which the leader gives things of value to followers—such as a sense of direction, values, and recognition—and receives other things in return—such as esteem and responsiveness—in their two-way dealings.

Crucial to the exchange between the leader and followers is the expectation that the leader will produce favorable results. In this view the leader is a valued resource. As Jacobs has put it, "The leader, who holds a position of 'high place,' should be the one in the group who can function best for the common good" (1970, p. 80). If the leader is not successful in this function, the followers are likely to feel that the exchange is not fair. After all, the organization and group members reward the leader more liberally than anyone else. A fair exchange would be one in which the leader performs well and deserves these advantages of status, including the trappings and benefits of being in a theater of high activity and high status. If the leader fails to do well, especially because of an evident lack of effort, then followers are likely to feel a sense of injustice. They may also be discontent if the leader seems to disregard their interests along the way, especially by self-serving actions and statements. When a leader's poor performance is seen to result from inattentiveness to followers, there may be resentment that blunders are being made because the leader is not "in touch." Followers may feel left out and blame the leader for not maintaining the other end of the transaction with them, that is, Responsiveness to them and their interests, which is one of the four Rs of IL.

Awareness of what followers know and need is of course essential to leadership, as emphasized in Chapter 1. However, it does not mean giving up judgment as a leader in a representative government, since to be informed about the will of the electorate is basic. The military presents other not so different considerations about follower input. Lecturing to seniors in the leadership course at the West Point Military Academy, one of the cadets who stood up afterward asked if I was "advocating voting on the battlefield." The obvious answer is no, but I said it may help to the extent possible in such a crisis to have a sense of your troops, what some may know about the enemy's position, the terrain, and the battle's success or failure.

The leader is usually the central figure in moving the group toward its goals. Where the leader has the resources but routinely fails to deliver, there is a basis for dissatisfaction. If, for example, the leader appears to be deviating from accepted norms, such nonconformity may be tolerated initially as a feature of possessing idiosyncrasy credit. However, when that nonconformity seems to produce unsuccessful outcomes, the leader is more vulnerable to blame. It is as if the group said "We expect good results from your actions. If you choose an unusual course, we will go along with you and give you some latitude. But you are responsible if the outcome is that the group fails to achieve its goals."

A fair exchange also involves a climate in which the leader is seen to be concerned that rewards are distributed equitably. Basic to the exchange process is the belief that rewards, such as recognition, will be received for benefits given. However, it is difficult to accomplish this routinely. Even if it were done, the rewards would take on less value due to their frequency, since the scarce reward is usually valued more than the abundant one (Homans, 1961). But there is no doubt there is an optimal range for rewards so that some attention to individual contributions is necessary, even occasionally, if people are to feel they are being treated fairly.

A process of social comparison appears to be basic to many human relationships. Therefore, it is not simply what a group member is able to get by way of praise or more salary. The member can compare these benefits with what others of similar standing are receiving or have received. If the ratio of a person's own benefits to costs is lower than that of some other comparable person in the group, there can be dissatisfaction. The possibility of minimizing such perceived inequities is a good reason why fairness is one of the attributes most valued in a leader.

There are in fact two related factors evident in a fair exchange: (a) system progress and (b) equity. System progress is summed up in the question "How are we doing?" It involves the effective use of resources to achieve desired outcomes for the group. Here the leader's competence in mobilizing group effort is one important issue, with respect to the inputs applied to gaining desired outputs. Equity is also seen in such matters as a sense of individual achievement and recognition.

Fundamentally, there is a "psychological contract" between the leader and followers, which depends on a variety of expectations and actions on both sides. The more dynamic qualities of leader-follower relations are emphasized in the transactional approach. Two key qualities are interpersonal perception and the fulfillment of expectancies. Among these expectancies are rights and obligations, many of which are understood but not formally written. However, organizational regulations and union contracts usually do contain some of them.

The transactional feature of the psychological contract grows out of the two-way nature of influence. Formal organizations grant some individuals the basis for having greater influence over others. Yet, if these others are dissatisfied with the way the contract is being fulfilled, they may feel a right to exert influence upward to change the position. This can lead to bargaining to establish a better understanding.

As indicated previously, a leader's legitimacy is less a fixed and more a dynamic attribute. It depends on the perception of the leader by his or her constituents, and their responsiveness to the leader as followers. They provide a leader with a benefit insofar as they do respond to his or her exercise of authority. Earlier, it was pointed out that the concept of legitimacy essentially refers to the leader's basis for exercising authority. Although legitimacy may be awarded by higher officials, it still requires the acceptance of constituents. Just as it is important that they give a form of consent to legitimacy, they can withhold it as well, although at some costs.

Authority in organizations is meant to fulfill assigned responsibilities, and constituents expect it to be used. However, there may be tension between the leader and constituents over limiting the leader's authority to those responsibilities. When the leader attempts to exercise authority in other areas, open conflict may be seen. The exercise of authority therefore requires enough trust in the relationship to allow some risks by followers as well as by the leader.

The leader's demands on the followers may be reciprocated by their demands on the leader. The social exchange view of leadership sees followers in an active role. Each follower is potentially a source of influence and to some extent can exert counter-influence. The leader directs communications to followers, to which they may react in various ways. The leader tries to take account of the actions and attitudes of followers. The followers, in turn, evaluate the leader's actions and attitudes, with particular regard to the responsiveness they show to the group and its needs. Especially important are the followers' perceptions of the leader's effectiveness and how they evaluate the leader's motivation.

As noted before, the leader can be viewed as a group resource—ideally one who provides for the attainment of the group's goals. In doing so, the leader derives certain benefits in status and increased influence, which serve as rewards. Therefore, in acting as a leader, an individual must necessarily transact with others in his or her environment, and the integrity of the relationship depends on some yielding to influence both sides. With it should be recognition of the contribution made by other participants in the enterprise, not just the leader.

The significant take away point is simply that relational factors such as listening and showing fairness hold a special place in maintaining a favorable leader-follower bond. *Whether leaders are called transformational, transactional, or inclusive, the common element of good leadership that unites them, in achieving "positive results," is respect for and attention to followers and their needs.*

Supporting this point is how much the leader's consideration toward followers matters, shown in the research of Fleishman and Harris (1962) and Fleishman (1998) on the reciprocal relationship of the leader's "consideration" and "initiating structure" behavior on performance of work groups in industrial settings. Using the Supervisory Behavior Description Questionnaire (Fleishman, 1953b, 1989b), they found higher "consideration" (in encouraging, communicating, and being concerned with employee needs) moderated the effects of "initiating structure" (in assigning tasks, organizing, and setting goals) on independent measures of their department's performance.

## MEASURING INCLUSIVE LEADERSHIP WITH A NEW SCALE

As discussed in Chapter 1, research using "critical incidents" with a group of 293 mainly organizationally based respondents provided accounts of their experiences with "good" and "bad" leaders. They were then asked further questions about the incidents and gave ratings about the leader's behavior, their own response, the effect these had on their relationship, and the eventual consequences. Content analyses were then done to relate major qualities to the quantitative findings and outcomes. Relational factors were again found to discriminate best between "good" and "bad" leaders. We then followed up by an extension of this work into further measurement, using excerpts from these accounts, in the respondents' own words, to create items for the Inclusive Leadership Scale (ILS), called an "Evaluation of a Person in a Leader Role."

The research and writing about IL has sought to emphasize the positives in leader-follower relations and reduce those negatives that interfere with successful outcomes. To capture those features, our ILS measure has been balanced with positive and negative items, then pretested with 160 respondents who had work experience. They were asked to indicate how much (Always, Often, Sometimes, Rarely, Never) the particular behavior describes the person they have known recently in the leader role. They also were asked to rate the effectiveness of that leader on a five-point scale (Excellent, Very Good, Good, Fair, Poor), and answer other questions about the relationship, including duration of the relationship and other background matters. Examples of items are these, the first three being positive and the last three negative:

Asks for my ideas about my work
Shows interest in how I am doing my job
Lets me make decisions about my work

Takes credit for work I did
Blames me in front of others when things go wrong
Makes comments to put me down

Research on the ILS has been done collaboratively with my Baruch College colleague Jaihyun Park. The results are presented in the Appendix. In the next section, consideration is given to resolving conflicts with an inclusive approach.

## EXTENDING INCLUSION: RESOLVING CONFLICTS

Much as it is desired, inclusion sometimes cannot readily be achieved. A failure to agree on rules, such as in sports or norms for conducting business, makes it difficult to engage in the activity. Sports represent a clear case of competition with a cooperative spirit that brings adversaries together for a contest of skill and determination. Respect for the opponent's ability is also necessary to bring performance up to the needed competitive level, rather than disparaging the opponent. In international relations, too, it is understood that it is a mistake to underestimate the capacity and intent of an adversary. Resolution of conflict, although better than war, is made difficult by incendiary language and signals of disrespect, which are more likely to result in armed conflict, as historian Barbara Tuchman presents in *The March of Folly* (1984).

Gaining a resolution of disagreements generally requires a common framework, which Sherif and Sherif (1953) advocated as important in finding "superordinate goals." These transcend individual ends to be achieved and show a way to have a "win-win" outcome, where both parties gain a benefit.

Leaders can offer conditions for conciliation of conflict, including proposed structure, for example, agreed tension-reducing conditions for outside mediation. This means letting the participants express their views about process, and their grievances, in a respectful atmosphere, separately and then together, as appropriate. The latter is made more productive if each adversary can state the position of the other side to indicate that there is an understanding of the conflict.

Brainstorming is another way to express ideas that may produce a solution, or solutions, to a problem, especially in an inclusive atmosphere. To achieve that benefit requires having many participants engaged, so it becomes a group enterprise to get "ideas out on the table." Then comments about them can be made, later, not before. Rankings of them by individuals can be done on a "preference" basis, indicating which they find acceptable and if desired how they would rank them from top down. This should be done on an open basis, if the group agrees, but closed balloting is acceptable in some conditions to maintain privacy, especially to avoid intimidation. In either case, the results are likely to be agreed upon and better received.

## USE OF THE IL SCALE

The ILS has utility not only for measuring qualities that leaders may possess but also for purposes of discussion about what should be encouraged as appropriate inclusive behavior. It may well serve to have participants in group discussions relate their experiences with those leaders who they encountered that revealed these or different tendencies. As leaders, it is also possible for individuals to reflect on how they might behave differently when situations arise that are referred to or implied in the ILS items, using this inclusive, participative process (Vroom & Jago, 1988).

A further caution is for the leader to avoid having a "groupthink" effect (Janis, 1972) or for other high-status members to state their views about the outcome or course of action before other participants are heard. Once established as the norm, group cohesiveness and loyalty to the leader virtually ensure that alternatives will either not be raised or dismissed with little consideration.

# PART 2

# Leadership-Followership Issues

# CHAPTER 4

# What Is the Crisis of Leadership?

## COMMENTARY

The paper presented in this chapter begins by examining some of the major historical themes and considerations emphasizing two-way influence in leadership-followership. This process is what I have subsequently called Inclusive Leadership, defined by taking account of the needs and expectations of followers. One illustration of it in practice is the use of such simple but meaningful questions as "How are things going?" and "What do you think is the problem?" when things are not going well. Another is in the involvement of followers, to the extent feasible, in decisions affecting them. In conferring, this basic value involves empowering others by distributing leadership. Bower (1997), for example, has made a particular point of encouraging a "leadership organization," with wide participation, as noted in Chapter 1 of this book. Vaill adds the caution that "Followers need very good reasons to take the increased initiatives empowerment intends; they need to trust that the leader's actions mean what they seem to mean" (1997, p. 79). For instance, is it authentic?

In practice, Hirschhorn (1997) says conferences with employees to raise issues and hear their ideas are important to acting strategically and achieving their commitment to these higher goals. He gives an example of hospital executives, trying to engage hospital staff, physicians, nurses, and others, to work cooperatively. Hirschhorn states that "These senior executives can succeed in guiding the enterprise only if they depend deeply on their employees' skills, their willingness to collaborate with one another, and their ability to recognize the impact of their work on the performance of the enterprise" (p. 5). He goes on to point out the inadequacy in such settings of control systems that depend on coercion and fear, even if these may be seen to be successful in the short term. Issues of coercive, fear-provoking, and other dysfunctional forms of leadership are covered well in two recent books dealing with case histories. Barbara Kellerman (2004) finds that the "bad leaders" are likely to be corrupt beyond incompetence, although these qualities can coexist. In our terms, noninclusiveness characterizes their relationships with followers, involving such deficiencies as arrogance. Lipman-Blumen (2006) says people are attracted to bad leaders who help reduce their fears, which they may themselves have instigated.

More positively, Vaill (1996) has emphasized leadership as a process of learning, captured in the sequence of listening and learning as a basis for thinking about ways of helping, which is essential to leadership. In practice, involving followers in this process is likely to foster mutual trust and loyalty. Another feature of this process is the sense of equity, a "fair exchange," which is one area where failings can produce a crisis. The absence of equity, or out-and-out perceptions of gross unfairness and injustice, allows forces of discontent to develop that can be contagious. Related to this central source is the need to inform and to be credible in the information presented. Another lack is not being accountable, which loosens the bonds of trust and loyalty. These characteristics are needed to keep constituents inside and participating, rather than outside and alienated, as the conclusion of the paper presented below states. At the time it was written, in 1978, some of the policies and practices in the leadership of government and corporations were criticized, and others had not yet been revealed. Revulsion followed from many more disclosures.

In the 1980s and 1990s, blatant leader self-serving behavior, failure of responsibility, dishonesty, and other dysfunctional patterns appeared to be more in evidence. Publicized cases of corporate cheating are exemplified by subsequent events at Enron, Tyco, and Global Crossing, among others involving massive fraud at the top executive level, abetted by major accountancy firms. Beyond those scandals are instances of mishandling and failure to disclose in two cases in 2007 of CEOs dismissed at Merrill Lynch and Citicorp, nevertheless awarded nine-figure severance sums. The atmosphere has likely been negatively toned regarding images of top leaders and leadership. The particulars of this shift and its implications are considered further in Chapter 14 regarding equity issues in leader-follower relations.

The U.S. presidency as a leader-follower phenomenon is mentioned in the original 1978 paper, republished here. Although the characteristics of the role are considered later, in Chapter 10, President Jimmy Carter's problems were used here as examples because they were current at the time of writing. Had it been earlier, during Richard Nixon's or Lyndon Johnson's administration, the matters say of deception and a "credibility gap" could have been cited. And, as noted before, expectations raised by President Bill Clinton were seen to create a problem when not met. These are not just individual matters but institutional ones. The enormity of the position and the widespread attention it commands make for large effects when, for example, there are disparities and disappointments, cross-cut by partisanship, in what has been called the "White House perpetual campaign mode," discussed in Chapter 10.

Reprinted, with permission of the Epiphany Association, from *Humanitas*, 1978, 14 (3), 285–296.

Leadership is critical to the health of a group, organization, or society. Given the expectations it raises, there is always the potential for a crisis of leadership to occur and to take on importance. The contemporary expression about a "lack of leadership" signals that importance and also indicates something about the general nature of the crisis. Recently, a friend used that phrase in describing the main problem in the organization in which she works. These words clearly conveyed a feeling of aimless drift and purposelessness, although little more was said.

Perhaps this malaise is a sign of existential alienation. However, whatever the label, there evidently are some expectations about leadership which are not being fulfilled and that may be characteristic of modern society, especially of the democratic form. Although leadership is present, even when it is "bad," the process called leadership very much depends upon the relationship between leader and followers. The leader is central to that process, and he or she is usually seen as the source of favorable or unfavorable features of the relationship and the results produced. But followers are not merely passive or inert, as the traditional view would have it. Leadership requires responsiveness, cooperation, and a distribution of labor. This fact necessitates a more active role for followers—"a piece of the action" in the vernacular—and its absence may be a major basis for the current crisis.

One difficulty is the categorical quality of words. For instance, there is still a common notion that "the leader" and "the followers" fit into sharp categories. But this overlooks the facts. All leaders, some of the time and to some degree, are followers. And followers need not be cast immutably in non-leader roles. They may, and sometimes do, become leaders. Even though only some people can occupy the status of leader, in a particular time and place, the qualities needed to be a leader are not possessed only by those persons. Furthermore, the leader cannot do everything, though he or she might try. In any group or organization, there are different leadership functions to be fulfilled, such as executive, problem-solver, arbitrator, and, advocate. Being a leader is, therefore, a complex role, and these functions frequently require delegation among several people.

These points take on a particular significance when seen against the historical backdrop of thought and study regarding leadership. A mystique has for so long permeated the concepts of leader and leadership that it is essential to understand the basis for the more contemporary viewpoints. We turn now to a brief review of that development.

## LEADERSHIP IN RETROSPECT

Beginning with the venerable "great man" theory, there have been various approaches to leadership which have attracted interest over the years. The quintessential expression of this theory is in the statement by a contemporary philosopher that "all factors in history, save great men, are inconsequential." Alternatively, an evaluation of the validity of this theory led an eminent sociologist to suggest that, if true, "the secret of greatness lies just in being born great ... " His more serious conclusion was that greatness was determined by a combination of individual, social, and historical circumstances."

Closely associated with this theory was the so-called "trait approach," stressing the personal qualities of those in leader roles. It was favored by psychologically-oriented investigators who studied the personalities and other attributes of leaders. These studies, mainly conducted during the first half of this century, dealt both with who becomes a leader and what qualities make a leader effective, sometimes disregarding the difference between the two. The assumption of a hereditary basis for leader qualities was also a feature of the classic trait approach, as in the work of Sir Francis Galton.

A review of the findings from studies of leader traits showed such mixed results that other factors had to be considered. This led to two interrelated developments. One was the study of the behavior of organizational leaders, initially through descriptive ratings by subordinates. The other was the emergence of a "situational approach," emphasizing the characteristics of the particular situation and task in which the leader and followers were mutually involved. The primary stress was on the demands made for particular leader characteristics there.

The situational approach gave needed attention to the varying demands made upon leaders and achieved a notable gain in putting to rest the trait-based conceptions of the past. However, it ran the risk of overstatement at the other extreme by tending to neglect the characteristics of leaders, when that was not the point at all. The situational approach also failed to distinguish between task demands, and the structure, history, size and setting of different social entities. Furthermore, the leader and situation cannot be so sharply differentiated since followers see the leader as part of the situation, who also helps to shape and define it for them.

An extension and refinement of the situational approach occurred through the relatively recent development of "contingency models." These models attempt to specify what leader attributes are appropriate, for certain contingencies in the situation. They emphasize factors calling forth different leader attributes to achieve effectiveness. In one of these, for example, the amount of follower participation in making decisions is viewed as a function of various contingencies. Among these are the amount of information possessed by the leader vs. the followers, the importance of decision quality, the degree of structure in the problem, the followers' motivation to attain the objective represented by solving the problem; how much their acceptance is necessary to the implementation of the solution, and the probability that the leader's decision made alone will he accepted by the followers.

Accordingly, while some decisions need to be made by the leader, there are conditions favoring greater follower participation. This particular model represents a break with the more traditional views of the leader-follower relationship which present an either-or contrast. One view asserts that the leader must do what he or she believes is the "right thing" without being overly influenced by followers.

The other view is that leaders must take into account the followers interests, needs, wishes, and so forth, in setting goals and directing action. We see now that neither view can be applied universally, and that a variety of considerations enter the picture. In that vein, a parallel development in time was the "transactional approach." It gave emphasis to the relationship between the leader and followers and the possibility of mutual influence.

## LEADERSHIP AS A TRANSACTION

Leadership is a process, and not a person, but the leader is usually seen as the active agent who commands attention and influence. While the leader may have the power of position, influence depends more on persuasion than on coercion. A two-way influence process ordinarily is not characterized by the exercise or threat of force. Instead it involves a "social exchange" between the leader and those who are followers, which means that benefits are given and received as rewards. Social exchange also has to do with the expectations people have about fairness, equitable treatment, and what is just.

In short, the leader gives something and gets something. He or she is usually expected to give direction producing successful results for the group, organization, or larger social entity. In return, the followers give the leader greater esteem, status, and the responsiveness which makes influence possible. However, some minimum degree of success is necessary for the leader's position to be supported, because a lack of success removes a major benefit which the leader can provide in a "fair exchange."

Therefore, a fair exchange would be one where the leader performs well and deserves the advantages of status. If the leader fails to do well, especially because of an evident lack of effort, then followers are likely to have a sense of injustice. They may also be discontented if the leader seems to disregard their interests along the way. Furthermore, when a leader's poor performance results from not listening to followers, there may be a feeling among them that blunders are being made because the leader fails to "be in touch." Followers may feel left out and blame the leader for not maintaining the other end of the transaction with them. This constellation of feelings represents a major source of the crisis in leadership, especially with the followers who have become more exposed to the wider-world through the cascade of mass communications.

Since leadership depends upon responsive followership, followers may justifiably feel that they have a vital role in the process. A counterpart to this is that poor leaders can create poor followers, insofar as the latter are not as much engaged and involved as they are capable of being. Therefore, a great waste of human potential can occur. One consequence is the despair that sets in when followers sense that gains are not being made, and opportunities are being lost, by an inept leader.

Ideally, the process of influence and counter-influence helps to use human talents and physical resources effectively for mutual goals. As already noted, any social entity has leadership in the sense of organized patterns of influence, even if it is poor leadership. The effectiveness of leadership depends on the character of this relationship of the leader and others involved in getting things accomplished. Poor leadership may result from many causes, including the leader's incompetence in moving on with the primary task, or the followers' failure to show some initiative. In general, groups carry out their functions best, and attain their goals, by having shared responsibilities of action and some delegation of authority.

In a simple transactional view, the leader directs communications to followers, to which they may react in various ways. The leader attempts to take account of the attitudes and needs of followers and they, in turn, evaluate the leader with particular regard to his or her responsiveness to these states. Especially pertinent are the followers' perceptions of the leader's effectiveness and how they perceive and evaluate the leader's actions and motives. For instance, where the leader has the resources but routinely fails to deliver, there is bound to be dissatisfaction. If, as another example, the leader appears to be deviating from the accepted standards, such nonconformity may be tolerated initially, especially if it seems to be yielding productive outcomes. This is a feature of the "idiosyncrasy credit" model, which emphasizes sources of earned status and the leader's related latitude for innovation.

The idiosyncrasy credit model confronts the apparent paradox that leaders are said to conform more to the group's norms and yet are also likely to be influential in bringing about innovations. Actually, these elements can fit together when seen as a matter of sequence. In the early contact between the leader, or would-be leader, and followers, credits are gained by signs of a contribution to the group's primary task and loyalty to the group's norms. As summary terms, these two factors are referred to as "competence" and "conformity."

The role of leader carries the potential to take innovative action in coping with new or altered demands; but how successful the leader is in effecting change depends upon the perceptions followers have of the leader's actions and related motivations. Accordingly, when a leader's nonconformity seems to produce unsuccessful outcomes, the leader is more vulnerable to blame. It is as if the group said, "We expect good results from your actions. If you choose an unusual course, we will go along with you and give you some latitude. But you are responsible if the outcome is that the group fails to achieve, its goals."

Given a fund of credits, an individual's assertions of influence become more acceptable. Furthermore, there is the expectation that, once accumulated, credits will be used to take actions which are in the direction of needed innovation. A failure to do so may result in the loss of credits. The leader who "sits" on his or her credits may be seen as not fulfilling role obligations.

Credits exist only in the shared perceptions which group members gain of the others over time. But credits have operational significance in allowing later deviations which would otherwise be viewed negatively, if a person did not have a sufficient balance to draw upon. As a case in point, a newcomer to the group is poorly positioned to assert influence or take innovative action. However, a particular individual may bring derivative credit from another group, based on his or her reputation. The credit concept may therefore apply to appointed leaders as well as to elected ones, even though followers are not the major source of legitimacy for appointed leaders. The credit concept assumes that a process of evaluation goes on. This means for instance, that maintaining a leader role, depends on showing results that can be judged. The process may vary considerably from situation to situation, but ordinarily there are "validators" who have some basis for judging the adequacy of the leader's performance. However, even if the judgment is negative, it may not be possible to displace the leader. For example, a term of office may be involved or a contractual arrangement. Also, the validators responsible for the leader's original placement in the position are likely to be unwilling to admit error.

This reluctance is even seen with an elected leader whose validators are the followers or constituents. They may have a sense of investment in the leader which makes them feel a greater responsibility for the leader's performance. When it is poor, there may be at least an initial rallying around to support the leader. Deposing an elected leader can offer considerable hurdles, especially in the midst of a fixed term. The matter of a leader's legitimacy in the role is at stake, and this requires additional comment.

## LEADER LEGITIMACY AND AUTHORITY

A leader's authority requires a legitimate basis. As suggested above, legitimacy may come through various sources: by appointment, election, or through the support of followers in a less, formal way. However, whatever the source, legitimacy depends on followers' perceptions about how the leader achieved his or her position. The essential point about legitimacy is that it produces the belief that the leader has the authority to exert influence. Legitimacy can also be seen to derive from a person's office, that is, an assigned status, or from a person's own qualities. A parallel point was made by Thomas Jefferson in distinguishing between social status based on an aristocracy of inherited position and a "natural aristocracy" of talent. A person might be admired for high position but not for individual qualities, or vice versa. In either case, when viewed from a transactional standpoint, legitimacy is related to the followers' perceptions of the leader.

A further point about legitimacy is the fact that a leader's high office does not necessarily insure follower responsiveness. The leader's personal qualities still matter. For instance, the president of a company has a position of leadership, which carries the legitimacy of high office. It is greater than that of a supervisor. Yet the president might be unsuccessful in achieving the desired response from subordinates. The supervisor might show a greater exercise of leadership by a more affirmative subordinate response. Fulfilling legitimacy through the use of authority, therefore, has a great deal to do with how followers respond to the leader's characteristics.

Authority can also be seen as a resource. The leader is expected to use it in meeting assigned responsibilities, just as the available material and personnel resources are there to be used. However, having authority is only a potential for action, and it may not be exercised for various reasons. Furthermore, as Chester Barnard long ago pointed out, followers will comply with an order only to the extent that: they understand it; believe on receiving it that it is not inconsistent with organizational goals or their own goals; and have the ability to comply with the order. Here again we see a stress on the importance of the followers' perception of the leader's legitimacy.

In sum, there are several factors which support the legitimacy of a leader's role. These are the manner by which it is attained and the followers' perceptions of the leader's competence and motivation. The latter perceptions deal with performance, which means the outcomes resulting from the leader's actions. A favorable situation for the leader occurs, therefore, when the followers consider the, leader's position to be valid and approve of his or her performance in moving the group toward, accepted goals.

In this regard, William Cowley many years ago made a distinction between leadership and headship. He said that a leader who depends entirely on the authority of a legitimated office is relying on headship and not leadership. Although "heads" are often called "leaders," they may have only the legitimacy of office. Without exercising authority through persuasion and influence, to achieve a program, there is not authentic leadership. Cowley acknowledged that a completely clean-cut distinction between leaders and headmen cannot always be made. Some headmen, he said are so clearly not leaders that everyone agrees they are not. But others, to the contrary, may be more like leaders.

The point should be clear that office-holding is not the same as leading, and that one factor in the difference is whether a leader is persuasive in pursuing a program. However, persuasion alone will not do. It needs to be tempered by credibility and accountability. Failings in these respects can be seen as irresponsibility, which is another source of the crisis in leadership.

## CREDIBILITY AND ACCOUNTABILITY

All problems are not of the leader's making, and all solutions do not depend upon the leader's wisdom or initiative. Yet, the leader's position is such that he or she is more often seen to be responsible for handling problems that arise and for finding solutions. Leaders not only have greater responsibility for the activities they direct, they also are the primary source of "social reality" for followers, which refers to a shared definition of the situation. In shaping social reality, the leader reduces uncertainty for followers and gives them a basis for action. However, a leader's statements and behavior have a positive impact only to the extent that the leader maintains credibility.

Although the concept of credibility may seem elusive, it has been found to be comprised of two major elements, expertise and trustworthiness. The so-called "credibility gap," which was said to have existed in recent presidencies, appears to have been caused more and more by a failure of trust. The leader needs to be trustworthy, most especially in fulfilling expectations by delivering on promises. Furthermore, there is a special significance to the presidency because of the model it presents in the society at large.

The recent spate of critical commentary on the Carter presidency often centers on the failure to match performance to the expectations raised. Indeed, the public does not take well to being disappointed by a president who does not live up to high expectations, such as that for the "new morality" of the post-Watergate era. The Burt Lance affair, with all of its denials, sounded too much like the "old cronyism," rather than the "new morality," and the president's credibility suffered on grounds of trust. The pity is that this problem can readily spill over into other areas and diminish the president's credits.

Unfortunately, in the late fall of 1977, a Harris poll found that a majority of people considered President Carter well-intentioned but wondered if he had the basic competence for the job. They felt that he suffered from inexperience and a failure to follow through. This is a problem of expertise. Early in 1978, *The Washington Post* editorialized on the "Perceptions of the President," and opened by saying, "The Carter Administration is now beginning its second year but, oddly, a great many Americans still say they have no clear view of it. For them, Mr. Carter and his central purposes have not yet come into focus." In another analysis, Thomas Ottenad, in the *St. Louis Post-Dispatch* said that: "Carter's performance has suffered from an awkward approach which made him appear uncertain and, at times, floundering." Although this may seem to be a matter of "style," it adversely affects the perceptions followers have of substance. There may be a sense that clarity of purpose is lacking. Such uncertainty undermines credibility and may increase frustration about the leader's accountability to followers.

Presidents and other leaders cannot evade the fundamental understanding that being a leader gives a person more influence over others, and the prospect of having more control over expectations and events. It also means having greater visibility and recognition, as a person of higher status. All of this comes at a price, a vital part of which is represented in the idea of accountability. There are good reasons why leaders should be held to account for failures, inadequate effort, or inaction in the face of problems or evident threats to the well-being of the group, organization, or nation. However, leaders do find devices to avoid it in practice, such as resorting to the *appearance* of collective responsibility vested in a committee or board. There are, of course, real situations of shared authority, which can be a good thing in principle. What provokes annoyance is the manipulation of such committees to make them nothing more than a sham, thereby providing further disenchantment with leaders.

Returning to the earlier theme, the leader-follower transaction requires that there be at least the sense of a "fair exchange." A follower usually is not a disciple who is obliged to accept the master's view uncritically. More appropriately, the leader-follower relationship needs balance. The follower has to be able to know and use his or her own critical ability in deciding some matters. A pattern of accommodation and two-way influence is required to produce mutual trust and the likelihood of positive results.

Simply put, followers need to have a basis for believing that they are being treated fairly and being informed properly. Such a belief will increase their inclination to remain inside and participate, rather than putting themselves at a psychological distance and opting out. In the latter event, the crisis in leadership will most likely be perpetuated and grow worse.

CHAPTER 5

# Contemporary Trends in the Analysis of Leadership Processes

### WITH JAMES W. JULIAN

## COMMENTARY

When the paper presented in this chapter appeared in 1969, it represented a departure from the major conceptions about leadership that were then current: the trait, the behavioral, and situational views. Its main thrust was to point the way to developments that help to bridge and go beyond them, such as contingency models, just then coming into fashion. It also highlighted the implicit exchange between leaders and followers, in a transactional framework, with the leader providing "added value" to be reciprocated by heightened status and influence. In Homans's terms, "The leader gives something, and gets something" (1961, p. 286). Indeed, as noted in Chapter 1, Burns defines leadership as a *relationship* between leaders and a multitude of followers. He says, "Leadership, unlike naked power-wielding, is thus inseparable from followers' needs and goals" (1978, p. 19).

Relatedly, the paper presented here furthered interest in the concept of interpersonal systems, presaging an emphasis on teams and their social structure and context. Also emphasized here was the assessment of performance effectiveness. Attention was given as well to perceptions and expectations about leadership, power, and authority, as part of cognitive and attributional developments.

The legitimacy of the leader, in regard to attainment and then maintaining his or her position, is a pivotal element in determining the character of leader-follower relations. The paper presented urges consideration of the entire interpersonal system implicated in leadership when assessing its effectiveness. Perhaps the most important point of departure is attention to the situation affecting perceptions and expectancies about leadership, power, and authority. Although these three terms are often employed almost interchangeably, they may usefully be distinguished from one another.

Figure 2.1, in Chapter 2, shows the three elements involved in leadership, with some of their relevant attributes. Note that these elements are represented by overlapping circles from largest for situation, to intermediate for followers, to smallest for leaders. The locus of leadership is shown in the crosshatched area, where they intersect. The arrows indicate the social exchange that occurs there between the leaders and the followers. (An early version of this figure appeared in 1974 in an article on emergent leadership that I wrote for a special issue of the *Journal of Management*. It then was revised for my book *Leadership Dynamics* [1978a, p. 8].)

Recently, the importance of the situation has been emphasized by Sternberg (2007), among others. Fleishman, Harris, and Burtt (1955) were among the first to look for and find situational moderators in ongoing complex organizations that affected the relations between leader behavior and the performance of their groups. Zacarro (2007), writing about traits, also promotes the idea that situational factors are important as contingencies. These views are in line with those stressed (Hollander and Julian, 1969) in this paper, not least the point that followers encounter the leader as a vital part of the situation. It might also be noted that Hackman and Wageman (2007) emphasize team activity, which relies on the variables in the situation that promote cohesiveness and group effort.

Transactional (TA) approaches have diverged from traditional leader-centric views by attending to the followers' part in the exchange process. TA approaches recognize that a leader's legitimacy, and potential for influence, is contingent on follower relationships, especially when directed toward change. Recall from the first chapter that Max Weber, major proponent of the charismatic leader concept, stated that if the leader was "long successful, above all if his leadership fails to benefit followers, it is likely that his charisma will disappear" (1946, p. 360). Therefore, charisma is not so much a possession of the leader, but rather something accorded by followers.

Political historian James MacGregor Burns presented a major development related to charisma in his 1978 book on transformational (TF) leadership. It opened the way for much psychological interest of the leader as a change agent who "transformed" followers. Although this mode of TF leadership is based on a change process, underlying it is a relationship that can be seen as essentially TA leadership. Ehrlich, Meindl, and Viellieu address this point in asserting that "Conceptually, the basis for either form of leadership is a relational and perceptual exchange developed between a leader and his or her subordinates" (1990, p. 231).

As noted here in Chapter 1, Burns (2007) has recently made the point that on reconsideration the dichotomy he postulated between TA and TF leadership is not valid. He now sees them on a gradient. However, the measure that Bass (1985) developed still presents a distinction between TA and TF leadership, with TA leadership portrayed unfavorably to make only TF appear to be the "good" mode. The research of Eagly et al. (2001) with women leaders found TF to be effective, but TA leadership providing recognition and rewards more often from them.

This distinction is furthered by considering only tangible rewards and not acknowledging the intangible ones followers receive from TF as well as TA leaders. But, even as defined by Bass (1985), TF leaders can be seen to provide intangible rewards to followers, such as personal attention and intellectual stimulation, among those on his list of TF qualities. He does not acknowledge them as rewards, though, nor did followers' reciprocation to the leader, found in giving credit, support, and trust. To do so would make plain that a transaction had occurred, which would breach the artificial view of TF as free of a transaction, with TA leadership as "less good," and even crass. This is far from the actual, richer TA conception that incorporated an earlier dynamic element (i.e., the idiosyncrasy credit model), dealing with acceptance of change by followers (see Hollander, 1995).

The TA and TF forms are not independent, but highly related, as research by various nonideologically committed investigators has shown. An example is the research by Curphy (1993), who studied ratings given by cadets to their officers at the U.S. Air Force Academy. Also, leaders wishing to bring about change need TA qualities to establish a relationship with followers based on trust. In that vein, Bensimon (1993) found that new college presidents who were successful had the ability to adapt by displaying TA qualities initially, before introducing changes. A study by Wallace (1996) found a parallel "middle way" of flexibility among corporate executives who were rated effective and could be seen to be both TA and TF in the situation that prevailed.

Furthermore, popular as the MLQ became, it did not include follower responsiveness to a leader, as Fiedler (1964) did in using "favorability" of the respondents to a leader in his contingency model. Two other problems with the TF concept is its leader-centric quality, assuming that the leader will do the "correct thing," morally and otherwise, in bringing about change. Even more basic is the assumption that change is always needed and desirable. A motivational issue is what followers believe about a leadership process that transforms them. Yukl (1999) also reports that the effectiveness of TF leadership is not in the change component as much as attention to followers. However, such attention has long been a feature of the leader-follower relationship, in TA leadership, before it was imported into TF, as if its own. Yukl also expresses reservations about the mechanisms that produce TF effects.

Basically, effective leaders, by whatever label, bolster their relationships by providing followers with what they need, not only in tangible ways but also through such intangible rewards as support, fairness, and trust. In return, followers affirm their loyalty and esteem by improved participation and contributions to their mutual goals. On this point, Chemers contends that intrinsic rewards of "self-esteem, a sense of purpose, or salvation ... become highly attractive and supremely motivating" when followers needs are intense enough. ... Under such circumstances charismatic or transformational leadership may be seen as a special, elevated case of the more mundane transactional exchange processes that are the basis for all, person-to-person, team leadership" (1993, p. 312).

Regarding good leader-follower relations, as part of good business practice, Fayol (1916) long ago advocated attention to worker well-being. In addition to providing remuneration, bonuses, and profit sharing, he saw the significance of intangible rewards. Yet, the focus on tangible rewards continues to leave a notable gap in understanding the role of the intangible ones, such as self-esteem, social identity, and responsiveness, in the leader-follower relationship and their consequences to satisfaction and performance. However, satisfaction is by no means a sure road to improved performance, since other variables, including expectations and other past-history considerations, may be involved. As Mulder (1971) pointed out, participation is fraught with such considerations as power and information differentials, which undercut favorable outcomes.

Although leaders and leadership are important to group and organizational processes, there has been a set of criticisms of this view. One of these is represented by the point that interpersonal influence is overstated, and that there are task and other organizational qualities, such as traditions, norms, roles, and rules, that are "substitutes for leadership" (see, for example, Kerr & Jermier, 1978). Indeed, these could be considered to be forms of leadership processes, insofar as they maintain an ongoing, stable enterprise. A *change of leaders* may alter this pattern, however, as is well known in the phenomenon of succession. It matters a great deal in everyday work life *who* the new boss will be. There are other views, however, such as the "Romance of Leadership" critique by Meindl and Ehrlich (1987), that point to an overemphasis on perceiving a person as a causal agent. Chapter 1 touched on this is connection with the "fundamental attribution error."

In a related vein, there is the attributional perspective, which contends that a good deal of leadership exists in preconceptions and other perceptions held by followers about leaders and leadership. Calder (1977) and Pfeffer (1997) are among the proponents of a position that considers "leadership" to be largely inferential and even attributed to leaders after the fact. The process may stem from an "implicit leadership theory" that is the basis for factors found in followers' ratings of leaders (Rush, Thomas, & Lord, 1977). Furthermore, positive or negative outcomes are also attributed more readily to the leader, and when things go wrong he or she is more likely to be faulted and even removed. In Pfeffer's causal attribution terms, leaders are symbols. If something goes wrong, the whole staff or entire team cannot be fired, but firing the manager can convey a sense of fixing the basis of the problem.

One effect of the attributional view is to make more explicit the significance of followers' and others' perceptions of the leader in shaping "leadership events." Clearly, to some degree, leader performance needs to be assessed objectively. Without the expectations that leader competence and motivation mattered and could be identified and enhanced, organizations would be unlikely to support executive and management training programs. The larger issue at stake is how to secure *better performance indicators*, which is the *outcome* question. It asks what a sequence of actions, presumed to be initiated by the leader, has produced by way of consequences. Too often in past research the answer has been based on whether the leader was influential and to what degree, as a sign of success, without asking *toward what ends*. Need it be said, *it matters*.

---

Hollander, E. P., & Julian, J. W. Contemporary trends in the analysis of leadership processes. *Psychological Bulletin*, 1969, 71, 387–397. Slightly abridged and reprinted with permission of the American Psychological Association.

Within the present era, characterized by a greater sensitivity to the social processes of interaction and exchange, it becomes clearer that the two research emphases represented by the trait and situational approaches to leadership afforded a far too glib view of reality. Indeed, in a true sense, neither approach ever represented its own philosophical underpinning very well, and each resulted in a caricature. The purpose here is to attempt a rectification of the distortion that these traditions represented, and to point up the increasing signs of movement toward a fuller analysis of leadership as a social influence process, and not as a fixed state of being.

## AN OVERVIEW

By way of beginning, it seems useful to make a number of observations to serve as an overview. First, several general points which grow out of current research and thought on leadership are established. Thereafter, some of the directions in which these developments appear to be heading are indicated, as well as those areas which require further attention.

One overriding impression conveyed by surveying the literature of the 1960s, in contrast to the preceding two decades, is the redirection of interest in leadership toward processes such as power and authority relationships (e.g., Blau, 1964; Emerson, 1962; Janda, 1960; Raven, 1965). The tendency now is to attach far greater significance to the interrelationship between the leader, the followers, and the situation (see, e.g., Fielder, 1964, 1965, 1967; Hollander, 1964; Hollander & Julian, 1968; Steiner, 1964). In consequence, the problem of studying leadership and understanding these relationships is recognized as a more formidable one than was earlier supposed (d. Cartwright & Zander, 1968). Several of the particulars which signalize this changing emphasis may be summarized under four points, as follows:

1. An early element of confusion in the study of leadership was the failure to distinguish it as a process from the leader as a person who occupies a central role in that process. Leadership constitutes an influence relationship between two, or usually more, persons who depend upon one another for the attainment of certain mutual goals within a group situation. This situation not only involves the task but also comprises the group's size, structure, resources, and history, among other variables.
2. This relationship between leader and led is built over time, and involves an exchange or transaction between leaders and followers in which the leader both gives something and gets something. The leader provides a resource in terms of adequate role behavior directed toward the group's goal attainment, and in return receives greater influence associated with status, recognition, and esteem. These contribute to his "legitimacy" in making influence assertions, and in having them accepted.
3. There are differential tasks or functions attached to being a leader. While the image of the leader frequently follows Hemphill's (1961) view of one who "initiates structure," the leader is expected to function too as a mediator within the group, as a group spokesman outside it, and very often also as the decision maker who sets goals and priorities. Personality characteristics which may fit a person to be a leader are determined by the perceptions held by followers, in the sense of the particular role expectancies and satisfactions, rather than by the traits measured via personality scale scores.
4. Despite the persisting view that leadership traits do not generalize across situations, leader effectiveness can and should be studied as it bears on the group's achievement of desired outputs (see Katz & Kahn, 1966). An approach to the study of leader effectiveness as a feature of the group's success, in system terms, offers a clear alternative to the older concern with what the leader did do or did not do.

A richer, more interactive conception of leadership processes would entertain these considerations as points of departure for further study. Some evidence for a trend toward this development is considered in what follows.

Whither the "situational approach"? What was the essential thrust of the situational approach, after all? Mainly, it was to recognize that the qualities of the leader were variously elicited, valued, and reacted to as a function of differential group settings and their demands. Hemphill (1949a) capped the point in saying "there are no absolute leaders, since successful leadership must always take into account the specific requirements imposed by the nature of the group which is to be led, requirements as diverse in nature and degree as are the organizations in which persons band together [p. 225]."

Though leadership events were seen as outcomes of a relationship that implicates the leader, the led, and their shared situation, studies conducted within the situational approach, usually left the *process* of leadership unattended. Much of the time, leaders were viewed in positional terms, with an emphasis on the outcome of their influence assertions. Comparatively little attention was directed to followers, especially in terms of the phenomenon of emergent leadership (cf. Hollander, 1961). With a few exceptions, such as the work of McGregor (see 1966) and others (e.g., Slater & Bennis, 1964), the leader's maintenance of his position was emphasized at the expense of understanding the attainment of it through a process of influence.

But even more importantly, the situational view made it appear that the leader and the situation were quite separate. Though they may be separable for analytic purposes, they also impinge on one another in the perceptions of followers. Thus, the leader, from the follower's vantage point, is an element in the situation, and one who shapes it as well. As an active agent of influence he communicates to other group members by his words and his actions, implying demands which are reacted to in turn. In exercising influence, therefore, the leader may set the stage and create expectations regarding what he should do and what he will do. Rather than standing apart from the leader, the situation perceived to exist may be his creation.

It is now possible to see that the trait and situational approaches merely emphasize parts of a process which are by no means separable. One kind of melding of the trait and situational approaches, for example, is found in the work of Fiedler. His essential point, sustained by an extensive program of research (see 1958, 1964, 1965, 1967), is that the leader's effectiveness in the group depends upon the structural properties of the group and the situation, including interpersonal perceptions of both leader and led. He finds, for example, that the willingness of group members to be influenced by the leader is conditioned by leader characteristics, but that the quality and direction of this influence is contingent on the group relations and task structure (1967). This work will be discussed further in due course.

Another kind of evidence about the importance to group performance of the leader's construction of the situation is seen in recent research on conflict. Using a role-playing test situation involving four-person groups, Maier and Hoffman (1965) found that conflict is turned to productive or nonproductive ends, depending on the attitude of the discussion leader. Where the leader perceived conflict in terms of "problem subordinates," the quality of the decision reached in these discussion groups was distinctly inferior to that reached under circumstances in which the discussion leader perceived disagreements as the source for ideas and innovation. In those circumstances, innovative solutions increased markedly.

A leader, therefore, sets the basis for relationships within the group, and thereby can affect outcomes. As Hemphill (1961) suggested, the leader initiates structure. But more than just structure in a concrete sense, he affects the process which occurs within that structure. Along with other neglected aspects of process in the study of leadership is the goal-setting activity of the leader. Its importance appears considerable, though few studies give it attention. In one of these, involving discussion groups, Burke (1966) found that the leader's failure to provide goal orientations within the group led to antagonism, tension, and absenteeism. This effect was most acute when there was clear agreement within the group regarding who was to act as the leader. Though such expectations about the leader undoubtedly are pervasive in groups studied in research on leadership, they are noted only infrequently.

## LEGITIMACY AND SOCIAL EXCHANGE IN LEADERSHIP

Among the more substantial features of the leader's role is his perceived legitimacy how he attains it and sustains it. One way to understand the process by which the leader's role is legitimated is to view it as an exchange of rewards operating to signalize the acceptance of his position and influence.

In social exchange terms, the person in the role of leader who fulfills expectations and achieves group goals provides rewards for others which are reciprocated in the form of status, esteem, and heightened influence. Because leadership embodies a two-way influence relationship, recipients of influence assertions may respond by asserting influence in return, that is, by making demands on the leader. The very sustenance of the relationship depends upon some yielding to influence on both sides. As Homans (1961) put it, "Influence over others is purchased at the price of allowing one's self to be influenced by others [p. 286]." To be influential, authority depends upon esteem, he said. By granting esteem itself, or symbolic manifestations of it, one may in turn activate leadership, in terms of a person taking on the leader role.

The elicitation of leader behavior is now a demonstrable phenomenon in various experimental settings. In one definitive study conducted by Pepinsky, Hemphill, and Shevitz (1958), subjects who were low on leader activity were led to behave far more actively in that role by the group's evident support for their assertions. Alternatively, other subjects known to be high on leader activity earlier were affected in precisely the opposite way by the group's evident disagreement with their statements. In simplest terms, an exchange occurs between the group and the target person. The group provides reinforcement which in turn elicits favored behaviors. In other terms, the reinforcement of a person's influence assertions substantiates his position of authority.

Other, more recent, work suggested that even the use of lights as reinforcers exerts a significant effect on the target person's proportion of talking time as well as his perceived leadership status (Bavelas, Hastorf, Gross, & Kite, 1965; Zdep & Oakes, 1967). Thus, the lights not only produced a heightening of leader acts, but also created the impression of greater influence with the implication of legitimacy as well.

In a similar vein, Rudraswamy (1964) conducted a study in which some subjects within a group were led to believe they had higher status. Not only did they attempt significantly more leadership acts than others in their group, but they even outdistanced those subjects who were given more relevant information about the task itself.

It is also clear that agreement about who should lead has the effect in groups of increasing the probability of leader acts (e.g., Banta & Nelson, 1964). Relatedly, in a study of five-man groups involving changed as against unchanged leadership, Pryer, Flint, and Bass (1962) found that group effectiveness was enhanced by early agreement on who should lead.

When a basis is provided for legitimately making influence assertions, it is usually found that individuals will tend to act as leaders. This, of course, does not deny the existence of individual differences in the propensity for acting, once these conditions prevail. In a recent study by Gordon and Medland (1965), they found that positive peer ratings on leadership in army squads was consistently related to a measure of "aspiration to lead." Similarly, research findings on discussion groups (e.g., Riecken, 1958) indicated that the more vocal members obtain greater reinforcement, and hence experience the extension of legitimacy.

The "idiosyncrasy credit" concept (Hollander, 1958) suggests that a person's potential to be influential arises out of the positive dispositions others hold toward him/her. In simplest terms, competence in helping the group achieve its goals, and early conformity to its normative expectations for members, provide the potential for acting as a leader and being perceived as such. Then, assertions of influence which were not tolerated before are more likely to be acceptable. This concept applies in an especially important way to leadership succession, since it affords the basis for understanding how a new leader becomes legitimized in the perceptions of his peers. Further work on succession phenomena appears, in general, to be another area of fruitful study. There are many intriguing issues here, such as the question of the relative importance in legitimacy of factors such as "knowledge" and "office," in Max Weber's terms, which deserve further consideration (see, e.g., Evan & Zelditch, 1961).

## THE PERCEPTION OF LEADERSHIP FUNCTIONS WITHIN GROUP STRUCTURE

A major deficiency in the older trait approach was its conception of "traits" within the framework of classic personality typologies. Personality measures were applied to leaders, often in profusion, without reference either to the varying nature of leadership roles or the functions they were to fulfill. As Mann's (1959) review revealed, such measures indeed do yield inconsistent relationships among leaders, variously defined. To take a common instance, dominance and extroversion are sometimes related positively to status as the leader, but mainly are neither related positively nor negatively to this status. On the other hand, Stogdill (1948) reported that such characteristics as "originality," "initiative," and "adaptability" have a low but positive relationship with leader status.

Granting that some essentially personality-type variables are more often found among those designated as leaders than among those designated as non-leaders, there can be no dismissing the widespread failure to treat the characteristics of the leader as they are perceived—and, what is more, as they are perceived as relevant—by other group members within a given setting. As Hunt (1965) and Secord and Backman (1961) pointed out, traits are viewed relative to the interpersonal context in which they occur. In short, followers hold expectations regarding what the leader ought to be doing here and now, and not absolutely.

One probable source for the disparate findings concerning qualities of the leader is the existence of differential expectations concerning the functions the leader is to perform. In simplest terms, there are various leadership roles. Without nearly exhausting the roster, it helps to realize that the leader in various time-space settings may be a task director, mediator, or spokesman, as well as a decision maker who, as Bavelas (1960) put it, "reduces uncertainty."

Whether in the laboratory or the field, studies of the perceptions of the leader's functions often have depended upon a sociometric approach (d. Hollander, 1954). Thus, Clifford and Cohen (1964) used a sociometric device to study leadership roles in a summer camp, with 79 boys and girls, ranging in age from 8 to 13 years. Over a period of 4 weeks, they had nine elections by secret ballot asking the youngsters to indicate how the others would fit into various roles, including such things as planner, banquet chairman, swimming captain, and so forth. Their results indicated that the perceived attributes of campers were tied variously to their election for different leader roles. In line with the earlier point about the interpersonal context of leader traits, these researchers say, "the problem should be rephrased in terms of personality variables required in a leader role in a specific situation, which is in turn a function of the follower's perceptions (p. 64)."

Apart from personality traits, one prevailing expectation which does yield consistent findings across situations is that the leader's competence in a major group activity should be high. Dubno (1965), for example, reported that groups are more satisfied when leaders are demonstrably competent in a central function and do most of the work associated with that function. This is seen, too, in an experiment with five-man discussion groups, from which Marak (1964) found that the rewards associated with the leader's ability on a task led to greater perceived as well as actual influence. In general, the greater influence of a leader perceived to be more competent was verified experimentally by Dittes and Kelley (1956) and by Hollander (1960), among others.

Another leader attribute which evidently determines the responsiveness of followers is his perceived motivation regarding the group and its task. This was seen in Rosen, Levinger, and Lippitt's (1961) finding that helpfulness was rated as the most important characteristic leading to high influence potential among adolescent boys. In a more recent study of the role dimensions of leader-follower relations, Julian and Hollander (1966) found that, aside from the significance of task competence, the leader's "interest in group members" and "interest in group activity" were significantly related to group members' willingness to have a leader continue in that position. This accords with the finding of a field study by Nelson (1964) among 72 men who spent 12 months together in the Antarctic. While those men most liked as leaders had characteristics highly similar to those who were most liked as followers, Nelson reported that perceived motivation was the major factor which distinguished the two. Hollander (1958) considered this as one critical factor determining the leader's ability to retain status, even though nonconforming. In Nelson's study, the highly liked leaders were seen significantly more to be motivated highly toward the group in line with his hypothesis that, "a critical expectation held of the leader, if he is to maintain esteem, is that he display strong motivation to belong to the group [p. 165]."

A study by Kirkhart (1963) investigated group leadership among Negro college students as a function of their identification with their minority group. In terms of follower expectations, he found that those selected most frequently by their peers for leadership roles, in both the "internal system" and the "external system" activities of the group, scored higher on a questionnaire expressing Negro identification. This quality of being an exemplar of salient group characteristics was noted long ago by Brown (1936) as a feature of leadership. Its relationship to processes of identification with the leader is discussed shortly.

## SOURCE AND NATURE OF LEADER AUTHORITY

The structural properties of groups affect the processes which occur within them. In leadership, the source of the leader's authority constitutes a significant element of structure. Yet, experimentation on leadership has given little attention to this variable, apart from some promising earlier work by Carter et al. (1951) with appointed and emergent leaders, and the work by Lewin and his associates on the style of the leader and its consequences to the group's social climate (Lewin et al., 1939; see also Preston & Heintz, 1949). More recently, Cohen and Bennis (1961) demonstrated that where groups could elect their leaders, the continuity of leadership was better maintained than where their leaders were appointed. In research on the productivity of groups, Goldman and Fraas (1965) found that differences occurred among four conditions of leader selection, including election and appointment.

With four-man discussion groups, Julian, Hollander, and Regula (1969) employed a multifactor design to study three variables: the source of a leader's authority, in either election or appointment; his competence, in terms of perceived capability on the task; and his subsequent task success. Their main dependent measure was the members' acceptance of the leader as a spokesman for the group. The findings of this experiment indicated that the latter two variables were significantly related to this acceptance, but that these relationships were differentially affected by whether the leader was appointed or elected. The shape of the three-way interaction suggested that election, rather than making the leader more secure, made him/her more vulnerable to censure if he/she were either initially perceived to be incompetent or subsequently failed to secure a successful outcome as spokesman for the group. While this finding alone does not sustain a generalization that the appointed leader necessarily is more firmly entrenched, it does support the conclusion that the leader's source of authority is perceived and reacted to as a relevant element in the leadership process.

Other work on a differentiation of the leader's role, through the social structure, was conducted by Anderson and Fiedler (1964). In their experiment with four-man discussion groups, half the groups had leaders who were told to serve as a "chairman" in a participatory way, and the other groups had leaders who were told to serve as an "officer in charge" in a supervisory way. They found that the nature of the leadership process was affected markedly by this distinction, thus paralleling the main findings of Preston and Heintz (1949). In general, the more participatory leaders were significantly more influential and made more of a contribution to the group's performance. But, more to the point, the relationship between leader attributes, such as intelligence and performance, was significant for certain tasks under the participatory condition, though not for any of the tasks under the supervisory condition. The conclusion that Anderson and Fiedler reached, therefore, is that the characteristics of a leader, including intelligence and other personality attributes, become more salient and more highly relevant to group achievement under conditions of participation by the leader, as against circumstances where a highly formal role structure prevails.

## EFFECTIVENESS OF THE LEADER

By now it is clear that an entire interpersonal system is implicated in answering the question of the leader's effectiveness. The leader is not effective merely by being influential, without regard to the processes at work and the ends achieved. Stressing this point, Selznick (1957) said that, "far more than the capacity to mobilize personal support ... (or) the maintenance of equilibrium through the routine solution of everyday problems," the leader's function is "to define the ends of group existence, to design an enterprise distinctively adapted to these ends, and to see that the design becomes a living reality (p. 37)."

As Katz and Kahn (1966) observed, any group operates with a set of resources to produce certain outputs. Within this system, an interchange of inputs for outputs occurs, and this is facilitated by leadership functions which, among other things, direct the enterprise. The leader's contribution and its consequences vary with system demands, in terms of what Selznick referred to as "distinctive competence." Taken by itself, therefore, the typical conception of leadership as one person directing others can be misleading, as already indicated. Though the leader provides a valued resource, the group's resources are not the leader's alone. Together, such resources provide the basis for functions fulfilled in the successful attainment of group goals, or, in other terms, group outputs.

Given the fact that a group must work within the set of available resources, its effectiveness is gauged in several ways. Stogdill (1959), for one, distinguished these in terms of the group's performance, integration, and member satisfaction as group outputs of a leadership process involving the use of the group's resources. Thus, the leader and his characteristics constitute a set of resources contributing to the effective utilization of other resources. A person who occupies the central role of leader has the task of contributing to this enterprise, within the circumstances broadly confronting the group.

One prominent exemplification of the system's demands and constraints on the leader's effectiveness is seen in Fiedler's "contingency model" (1964, 1965, 1967). He predicted varying levels of effectiveness for different *combinations* of leader and situational characteristics. Thus, depending upon the leader's orientation toward his co-workers, in the context of three situational variables—the quality of leader-member liking, the degree of task structure, and the position power of the leader—he finds distinct variations in this effectiveness.

In a recent test of his model, Fiedler (1966) conducted an experiment to compare the performance of 96 three-man groups that were culturally and linguistically homogeneous or heterogeneous. Some operated under powerful and others under weak leadership positions on three types of tasks varying in structure and requirements for verbal interaction. Despite the communication difficulties and different backgrounds, heterogeneous groups performed about as well on the nonverbal task as did the homogeneous groups. Groups with *petty* officers as leaders (powerful) did about as well as the groups with recruits as leaders (weak). The main finding of the experiment was support for the hypothesis from the contingency model that the specific leadership orientation required for effectiveness is contingent on the favorableness of the group-task situation. Partial support for this hypothesis came also from a study by Shaw and Blum (1966) in which they manipulated some of the same variables with five-person groups, and with three tasks selected to vary along a dimension reflecting different levels of favorability for the leader. Their results indicated that the directive leader was more effective than the nondirective leader only when the group-task situation was highly favorable for the leader, but not otherwise.

## IDENTIFICATION WITH THE LEADER

For any leader, the factors of favorability and effectiveness depend upon the perceptions of followers. Their identification with him/her implicates significant psychological ties which may affect materially his ability to be influential. Yet the study of identification is passe in leadership research. Though there is a recurring theme in the literature of social science, harking back to Weber (see 1947), about the so-called "charismatic leader," this quality has a history of imprecise usage; furthermore, its tie with identification processes is by no means clear. Putting the study of the sources and consequences of identification with the leader on a stronger footing seems overdue and entirely feasible.

Several lines of work in social psychology appear to converge on identification processes. The distinction made by Kelman (1961) regarding identification, internalization, and compliance, for example, has obvious relevance to the relationship between the leader and his followers. This typology might be applied to the further investigation of leadership processes. The work of Sears (1960) and of Bandura and Walters (1963), concerning the identification of children with adult models, also has implications for such study.

One point which is clear, though the dynamics require far more attention, is that the followers' identification with their leader can provide them with social reality, in the sense of a shared outlook. An illustration of this is seen in work on the social psychology of political leadership by Hollander (see 1963). In two phases, separated by an interval of 8 years, he studied Republicans in 1954 who had voted for President Eisenhower in 1952 and who would or would not vote for him again in 1954; and then in 1962, he studied Democrats who had voted for President Kennedy in 1960 and who would or would not vote for him again in 1962. He found that continuing loyalty to the President of one's party, among these respondents, was significantly associated with their views on issues and conditions and with their votes for the party in a midterm congressional-senatorial election. The defectors showed a significant shift in the precise opposite direction, both in their attitudes and in their voting behavior. In both periods, the ideology of loyalists was highly consistent with the leader's position. In the economic realm, for example, even where actual well-being varied considerably among loyalists, this identification with the President yielded highly similar attitudes regarding the favorability of the economic picture facing the nation. [See Chapter 10 here on Presidential Leadership.]

With appropriate concern for rectifying the balance, there may be virtue in reopening for study Freud's (1922) contention that the leader of a group represents a common "ego ideal" in whom members share an identification and an ideology. Laboratory experimentation on groups offers little basis for studying such identification in light of the ephemeral, ad hoc basis for the creation of such groups. In fact, a disproportionate amount of our current knowledge about leadership in social psychology comes from experiments which are methodologically sophisticated but bear only a pale resemblance to the leadership enterprise that engages people in persisting relationships.

There also is the problem of accommodating the notion of identification within prevailing conceptions of leader follower transactions and social exchange. But that is not an insurmountable difficulty with an expansion of the reward concept to include, for instance, the value of social reality. In any case, as investigators move increasingly from the laboratory to studies in more naturalistic settings, one of the significant qualities that may make a difference in leadership functioning is precisely this prospect for identification.

## SOME CONCLUSIONS AND IMPLICATIONS

The present selective review and discussion touches upon a range of potential issues for the further study of leadership. The discussion is by no means exhaustive in providing details beyond noting suggestive developments. It is evident, however, that a new set of conceptions about leadership is beginning to emerge after a period of relative quiescence.

In providing a bridge to future research here, these newer, general ideas are underscored in a suggestive way. The methodologies they demand represent a challenge to imaginative skill, especially toward greater refinements in the conduct of field experiments and field studies which provide a look at the broader system of leadership relationships. Then, too, there is a need to consider the two-way nature of the influence process, with greater attention paid to the expectations of followers within the system. As reiterated here, the key to an understanding of leadership rests in seeing it as an influence process, involving an implicit exchange relationship over time.

No less important as a general point is the need for a greater recognition of the system represented by the group and its enterprise. This recognition provides a vehicle by which to surmount the misleading dichotomy of the leader and the situation which so long has prevailed. By adopting a systems approach, the leader, the led, and the situation defined broadly, are seen as interdependent inputs variously engaged toward the production of desired outputs.

Some release is needed from the highly static, positional view of leadership if we are to analyze its processes. A focus on leadership maintenance has weighted the balance against a more thorough probe of emerging leadership and succession phenomena. Investigators should be more aware of their choice and the differential implications, as between emerging and ongoing leadership. In this regard, the significance of the legitimacy of leadership, its sources, and effects, requires greater attention in future investigations.

In studying the effectiveness of the leader, more emphasis should be placed on the outcomes for the total system, including the fulfillment of expectations held by followers. The long-standing overconcern with outcome, often stated only in terms of the leader's ability to influence, should yield to a richer conception of relationships geared to mutual goals. Not irrelevantly, the perception of the leader held by followers, including their identification with him/her, needs closer scrutiny. In this way, one may approach a recognition of stylistic elements allowing given persons to be effective leaders.

Finally, it seems plain that research on task-oriented groups must attend more to the organizational frameworks within which these groups are imbedded. Whether these frameworks are industrial, educational, governmental, or whatever, they are implicated in such crucial matters as goal-setting, legitimacy of authority, and leader succession. Though not always explicit, it is the organizational context which recruits and engages members in particular kinds of tasks, role relationships, and the rewards of participation. This context deserves more explicitness in attempts at understanding leadership processes.

# CHAPTER 6

# The Essential Interdependence of Leadership and Followership

## COMMENTARY

The paper presented in this chapter is a distillation of many key points associated with my conception of leadership as a unity with followership. Although it duplicates other material presented in this book, I decided to keep it *as is* so that the points made are available in brief form. As background, note that an earlier version of the paper was presented in the Invited Symposium on "The Duality of Leadership and Followership: Social, Cognitive, and Organizational Perspectives," organized and chaired by Ann Howard, at the 1991 Annual Convention of the American Psychological Society (APS, since 2006, the Association for Psychological Science).*

After my talk at this APS convention, Sandra Scarr, who had recently been installed as the first editor of the new APS journal *Current Directions in Psychological Science*, asked me to submit it for publication. I am glad to acknowledge my debt to the two valued colleagues just mentioned for their supportiveness. The other is Virginia Vanderslice (1988), a former doctoral student in my leadership seminar at SUNY Buffalo, who presented the useful idea of separating leadership functions from leaders.

One misunderstanding in looking at this interactive process is to see responsiveness to followers as an abdication of a leader's role in giving direction. First, this view overlooks other functions such as information seeking, problem solving, advocacy, and conflict resolution, which are part of what *leadership* needs to do, *not just the leader*. Second, these are among important shared functions that can benefit from follower input, with the leader still responsible. However, distributing these functions is of primary importance.

Much of research on leadership has been directed to the effects of leaders on followers, so that the bases for leader actions have been neglected. Furthermore, as already stated, all leaders to some degree are at times followers, and followers are not forever cast as "passive nonleaders." Fleishman's (1953b) early work demonstrated the importance of "leadership climate" in lower-level management's leadership. The effects of training were found to be negated by the climate. The phenomenon of "upward influence" is an active followership role too often neglected (Hollander, 2004). Also ignored is the motivational question of *origins* rather than of *effects* (see Green & Mitchell, 1979). One result of these omissions is a poorly developed picture of the instigating factors that underlie the actions of individual leaders. An enlarged perspective on the foundations of leader action could consider the constraints that followers create by their expectations and the intentions perceived to be behind it. For leaders to be able to do different things in different ways, there needs to be positive responsiveness from followers, which depends on how they perceive the leader's course and motives; on the other side of this coin is the leader's need to preserve the basis for discretionary choice (Stewart, 1982). More in-depth research, extended over time, is required to establish the links between leader's motives, aspirations, and actions.

---

* Washington, DC, June 16, 1991. It also had origins in the March 31, 1989, presidential address I gave to the Eastern Psychological Association (EPA), "Character, Credit, and Charisma: Reconsidering the Leader-Follower Connection" at that year's Annual Convention in Boston.

Republished with permission of Blackwell Publishing, from *Current Directions in Psychological Science*, 1992, 1(2), 71–75.

## LEADERSHIP AND FOLLOWERSHIP AS A UNITY

There are many reasons to attend to the unity of leadership and followership. Yet, by convention, these phenomena are treated apart. Both leadership and followership represent active roles, given the reality that organizational functions require them at every level. The usual expectation of the leader role as active and the follower role as passive is misconceived even in traditional hierarchies. Barnes and Kriger (1986) observed that leadership does not rest with a single individual but is pluralistic and fluid, in part due to the crossing of the formal structure by informal networks. In short, leadership is a process, not a person. Because of the common misconception that it belongs to one person, the prospect of leadership coming from sources other than designated leaders in a hierarchy is still obscured (Vanderslice, 1988). Leaders do command greater attention and influence, but followers can affect and even constrain leaders' activity in more than passing ways, as has been shown in a variety of studies (Hollander, 1985). Although the early interest was in who becomes a leader, with what traits and effects, new emphases address questions about how leadership functions are performed in particular situations presenting varying demands. Not least among these are the qualities and responsiveness of followers, with their needs, expectations, and perceptions. The role of follower can therefore be seen as holding within it potential for both assessing and taking on leadership functions. In addition to directing activity, these include decision-making, goal setting, communicating, adjudicating conflict, and otherwise maintaining the enterprise. To some extent, all these functions may be dispersed through a degree of delegation to followers. Furthermore, qualities sought in good leaders, such as dependability, competence, and honesty, are also included among attributes of good followers (Hollander & Webb, 1955; Kouzes & Posner, 1987). Despite the imbalance of power, influence can be exerted in both roles, as part of a social exchange. Homans (1961) long since noted that effective leadership is more likely to be achieved through reciprocity and the potential for two way influence than through a reliance on power over others (Hollander & Offermann, 1990).

The traditional view of the leader-follower relationship assumed a relatively closed system, less open to dynamism than to stasis, with the leader giving top-down direction. In that familiar view, beginning with parent-child relations, a leader is presented as the font of wisdom, with followers relatively unknowing and supposedly unexposed to alternative views. Leaders themselves may still be comfortable seeing their relationships with followers in closed system terms, but this view is no longer viable in many settings. As Meyer (1982) put it, "Oversimplification of leadership roles and adherence to anachronistic models of leader-follower relationships have precluded consideration of how the changing complexities and problems of organizations ... require profound changes in leader-follower interactions" (p. 930).

## LEADER TRAITS AND FOLLOWER ATTRIBUTIONS

A focus on leaders largely to the exclusion of followers is exemplified in the venerable tradition of attention to leader traits. Today, leader traits are still considered important (Kirkpatrick & Locke, 1991), but more likely as they fit followers' attributions about leaders and elicit a response, affirmative or otherwise, from followers. Lord and Maher (1990) said that followers check their perceptions of a leader against their prototypes of leader attributes, such as intelligence, and expectations of how leaders should perform. In this conception of leadership, perceptions are the key link between the leader's past performance and expectations about his or her future performance. Positive or negative outcomes also are more likely to be attributed to the leader than to others or external factors (Meindl & Ehrlich, 1987; Pfeffer, 1977). In general, this work is part of the heightened attention being given to cognitive elements in leader-follower relations, represented by followers' implicit leadership theories, among other concepts. Context is also important. Among the many factors now recognized as affecting the leadership process are the nature of the task or activity, its history and actors, the availability of human and material resources, and the affective tone of leader-follower relations. These relations are, of course, shaped by the perceptions of a leader's attributes, including his or her perceived competence, motivation, and personality characteristics, as these are connected to followers and the demands of the situation. All of these attributes can play a part in influencing followers' perceptions of and responses to a leader's actions. In studies of attributions of leader performance, there now is increased attention to accountability and evaluation by followers. But in line with the aphorism that "an ounce of image is worth a pound of performance," imagery and self presentation can obscure the realities of a leader's performance in dealing with other people, including followers, peers, superiors, and adversaries. Still, obvious instances of unfairness, self-seeking at others' expense, weakness, vacillation, and outright misconduct will jeopardize relationships and have negative consequences. Some leaders may become so detached from followers that the leaders cease to be concerned about how their actions will be perceived by and affect followers and their mutual activities. A current illustration of this pattern is seen in the heightened criticism of excessively large salaries and bonuses paid to American chief executive officers, as compared with foreign competitors, even in the face of layoffs, declining earnings, and other poor performance outcomes for their firms.

## RELATIONAL QUALITIES OF LEADERSHIP

The follower's perspective has proved to be a useful avenue to understanding leadership, and has been increasingly employed. This approach is illustrated in McCall, Lombardo, and Morrison's (1988) study of derailment among 400 promising managers who were seen to be on a fast track. Those failing to reach their expected potential tended to show various kinds of inconsiderate behavior toward others, but rarely lacked technical skills. Kouzes and Posner (1987) asked a sample of 2,600 top-level managers about qualities they admired in their leaders. Being honest and providing inspiration were among the most frequently chosen ones, in addition to being competent and forward-looking. Here again, the interpersonal, or relational, realm was seen to play a significant role. More recently, Kelly and I analyzed critical incidents of good and bad leadership we obtained from an initial sample of 81 mainly organization-based respondents, both male and female. They also answered follow-up questions and completed rating scales regarding the superiors involved in the incidents. We found that relational qualities were emphasized in distinguishing good from bad leadership, and that four rating scales—perceptiveness, involvement, trustworthiness, and rewardingness—most consistently confirmed the distinction. Sensitivity to followers, support, and praise dominated good but were absent in bad leadership. Neither salary increases nor promotions were mentioned with any frequency in differentiating the two. These results have since been corroborated with a second wave of 120 similar respondents. Gender provides an example of the effect of expectations [see Chapter 7]. Comparisons between women and men in the leader role often fail to consider that women begin with an initial hurdle to attaining legitimacy, even though neither men nor women appear to be more "effective" as leaders across mixed gender situations. Individual differences among leaders, including differences in style and self-oriented actions, are perceived as real and do play a role in follower satisfaction and performance outcomes. However, a leader's style may be a function of the particular followers with whom the leader has a relationship, as Graen (1975) and Dienesch and Liden (1986) have pointed out in the leader-member exchange model. Positive response from followers depends on how they perceive the leader's course of action and motives. These perceptions of intentions can limit the leader's discretionary choice. Also noteworthy is how followers' perceptions of leaders' qualities can affect the emergence of leaders in the first place. Another perspective on this process, recently investigated by Fiedler and Garcia (1987), is the ability to use cognitive resources, essentially intelligence, which can be constrained by a leader's superior.

## TRANSACTIONAL LEADERSHIP AND THE ACTIVE FOLLOWER

Transactional models of leadership emphasize the implicit social exchange, or transaction, that exists between leader and followers as a feature of effectiveness. In the transactional view, the leader gives benefits to the followers, such as a definition of the situation and direction; the followers reciprocate with heightened esteem for and responsiveness to the leader. This transactional approach emphasizes a more active role for followers, with the potential for two-way influence, rather than coerced compliance. The idiosyncrasy credit (IC) model of innovative leaderships is a related concept dealing with the latitude a leader has to bring about change. According to the model, this latitude is a function of followers' perceptions of the leader's competence and signs of loyalty that engender trust. This credit-building process, and its consequences, resonate with modern-day attributional concepts. The essential point of the IC model is that leadership is a dynamic process of interpersonal evaluation: Individuals earn standing in the eyes of present or eventual followers and then have latitude for actions, including innovations associated with the leader role, that would be unacceptable for those without such status. Credits are essentially a form of accorded status that accrues primarily from perceived competence and conformity to group norms, as a sign of loyalty. The idea of credit is embedded in everyday language, in terms such as "receiving credit," "taking credit," and "being discredited." In its refinement, the IC model points out the way credits accumulate and have operational significance in permitting innovations. For instance, it has been found that a leader's source of authority from election signals a greater accumulation of credits than does appointment and therefore allows greater latitude for disagreeing with group judgments. An appointed leader often requires more time for building a relationship and constituency to assert influence in the direction of change.

## LEADER RESPONSES TO FOLLOWERS

Attributional analysis makes explicit the significance of followers' and others' perceptions and expectations of the leader. But the reverse process, the leader's response to followers, also is significant. In an experiment by Crowe, Bochner, and Clark (1972), for example, supervisors who preferred autocratic or democratic managerial styles accommodated when put in charge of workers with opposite expectations. Other research has studied the content of followers' feedback as a source of influence on the behavior of leaders. A recent experiment in this vein compared how appointed and elected leaders evaluated followers in a group problem-solving task. In a 2 x 2 design, the followers displayed either positive or negative feedback (agreement or disagreement) with either high or low task activity (five proposals or one). The main hypothesis was that appointed leaders would respond less favorably than elected ones to followers giving negative feedback, because of a greater threat posed to the leaders' status, especially under the high-activity condition. Forty-six subjects, 20 female and 26 male, were randomly placed in the appointed or elected condition of leader legitimacy and told they were leading four same-sex followers in a group problem-solving task. The dependent measure was a composite score made up of 10 semantic differential ratings of each follower. Figure 6.1 shows the results. In general, a main effect showed that elected leaders were more positive than appointed

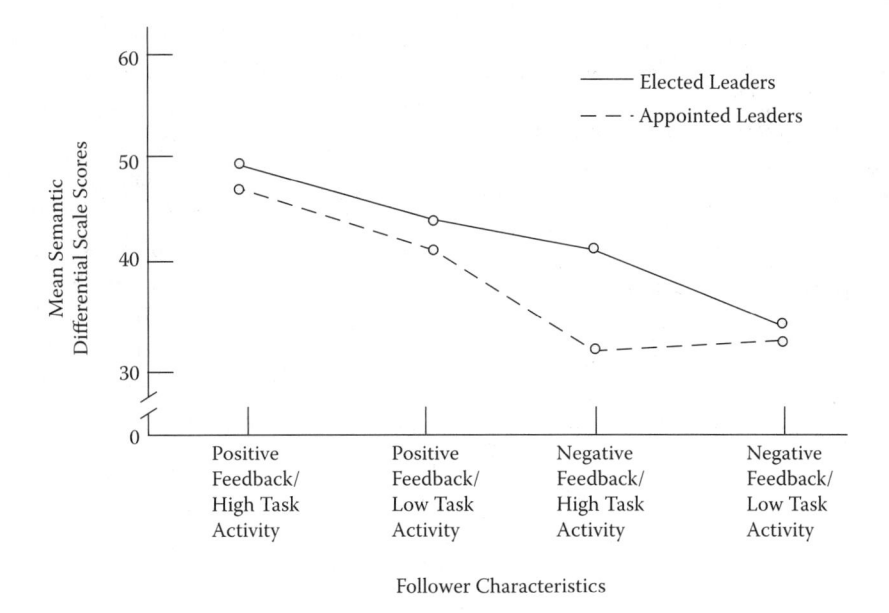

**Figure 6.1** Mean semantic differential score scales assigned by two types of leaders, elected or appointed, to four types of followers, by whether positive or negative in feedback to leaders and high or low in task activity. From Elgie, Hollander, and Rice, 1988, p. 1367.

leaders in judgments of their followers. As predicted, however, appointed and elected leaders responded differently to high- and low-activity followers, particularly under the negative feedback condition, and more similarly under the positive feedback condition.

## TRANSFORMATIONAL LEADERSHIP AND CHARISMA

Burns's (1978) idea of the leader as a transforming agent has been applied to organizational leadership by Bass (1985) and Bennis and Nanus (1985), especially as a source of exceptional performance. The essential point is that the leader strives to go beyond the bounds of the usual to bring about a change in followers' thinking that will redirect their action. This function can be accommodated within transactional leadership, as part of granting rewards such as a "vision" that reduces uncertainty by providing a clear definition of the situation. Transformational leadership can be seen as an extension of transactional leadership, with greater intensity of the leader and arousal of the follower. Indeed, the research by Bass (1985) and Yammarino and Bass (1990) involves a measure with two transactional factors in addition to charisma, intellectual stimulation, and individual attention to followers. Charisma is not just a quality possessed by a leader, but something accorded by followers. Indeed, it can be considered to represent a great fund of idiosyncrasy credits. There is, however, the potential for damage from a leader who has charismatic appeal, as Post observed in considering how this quality is associated with narcissistic needs for continual approval from others. Coupled with personalized power needs, the outcome of a charismatic appeal can be destructive, as Hogan, Raskin, and Fazzini (1988) observed in their work on "the dark side of charisma." Other flawed leader types may appear to have good social skills and rise readily in organizations, but take a financial and human toll in reduced productivity, poor morale, and excessive turnover.

## BRINGING FOLLOWERS INTO THE PROCESS

Vanderslice (1988) is among the latest observers to point the way to detaching leadership functions from leaders in hierarchical structures: "Not only is it possible to fulfill leadership functions without creating static leader roles, but also, there may be negative organizational consequences to leader-follower distinctions." In conclusion, our understanding of leadership is incomplete if we do not recognize its unity with followership. One implication of this is to allow more latitude for inputs from various sources by bringing followers into the process to a larger extent. Every initiative need not come from a designated leader. But the strategic position of such designation can be employed to facilitate implementation of ideas and other participatory activities. Even while retaining authority and responsibility, a designated leader can interpret the role in facilitating and even coaching terms instead of conventional top-down, directive ones, so as to develop leadership skills in others. A large increase in understanding comes with the recognition that finding "new" or "better" leaders requires attention to their ability to engage followers in mutually productive and satisfying enterprises.

# CHAPTER 7

# Women and Leadership

## COMMENTARY

An optimistic view 25 years ago held that women would achieve greater parity with men regarding compensation and status in the workplace, among other signs of progress. Recent data, however, reveal that the "pay gap" in the United States has not narrowed, and indeed may be at best steady, or even slightly larger, depending on the occupation. Similar pay results were found in a current worldwide study by the International Labor Organization (ILO), a United Nations agency. Women's work was still found to pay less than men's by a considerable margin, although the differential may vary by activity and nation. In manufacturing, women often represent as many as 80% of line workers, especially in such fields as garment and electronic production, although usually at a lower average pay than men. Women also represent a minority of supervisors as compared to men at the workforce level and above.

In a study of whether male or female leaders differed in ways of leading, Eagly, Johannesen-Schmidt, and van Engen (2003) conducted a metaanalysis comparing findings from 45 research studies of managers. They found female leaders inclined more to transforming (TF) leadership than were male leaders, but exceeded the males in rewarding subordinates for doing a good job. This reveals a higher transactional (TA) practice, which is showing responsiveness to followers, a form of inclusion, not necessarily indicative of the change element imbedded in TF leadership. Eagly and Carli (2007) have recently published research on the erosion of gender differences that increase the prospects for women taking on high-level executive positions, including their more interpersonal qualities.

At the very top, however, the number of women in executive roles continues to be only a fraction of hoped for results, just marginally greater than when the paper presented in this chapter was written. At the CEO level, fewer than 5% of the Fortune 500 companies have a woman in that role. One reason given for this is *stereotyping* that discounts a woman's capability to occupy leadership roles.

A recent study titled "Women 'Take Care,' Men 'Take Charge,'" was reported by Catalyst (2005), a major research and consulting organization concerned with women's advancement in business and the professions. These gender stereotypes, as stated in the title, are patterned after the traditional conception of mother and father roles. However, in practice, they were found to portray women "as relatively poor problem-solvers" so "their power to motivate followers may be seriously undermined" (p. 4). Accordingly, "women leaders are rated more harshly at stereotypically male, 'take charge' behaviors … and may be especially at risk for such criticism in traditionally masculine fields, such as general management. Further, adding insult to injury, it may be difficult for women leaders to prove stereotypes about their leadership wrong" (p. 30). A profound reason for this psychologically is the tendency to pay more attention to evidence that confirms a stereotype rather than evidence that does not.

The few women who reach the top ranks of organizations as CEOs are usually presented by media and others as exceptional, or "tokens." They are in any case treated as "different," and may not as readily gain a following, or earn credits, as revealed in research on the idiosyncrasy credit model (Wahrman & Pugh, 1974). One such groundbreaker was Carly Fiorina. Appointed Hewlett-Packard's CEO, she led the merger with Compaq, which ultimately proved beneficial to the firm, but was ousted by her board, nevertheless. Being considered as someone exceptional is not necessarily favorable to women in her position. In that regard, Yoder (2001) has provided an insightful analysis of the particular difficulties faced by women, such as Fiorina, who are constrained by gender biases, including stereotyping, and by women as well as men. Indeed, women have been found to be more critical at times of other women in leader roles than they are of men (e.g., Carrieri et al., 1990).

On the U.S. political scene, the 2006 elections placed a woman, Nancy Pelosi, into the speakership of the House of Representatives, which is a historic first, given the more than 200 years in which only men have filled that role. Importantly, it is just behind the vice president in the line of succession to the presidency. In the cabinet, for the second time, a woman has been appointed secretary of state, but the cabinet continues to be overwhelmingly male.

Although the 2006 election also produced a high point of 16 women in the U.S. Senate, that figure does not compare favorably with many of the developed nations of the world, where women in national legislatures routinely are far higher in number. In the U.S. House, the recent election netted some 70 women members out of 435. On a proportional basis, that figure represents a small percentage of women members not far different from the Senate. It appears that reaching even 20% might be considered in either or both bodies to be a great accomplishment. True enough, there are women governors, in such dispersed states as Arizona, Connecticut, Kansas, and Michigan, but again their numbers are small, proportional to men governors. Similarly, women occupy mayoral positions in many cities, but far fewer than do men. Women have organized to have more of their numbers in elective and appointive political positions, such as the nonpartisan National Women's Political Caucus (NWPC) started in 1971. It strives for more equitable representation of women and publicizing women's issues in elections at all levels. Women in legislatures have been found by political scientists to make a significant difference in what gets discussed, but also in the kinds of legislation advanced, by a style that is more integrative in facilitating interaction (O'Conner & Yanus, 2004).

In graduate and professional schools, for academic fields, and law, medicine, and dentistry, women have fared far better in numbers, achieving parity in these institutions as students. Indeed, at the undergraduate level women exceed men in numbers and quite often in performance, as measured by grades. As for faculty positions, in some fields women have advanced with men to full professorships on a comparable schedule, while in others they have been held back. At the levels of partnerships in law firms and major directorships at hospitals and chairmanships at medical and dental schools, women lag behind men, who predominate at the top. However, women have achieved the presidencies of academic institutions in far larger numbers now. Several Ivy League universities have lately chosen women as presidents, so that four of eight are women, along with MIT, Harvard's neighbor on the Charles River, where Susan Hockfield has been president since 2005. Harvard also joined Brown, Penn, and Princeton recently in making the choice of a woman, history professor Catherine Drew Gilpin Faust (Rimer, 2007). She had been the founding dean of the Radcliffe Institute, which brings 50 scholars yearly to study on campus. She also was an advisor on women's issues among others for President Lawrence Summers after the difficulties leading to his resignation. Faust says she wishes to be Harvard's president, and not be defined by gender as the woman president (R. Wilson, *Chronicle of Higher Education*, February 23, 2007, pp. A1, A24).

The military services in the United States have become more accessible for women, where they can take on a greater variety of roles, especially since the military academies were opened up to them, almost 30 years ago. Nonetheless, service institutions continue to affect women adversely by harassment and impediments to their careers (Offermann & Malmaut, 2002). Military superiors have sometimes been guilty of turning a "blind eye" to complaints of such practices and have targeted the victims for additional difficulties. Consequently, many instances of such behavior go unreported, including those as serious as rape (S. Corbett, March 18, 2007, *New York Times Magazine*). Despite these problems, women have performed very well, including those who are helicopter pilots flying missions over enemy forces. This is one of few positions that involves women in combat, although in current warfare there often is far less distinction between noncombat and combat functions at a "front." Harassment of women in the federal workforce continues to be at a relatively substantial number, 42% of women reporting incidents of such behavior, in a large-scale 1994 survey. It remained at that level from earlier surveys done in 1981 and 1987 (Cleveland, Stockdale, & Murphy, 2000, p. 230).

Although there are more women now in police and fire departments, and even some who hold chief's positions, women have had a harder time being accepted. Gerber (2001) found that male officers in a major city's police force she studied were more often assigned to higher-status positions in two-person police partnerships than were female officers. She related this to attitudes about gender, namely, the expectation that when they worked as partners, the man had higher status than the woman. Women officers were also found to use indirect power in dealing with men partners, so as not to challenge the leadership position of the men. Gerber concluded that superiors' attitudes about gender and personality, although faulty, reflected cultural stereotypes used as the basis for evaluating the performance of women, to their disadvantage. Research by Offermann and Schrier (1985) on sex, role, and the impact of power has contributed to understanding the dynamics of this process. A new book by Kellerman and Rhode (2007) treats a range of such issues concerned with women and leadership.

The ultimate value of diversity in the workforce has been long established in the research done by Catalyst, among other organizations. Morrison (1992) has done landmark research on the topic, showing the way that organizations benefit by having multiple elements among their employees. One example is in the differential range of experience that is brought to bear in deciding solutions to problems, including marketing and other dealings with customers. All male or all white workforces are examples of clearly inadequate resources to meet these challenges, although highly diverse ones require special sensitivities for leadership (Offermann & Matus, 2007).

Reprinted with permission of John Wiley & Sons Ltd., from *Small Groups and Social Interaction*, Vol. 1, Edited by H. Blumberg, A. P. Hare, V. Kent, and M. Davies, 1983, London: John Wiley & Sons Ltd.

Despite some notable cases of women who have become leaders in business, politics, and elsewhere, leadership has been and still is largely a male domain. In a parallel way, the study *of* leadership in groups has been done mainly with men (Borgatta and Stimson, 1963). Hare's revised *Handbook of Small Group Research* (1976) indicates that the situation had not changed much with regard to group composition. Evidently, our knowledge about leadership in groups has largely been founded on studies with men and far less with studies of women, or of men and women in groups of mixed composition.

## GENDER DIFFERENCES IN SOCIAL BEHAVIOR

Conventional wisdom accepts that women and men differ in certain aspects of their social behavior. While there are data to support that view, as Deaux (1976) and O'Leary (1977) have noted, they have to be interpreted cautiously because of a good deal of confusion about femininity and masculinity based on social roles or on characteristics of gender (see Heine, 1971). Moreover, the basis used to establish so-called 'sex differences' in social behavior often rests on stereotypes rather than on observations of interaction. For example, McKee and Sherriffs (1957) found that men were more favorably rated than women on a variety of evaluations by both women and men. Heilbrun (1968) looked at differences in instrumental and expressive behaviors of men and women and found that women were seen as more expressive than instrumental in their behavior by both sexes. However, men were rated by both women and men as being expressive and instrumental. Broverman et al. (1972) found that the male stereotype was laden with competence items and the female stereotype with a cluster of warmth and expressiveness items.

A second area of comparative research on gender has investigated the responses of women and of men who have been in interaction. Many of these studies have included groups of two (dyads), or of three (triads). Dyads are a particularly special group because the departure of either member effectively destroys it. Among the classic experiments in this vein are those by Bond and Vinacke (1961) and by Strodtbeck and Mann (1956). Overall, they found that the performance of men tended to be exploitative and competitive in these groups, and that of women tended to be more accommodative. Although such results neatly fit the Bales and Slater (1955) distinction between the father's task role, and the mother's socioemotional role, they are not conclusive on the point because of the effects of social learning and society's expectations. Women, for instance, have long been discouraged from too openly displaying competitive behavior with men, given the anticipation of men's negative attitudes toward such displays (see Tavris and Offir, 1977, Ch. 6).

Furthermore, the existence of such gender differences does not substantiate a predetermined quality of masculinity and femininity. Instead, gender distinctions in leadership behavior can be attributed to role expectations, style, and the task demands in the group (Hollander and Yoder, 1980).

As suggested earlier, dyads are special groups because accommodation is so important to their persistence. Therefore, the family's continuity as a parental unit depends upon it, which may account for the traditional expectation that women be oriented toward harmonious relations to keep the unit intact. The Bales and Slater (1955) distinction also overlooks the reality that married women perform tasks, even if they are not working at a job, in being a housewife and mother.

The point goes still further. The distinction between the mother and father roles in the family seems to underpin the usual findings in the experimental vein. This may well be because the stereotype of the father as the task specialist and mother as supporter is still relatively entrenched among experimenters and subjects alike.

In fact, the comparative activity of women and men is not so clearly divergent. In modern society, the altered pattern of women at work is something which demands a re-examination of the stereotypic view. According to the 1979 *Statistical Abstract of the United States,* almost half of American married women *with husband present* hold jobs outside the home. That does not include women who are widowed, separated, or divorced, and who work *and* also are heads of households. There are more of these than ever before (see Hollander, 1981, pp. 187–196).

Although there have been observed differences in the aggression and dominance shown by women in groups versus men in groups, the nature of the activity and its context are important. If physical aggressiveness is what is meant, then women show less of it, bearing in mind of course that there is considerable cultural encouragement for boys to engage in physically aggressive contact sports as testimony to their 'manliness,' as Mead (1949) has long since noted. Girls may be 'aggressive,' but not so much in physical ways.

Indeed, Deaux (1976) contends that women are as active as men, but that the areas in which they strive to achieve are different. With respect to being dominant or assertive, women in mixed-sex company tend to be less obviously so than men. However, the social context matters, with respect to who is present and for what purpose. A masculine orientation in traditional culture has been associated with 'taking charge,' while the feminine orientation has been traditionally associated with 'harmonious interpersonal relations' (cf. Eagly, 1978).

## TAKING THE LEADER ROLE

Associated with dominance, and aggressiveness in the assertive sense, is the emergence of leaders in groups. Members who participate more are likely to be more influential and to be seen as leaders.

In groups composed of men and women, a standard finding is that women generally are less likely to become the leader, and are less inclined than men to seek that role (Eskilson and Wiley, 1976). In another experiment, Megargee (1969) showed further that, regardless of the dominance of the women paired with a man, she was unlikely to become leader. Interestingly, a dominant woman was more inclined to assign the leader role to the man than the reverse.

Recognizing that there are individual differences, and that groups and their activities vary widely, women generally do participate less in the presence of men than men do with men. For example, in their classic study of jury deliberations, Strodtbeck and Mann (1956) found that men talked significantly more than women. A more recent study by Aries (1976) found that men initiated and received 66% of the communications in the group. Aries also examined participation rates over time, which are considered to indicate the stability of the group' dominance hierarchy, or status ladder (Bales, 1950). Men in both all-male and mixed-sex groups were found to have more stable rates than did women. But women *did* have an impact insofar as men in mixed-sex groups increased their expressive remarks, which is more characteristic of the content of women's communications (Aries, 1976).

The differences in the participation rates of women and men in groups can be explained, where found, by the task ability which is required, and what is perceived to be expertise, and not by a gender-specific attribute. As Maccoby and Jacklin (1974) have observed, the choice of a task can itself create a biased condition for men or for women.

There is also the factor of expectations. A good deal of research evidence indicates or implies that people generally expect the leader role to be filled by a man. For instance, in a study by Schein (1973), male middle managers rated women in general, men in general, or successful middle managers on their overall characteristics, attitudes, and temperaments. On 60 of these 86 items, men and successful managers were rated similarly, while on only eight items were women and successful managers rated similarly.

As O'Leary (1974) has pointed out, a basic concern exists among women and men about whether or not the leader role is appropriate for a woman in a mixed-sex setting. The success of women therefore may be inhibited not only by external expectations, but by attitudes held by the woman herself. While an ineffectual male leader may have to cope with a stronger sense of failure for mismanaging his role, a successful female leader might have to face the fact that societal attitudes do not readily recognize her success in the leader role (cf. Jacobson and Effertz, 1974).

There are still comparatively few studies of women who serve as leaders of mixed-sex groups, whether through appointment, election, or some informal process of emergence. In one attempt to rectify this, Fallon and Hollander (1976) studied 32 groups, each of two men and two women undergraduate students, who were able to elect a leader in a discussion task concerned with urban problems. Each group talked about the first two problems for about 10 to 15 minutes, and made a group ranking of the alternative action programs for each. A secret ballot was then distributed. Of the 32 groups, 14 elected men and 10 women as leaders; 2 men tied and a coin toss yielded the choice. In 6 groups a woman and a man tied and the woman was made the winner to offset what was an overall tilt to elect men. However, by the process used, the leader was *always* the most or equal to the most chosen person in the group. Following the first two phases, half the groups were given success feedback and half failure feedback on performance. Regardless of the type of feedback, we found that the men leaders were significantly more influential than women leaders in the last phases. There was, however, no difference by the sex of the leader in the satisfaction item of the post-interaction questionnaire, although men as leaders were seen by both men and women as having significantly *more task leadership ability*. It may be that we had a sex-biased task, but our pretesting certainly did not reveal it. Therefore, we must take seriously the fact that men evidently fared better than did the women as leaders, and that the women generally joined men in seeing women leaders as less able on the task.

In a recent study at the US Military Academy at West Point (1980), my colleagues Robert Rice and Lisa Richer Bender, together with Captain Alan Vitters of the staff there, compared men and women cadets as leaders of three-man cadet groups. They had previously measured the attitudes toward women of those men, using the Spence-Helmreich Attitudes Toward Women Scale (1972). While the sex of the leader did not appear to affect performance and morale, these attitudes proved to be quite decisive in determining the attributions made about the women as compared to the men leaders. When the group was 'successful' with a woman leader, both the leader and men followers tended to attribute it to 'luck.' With a man leader they attributed success more to the leader's ability.

## PERFORMANCE AS A LEADER

As indicated, the factors that affect the leadership behavior of women and men are quite often complex and interactive. There also are subtle differences which go unnoticed. For instance, in a recent analysis I did with Jan Yoder (Hollander and Yoder, 1980), we concluded that there appear to be two distinct approaches to studying differences between women and men as leaders: assign women or men to the role of leader, keeping other factors constant; or, examine the leader's and group's reactions to women or men who are already in place as leaders, for example, those who are managers. The first procedure addresses the general question of whether women *assigned* to be leaders can be as effective as men. The second asks if women who *choose* to be leaders are as effective as men who choose the leader role.

Not surprisingly, when one reflects on it, these two approaches produce conflicting research findings. Studies supporting sex differences in leadership behavior tend to take a sample from the general population of women, and to thrust those into the leader role. Studies finding few differences between women and men leaders tend to sample the population of actual leaders. The factor which appears to be critical is whether the individual has the initiative in assuming the leader role.

What happens if a woman is put in charge of a group or an organization as an executive or a manager? For one thing, she is likely to be at an initial disadvantage. However, in her book *Men and Women of the Corporation*, Rosabeth Kanter (1977) concludes that individual differences matter more than a woman's gender in managerial roles. This is despite the fact that women will often face the extra burden of overcoming negative attitudes in managing mixed-sex groups, as Virginia O'Leary (1974) has indicated. On this point, Florence Denmark (1977) has said:

> Many of the assumptions that women managers are basically different from men are just not supported by data. The one difference investigators generally agree upon is women's greater concern for relationships among people; this should be considered a plus in terms of leadership effectiveness. Alleged sex differences in ability, attitudes, and personality have been based on sex-role stereotypes, rather than empirical observations of women leaders (pp. 110–111).

Nevertheless, women in managerial and executive roles are likely to be treated differently by their male associates. For example, there are instances of attempted or actual sexual harassment which present a social problem that has gained increased attention. In another vein, there is a tendency for women's comments to be interrupted, overlooked, ignored, or 'unheard' by men not used to paying attention to what women say in mixed-sex groups (Bunker and Seashore,

1975). Unfortunately, women may themselves ignore other women.

It seems true, in sum, that serving as a leader of a group made up of men and women presents extra difficulties for a woman. As noted here, this is usually considered to be an outgrowth of the stereotype associating masculinity with dominance and leadership (see McGregor, 1967; Lockheed, 1977). However, viewed as a transactional process between a leader and followers, leadership basically depends upon competence and a sense of fairness (Hollander, 1978). Therefore, even with the impediments presented to women, they can be effective in these functions if the primary task is not sex-biased. Indeed, recent evidence from two organizations suggests that the leader's gender was not related either to leader behavior or subordinates' satisfaction (Osborn and Vicars, 1976).

The overall picture is therefore not quite so disheartening as might appear, especially since many of the studies which show women at a disadvantage may become increasingly dated. As more women move into leader roles, and perform capably, their numbers may well reduce the disadvantages they have encountered.

# CHAPTER 8

# Leadership, Followership, Self, and Others

## COMMENTARY

The paper presented in this chapter reviews the development of an approach to leadership based on a more active conception of the follower role in reacting to leader qualities. The leader-follower relationship is seen to be affected by perceptions, misperceptions, and self-oriented biases by both parties. Greater attention to follower expectations and perceptions is emphasized. The importance of reciprocal influence in the context of an exchange relationship is clear. The paper deals in part with transactional (TA) leadership, but has implications as well for the transformational (TF) leadership put forth by Burns (1978). In practice, as Yukl (1999) has pointed out, there are rewards associated with both forms of leadership, although Bass (1985) maintained that the transformational form did not necessarily involve rewards.

Issues of dominance and submission are seen to be important in this relationship. Robert and Joyce Hogan (1995), for example, consider these to be orthogonal dimensions with dominance associated with leadership, and submission with conformity. That is one useful interpretation of interest. Another is derived from conceptions of top-down leadership, which is considered to be controlling, as in many military situations. By contrast, Wheatley (2007, p. 113) speaks about her military experience as having the desired feature of mutual concern, with command responsibility involving a form of dedication to the well-being of individuals and units. My impressions from my own service time in the army as a private, and my navy experiences as a junior officer, support her observations, granted that this is not necessarily generalizable. However, the emphasis on teams and "comradeship," along with the sense of mutual sacrifice, usually moderates the motivation for individual gain.

The factor of support accompanies control, and both may be high in a military situation. Fleishman and his colleagues (1998) found in earlier work that consideration for employees in an industrial situation gave the manager more latitude to exert influence, and even control. This is in line with the idiosyncrasy credit model, insofar as the person in a leadership position can gain such latitude by a more favorable position in the eyes of subordinates.

Reprinted from *Leadership Quarterly*, 1992, 3(1), 43–54, with permission of Copyright Clearance Center's Rightslink.

Attempts to understand leadership as a function of leader qualities still represent a challenge in the field (see e.g., Kenny & Zaccaro, 1983; Lord, DeVader, & Alliger, 1986; Kirkpatrick & Locke, 1991). As a starting place, that venerable approach gained credence if only because the leader is usually seen as the major actor in leadership. It is easier to focus on one individual as the center of action, influence, and power than many in making attributions.

Another practical reason for attention to the leader is that leader action or inaction can have multiple effects on other people, not only in the success of the enterprise, but also in the "social health" of a group, organization, or larger entity, including a nation. Indeed, a reasonable question, not asked enough, is what are the *costs* of putting this person in a position, of authority, and responsibility? Another might be, how does he or she respond to disconfirming information from subordinates?

Despite the understandable focus on the leader, the concepts of leader and leadership do not exist in isolation. To be viable, both depend upon followership (see Hollander &, Offermann, 1990a,b). Accordingly, this paper takes a relational approach to leader qualities, whose significance lies in how they are perceived and responded to by followers within the situation experienced with the leader. As Gibb (1947) long ago indicated, "Leadership is a concept applied to the personality-environment relation" (p. 267).

Although leaders are usually directors of activity, all initiatives need not come from the leader. Followers also have the potential for making significant contributions to successful leadership. Indeed, at every level in organizations, leaders are called upon to be responsive also as followers. Not least is the reality that leaders typically rise from among those who have shown ability in the follower role, and are thereby given a boost.

President Dwight D. Eisenhower's career presents a dramatic case in point. Long a junior staff officer before World War II, he was mentored by Generals [Douglas A.] MacArthur and [George C.] Marshall. Promoted to Colonel near the onset of war, twenty-six years after graduating from West Point, he was made a Major General and Commander of U.S. forces in Europe the very next year, elevated over 366 eligible officers. What were the qualities he displayed as a follower [less senior leader] that eventually advanced him to Supreme Commander of Allied Forces and beyond? Without knowing them in detail, it is reasonable to surmise that they fit the task demands of the situation and that not just desire, nor geniality coupled with keen intelligence, could account alone for his dramatic rise and evident success.

## LEADER QUALITIES BY STAGES

Maccoby (1987) is among those who have made the essential point that the style that gets the leadership position is not the same as what is required for effectiveness later. There are even more distinctions, however, in addressing leader qualities needed at successive stages (cf., e.g., Howard & Bray, 1988; Kraut et al., 1989). Moreover, there are the more fundamental questions of who seeks the leader role? What motivates that quest? What features of leader style go with which motives?"

Viewed sequentially, at least four distinctive, if partially overlapping, stages can be identified where certain qualities are more likely to be seen. Put briefly, these stages are definable as *wanting, getting, doing,* and *maintaining the job.* Motivational elements in seeking a leader role obviously take precedence, including needs for personalized power, achievement, and affiliation (see McClelland, 1975), as well as self-efficacy (Bandura, 1977), to touch on only some.

At the next stage come the qualities perceived to be important in securing it, such as self-presentation skills directed at seeming to fit legitimators' prototypes and perhaps serving their needs, which may involve self-monitoring (Snyder, 1979). Finally come those qualities involved in succeeding in leadership and maintaining the leader role, assessed by various, often indeterminant, performance criteria. As noted, the latter stages may call forth manipulative skills aimed at impression management to achieve favorable' outcomes for one's self, often at the expense of others and the broader enterprise (see e.g., Conger; 1990, on John DeLorean). In any case, leader qualities are more likely perceived by followers relevant to the present and future, in the context of the situation, rather than as desirable absolutely (see Hollander & Julian, 1968; Hollander, 1985, p. 493).

An illustration of this is provided by the characteristic known as Machiavellianism (Christie & Geis, 1970). Those high on this measure see the world in manipulative and power-oriented terms, and look for situations where he or she can gain control, especially where there is low or less structure. An experiment by Gleason, Seaman, and Hollander (1978) was directed to precisely this point. Sixteen four-man task groups were constructed composed of one Hi Mach, one Lo Mach, and two middle Machs, based on pretesting introductory psychology students with the Machiavellianism Scale. As expected, the Hi Machs were observed to show greater ascendance than the others, especially under the low structure condition. Even more, relevant in revealing the followers' perspective, their post-interaction ratings of those preferred as future leaders of the group showed the Middle Machs to be significantly more desired for the leader role than either the Hi's or Lo's. Without knowing precisely why these others were different, follower preferences clearly avoided those who scored at the extremes.

As leaders move through the stages of getting, to doing and maintaining the job, qualities like empathy, creativity, and flexibility loom larger as mediators of performance beyond the drive to get the position. In general, this helps to account in part for why qualities that seemed appropriate at the wanting and getting stages fail to be satisfactory at the doing and maintaining stages. An obvious instance occurs when high expectations are created at the getting stage which are not sustained in doing the job. This phenomenon of heightened follower perceptions and expectations, which are disconfirmed, has been called "anticipointment."

## FOLLOWER PERCEPTIONS AND EXPECTATIONS

Recent developments in the study of leadership have made evident the practical importance of follower perceptions on the leader-follower relationship. The nature of this linkage increasingly is recognized as central to affecting the success or failure of leadership (Hollander & Offermann, 1990a,b). One instance of this is shown in the work on "derailment" (McCall, Lombardo, & Morrison, 1988), with four hundred promising managers seen to be on a fast track. Those failing to reach their expected potential were often perceived to lack interpersonal skills. Other research by Kouzes and Posner (1987), with a sample of 2600 top level managers, dealt with qualities they admired in their leaders. Among the most frequently chosen qualities were being honest and inspiring, in addition to being competent and forward looking. Again, the interpersonal or relational realm was perceived to play a significant role. Clearly, the followers' perspective is useful as an avenue to understanding leadership.

Hollander and Kelly (1990) gathered critical incidents and ratings of good and bad leadership from 81 respondents (40 men and 41 women) with organizational work experience, preponderantly of two years or more. Content analyses of the rewards in the situation described indicated that sensitivity to followers, support and praise dominated good but were absent or negative in bad leadership. Respondents in good leadership reported increased participation/productivity, satisfaction, and a sense of being valued. This effect has been confirmed now with 120 more respondents.

## LEADER-FOLLOWER RELATIONSHIPS

This newer approach considers leadership to involve a set of relationships which includes the leader, follower and their situation, most notably the task or function at hand. Especially now, the emergence of a diverse workforce demands more attention to the complex interrelationships in the workplace that are vital to what comes out of the process. This reflects a growing recognition of leadership as a process, and not just a person.

The functions performed by leadership include the obvious one of directing activity, but also decision-making, goal-setting, communicating, adjudicating conflict, and otherwise maintaining the enterprise, among others. These dispersed functions often need some delegation to followers, which reveals the interlocking system of relationships between leaders and followers, and their commonly desired characteristics (Hollander & Webb, 1955; Kouzes & Posner, 1987).

Leadership also operates within constraints and opportunities that are presented by followers (Stewart, 1982). The constraints include the expectations and perceptions of followers which can influence leaders (Hollander, 1985, 1986; Lord & Maher, 1990). One early exponent of this general view,

Fillmore Sanford (1950), asserted the proposition that followers are crucial to any leadership event. In addition, the repeated finding that follower behavior is affected by leader behavior is also shown to be reciprocal. Followers affect leaders in a variety of ways, not least as an audience to which leaders orient and address themselves (Hollander & Offermann, 1990a).

Given their need for mutual responsiveness, leadership and followership can be considered to be reciprocal systems requiring synchronization. Leadership is usually seen as the more active system, but followership can be proactive, not only reactive, as seen especially in social movements. Empowerment in some sectors of activity would be another instance of giving followership a more proactive role, as an accompaniment to leadership in the traditional directive mode.

## ROLE OF FOLLOWER ATTRIBUTIONS ABOUT LEADERS

Follower attributions about leaders affect followers' responses to and relations with their leader. These are affected by the leader's *perceived* attributes, including his or her competence, motivation, and personality characteristics, as related to followers and the prevailing situation. Lord and Maher (1990) consider these perceptions to be checked against prototype held by followers of leader attributes, such as intelligence and expectations of how leaders should perform. In this feature of leadership, follower perceptions are seen as the key linking past performance and future performance, as part of the greater attention now to cognitive elements in leader-follower relations. This development is well represented by follower "implicit leadership theories" (ILTs), among other concepts (see Calder, 1977; Lord, DeVader, & Alliger, 1986; Rush, Thomas & Lord, 1977). A precursor of this was the relating of followers' expectancies of leader attributes to perceptions of leader behavior (Hollander, 1964).

Indeed, the link between perceptions and behavior is the essence of the interest now in leader attributes *as perceived by followers*, and the response that ensues. For example, Calder (1977) and Pfeffer (1977) are among the proponents of a perceptual/attributional perspective which says that leaders are credited or blamed for outcomes over which they alone had little effect. Because positive or negative outcomes are more likely to be attributed to the leader, he or she is more readily faulted and even removed as a symbol when things go wrong, rather than firing the whole staff or team.

## SELF AND OTHER: DOMINANCE AND IDENTIFICATION MOTIFS

Fundamental to the leadership process is the way the leader perceives his or her social self relative to followers. A traditional view of the leader role associates it with authority as the basis for using power, which puts distance between the leader and followers (see Kipnis, 1976). Such a view sees followers as essentially compliant and manipulable, within a dominance motif. One expression of this is a quote from a corporate CEO that "leadership is confirmed when the ability to inflict pain is demonstrated" (Menzies, 1980).

An alternative view, more in keeping with a participative ethos, sees the leader-follower relationship within a mutual identification motif. This includes the prospect of two-way influence, and the perception and counter-perception of leader and followers. Cantril (1958) has said that the leader must be able to perceive the reality worlds of followers and have sensitivity to guide intuitions, if a common consensus and mutual trust rather than "mere power, force, or cunning" are to develop and prevail (p. 129). In practical political terms, Kellerman (1984) has observed that presidential leadership has to be accomplished from "within the world of other people."

The identification with the leader motif is exemplified in Freud's (1921) concept of the leader as a shared "ego-ideal" with whom members of a group mutually identify. Fromm (1941) extended this contention in personality terms by writing that "the psychology of the leader and that of his followers are, of course, closely linked with each other" (p. 65). Erikson (1975) made an associated point about this linkage in asserting that followers "join a leader and are joined together by him" (p. 153).

A good part of the imbalance in treating the leader-follower relationship arises from the lingering mythology that leaders simply exercise authority and power. Cowley (1928) called this "headship," rather than leadership, which by contrast engages followers in a concerted program of action. More recently, Kipnis (1976) has shown that assertions of power effectively undermine the goals of authentic leadership. Such assertions also are limited in creating positive identifications.

## LEGITIMACY AS A BASIS OF AUTHORITY

Followers' perceptions and identification with the leader begin with how he or she attained the role. This is the leader's basis of authority, which is the issue of legitimacy. Such perceptions also are a function of follower expectations, and of persisting "implicit theories" about leaders and how they are perceived to act or should act.

Election and appointment are two contrasting instances of legitimacy, which have been found to produce different effects on followers, insofar as they generate varying commitments to the leader. Election creates a heightened psychological identification with the leader, but also more vulnerability to criticism and the withdrawal of support by followers. The evidence indicates that a leader's legitimacy has a considerable effect in shaping follower's perceptions (e.g., Ben-Yoav, Hollander, & Carnevale, 1983), and on group performance and the leader's perception of followers (cf. Green & Mitchell, 1979).

The election case is of course a more obvious instance of leader emergence with the consent of followers. In that regard, election gives followers a greater sense of responsibility for and investment in the leader. But they also may have been found to have higher expectations about the leader, at least initially. Elected leaders who fail to perform to expectations have been found to be more vulnerable to criticism than appointed leaders, particularly if they were seen to be competent in the first place (Hollander & Julian, 1970, 1978). While election and appointment create different psychological climates between leaders and followers, organizational leaders *can* attain a "following" by doing more than exercising authority, as Katz and Kahn (1978) have observed.

One effect of the current attributional view is to make even more explicit the significance of followers' and others' perceptions of the leader as a constraint or check on leader behavior. There also are the related expectations about such leader characteristics as their requisite level of competence and motivation. The reverse perspective of the leader's perception of followers also is significance (see Mitchell, Green, & Wood, 1981).

This is illustrated in the findings of an experiment by Elgie, Hollander, and Rice (1988). Leader evaluations were studied of four types of followers, who provided either positive or negative feedback with either high or low task activity. The outcome measure was a score made up of their ratings of each follower on ten semantic differential scales. An overall result showed that elected leaders gave more positive ratings generally than appointed leaders in ratings of their followers. A specific finding of interest was that elected and appointed leaders responded differently to high and low activity followers under the negative feedback condition, but similarly under the positive feedback condition. With the lower ratings they assigned, appointed leaders evidently viewed such negative feedback more critically, possibly as a greater threat to their status.

## TRANSACTIONAL MODELS OF LEADERSHIP

Process-oriented "transactional" models of leadership developed initially out of a social exchange perspective, emphasizing the implicit social exchange or transaction that exists between leader and followers as a feature of effectiveness (see Hollander, 1964, 1978; Hollander & Julian, 1969; Homans, 1961). In the transactional view, the leader gives benefits to followers, such as a definition of the situation and direction, which is reciprocated by followers in heightened esteem for and responsiveness to the leader. This transactional approach is part of the current organizational theme emphasizing a more active role for followers, and the potential for two-way influence (see Hollander & Offermann, 1990a). It also conveys the sense of the leader earning or deserving a following.

Followers' perceptions of and expectations about the leaders actions and motives are generated in accordance with an attributional process. Such interpersonal perceptions are seen in Heider's (1958) distinction between "can" and "will." When a leader is perceived to be able to achieve a favorable outcome, but does not because of a perceived failure of will, this causes a greater loss of following than the reverse, that is, an inability to achieve something desirable but still with an apparent try.

## IDIOSYNCRASY CREDIT

This attributional analysis is related to a social exchange concept, the "idiosyncrasy credit" (IC) model of innovative leadership (Hollander, 1958, 1964). The model deals with the latitude a leader has to bring about change as a function of followers' perceptions of that leader's competence and signs of loyalty that engender trust.

Credit is a term in common usage which emphasizes an interpersonal process long recognized. We give credit, take credit, and are discredited, as examples. It has its root in the work creed, referring to, the belief, confidence, trust, and faith we have in another. In leadership it applies to attributions of a leader's intentions, and expectations of action, and likely consequences. An essential virtue of the credit perspective is to make plain the leader's need to establish himself or herself with followers as perceivers and evaluators who 'give' or withhold credit.

In the IC model, leadership is viewed as a dynamic process of interpersonal evaluation in which credits are earned in the eyes of followers. These credits provide latitude for deviations that would be unacceptable for those without such credit. Credits come from perceived competence and conformity to group norms, as a sign of loyalty, and then can be used to take innovative actions expected as part of the leader's role.

Other factors may contribute to the accumulation of credits. Seniority is one of these that operates widely, though obviously not with uniform impact. A person may also benefit by having "derivative credit," in the form of a favorable reputation from another group, or from the society at large, as seen for example in high socio-economic status.

Most usually, however, a new member of a group is in a poor position to assert influence, especially in the direction of change, unless he or she has a unique qualification, such as an idea that helps deal with a major group problem, or a badly needed skill. In these circumstances their credit is gained by maximizing on the competence factor.

A benefit may also result from calling attention to oneself in a figure-ground sense, if the outcome for the group is positive. This is verified in the research by Sorrentino and Boutillier (1975) who found that initial quantity of participation in a group was viewed by others as a positive sign of a group member's motivation, while later participation was evaluated more as to quality. Relatedly, Ridgeway (1981) has contended that nonconformity may be a greater initial source of influence and has presented experimental evidence that appears contradictory to the IC Model. Certainly it is, true that within a brief time a person may call attention to himself or herself by manifest nonconformity to prevailing norms. However, this will be evaluated in due course by the standard of the task contribution made, and a point of dysfunctionality may be reached where rejection may result.

An experiment pertinent to the expenditure of credits was conducted by Hollander, Julian, and Sorrentino (1969). They studied the effects on appointed or elected leaders of disagreements with their followers. Elected leaders who had been told they had strong group support in attaining that position were significantly more likely to make total reversals of their group's decision—indeed on about half the critical trials—than were those in the other conditions. In addition, elected leaders with strong support showed lower conciliation in their responses to group judgments, based on a content analysis of their messages to the group. Evidently, the elected leader in this condition felt freer to challenge group judgments, as a likely function of idiosyncrasy credit.

Unused credits can be lost by failing to fulfill follower expectations for that role, including inaction in the face of need. Also, the leader's self-serving and other negatively viewed behaviors can drain credits, as can perceptions of weak motivation, incompetence, and the responsibility for failure (see Alvarez, 1968).

Perceiving how and when credit is earned and expended therefore seems to be an essential interpersonal task. On the earning end, as one example, Porter (1985) says, "Managers are reluctant to spend the time and resources on interrelationship projects if they are uncertain to receive credit for them" (p. 389). On the expending end, situations may be perceived by a leader as risky to his or her status, and thereby cause restraint in taking action, especially for fear of a loss of personal power (see McClelland, 1975).

## SOCIAL SELF, SOCIAL PERCEPTIVENESS, AND SELF-MONITORING

As already noted, the study of leadership requires attention to the leader's self-concept. More pointedly, it is the social self that is pivotal to understanding the leader-follower relationship. If the leader's self-perception is inaccurate with respect to others' perceptions, the relationship is likely to be affected adversely. Misperception of others' perceptions and desires becomes magnified as a problem in leadership. It also accounts for a failure to know whether and when to use credit, as exemplified when a leader takes no action in the face of manifest need.

One quality that has been postulated as a significant ingredient in gaining and doing leadership successfully is social perceptiveness, that is, alertness to the surrounding environment and understanding of situations (see Stogdill, 1948; Hollander & Julian, 1968). A related feature of this quality is "self-monitoring," which Snyder (1979) identified as the ability to monitor and control one's expressive behaviors. Among the three characteristics included within this quality is "sensitivity to social cues." Recent research by Zaccaro, Foti, and Kenny (1991), using a rotation design, found that self-monitoring was stable as a characteristic correlating significantly with overall leader ranking.

## SELF-SERVING BIASES

More than the usual tendency, leaders may be given to self-serving biases that exist in many relationships. This is revealed in such everyday comments as "You are stubborn, but I am acting out of principle," or "I am only doing this for your own good." The role of leader may enhance this tendency, even in the absence of power over others, but especially with it (Kipnis, 1976). This brings about self-absorption and self-deception, which may readily be fed by followers, and result in what is commonly called an "ego-trip." More significantly, in executive suites, it can lead to calamitous results for the organizations involved (see, e.g., Conger, 1990; Byrne et al., 1991).

In an analysis of some psychological elements involved, Greenwald (1985) has presented an interpretation of how the leader's ego or self incorporates several distinctive cognitive biases. These include the self as the focus of knowledge, "beneffectance" as the perception of responsibility for desired, but not undesired, outcomes, and resistance to change.

A necessary corrective is to be aware of the perception, motives, and more about others. But the narcissism associated with leaders who draw on the affection of followers, as in "charismatic leadership," deprives them of this corrective (see Post, 1986). Followers, also, may be vulnerable to perceptual distortions as a feature of the self-serving bias and identification with the leader that can serve a need to bolster the self.

## CHARISMATIC AND TRANSFORMATIONAL LEADERSHIP

The concept of the "charismatic leader" (Weber, 1921) deals with leaders who have considerable emotional appeal to followers and a great hold over them through an identification process. While charisma refers to a quality usually seen to be possessed by a leader, it manifests itself in followers who accord it. Without their responsiveness, charisma is hollow.

More recently, from a political science perspective, Burns (1978) proposed a related concept of the "transformational leader." Burns' idea of the leader as an agent who may transform the outlook and behavior of followers has been applied to organizational leadership by Bass (1985) and Bennis and Nanus (1985). Their main point is that such leaders strive to go beyond the bounds of the usual to bring about a change in followers that will create a climate for exceptional performance (see Fiedler & House, 1988).

In one view, transformational leadership can be seen as an *extension* of transactional leadership, with greater leader intensity and follower arousal (Hollander & Offermann, 1990a). Research by Bass (1985) and Yammarino and Bass (1988) on transformational leadership in fact involves a measure with two transactional factors in addition to charisma, intellectual stimulation, and individual attention to followers. However, charisma also may be negative when primarily directed to the leader's self-serving ends, not least the manipulation of others primarily for the leader's ego gratification, as well as for other dubious causes, that can have disastrous effects for the broader good.

The potential for damage from a leader with charismatic appeal is evident. Such a leader is "mirror hungry" and has narcissistic needs for continual approval from others (Post, 1986). Coupled with personalized power needs, a charismatic appeal also can be destructive, as Hogan, Raskin, and Fazzini (1990) have observed in writing about "the dark side of charisma." Moreover, the charismatic leader fosters an atmosphere where imagery substitutes for, or is elevated above, performance (see, Drucker, 1988).

All charismatic-transformational leaders do not provide problems in these ways, but their potential for affecting large numbers of others adversely requires attention, if only because appeals based on emotional arousal provide ample opportunities for abuse. It is not enough to say, for instance, that charismatic-transformational leaders transmit a vision—as if they were the only kind of leader who did so—without examining that vision and its probable or known consequences.

## CONCLUSIONS

Granted that the study of leadership has usually assumed the existence of followers, their role nonetheless has been seen as mainly passive. This is so despite the truth that followers are more likely to see and know the reality of the leader's day-to-day approach to leadership. Recent models and applications have increasingly sought to integrate followers more fully into the understanding of leadership phenomena. Building on the foundation provided by newer conceptions of leadership, such as the operation of attribution processes, leader-follower relations now have been examined with heightened attention.

A major implication of what has been presented here is to accord a more active role for those considered followers. In this newer view, leaders and their qualities are important particularly as they engage followers toward productive ends. Central to this process are the self-other perceptions, and misperceptions including self-serving biases, that can exist in leader-follower relations. The impact of these transcends the usual way of viewing leader qualities as personal possessions. Leader "charisma," for instance, needs to be seen as essentially interpersonal, since it depends upon the followers' recognizing the leader's special attributes. An essential question, therefore, is what leader qualities elicit a favorable response from particular followers, as well as generally. Some suggestions in that direction have been offered within a relational conception of leadership.

CHAPTER 9

# College and University Leadership from a Social Psychological Perspective*

## INTRODUCTION

Higher education represents a particular challenge for Inclusive Leadership because of the diverse constituencies and expectations that it comprises. These are schools for adults, who are students, and also clearly the consumers of the educational product. These roles are not always compatible. They award degrees that necessitate compliance to academic requirements and rules of conduct that they set. Since they are voluntary organizations, enrollees come with this understanding, and can leave at their own will, without the degree. Students benefit from participation, but their governance is not the same as that of a political entity, such as a city or nation. There are instead dual lines of authority, one from trustees through the president and administration, and another from the faculty, yielding both a bureaucratic and a collegial structure. There can serve diverse internal and external constituencies whose interests will differ at times. They therefore rely on a balance of mutual understandings of faculty-students-administration interests to yield a satisfactory product, preferably through influence, rather than coercion, to achieve a sense of inclusion. There are also relatively ambiguous criteria for success because of complex, multitask goals, which can present a range of conflicting demands on leaders. Presidents are easy targets for anger because of the discontent of one or more constituencies.

## INCLUSIVE LEADERSHIP ON CAMPUS

There are many leadership activities that take place on a college or university campus. The president and trustees, with their administrative staff, have a formal leadership role, in the institution. (The term "institution" is used here generically for a single-campus college or university. The term "president" refers to the senior campus officer.) However, the faculty

---

* This chapter is mostly new material, or largely rewritten and updated parts of a report originally commissioned by the National Center for Postsecondary Governance and Finance with support from the U.S. Department of Education. It served as the basis for the Invitational Interdisciplinary Colloquium on Leadership in Higher Education at Teachers College (TC), Columbia University, on May 7, 1987, which was hosted and Chaired by Professor Robert Birnbaum of TC, a former public university president in the University of Wisconsin system, who headed this program at TC. I was one-time Provost of Social Sciences and Administration at the State University of New York at Buffalo, a large public university, and was previously founder and longtime director of the doctoral program in social and organizational psychology there. The particular focus in this report originally was requested to be leadership at the campus president level. Obviously, there are many other leaders and leadership events that occur there. An important one is leadership in the departments, particularly in the chair role, about which I developed observations that have been included in this revision. Reproduced by permission.

has its leadership functions that are seen at the micro level in the departmental chair role and perhaps in an elected executive committee. The chair may be elected or appointed by the administration, often on the recommendation of the faculty. There also is usually a faculty senate or some organized body elected by the faculty to represent its interests and give their views to the institution. Typically it speaks as well to its needs and to practices and proposals that come from the administration. The students also have leadership activities, formalized in a student senate and other bodies, such as clubs and other interest groups.

The staff as well as faculty and students may have employee unions. Each of these constituencies, and others, is concerned with having a role, perhaps a voice at the table. However, as others have pointed out, a college or university is not the same as a nation with citizens having equal votes. A departmental faculty, for instance, may change curriculum and decide on whether a student qualifies for a degree in their major, but not on how much a new building should cost. However, the department chair role clearly is an important one involving leadership. Shortly, the leadership functions needed at the departmental level will be considered. First, though, it is useful to consider the presidential role, which has the greatest visibility and responsibility.

## THE PRESIDENTIAL ROLE OR SET OF ROLES

A challenge to presidential leadership on campus is the divergent conceptions of the presidential role, which is in fact a complex of functions that in themselves may make differing demands. At one time, it was said, semiseriously, that the issues a campus president had to be concerned about were parking for the faculty, drinking for the students, and varsity teams for the alumni. At the other end of the scale, Kingman Brewster, when president of Yale, stated that every university needed to have "a theory, or at least a way of thinking about its functions" (1968, p. 1). He made that statement in an annual report to the trustees of the Yale Corporation in which he addressed the university's role in dealing with certain social problems of the time. More to the point, he was manifesting the significance of higher order values a leader and others needed to be able to share in handling contending interests on a campus.

In one respect, for instance, Cohen and March (1974) contrasted two distinct organizational systems, a bureaucratic-administration one or a political interest–group bargaining one. The former calls forth the image of a military commander and the latter a mayor (p. 41). Add to that a cross-cutting set of dimensions, having to do with size and function, among other variables. Although often not differentiated as much as they should be when the general term "higher education institutions" is used, they have distinctive characteristics. These merit recognition as to mission and scope, enrollments, and setting, from community colleges through public or private research universities. Note that public institutions operate with certain governmental constraints and expectations, including due process (P.a. Hollander, 1978).

## EXPECTATIONS AND PERCEPTIONS

In general, there also are multiple ways of construing what are the features of leadership itself, and many onlookers who are ready to define them approvingly or otherwise (Fiedler & Garcia, 1987). Indeed leaders must inevitably deal with the expectations and perceptions of followers and others, and the results of the differences between these expectations and perceptions of reality, and their own. Indeed, many of these are unspoken and less accessible to view on both the leader and follower sides. Once spoken, a leader's views may be judged by a higher standard, especially if seen to lack a sufficient factual basis, and in addition may be offensive to a particular constituency. In short, attention to follower perceptions and related responses is basic to the leader role and is likely to be important in achieving mutual goals.

A failure in this realm appears to be what happened in the case of Lawrence Summers, recent president of Harvard, who at a conference made an offhand statement about why women were underrepresented on science faculties. His point essentially was that women lacked the necessary qualities to excel in these fields. Many at the event, and others later hearing about it, considered his comment to be uninformed and prejudicial to women. Despite his attempts later to acknowledge error and take action to bring more women to those departments at Harvard, he still had a turbulent relationship with some constituencies. After receiving a vote of no confidence from the large arts and sciences faculty, he resigned from the presidency, effective at the end of the 2005–2006 academic year. His successor named in 2007 is a woman history professor, Catherine Drew Gilpin Faust, founding dean of the Radcliffe Institute at Harvard (Rimer, 2007).

Another point is that attributions made about a leader, regarding favorable or unfavorable outcomes, may have less to do with the leader's actions than they do with circumstances and other actors (Calder, 1977). This happens when a successor gets credit or blame for programs initiated or under way when his or her predecessor was in office. Also, these misattributions illustrate a well-established principle in social psychology, called the *fundamental attribution error*. Essentially, it refers to the tendency to perceive other individuals as the source of their actions, especially if things turn out badly, but not so readily if they are good. Then, situational factors would be likely seen as sources. When it is a case of self-perception, though, as in doing poorly on an assignment, the attribution is likely to be made to situational factors, and not oneself, as Jones and Nisbett (1971), among others, have found. The effect simply is self-protection from bad outcomes and self-enhancement for good ones.

## THE DEPARTMENT CHAIR AS A LEADER

The heart of academic institutions resides in their departments, in which disciplines can thrive or decline. The selection of a Chair is a serious matter, since he or she is the department's leader. However, it may be determined simply by passing it to the next insider due to have it, if an outside search is not contemplated. This pattern is still current, although not everyone is interested or qualified to take on the position, as seems obvious enough. It requires administrative ability and concerns, not least fairness, and academic astuteness regarding programs and personnel.

Especially at this close-in, working level, academic leadership can affect people's lives, hopes, and well-being. To have it in the hands of a disinterested and unqualified chairperson is fraught with peril. Or, indeed, to have a power-oriented person wanting the role to wield it can be calamitous. Even a diligent faculty and attentive student constituency may not be enough to avoid the worst results. In short, active and critical followership is essential, in any case. On the positive side, what constitutes good leadership in a department Chair?

### BUILDING CONSENSUS AND A COMMON MISSION

The Chair should encourage cooperation, participation, and agreement among faculty members about where the department stands and should be headed regarding its strengths and weaknesses. With input from faculty, the Chair should help formulate its mission and articulate its place within the institution, as well as presenting a good grasp of the discipline and its front-line research trends, in and outside the academic world.

## PROMOTING COOPERATIVE RELATIONS

The Chair is the liaison between the department and all other departments, as well as with the upper administration. To represent his or her department and discipline effectively, the Chair must foster cooperative relations with other Chairs and administrators, by sharing information. It is essential thereby to seeking a reasonable allocation of resources, with participation in mutually beneficial joint programs and functions.

## SECURING RESOURCES

The Chair should be active in creative and assertive pursuit with faculty of both human and material resources to implement departmental programs in research and teaching. An atmosphere ought to be present that encourages interest in bringing resources to the department, through grants and contracts for research and academic programs.

## MANAGING THE DEPARTMENT

The Chair is responsible for overseeing the administration of the department, to see to it that management functions are performed in a timely and accurate manner. Effective delegation is necessary toward that end, but with an insistence on accountability, and the maintenance of fairness as a standard.

## MOTIVATING SCHOLARSHIP AND AN EDUCATIONAL ENVIRONMENT

The Chair should facilitate a supportive and stimulating educational environment for students. He or she should encourage faculty growth, development, and productive scholarly research and provide guidance to junior faculty for tenure and promotion, while helping all the faculty in their academic commitments, including participation in meetings of disciplinary organizations.

# DECISION PROCESSES AND FUND RAISING

At the macro level of institutional needs, a major presidential role is that of fund raiser. This presents the incumbent with a set of decisions and tasks that have many ramifications beyond the routine of sponsoring and attending alumni dinners. Most critically, it can become what is seen at least as the sanctioner of a sale of the name and resources of the institution. It is not just athletics, where coaches are often paid salaries that are underwritten by outside persons or companies with a contractual tie to a coach. These deals pay at or near the highest individual compensation on campus. Nor is it about awarding honorary doctorates and naming buildings. The thorniest issue is what comes under the heading of "commercialization," which sometimes makes news at elite universities, although it exists as well at major public research ones and elsewhere in academe. These profitable business arrangements, for example, in specialized research fields, have the university engaging in a joint venture for sometimes substantial sums. That in itself may be quite legitimate and is more prevalent with passing time. Mainly, it is in the way the contract is negotiated, written, and operationalized that problems may arise. Since participating faculty members gain as special beneficiaries, they may be the object of envy and need to be monitored or at least supervised by the institution, which may be the source of some resentment. Those faculty who are involved also may act as if they have at least tacit approval from above to effectively give authority to outside others. These are all manageable issues if recognized as requiring attention and specification in the first place. Otherwise, things that can go wrong may go wrong with attendant problems and publicity.

The eminent sociologist Thorstein Veblen addressed the problem of commercialization, early in the 20th century. He saw institutional competition as analogous to the retail trade. However, it also exposes internal rivalries on campus that need to be considered, and at least brought into balance by a president's inclusive decision process. In this vein, Derek Bok (2003), a former president of Harvard, says in his book that money-making ventures in education and research can undermine academic values. However, he reveals the challenges and how to avoid those pitfalls. He writes:

> [D]eans and professors had brought me one proposition after another to exchange some piece or product of Harvard for ... often quite substantial sums of money. ... Nevertheless, nagging questions kept occurring to me. Was everything in the university for sale if the price was right? ... [M]ight the lure of the marketplace alter the behavior of professors and university officials in subtle ways that would change the character of Harvard for the worse?" (p. x)

Among the antidotes to this kind of competition he urges discussions and decisions with openness versus secrecy and insistence on maintaining higher order academic and institutional values and traditions.

Here we see the crucial role of a leader in setting a pattern that serves as a standard conveyed to others. This is an essential feature of a social psychological perspective on the leader's role in these institutions. In particular, it looks at constituents as followers involved in a relationship over time that includes the prospect of two-way influence. A key point is that the leader gives things of value to followers, including direction of necessary functions, the affirmation of the goals and values, and a picture of their situation. In return, a leader exerts influence and may receive esteem and responsiveness from them.

This transactional conception is basic to "inclusive leadership," which is achieving and maintaining collegiality, insofar as the president is seen as first among equals. This pattern accords well with the spirit of recommendations made by professional associations such as the American Council on Education, and others.

Note also that presidents and other administrators are referred to here as leaders insofar as their roles have the potential for acts of leadership, including engaging others in furthering a program, responding to needs, and bringing about desired change. Not all, by any means, operate mainly in that mode to engage their constituents. However, they are nonetheless susceptible to the expectations of these constituents for such actions. The term constituent is itself indicative of a potential for being a follower, but many constituents are relatively autonomous and, therefore, cannot be expected as a routine matter to follow the leader. Exceptions would be for firmly fixed institutional rules, or a religious identity that undergirds adherence. Granting such obvious exceptions as these, there also is the case of a crisis, which usually directs the leader-follower relationship toward more compliance to authority, all other things equal, or mostly so.

## INTERPERSONAL RELATIONS AND SELECTION OF ADMINISTRATORS

Because of its distinctive setting and nature, college and university leadership is clearly based more on mutual dependency than on power. This fact makes imperative an understanding of the importance of consultation rather than coercion as a model of operation. The balance of administration-faculty-student relationships can be upset when this is clearly disregarded. A case in point comes from a study by Benezet, Katz, and Magnusson (1981) on the patterns on 25 campuses. As an example, one president, a newcomer who arrived from a nonacademic post, decided to establish a professional school without consulting the arts and sciences faculty. Although he expressed "respect" for faculty members, he said that he looked not to them but to administrators for "initiative." These writers add: "This president has since learned to consult faculty. Some are still resentful, however, and sense an alliance between him and the board of trustees" who are seen as unresponsive to education concerns (p. 30).

Two points that are especially noteworthy in this example are the president's inadequate "credit" with the faculty and the multiple constituencies that were to be served. Having come from a nonacademic position elsewhere, he had neither an obvious reservoir of common values and interest with the faculty, nor, as a newcomer, a ready following. Hence, there was a high hurdle to be surmounted if he were to gain faculty respect and be able to innovate with their support. Regarding the second point, credit balances may be variable between constituencies because of different priorities and goals, represented in this case by the trustees and the faculty. These balances are not fixed, however, but available to revision. More important here, beyond doubt, was a failure of a process that if handled better might in the end have yielded a less acrimonious result. Regrettably, the tendency of a top executive to make insular decisions, often with inadequate information and advice, occurs among university and college presidents, too.

At one major public university a colleague reported hearing the president candidly disparage leadership from others whom he saw as not being designated to make leadership decisions. In my experience, I heard the president of a similar university speak to a group of student leaders with a discordant message. They had just completed a leadership workshop with me that met once a week for 6 weeks. He came there to congratulate them on completing it. However, he added the decidedly questionable point that he was a born leader, and that those who had the right traits like himself would be successful as leaders. This message, in conflict with what I was trying to convey, led me to send him soon after a recent chapter of mine about leadership, which he acknowledged and said he would read. I heard nothing further, nor had I expected I would. In fairness, he was a great success, by the usual performance criteria, and continued on to bigger and better things.

## STUDENT LEADERSHIP

Among students on campus, there are many opportunities for leadership to develop, both formally and informally. The likelihood of inclusion is many times at stake, especially with self-serving leaders who wish to take over the enterprise. Often they are motivated by a desire for power. For that reason and others, it is important to have leadership development for students, as part of the teaching of skills and institutional citizenship. There are now programs for majoring in leadership available at a growing number of institutions, such as the University of Richmond, which has the Jepson School of Leadership.

Student protest movements are a more spontaneous mode of leadership, which can reveal a breakdown in processes of communication that would have given needed attention to a grievance. An instance in 2006 occurred at Gallaudet University in Washington, D.C., the major higher education institution for the deaf. The selection by the trustees of the provost as the successor to the retiring president was objected to by many students, with support from some faculty and alumni. The *New York Times* story on the trustees' withdrawal of her appointment indicated protesters' long-standing complaints that "she lacked leadership ability and did not embrace the primacy of American Sign Language." These objections, based on her performance, were raised during the search process but said to be dismissed at the time. The protest centered on giving the students a voice, and it led to many of them being arrested one night on campus. The trustees' announcement that the search would reopen was greeted with enthusiasm. The president of the student government issued a statement that this time it would have to demonstrate "inclusion, transparency, and equality" (A. Schemo, *New York Times*, October 31, 2006, p. A17). The reversal by the trustees had a precedent in the way the retiring president, then a popular dean there, had been selected to replace another candidate objected to by student and other constituencies, 18 years before.

The issues in this student protest were clearly pertinent to academic concerns, as contrasted with those in which political agenda are more central. During the Vietnam War, it was often the case that the campus became an arena for political conflict. Roger Rosenblatt's (1997) painstaking account of the spring 1969 takeover of Presidents' Hall, the administration building at Harvard, led by a group of dissident students, shatters illusions about seemingly solid institutions. Then a junior faculty member in English, he reveals the breakdown of trust and loyalty that occurred. Such institutions require these understandings, or their vulnerabilities are readily exposed.

The university gave in to demands to eliminate the Reserve Officers' Training Corps from campus and establish a Black Studies unit, among other actions. The faculty was split on these, as well as on the prior handling of the initial protest and the sanctions later imposed on those students who physically mishandled staff in the takeover. Rosenblatt was on the Committee of Fifteen that investigated the unrest and its aftermath to give a report with recommendations on those sanctions. Although he says he did not doubt the sincerity of the majority of the protesters, "what had occurred in those two months was devastating to the University" (p. 215). He blames the administration who "cooperated with those who wanted to take the place apart merely by overreacting and behaving stupidly," and criticizes the faculty's failure to speak out and "instruct their students usefully merely by voting the right vote and by saying the right things ... in which they supposedly believed" (p. 216). He expresses dismay at the readiness of many faculty members to give up their support of the institution and its higher order values for their self-interest. His disillusionment led him to leave academe within a few years to become a successful writer, editor, and commentator.

Institutional loyalty is challenged at times by the self-interest of faculty members who are bound instead to professional and guild identities to achieve benefits. This increases their likelihood of mobility, in gaining richer returns, not only financially, but also in space, equipment, and prestige, among other rewards. Career interests of this variety present a problem especially in large research universities.

In the selection of top academic administrators, from presidents on down, it is useful to know their approach to interpersonal relations, particularly in such difficult situations. The ability to charm, intimidate, or otherwise impress by status and/or appearance is often inadequate when problems involving conflict arise. For instance, how do they react to hearing information from subordinates that defies their expectations, such as bad news? Do they adapt in the face of disconfirming evidence, or discourage such reports? In general, are they capable of learning from followers about new circumstances, which Vaill (1996) among others has identified as essential to good leadership? Do they have a conception of how to deal with change, or seek to implement it, and if so what is it? If not, why not? What, then, is their notion of the need for adaptation?

When serving as a member of search committees for such positions, I have tried to get at examples of these matters from candidates, verified if possible from other information. This is a necessary alternative to the usual practice of just having a polite but limited interview of maybe 50 minutes and review of a resume and letters of recommendation. Those rarely will reveal behaviors that fit this concern and describe accurately the situation in which observed, if in fact they were.

The meeting with the committee is possibly disorganized, with each member given a brief time to ask a question or two, usually with less than needed planning about priority issues and questions to be raised and pursued. This can result in a chaotic hit-or-miss event in which a well-prepared candidate may give a "good performance," that is slickly delivered to cover any failings. Similarly, if there is a general meeting with the faculty or students, questions can be quite wide ranging. In that case, a candidate may evade important issues of the kind raised above and deal with "glittering generalities" about past experience, plans, and other matters. In the case of both the committee and general meeting, coordination is needed by a chair or moderator who tries to have certain mutually understood points of importance covered by selecting and grouping written questions invited from the larger audience.

## DEFINING SUCCESS

In his book Derek Bok, former president of Harvard, observed:

> Leading a university is also a much more uncertain and ambiguous enterprise than managing a company because the market for higher education lacks tangible measurable goals by which to assess success. Academic leaders cannot look to precise indicators comparable to market share, return on investment, stock prices, or cost per unit of production to determine how well their institution is progressing. No university can measure the value of its research output or determine reliably how much its students are learning. For this reason, efforts to adapt the corporate model by trying to measure performance or "manage by objective" are much more difficult and dangerous for universities than they are for commercial enterprises. (2003, p. 30)

Although traditional organizational issues apply to leadership in colleges and universities, they have peculiarly distinctive characteristics. In addition to those mentioned at the outset, it should not be overlooked that their constituents are relatively autonomous, particularly those who are full-time faculty members. This produces the phenomenon of "loose coupling," which has been commented upon by various observers. Given this circumstance, the evaluation of success is complicated by the varying perspectives of those autonomous constituents and the entities to which they may feel primary allegiance, such as disciplines, department, programs, institutes, centers, and schools.

Because leaders stand out they are likely to be seen more as causal agents. This is obviously so when appointed to significant executive functions. Perceived competence, which is widely regarded as essential to seeing a leader as successful, or not, can be highly dependent on extraneous factors. Cohen and March (1974) report that their 35 responding presidents most frequently mention "quality of faculty" and "growth" as criteria of success, but with considerable dispersion, including "quiet on campus" and "respect of faculty" also frequently mentioned. They aggregated these criteria into three main categories: (a) personal,

(b) constituency, and (c) administrative, plus other noncodable mentions. These criteria come from the perspective of the presidents and are not a necessary match to what various constituencies might cite as evidence of success. Moreover, their judgment of competence also relies on a reputation that comes from having been successful in other posts. However subjective, judgments of "getting result" or "showing ability" and other such qualities carry weight in yielding positive perceptions.

Quiet, less obvious acts of competence may be important but still go unnoticed. Usual activities are not as compelling as are dramatic ones, exemplified by crises. Typically, there is less interest in the leader who prevents crises from ever happening, but in less visible ways. The president who manages with little fanfare to anticipate problems and keep them from erupting may go unappreciated. The irony is that things that do not happen are unlikely to be so easily credited. Although it is difficult to know the number of crises that were averted by such unheralded efforts, behind-the-scenes activity is a potentially important criterion of effectiveness.

## CONVEYING STRUCTURE AND STYLE

There also are factors in the organization's structure that can shape and limit the attainment of success. Some years ago in London, while a postdoctoral fellow at the Tavistock Institute, I became acquainted with the now late A. K. Rice, who was well know for his systems analysis approach to organizations (see Miller & Rice, 1967). Among the conclusions from his work was that organizations should recognize when they might not allow, let alone facilitate, competent performance, but instead might be unwittingly preventing it.

A case in point at a major university occurred when two top administrators were locked in a struggle over various turf issues, notably control of the library. More than an obvious element of organizational structure was behind the festering conflict that had become an explosive feud. Evident to all was a failure in the president's exercise of the leadership functions of decision making and adjudication, at the very least.

In practice, not just structures but individual actions clearly are important in college and university leadership. The nature of the situation obviously does not dictate all of the outcomes nor do individual differences. But when performance, however defined, improves after a new president has taken over, there are bound to be reasonable attributions about his or her personal qualities (Birnbaum, 1987; Pfeffer, 1977). Indeed, there has been a resurgence of interest in who holds the leader role. This includes their interests and values, but also personality dimensions such as autocratic-democratic, task-, or human-relations orientation. But each of these needs to be understood in the context of particular situational demands. Although individuals carry their dispositions from situation to situation, they still need to be adaptable to those role demands in changing circumstances. Illustrating this phenomenon is the research with new college presidents by Bensimon (1993). She focused on their inclination to use transactional (TA) and transformational (TF) leadership patterns and with what effect. Those found to be successful showed adaptability in behaving as needed, usually building a constituency by a TA pattern and only then when change was required using a TF one. Birnbaum (1992, p. 30) reported further that TF leadership is not as successful, however, when values-oriented TA leadership is employed.

Jennifer Wallace (1996) subsequently did a dissertation studying executives considered to be effective. She found that they showed a parallel pattern of flexibility in being neither TA nor TF so much as they were able to adapt in using what was appropriate. The take-away point from these findings is that no one categorical style of leadership is entirely "correct" and likely to be successful, if it does not allow for adaptability. That is the essential element of the Vroom and Yetton (1973) contingency model of leadership and decision making and its later version by Vroom and Jago (1988). The contingencies that affect what is appropriate in the decision process include time available to make it and the degree to which information about it is available to be shared. Let it be understood, however, that an openness of mind is needed, too, in Rokeach's (1960) cognitive sense of avoiding "mental rigidity," but being open to new alternatives.

Leader style, therefore, should be understood to be more complex than just typical behavior. Among other situational variables, Boyatzis (1982) has also found it to be related to a leader's level of status in an organization. Style is also a function of the particular followers with whom the leader interacts, as Graen (1975) and Dienesch and Liden (1986) emphasize in the leader-member-exchange (LMX) model. Briefly, it asserts that leaders do not have a single uniform style with all their followers, but instead develop a variety of relationships depending first on whether particular followers are in the leader's inner or outer circle.

## LEADERSHIP AND MANAGEMENT

The terms leadership and management are frequently linked in a comparison that provides various distinctions attempting to differentiate them. Often they refer to similar or overlapping functions, such as the requirements of providing direction of activity and planning. This is also true for the terms supervision and administration. However, the key distinction seems to be in the latitude for deciding a course of action, as in an epigram from Bennis and Nanus, that "Managers do things right. Leaders do the right thing" (1985). Clever though it seems, it does not deal with the practicality that at times leaders need to manage and managers to lead if successful outcomes are to be achieved. Mintzberg (1973) especially stresses the latter from his study of how managers function on the job. A failure to attend to both of these can result in poor performance, whatever label is affixed to the role. Furthermore, career progression usually brings administrators through a series of positions that expose them to demands for such activities.

In the university presidency, most management functions are usually delegated, not least because he or she needs to give attention to the broader policy role. The internal-external dimension of the president's activity necessitates another division of labor. Demands for fund raising and community relations compete with constituencies for attention on campus. These dealings may occupy the provost or executive vice president as officers delegated to handle them, but the president may be called on at times to be included, or at the very least to know about the persons and issues involved. However, the duality of external and internal concerns may produce "role conflict," with accompanying "strain." Kauffman (1980) describes the situation of a new president called upon to heal a campus in the aftermath of past protest riots, who was informed just a month after taking office that a several million dollar deficit also needed to be rectified, with budget cuts necessary.

Given its multiple demands, performance criteria for assessing presidents may be imprecise, and in any case are complex (Benezet et al., 1981; Cohen & March, 1974; Demerath, Stephens, & Taylor, 1967; Kerr & Gade, 1986). Yet there is often agreement about those presidents who are succeeding and those who are not. Some of the reasons for this judgment have been suggested here, although without specifying absolute criteria. There also is the experiential or personal side of succeeding or not, which has to do with how a president "feels" about what is traditionally called the "exercise of power." In this vein, Harold Stokes (quoted in Hollander, 1987), a former high-level administrator, said, "Those who enjoy exercising power shouldn't have it, and those who should exercise it are not likely to enjoy it" (p. 20). To this point can be added the matter of sheer stamina needed to carry out the usually heavy and persisting load of activities. Furthermore, stamina helps in meeting the difficulties and sometime disappointments of the multiple demands on presidents presented here. Peters and Waterman (1983) contributed a good deal to this understanding from their study of various factors that make for excellence in organizations generally. The nature of their "culture" is one of the important ones deserving attention (Kilmann et al., 1985; Schein, 1985).

## SOME IMPLICATIONS AND CONCLUSIONS

A social psychological perspective on institutional leadership in higher education requires a broad view of the complex system of relationships within it. At the same time, it is essential to understand the pertinence of the individual expectations and perceptions of the people who make up the constituencies there. This does not mean omniscience, but an openness that provides awareness of "what is going on," in fact and in outlook. A primary feature associated with such understanding is two-way communication, in both listening and making clearly known the goals and values of the enterprise. Although seemingly obvious, this mission is not so evident in practice.

As Selznick (1984) observed, an institutional leader needs a "system perspective," which has to be shared. This point is related to the earlier quote here from former President Kingman Brewster of Yale on needing to have a theory of the university's functions. Selznick says that promoting and protecting values is the larger task for institution building through communication. He adds that "A university led by administrators without a clear sense of values to be achieved may fail dismally while steadily growing larger and more secure" (p. 27), such as feeling smug.

Basic to the social contract between leaders and their constituents is the expectation that they will serve with responsibility, respect, fairness, and honest dealings. Essential to this is accountability. Considering their grant of higher status, with the material and other benefits it provides, as well as added influence, leaders who fail in this realm are faulted and disdained. Their lapses may be compounded by perceptions of arrogance and aloofness that further diminish their effectiveness with constituents. Stewart (1982) observes that they can then constrain or limit a leader's course of action. This dynamic is associated with the concept of losing idiosyncrasy credits (Hollander, 1958, 1964) that have been accorded a leader for taking needed actions and other initiatives. In plain terms, constituent beliefs about their leaders are ultimately relevant to an institution's functioning. They also play a consequential role in presidential succession, and its aftermath, as Birnbaum (1987) notes.

Essentially, when they believe they are being adequately informed and fairly treated by a reasonable leader, constituents are more inclined to be trusting of and responsive to that leader. With trust, there is a greater prospect that they will participate in the institution by feeling included, rather than opting out, perhaps with discontent still in place.

In sum, a leader's pattern of showing concern for both the processes and people on a campus gains followers, with the prospect of achieving larger purposes. Given their multiple constituencies, this challenge is particularly seen in institutions of higher education where the president's attention to inclusive leadership is eminently appropriate and desirable and likely to be productive.

CHAPTER 10

# Presidential Leadership*

## INTRODUCTION

The U.S. president is provided enormous legitimation from the power of election. Since its inception, the presidency has contained the fixed-term elective office of "head of government" with the office of "head of state," a role traditionally associated with royalty. This paradox led Patrick Henry to say disapprovingly, "It squints toward monarchy" (quoted in Burns, 1965, p. 8). Others at the time also feared that the president would become a king. Although George Washington rejected that role, the latest evidence of such concern is expressed in the alarm over the "imperial presidency" (Schlesinger, 1973; see also Savage, 2007) and the resurgence of what the late Senator William Fulbright (1966) deplored as the "arrogance of power." These tendencies are seen still in aggressive initiatives abroad, even without consultation, and secret assertions of presidential power (Dean, 2003). The Gallup Poll director reported that the issue's intensity underlies President George W. Bush's approval rating of just 37% on the sixth anniversary of his inauguration, on January 20, 2007 (Newport, 2007). It was the lowest of all his prior ones. Respondents mostly disapproved of the president's assertion of his latitude to do what he decides without taking account of the expectations of constituents and Congress.

Ricks (2006) reports that candidate Bush, in the October 3, 2000, debate with candidate Al Gore, said "I will be very careful about using our troops as nation builders. I believe the role of the military is to fight and win wars and to prevent war from happening in the first place" (p. 24). Subsequent events were clearly adverse, from the unpopular Iraq War over which President Bush was presiding, and the election in November 2006 of a democratic majority in both the House of Representatives and Senate. An unfulfilled expectancy and noninclusive stance evidently were not popular. A so-called credibility gap arose under President Lyndon Johnson, who escalated U.S. forces in Vietnam in 1964. His actions followed the passage by Congress of the Gulf of Tonkin Resolution that August, after he produced the unsubstantiated story that Vietnamese gunboats had attacked an American destroyer. In his recent autobiography, the now late Jack Valenti (2007), a major Johnson aide then, reported the president's willingness to try listening to criticism of the recommended military escalation. But Johnson noted as a powerful persuader, ultimately dismissed alternative courses of action.

There are clear grounds for concern about the extent of the dominant role played by a president as commander-in-chief, especially in time of war. However, as Wills (2007) points out, the president is commander-in-chief only of the military forces, but the National Guard

---

* This chapter is newly written with some material drawn from my prior works. Portions are from an invited address to the American Psychological Association Division 8 (Personality and Social Psychology) in August 1983 annual convention at Anaheim, California. Some points also appeared in chapter 22 on "Leadership and Power" (pp. 487–537) in the *Handbook of Social Psychology,* 3rd ed., edited by G. Lindzey and E. Aronson, published by Random House, and reprinted with permission of the McGraw-Hill Company.

reports to him only if it is federalized. Applying this role's reach to civilians is akin to an absolute monarchy, says Wills, in keeping with what Patrick Henry feared. Critics have argued that when the president asserts that he is "the decider," as he rejects the views of others, this bypasses authentic consultation and the need to persuade, which are vital to a democratic society, more than just being elected.

Yet, realistically, a president has enormous legitimation as an officeholder said to have "powers that are the greatest that our nation can bestow." George Reedy, a onetime White House press spokesman for President Lyndon Johnson, states: "There are all sorts of reasons why a man might have only 51 percent of the votes, or even less, and still be able to make some rather sweeping changes. ... Many Presidents have found their following has increased enormously the day after election" (1973, p. 26). Clearly, legitimacy is not just vested in the role but in responsive followers.

Consider the meaning of two recurrent sayings and an evident fact, in the broad context of presidential power. The slogans are: "We only have one president at a time," and "The president is president of all the people." A past president—even one who has "fallen" or "failed"—is assured of a place of virtual reverence as well as extremely generous outside income, "beyond the dreams of avarice," in Samuel Johnson's phrase. James David Barber (1972) says the president is the "most personal officer" in government, which may account for identification that could take the form of such adulation, even with a profound sense of disappointment for his behavior.

Indeed, after President Richard Nixon's pardon, he continued to write and speak without an admission of guilt or apology. The understanding that President Gerald Ford thought he had when he issued the pardon was not fulfilled when Nixon refused to give a statement along those lines. Many people were incensed at the pardon, and the *New York Times* was among many newspapers that editorialized against it at the time. The issues raised included the bad example set for the requirements of justice, and the failure to learn the truth by a legal proceeding. In the aftermath of President Ford's death at Christmastime in 2006, the pardon issue resurfaced with comments on his role as a "national healer." However, the *New York Time*'s editorial (December 28, 2006, A34) said that the nation could have borne the truth that the pardon did not reveal. Not conceding the critical points, the editorial concludes that "Ford deserves to be remembered by more" than it alone.

## PARTY, POPULARITY, PROMISE, PERFORMANCE

Various political scientists have listed the multiple roles fulfilled by a president. Clinton Rossiter (1956), for one, lists these as the primary roles: chief of state, chief executive, commander-in-chief, chief diplomat, chief legislator, chief of party, and voice of the people. All of these rightly belong in any such list, but they are by no means independent. Blurring of the roles frequently occurs, as Richard Neustadt (1960) said in referring to the president mainly as "chief clerk" carrying out those functions demanded by many forces that can affect the office. That may be partially so, and trivial. Recent presidents—Jimmy Carter, Ronald Reagan, and on through George W. Bush—try to serve as the "voice of the people" in "cheerleading" aimed at the "players" in Congress, while also acting as chief legislator and chief of the party. Interestingly, although with different positions on the political spectrum, all of these presidents can run "against Washington," as a theme. During the 1980 presidential campaign, the political humorist Mark Russell commented that in 1976 Jimmy Carter said "Washington is rotten, and I want to go there." "Now," said Russell, "four years later, he's the guy he warned us about." As for Ronald Reagan, when it suited him, he continued to detach himself from government by referring to it in the third person as "they" or "them" in public statements, and by calls for people to "send a message to Washington."

## A SOCIAL PSYCHOLOGICAL PERSPECTIVE

As stressed here, leadership is critical to the health of a group, organization, or nation. Because of its vital function, there is always the potential for a so-called leadership crisis to occur and take on importance. In Chapter 4, it was observed that one form of such a crisis is revealed in the expression about a "lack of leadership," which suggests aimless drift and purposelessness. The remedy may be clarification through transparency to bring about inclusion. However, a call for "strong leadership" may be voiced instead, as in former New York City Mayor Rudolph Giuliani's response to interviewer Larry King's question (CCN, February 14, 2007) about what quality he would distinctly bring to the presidency. This quality is an unfulfilled expectation among some about the dominance of a leader, not only in the presidency. It is quite the reverse for others who want a balance yielded by authentic participation by inclusion.

With the volume of writings about the presidency by journalists, historians, political scientists, and even presidents, there is no evident major behavioral approach to it. However, when "psychological" factors have been considered, they have been seen mostly with regard to the personality qualities of a particular president, as in "psycho-history." Barber (1972) has contributed a variant of defining character typologies (i.e., positive-negative crossed with active-passive). In that system, Franklin Roosevelt was an active-positive and Richard Nixon an active-negative.

Clearly, it is important to recognize how individuals affect the way the institution functions. Laski emphasized this theme in his classic work *The American Presidency* by asserting at the outset that political institutions "change with changes in the environment within which they operate, and ... differ, from one moment to the other, in terms of (those) who operate them" (1940, p. 1). McClelland (1964) has emphasized motives of achievement, power, and affiliation as a leadership-need system. His colleague, Winter (1973), found that content analyses of 20th-century presidential inaugural addresses were useful in assessing these needs, and that power was associated with presidents involved in the onset of wars. Relatedly, presidents dubbed "great" were most often wartime presidents. Is there some advantage, therefore, in claiming "I am a wartime president"?

The traditional social psychology literature on leadership deals primarily with small groups. In this microleadership study, face-to face discussion groups predominate, although some work is concerned with supervision and management of production groups and other work with decision making. Yet, the sum total of it does not translate well to the macroleadership scene of presidential leadership on a national, indeed global, scale.

Many things are different as one goes from micro- to macroleadership events. Not least among them are the intensity and consequences of exercising power on a large scale. However, there is a parallel process both in small groups and in mass society: an elected leader has a particular commitment from constituents. The extent of their psychological investment can be affected by whether they voted for the incumbent, but its effect is felt nonetheless. The most probable source for this, as noted earlier, is respect for the integrity of the electoral process and its outcome. The legitimacy of a leader, through election or appointment, has been routinely found to create differing effects on U.S. subjects in relating to leaders (see

Hollander & Julian, 1978). In general, an elected leader benefits from the legitimation by followers who are committed to a term of office and tend to rally around if the leader is not performing well—at least initially.

The process of Inclusive Leadership depends on the relationship between the leader and followers. In a healthy, productive relationship, although the leader is usually central to the process, the followers are not passive but are involved in an active role that necessitates their being informed. The leader has the power of position, but requires follower support through persuasion rather than coercion.

The idiosyncrasy credit concept (Hollander, 1958, 1964) proposes that leaders can be influential by signs of perceived contributions to the group goals and perceived loyalty to the group norms. With a fund of credits, a leader's introduction of innovation becomes appropriate. Therefore, the role of leader carries the potential to take innovative action in coping with new or changing demands. But how successful the leader is in effecting change depends on the perceptions followers have of the leader's actions and related motivations. When a leader's nonconformity seems to produce unsuccessful outcomes, the leader is more vulnerable to blame. It is as if followers say "We expect good results from your actions. If you choose an unusual course, we will go along with you and give you some latitude. But you are responsible if the outcome is that we fail to achieve our goals."

When President John F. Kennedy took responsibility for the disastrous Bay of Pigs invasion of Cuba in 1961, his ratings in opinion polls went up. From firsthand experience as a Kennedy aide, Sorenson observed that the president "need not make a fetish of consistency but he must avoid confusion or the appearance of deception" (1963, p. 34).

Furthermore, there is the related expectation that once accumulated, credits will be used to take needed actions; a failure to do so can result in the loss of credits because the leader who "sits" on his or her credits may be seen as not fulfilling role obligations. But what they can do about it depends on such factors as elections can provide.

To review, this transactional (TA) view of leadership involves a social exchange in which the leader gives something and gets something (Homans, 1974, p. 286). A "fair exchange" would be one where the leader performs sufficiently well to deserve the advantages of status (Jacobs, 1970). Followers may have a sense of inequity if the leader fails to do well because of an apparent lack of effort, or from a disregard for followers interests, thereby producing blunders from being a leader who is "out of touch" (Hollander, 1978). Followers may then experience a loss of enthusiasm, even despair and alienation, from the process. It is in this way that poor leaders can create poor followers, with a considerable loss of human potential.

There are numerous benefits a leader can provide, but the major ones are *defining a situation* and *giving direction to activity* (Hollander & Julian, 1969; Chapter 5 in this book). In the political realm, Tucker (1981) delineated three phases of this function: *diagnosing* the problem facing the constituency; *prescribing* a course of action, which is "policy formulation"; and *mobilizing* action, which is "policy implementation."

Also from a political science base, Burns (1978) says that transformational (TF) leaders function to bring people together for higher purposes. They are interested in more than garnering votes; they want to bring about change. However, persuasion alone will not do. Responsibility and accountability are also essential. As noted elsewhere, Sartre was supposed to have said that to be a leader is to be *responsible*.

However, a president needs to provide a version of "social reality" that becomes shared and that is credible. This definition of the situation is the basis for the president's credibility, which is essential. During the Vietnam War, President Johnson's decision not to run for reelection in 1968 was attributed to his "credibility gap," a reason for his loss of standing among constituents.

## POSTELECTION SURVEYS OF EFFECTS OF PRESIDENTIAL IDENTIFICATION

In 1954, immediately following the congressional election that year, I was able to study the psychological mechanisms of identification with a president, especially of one's own party. With the help of my students at Carnegie Tech (now Carnegie-Mellon University, or CMU), I conducted a survey in Pittsburgh among a representative sample of over 400 eligible voters. The first midterm election for the House and Senate, after the victory of President Dwight D. Eisenhower in 1952, was held in 1954. We could therefore study voting patterns for Congress and attitudes associated with such psychological considerations as identification with him.

Using some findings from that Pittsburgh survey, new data from a 1962 postelection survey in Buffalo, and other material, we tested two propositions that are given wide credence: first, that the electorate is more moved by domestic, bread and butter issues, and may be unmoved by international issues except in times of dire crisis; and second, that the president cannot readily trade the electorate's loyalty to him for the election of his supporters in midterm congressional elections.

Among other findings from the 1954 Pittsburgh survey reported some years ago, I found, as have others, that economic issues weighed heavily in the voting behavior of respondents. It went like this: the preponderance of republican respondents felt that economic conditions were good that year and the majority of Democratic respondents felt they were *not* good. When we looked at only those people who reported they had actually experienced an increase in income from 1952 to 1954, Republicans and Democrats continued to be significantly different in their respective perception of economic conditions. So this was not a matter of personal economic experience but something more like a guided perception, an orientation associated with a party, as in the work of Campbell and his colleagues in *The American Voter*. More important, adherence to this perception was systematically and significantly related to party voting among registered Republicans; for them, a descending proportion of votes for the party candidates was found in viewing respondents from the "very good" response on down to the "bad" response on the economic question. As for President Eisenhower's "pull," those who had voted for him in 1952, but who would *no longer* have supported him as of 1954, were inclined to have a significantly less optimistic view of the 1954 economic picture than those who continued to support him at that time, and this was seen in a marked and statistically significant drop in party support at the polls in the 1954 election. For democrats who continued to support Adlai Stevenson, no such relationship was found.

It appeared, therefore, that continuing loyalty to Eisenhower as president was interrelated with the perception of economic conditions and served to elicit two related consequences: first, actually turning out to vote, and, second, voting for party candidates. Finally, without asking directly about international issues, we found, as others before and since, that on self-reports by respondents to open-ended questions on reasons for voting as they did, only meager mention was made of *international issues*. This does not mean that such issues were not influential in 1954, but only that people did not spontaneously refer to them as being influential.

### INTERNATIONAL ISSUES

In 1962, at a comparable stage in President Kennedy's term, I directed a similar survey in the City of Buffalo, with many students from the SUNY Center there. We had 300 respondents drawn from among eligible voters and asked many of the same questions employed in the Pittsburgh survey of 1954. This time, however, we added a number of items having to do specifically with international issues. Subsequently, we were able to make some comparisons between the pull of economic and other domestic issues and such things as attitudes toward international affairs, including, for example, a disarmament pact and the Cuban missile crisis of October, in turning out a party vote.

We had several findings of note, based on 40 items of data gathered in 1962. This report deals only with a segment of these. Also, only the congressional and senatorial voting patterns were attended to. Although we were *not* attempting to *predict* an election, but rather to discern factors affecting voting patterns in an election that has already occurred, we had a satisfactory degree of accuracy in terms of correspondence with the actual vote. And, not incidentally, we found approximately 85% of the Republicans and the Democrats sampled in Buffalo reported voting in 1962.

## ECONOMIC ISSUES

Concerning the economic situation, we asked the same question in 1962 in Buffalo that had been asked in 1954 in Pittsburgh. We found that once again being a registered Democrat or Republican led overall to a significant difference in the perception of the economic picture. At the time, however, the Democrats differed significantly from the Republicans by having a more positive view of economic conditions than did the Republicans. Furthermore, 90% of *Democrats* who reported the economic picture as "good" or "very good" in 1962 voted for the Democratic congressional candidate; only 63% of those who saw it as bad or very bad voted for the Democratic congressional candidate. This is a reversal of what was found in Pittsburgh in 1954 and leads to the reasonable conjecture, bolstered by a number of additional analyses and other studies, that those whose party holds the White House are likely to view many conditions in a more partisan fashion, especially if they continue to be loyal to the president. Thus, *Republicans* did *not* show a significant or systematic relationship to party support, precisely reversing the 1954 finding where the Republicans were similarly affected while the Democrats were not.

We also found in 1962 that 90% of the Democratic respondents tended to be satisfied with President Kennedy's performance, based on a series of questions having to do with "the way the president is doing his job." Furthermore, on an open-ended probe Democrats spontaneously gave a high percentage of responses, 35% indicating their satisfaction for the president's handling of the then recent Cuban missile-base crisis of October, or in the general category of foreign affairs. The data also indicated that those Democrats who were not satisfied (but not necessarily dissatisfied) with the president's performance were not as likely to turn out to vote. The data clearly do establish a basis for seeing party support at the polls in terms of issues and identification with the president.

## PARTY LOYALTY

A virtually indispensable vehicle for attaining the presidency is the national political party. But *presidential partisanship* presents a paradox that is especially annoying to those of the opposition party who are on the awkward side of the "president of all the people" concept. As Rossiter said:

> It troubles many good people, not entirely without reason, to watch their Chief of State dabbling in politics, smiling on party hacks, and endorsing candidates he knows to be unfit for anything but

immediate delivery to the county jail. Yet if he is to persuade Congress, if he is to achieve a loyal and cohesive administration, if he is to be elected in the first place (and re-elected in the second), he must put his hand firmly to the plow of politics. (1956, p. 29).

Many political scientists and other commentators have elaborated this theme regarding the president's need for party support. A further paradox, however, is imbedded in the process of gaining the party's nomination and holding the allegiance of party loyalists who dominate primaries and nominating conventions. In appealing to these partisans, a narrow band of positions on issues is established. Once in possession of the nomination, there is then a need for a "joining of hands" across party factions with differing positions to heal intraparty wounds. Especially in a first presidential candidacy, compromises need to be struck to be able to achieve victory in the national election. Party adversaries may be forced into uncomfortable alliances for the general campaign, such as Kennedy with Johnson and Reagan with Bush. The latter's primary contest crack about Reagan's "voodoo economics" was often trotted out by the opposition and illustrates the problem in going from one phase to the next.

The party issue also has another dimension. In *The Deadlock of Democracy*, James MacGregor Burns (1963) has trenchantly observed that there are two presidential parties and two congressional parties—four in all. The weakest is the presidential party out of power. Although presidents are expected to exert party leadership, they primarily lead a presidential party organized for the personal ends of winning office and mobilizing support while in office. Burns said:

The presidential party in power is headed by the President, his political staff, his Cabinet and other politicians; it embraces much (but usually not all) of the regular party organization; it has its own leadership cadres in the states and cities. Collectively these people comprise the "presidential politicians" who supply relatively firm political support for the President and the central decision makers. (1965, p. 159)

The chief contenders for national power who vie with the president are the congressional parties. Although not as powerful as they were before reforms, when utterly dominated by the barons of one-party states and districts, congressional party leaders continue to be forces on Capitol Hill—particularly in blocking legislation through their seniority on committees and their ability to employ parliamentary devices to stall or kill bills.

Nonetheless, the president can be quite formidable.

Under activist Presidents the presidential party extends far beyond the White House ... the national chairman of the party has become wholly absorbed into the presidential orbit. ... It has become definite practice that the newly nominated presidential candidate chooses his own national chairman, who then takes over the whole national party organization. Almost always the presidential politicians control the national convention lock, stock and barrel. (Burns, 1965, pp. 168–169)

It is noteworthy, too, that neither major party in recent times has denied the nomination to an incumbent who desired it. Ford, Carter, and George H. W. Bush, in 1976, 1980, and 1992, respectively, held out for the nomination, and each lost in the general election. The Carter renomination was especially striking because of the strong convention challenge mounted by Senator Ted Kennedy in the face of the considerable delegate votes that President Carter held and would not free for so-called open balloting. As the adage has it, "The problem with regicide is: what if it fails?"

For various reasons, then, the national party apparatus largely functions in behalf of the president, in either party. It can be quite "partial" about the president's nomination, as has happened, the Republican National Committee mailed a solicitation letter to over a million people urging that they sign and return a card asking President Reagan to run again. Why the so-called presidential party matters will be evident in some consistent findings to which I now turn.

## IDENTIFICATION WITH THE PRESIDENT, PERCEPTION, AND VOTING BEHAVIOR

A major concept in social psychology is that an individual's perception of the environment is less dependent on objective realities than on subjective interpretations of them. W. I. Thomas formulated this in his classic statement that "situations defined as real are real in their consequences" (quoted in Janowitz, 1966, p. 301). Indeed, situational determinants can weigh heavily enough to cause people to misinterpret objective realities, even the most obvious "facts." Why? It is fairly clear that they identify with a political leader and the interpretation of reality the leader offers.

As stated earlier, leaders provide followers with a ready "definition of the situation." This effect is made particularly salient in a democratic society when there is a national election, in which a president is heavily involved. For a long time I pursued this phenomenon of *identification* with a president by conducting postelection surveys, with the help of graduate and undergraduate students as interviewers and researchers, at three intervals. The first was done in Pittsburgh, following the 1954 midterm election; the next two were carried out in Buffalo, one after the 1962 midterm election, and the next after the 1972 presidential election.

In the 1954 survey in Pittsburgh, among a representative sample of over 400 eligible voters, a representative finding was that the preponderance of registered Republican respondents reported economic conditions as good, while the majority of registered Democratic respondents reported them as *not* good. When we looked only at those who said they had *actually experienced an increase in income* from 1952 to 1954, registered Republicans and Democrats continued to be significantly different in their respective perceptions of economic conditions. Therefore, this was not a matter of personal economic experience but something more like a guided perception by party orientation and leader identification, such as that reported by Angus Campbell and his colleagues (1954) in *The Voter Decides*.

More important, adherence to this perception was systematically and significantly related to party voting among registered Republicans: for them, a descending proportion of votes for the party candidates was found among respondents going from "very good" to "bad" on the economic question. Kernell (1978) is among those who substantiate the point that poor economic conditions (i.e., high prices and high unemployment) generally affect the evaluation of an incumbent president adversely (see Sigelman, 1979). However, this negative view is considerably moderated among loyalists. Kinder (1981) finds, nonetheless, that if economic conditions are bad enough, even those who are not personally subject to hardship may blame the president for not coping adequately with national economic distress.

President Dwight Eisenhower's "defectors" were those who had voted for him in 1952 but who would *no longer* have supported him in 1954. They showed a significantly more negative view of the 1954 economic picture than those who continued to support him. Among defectors, this also was seen in a marked and statistically significant drop in party support at the polls in the 1954 election. No marked contrast was found, however, for registered Democrats who did or did not continue to support Adlai Stevenson. Therefore, persisting loyalty to President Eisenhower was related to a favorable perception of economic conditions and served to elicit two effects: first, actually turning out to vote, and, second, voting for Republican congressional candidates.

As noted, in 1962, at a comparable stage in President Kennedy's term, we conducted a similar survey in Buffalo, with over 300 respondents drawn from among eligible voters, asking many of the same questions employed in the Pittsburgh survey of 1954 and adding others to total 40 questions. Using the identical question about the economic situation, which had been asked in 1954 in Pittsburgh, we found in 1962 in Buffalo that this time the Democrats were the ones holding a significantly more *positive* view, not the Republicans, an almost exact mirror image of the Pittsburgh findings in 1954. This supports the reasonable conclusion from still other analyses that *those whose party holds the White House are likely to view economic and other conditions in a favorable fashion*—and most of all if they would still vote for the president. In short, the effect of Eisenhower on Republicans in 1954 was matched by the effect of Kennedy on *Democrats* in 1962, in two northeastern cities. Percentages of turnout to vote for party candidates were higher by at least 25% for each president's "loyalists," compared with "nonloyalists" of the same political party. The "presidential party" delivered the votes.

In 1972 I pursued these relationships further by directing a survey in Buffalo with another random stratified sample of more than 300 eligible voters, soon after the Nixon–McGovern presidential election, in which Nixon ran successfully for his second term. Paralleling the analyses done previously, a highly significant difference was found in responses to the question regarding the state of the economy. Senator McGovern's supporters saw the economy in much bleaker terms than did President Nixon's supporters. Although less marked, a comparable finding was found for a comparison of registered Democrats and Republicans. Most strikingly, registered Republicans who "crossed over" and voted for Senator McGovern had the *least* favorable mean, rating the economy as "bad" (i.e., 4.00 on a scale from 1 (Very Good) to 5 (Very Bad). The *most* favorable mean, on the contrary, was again among registered republicans, by those who voted for President Nixon (i.e., 2.54, between "Good" and "Average"). Once again, the differential effect of loyalty to the president was clearly evident.

Finally, among the questions on the 1972 interview schedule were four items testing the respondents' knowledge of current political affairs. Using a total "knowledge score" derived from summing the number of correct answers to these factual items, voters for Nixon and McGovern were *not* found to differ significantly in their means, although they had shown significant differences in perception of the state of the economy and of international relations. However, with a median split of knowledge scores, a significant effect was found by a chi-squared test indicating that Democrats crossing over to Nixon were lower in these scores and Republicans crossing over to McGovern were higher.

When McGovern and Nixon voters were compared without regard to party affiliation, taking account of *their own self-reported economic situation* on the income shift question and their response to the *state of the economy* question, as just noted, Nixon voters showed up viewing the economy significantly more favorably than did McGovern voters. In fact, even the Nixon voters indicating "income *down*" saw the economy as *better* than the McGovern voters indicating "income *up*"! Nor was socioeconomic status found to have a significant effect on this relationship. Therefore, the evidence again supported the impact of presidential leadership in defining politically laden issues for the presidential party loyalists.

Clearly, the occupant of the White House is a *definer of reality* who has a powerful effect on the attitudes of his adherents, especially from his own political party, and on followers brought along from the other party. This process also affects so-called independents who could lean either way. A counterpoint to this is evident too in these findings; that is, *not* voting for the presidential candidate of one's party is associated with holding attitudes that run counter to those of the presidential party loyalists.

## POPULARITY

Generally, shifts in a president's popularity may be predictably linked with certain events. Opinion polls usually show increased support when there is a dramatic crisis abroad, but prolonged conflicts, such as the Korean, Vietnam, and current Iraq War, have drained support for the president. Also, there are sequence effects, such as the usual finding that a new president benefits from a "honeymoon period." This initial "era of good feelings" may be a function of hope, respect for the integrity of the electoral process, if not for the person. However, there also is typically a slump for presidents at about their second anniversary in office—at least partly due to a "disappointment effect" from raised expectations unfulfilled at an obvious time for stock-taking. Although Ronald Reagan was often regarded as more popular than Jimmy Carter, in fact they both reached a point in the low 40s in percentage of approval ratings at the time of the "midterm slump."

Sometimes popularity is stated as "favorableness" or "approval," which politicians and pollsters believe equates with support on issues, although not necessarily liking. In opinion polls, President Reagan continued to show the obverse, that is, stronger ratings for liking of his personality than for support of his positions on many issues. Liking for a president's personality may give him a special ability to bounce back in the polls, as President Reagan did after a 1982 congressional veto override, and later the Iran-Contra scandal. Kaiser commented that President Reagan "seems to lead a charmed life, getting away with things that would have sent his predecessors to the woodshed" (1983).

Great efforts are expended on many fronts to improve a president's "favorableness" rating by actions and by statements that can serve as action. This image building is familiar in social psychology, termed *impression management.* Barber (1972) says that its extremity, where presidential candidates are impelled more by image than by reality, is akin to the mother who is complimented on her darling young child and says, "But you should see her pictures!"

"Popularity" based on appearances is frequently achieved as a manipulated mass media effect, especially in fast-paced campaigning. The president can be seen to be perpetually campaigning to maintain and enhance his political base from the White House and his following nationally. News management becomes an everyday task in the service of these goals that perpetuate power.

## PROMISE AND PERFORMANCE

An obvious fact of political life is that what is promised to voters in order to get elected may bear little relationship to what is delivered eventually. Looking back to an oft-cited classic example, President Nixon pledged for some time that he was opposed to wage and price controls to hold down inflation, but, later, introduced them to a considerably surprised public.

The paradox in campaigning is simply that candidate "promises" will inevitably disappoint many or at least some supporters once the president is in office. Beginning with primary contests, and omitting now the record before, a candidate makes a host of statements in set speeches, responses to press questions, and off-the-cuff remarks. These have highly variable applications to a coherent and workable administration program. The political party convention "platform" is still another statement that usually represents varying degrees of compromise between the candidate and factions of the national party. Beyond a general ideological orientation, there is an imperfect basis for knowing what the candidate will do as president.

This perplexity is revealed starkly in what one prominent supporter said of Jimmy Carter during the 1976 campaign: "what bothers me most about the Carter candidacy ... is that I have no way of predicting what he is going to do" (quote from Julian Bond, *Newsweek*, July 19, 1976, p. 26).

Indeed, Carter did have a program or pieces of a program, some of which were part of his promise. But, as a case in point, he established one basis for his own demise when, in the 1976 campaign against Ford, he calculated a "misery index" that showed an inflation and unemployment rate each over 6%, thus yielding 12% for Ford, which Carter said was an unacceptable rating, and more. So Carter went on to win and was set up for a challenge by Reagan, pointing out that the misery index was then over 20% for Carter. Whatever was intended or desired, Carter came out badly from just a simple "contrast effect," psychologically. In this vein, Arthur Schlesinger, Jr., said during the campaign that in retrospect he could not forgive Carter for having made Ford look like a great president.

## THE "MANDATE"

Once elected, a president is often regarded as having a "mandate" to put new or different programs into effect. This poses some troublesome problems of definition insofar as supporters may have highly discrepant conceptions of what was promised. More to the point, constituencies are often brought together who have interests at variance and who also feel differently on the three important factors that are most consistently mentioned as sources of support for a candidate: *party*, *personality*, and *program*.

President George W. Bush took his reelection in 2004 as a signal of a continuing mandate to do what he intended in the Iraq War, and in such domestic matters as a change in the Social Security program. Soon after election he said he had "political capital" and he "intended to spend it." However, not all of his intentions where fulfilled, especially in the domestic realm. Also, realistically, changing circumstances can be invoked to allow the bending or reinterpretation of a mandate. Furthermore, determining what part a president's program was supported by voters is made especially difficult by special appeals to "splinter constituencies." The relevant questions, therefore, may be: What was promised? When? To which constituency? Perhaps the most that can be assessed is the ideological leaning conveyed in the campaign as a general theme.

In evaluating presidential performance, the paradox is that the president is not just the performer but is also the executive producer and a formidable critic. Given his status, the president is uniquely capable of gaining the airwaves and headlines as a super mass media figure. President Johnson's news secretary said that a president "can call upon the television industry to turn over its networks to him anytime he wants them" (quoted in Reedy, 1973, p. 9). A president, therefore, has an immense advantage by being seen and heard in one or more segments on the nightly television news, by holding press conferences in prime time, preempting other programming, and by virtually setting the agenda for major items of news attention in the press. In recent decades, a major manifestation of this phenomenon is the institutionalized presidential Saturday noon radio broadcasts to the nation. They reach a potentially vast listening audience, especially with rebroadcasts, and then command a story in the Sunday newspapers. The token "rebuttals" allowed to a mostly faceless, rotating cast of opposition spokespersons are no match for the one visible president atop a massive communications enterprise dedicated to gaining and holding the support of public opinion.

Yet recent presidents, even with this enormous apparatus at hand, have suffered from communication problems, lapses, gaffes, and gaps. The public, in effect, can and does assign other meanings to events than the processed interpretations offered by politicians, even those by the president. The paradox here is that the public generally evidences a desire to believe and depend on the view projected by the highest national leader. But the public also is made wary by the very majesty of the presidency, which has been characterized as having a "remote aloofness" from the citizenry and their everyday concerns. As numerous observers have commented, a president is too insulated from such concerns. On the other hand, the portrayals of presidents in settings with ordinary people—as "just like other folks"—often are seen as contrivances, however sincerely motivated. When President George H. W. Bush was shown at a supermarket checkout counter, confronting a price scanner whose workings he seemed not to know about, it showed him distinctly at a disadvantage. Earlier, President Carter tried to appeal to the public by such populist gestures as walking down Pennsylvania Avenue with his wife, Rosalind, after his inauguration and wearing a cardigan sweater for his first television "fireside chat," to emphasize energy savings.

## POLICY MAKING

When making policy, the presence of deferential staff members keeps a president from the give and take of informed, frank appraisals of alternative policies. Problem solving is altered in the president's presence. Reedy said:

> White House councils are not debating matches in which ideas emerge from the heated exchanges of participants. The council centers around the President himself the first strong observations to attract the favor of the President became subconsciously the thoughts of everyone in the room. (1970, p. 12)

This convergence of expressed view, centered in a manifest sign of loyalty to a leader, is a major basis for Janis's (1972) "groupthink" phenomenon. It underlies many cases he cites of catastrophically bad group decisions by otherwise capable advisors.

In addition, the presidential personage is usually quite intimidating to all but a few. Reedy said:

> [T]he presidency is about as close to total estrangement as one can get in the modern world. The only time he ever meets a peer is during the rare visit of some foreign potentate, and ... most of the potentates who visit ... feel a bit diffident. (1973, p. 20)

Reedy once asked an elder statesman Democratic senator, who had been a Johnson ally since his senatorial days, why he did not have a "heart-to-heart talk" with President Johnson about some national problems they agreed were bad. The senator said, "I can't talk to a President the way I can to a Senator." Reedy adds that "Politicians need peers and without them they become remote from reality" (p. 30).

Taking account of these factors, it is no wonder that in the White House images may easily come to represent reality in assessing presidential performance. A statement by President Reagan that he was "not a bigot" illustrates the point by clearly begging the question of why some people might think so. In a comparable but not entirely parallel fashion, President Nixon said he was "not a crook," and President Carter told the public, "I will never lie to you."

President Reagan handled this problem of alleged bigotry by attributing it to a misperception fostered by the media, and not to any action of his. Similarly, his assertion that he is "perplexed" about the "allegations" concerning hunger in this country raised eyebrows about the degree to which he was aware of the extent of his administration's cuts in basic nutrition programs, such as food stamps and school lunches. Not uniquely, he makes the self-attribution that his intentions were good and, as obviously, should be seen to be good. If they are not, then somebody is misleading the public to judge him wrongly.

## IMAGES VERSUS PERFORMANCE

Imagery, not substance, may come to matter more, as is well known. Presidents are not wrong in thinking that the mass media influences public images. Indeed, politicians are convinced that "saying the right thing" effectively "deals" with a problem. Here I am reminded of the subtitle, "Words That Succeed and Policies That Fail," from Edelman's (1977) book *Political Language*. Lakoff's (2004) book on political language is another contribution in this area. A warning still is the dictum regarding politicians' speech: Watch what we do, not what we say.

Another element in evaluating presidential performance is the atmosphere created by an administration. Democratic leadership has been said to have two main functions, among others: to *reduce provocation* and *act positively to increase opportunities for participation* (Lasswell, 1948). These are achieved through goal clarification, consultation, and other signs of respect for individuals, including power sharing. Although this is an expression of ideal-type values, which may largely be unattainable, it is worthwhile to consider the two categories as basic.

With regard to provocation, there is a reasonably clear issue of the degree to which political appeals embody threats, or avoid them. In his analysis of the rioting by African Americans in 1960s Los Angeles, the sociologist Ralph Turner (1969) at the University of California–Los Angeles discussed the balance needed between trying to make a statement about injustice and avoiding an excessive load of threat in doing so, thereby producing "backlash." Riots of course are not calculated so rationally, as Turner acknowledges. However, the basic point of *arousing without excessively threatening* fits psychological formulations regarding moderate arousal, through limited fear appeals, to gain desired actions.

## CRISES CREATE EVEN MORE POWER

A truism of the presidency is that in a crisis greater power flows to the White House. The clearest danger lies in the obvious temptation to present some situation in more dramatic, threatening terms, even unwittingly. This may apply to national as well as international events, although the latter can serve better as a rallying point. In such a crisis, Lasswell's second function—increasing opportunities for participation—is largely swept aside. Power, jealously guarded even under usual circumstances, is even less likely to be available for sharing in a crisis. Not least, a president in difficulty may find that he can "ride it out," and possibly can gain by being seen as performing better when handling a crisis.

Still another problem is created, however, by the heightened turbulence, uncertainty, and anxiety unleashed in a crisis atmosphere. A president can be hyperreactive, as in the case of Carter with the Afghanistan and Iran crises. His decision to have U.S. athletes boycott the Olympics in Moscow aroused much annoyance in the populace. The frustrating combination of strong talk with weak follow-through was a further source of aggravation. Of course, *strong* talk with *strong* follow-through may also have deadly consequences. One such case is President Johnson's continued use of the dubious Gulf of Tonkin incident, later proven to be false, as the pretext for a massive escalation of the Vietnam War. All the while he told the American people that "our national honor is at stake." Such incendiary language may indeed have its place in times of war when arousal is essential, as was the case with Churchill's stirring phrases on the eve of the Battle of Britain. However, as a basis for diagnosing a problem and proposing needed action, it can be counterproductive and therefore has to be used judiciously.

There also is an element of "public haranguing," which an activist president can produce by excessive media exposure. Loyalists ordinarily do not require regular doses of persuasion. Those who are unpersuaded to begin with are unlikely to be affected positively by the frequency of presidential appeals on television. Among those who occupy the middle ground, there is quite likely to be indifference at best from such media saturation.

If a president is to perform in behalf of the common good, one standard must be whether he is *introducing stress and diminishing a sense of security unnecessarily.* That last word is the critically operative term, since what a president thinks is *necessary* may readily prevail at the time—even if not in history. For the present, it is certainly appropriate to ask whether a needless psychological toll is taken on the body politic by intemperate or disproportionate statements and action, not least in repeatedly raising expectations and making promises that go unfulfilled.

## CONCLUSIONS

Presidents and other elected leaders have a fundamental social contract with constituents. An elected leader has a grant of status with more influence over others and the prospect of exerting power over expectations and events. But all of this comes at a price, a vital part of which is represented in responsibility and accountability. There are good reasons why presidents and other public officials should be held accountable for failures, inadequate effort, or inaction in the face of problems, or evident threats to the well-being of the constituency and its interests. Avoiding this responsibility can produce public cynicism with "the system."

Above all, clarity of purpose is necessary if the leader-follower transaction is to be soundly based. Followers need to believe they are respected by being informed properly, treated fairly, and able to participate meaningfully. Such a belief will keep them inside the system and participating rather than opting out, as even seen in presidential elections when barely half of the population participates through voting.

CHAPTER 11

# Power and Leadership in Organizations

WITH LYNN R. OFFERMANN

## COMMENTARY

The article reproduced in this chapter appeared in a special issue of the *American Psychologist on Organizational Psychology*. It is one of three publications in which I collaborated with Lynn Offermann (1990a, 1990b, 1997), in addition to working on the Kellogg Leadership Studies Project (KLSP) with her for several years, beginning in 1993, as conveners of the Leadership-Followership Focus Group. She generously arranged the site and hosted most of our meetings at George Washington University. Together we coedited *The Balance of Leadership and Followership* (1997), published by the Burns Academy of Leadership at the University of Maryland. Our Introduction to it is republished in this book as Chapter 15. The important emphasis on follower participation in organizations is central throughout the 1990 paper and the 1997 publication, which includes articles by Ann Howard, Peter Vaill, Lynn Offermann, and myself.

Abridged from E. P. Hollander & L. R. Offermann. Power and leadership in organizations: Relationships in transition. *American Psychologist*, 1990, 45(2), 179–189, with permission of the American Psychological Association.

Over the past decade or more, significant developments have occurred in thinking about the participation of followers in leadership and the exercise of power in organizations. Concepts of empowerment and power sharing reflect a shift in focus from a leader-dominated view to a broader one of follower involvement in expanding power (see e.g., Burke, 1986; Kanter, 1981). This development has been affected by the greater attention to groups and team effort in the workplace attributable in part to Japanese management practices (e.g., Ouchi, 1981), which had precursors in the "human relations" approach (e.g., Likert, 1961; McGregor, 1960). Accordingly, there now is a context of thinking encouraging the value of participative leadership, at least in organizational psychology. In this article, we present the background of the expanding power of followers, review some of its current features and applications, and point to new directions of effort.

Leadership clearly depends on responsive followers in a process involving the direction and maintenance of collective activity. Central to this process are one or more leaders who are the primary actors serving vital functions, especially defining the situation and communicating it to followers. Other leadership functions are such roles as problem solver and planner, adjudicator of conflict, advocate, and external liaison. Because the leader cannot do everything alone, these functions need to be dispersed and involve sharing power and engaging others' talents through empowerment. Leadership is therefore a system of relationships with constraints as well as opportunities (see Stewart, 1982). System constraints include not only task demands but also the expectations and commitments of followers.

Power is not the same as leadership, but often is seen, as a feature of it (see Maccoby, 1976, 1981; McClelland, 1975; Zaleznik & Kets deVries, 1975). Power in organizations has three identifiable forms, which often exist together as a result of an individual's position in a time and place, as well as his or her personal qualities. The most familiar form is power over, which is explicit or implicit dominance. Clearly, leadership in organizations involves such power in varying degrees. But Freud (1921/1960), for one, compared dominance unfavorably with leadership, and Cowley (1928) called such authority-based power "headship." A leader's dependence on this kind of power has costs in undermining both relationships with followers and goal achievement (Kipnis, 1976). A second form is power to, which gives individuals the opportunity to act more freely within some realms of organizational operations, through power sharing, or what is commonly called empowerment. A third form is power from, which is the ability to resist the power of others by effectively fending off their unwanted demands. High status carries the potential for all of these power forms, while lower status participants may at best have one or two of the latter forms available to them.

Both leadership and followership can be active roles, given the reality that hierarchical organizations require both at every level. The traditional view of the follower role as mainly passive is misconstrued. Although leaders command greater attention and influence, there is more awareness now of follower influence on leaders, especially insofar as follower expectations and perceptions affect the process of leadership (see Hollander, 1985, 1986; Lord & Maher, 1990), as will be discussed in more detail later. [Historical Developments that appeared in the original have been omitted here since they largely duplicate material covered in Chapter 2.]

## FROM TRAITS TO ATTRIBUTIONS

Today, the emphasis has shifted from traits to follower attributions of leaders that make followers respond affirmatively or otherwise to their leader's qualities (Lord, DeVader, & Alliger, 1986). These perceptions are checked against prototypes held by followers of leader attributes and how leaders should perform (see Lord & Maher, 1990). This line of work is part of the greater attention being given to cognitive elements in leader-follower relations, exemplified by follower expectations and attributions. Such an integration of cognition and leadership is but one example of how the increasing prominence of cognitive approaches in psychology in general can be seen in organizational research (e.g., Gioia & Sims, 1986).

A related approach to leader cognition considers it to be based on relatively stable cognitive qualities, a style. This is illustrated by the work on "integrative complexity" in cognition by Suedfeld and Tetlock (1977), which refers to the richness of a leader's cognitive elements, revealed by content analyzing his or her verbal materials. Another approach is the work of Fiedler and Garcia (1987) on "cognitive capacity," essentially intelligence, whose applicability Fiedler and Leister (1977) found was limited by what a leader's superior would allow.

## LEADER AND FOLLOWER ROLES

Ideas about leadership have viewed the leader and followers in highly differentiated roles, although being a follower can be an active role that holds the potential of leadership. Indeed, behaviors seen to represent effective leadership include attributes of good followership, such as dependability and responsiveness (see Hollander & Webb, 1955; Kouzes & Posner, 1987). Granting that there is an imbalance of power, influence can be exerted in both roles, as part of a social exchange (Homans, 1961). To some degree, effective leadership depends on reciprocity and the potential for two-way influence and power sharing. This is so despite the extremes of leaders shrinking from using power and seeing it as necessarily bad or, alternatively, seeking it at the expense of abusing less powerful others and damaging their relationships with those others. The latter difficulty is seen in Kipnis's (1976) work on the "metamorphoses of power," dealing with the changes that may be brought about in the "powerholder" by having high power over others, including exalted self-worth and isolation from and devaluation of less powerful others.

## TRANSACTIONAL APPROACHES

A process-oriented transactional approach to leadership developed out of a social exchange perspective. It emphasizes the implicit social exchange or transaction over time that exists between the leader and followers, including reciprocal influence and interpersonal perception (see Hollander, 1964, 1978; Hollander & Julian, 1969, appearing as Chapter 5 here; Homans, 1961). The leader gives benefits to followers, such as a definition of the situation and direction, which is reciprocated by followers in heightened esteem for and responsiveness to the leader. This transactional approach fits other contemporary social science views emphasizing the significance of persuasive influence, rather than coercive power and compliance in organizational leadership.

Furthermore, a transactional approach gives special emphasis to the significance of followers' perceptions of the leader. Relatedly, Graen (1975) developed a Leader Member Exchange (LMX) model of leader-follower relationships emphasizing role-making between a leader and particular followers (see Dienesch & Liden, 1986). Briefly, the LMX model distinguishes between followers who are close to the leader and those who are more distant. The first have a better quality relationship with the leader, but the leader also has higher expectations for their performance and loyalty. For the others, the leader makes fewer personal demands and gives fewer benefits. For example, subordinates who reported a high-quality relationship with their supervisors assumed more job responsibility, contributed more, and were rated as higher performers than those with low-quality relationships (Liden & Graen, 1980).

Transactional approaches center on the followers' perceptions of and expectations about the leader's actions and motives, in accordance with attributional analysis. Heider's (1958) earlier work on the attribution of intentions through interpersonal perception is exemplified in the distinction between can and will. If a leader is perceived to be able to achieve a favorable outcome, but does not because of an apparent failure of will, this causes a greater loss of following than if he or she is unable to achieve something desirable but has made an evident effort, nonetheless.

[The section on the IC Model has been omitted here since it is presented in Chapters 1 and 16.]

A closely associated question concerns how followers perceive the leader's source of authority, or "legitimacy," in responding to that leader. A leader's legitimacy affects group performance, the followers' perceptions of the leader (e.g., Ben-Yoav, Hollander, & Carnevale, 1983), and the leader's perception of followers (cf. Green & Mitchell, 1979). Generally, election creates a heightened psychological identification between followers and the leader, insofar as they have a greater sense of involvement with someone for whom their responsibility is greater. But they also have higher expectations about the leader and may make more demands on the leader. Elected leaders who fail to perform well are more vulnerable to criticism than appointed leaders, particularly if they are seen to be competent in the first place (Hollander & Julian, 1970, 1978). Although election and appointment can create different psychological climates between leaders and followers, this does not deny the very real possibility for organization leaders to attain a "following" by doing more than exercising authority, as Katz and Kahn (1978) have observed in saying that organizational leadership is an increment of influence above compliance based in authority.

This would be seen in showing attributes such as trustworthiness and credibility that engage followers and evoke commitment from them.

One effect of the current attributional view is to make even more explicit the significance of followers' and others' perceptions of the leader. These perceptions set up expectancies that may affect the leader's own sense of latitude to take or not take actions affecting followers. In this way, follower perceptions can serve as a constraint or check on leader behavior. There also are associated expectations about leader characteristics such as appropriate competence and motivation, as well as the perceived motives behind leader behavior, especially in dealing with followers, peers, superiors, and adversaries. However, the reverse perspective of the leader's perception of followers also is significant in determining leader behavior (see Mitchell, Green, & Wood, 1981). For example, when an employee's performance is unsatisfactory, coercive corrective actions are seen as most appropriate if failure is perceived to be due to the subordinate's lack of effort; by contrast, taking no immediate corrective action is seen as more appropriate when failure is perceived to be due to factors outside the subordinate's control, such as luck or task difficulty (Pence, Pendleton, Dobbins, & Sgro, 1982).

[The section here, dealing with Charismatic and Transformational Leadership, is abbreviated since it is covered elsewhere, beginning in Chapter 1, and in the commentary for Chapter 5.]

Transformational leadership can be seen as an extension of transactional leadership, but with greater rewards in leader intensity and follower arousal. Indeed, according to Bass (1985) transformational leadership has two transactional factors (i.e., contingent reward and management by exception), in addition to charisma, intellectual stimulation, and individual attention to followers. However, it is important to note whether charisma is primarily directed to the service of the leader's self-oriented ends or to mission-oriented ends, which is a distinction Burns (1978) had made. Coupled with personalized power needs, the outcome of a charismatic appeal can be destructive, as Hogan, Raskin, and Fazzini (1988) have observed in their paper, "The Dark Side of Charisma."

## ORGANIZATIONAL CULTURE AND LEADER STYLE

Also significant today is the attention being given to organizational culture, as seen in the recent works of Deal and Kennedy (1982), Schein (1985), and Kilmann, Saxton, Serpa, and Associates (1985). This emphasis has broadened an earlier interest in organizational climate, exemplified by Likert's (1961) observation that the top leader sets a climate or tone in an organization that permeates the leader style there. For instance, a highly placed autocratic leader, who is low on input and participation from subordinates, can set a climate that limits the ability of leaders below to be participative. Therefore, style in some degree is a function of the climate and culture of the organization.

Individual differences among leaders are perceived as real and do play a role in follower satisfaction and performance outcomes. Leader style now is understood to be more complex than just being typical behavior, as was thought earlier. Obviously, it is affected by such situational constraints as role demands, which are related to the leader's level in the organization (see Boyatzis, 1982) and the expectations of followers. Style also is a function of the particular followers with whom the leader interacts, as pointed out in the leader-member exchange model already noted.

## NEWER DEVELOPMENTS AND ORIENTATIONS

The conceptual and research developments described show increasing attention to the follower in the leadership process. Although the study of leadership has always presumed the existence of followers, their roles were viewed as essentially passive. Recent models have increasingly sought to integrate followers more fully into an understanding of leadership, building on the foundation provided by contingency and transactional models.

Attribution approaches provide a richer perspective on the leader-follower dynamic, focusing both on follower behavior as the stimulus for leader behavior and the obverse, thus expanding leadership as a process worthy of study as either a dependent or an independent variable. As noted earlier, ILTs examine the way in which follower perceptions and expectations about leaders may structure the leader-follower relationship and may adversely affect the validity of subordinate evaluations of leader behavior. Dynamic leader-member exchange relationships are key features in models by Hollander (1958, 1978) and Graen, (1975; Graen & Scandura, 1987), with an increasing interest in follower influence and follower perceptions of leaders. Furthermore, charismatic leaders and, therefore, the charismatic component of transformational leaders, are identified by the effects they have on their followers.

Do these changes in views of leadership benefit organizations that seek to use current leadership concepts? Clearly, they do. Greater attention to followers, and their role in understanding and promoting leadership, is compatible with changes in the organizational environments faced by today's leaders. A climate of participative management with greater follower involvement in decision-making appears to be more common in organizations and appears to increase commitment and profitability (Burke, 1986).

Quality circles, groups of employees meeting regularly to discover and solve work problems in their areas, are on the rise (Ledford, Lawler, & Mohrman, 1988). Employee stock ownership programs (ESOPs), such as the one at Weirton Steel in West Virginia, are breaking down traditional distinctions between management and labor. The development of self-managed work teams (Goodman, Devadas, & Hughson, 1988) shows that there may be new roles for corporate leaders, with some functions associated with traditional leadership being performed by committed peer groups. All of these workplace trends underline the importance of developing and expanding the roles of followers in the leadership of organizations. These trends also presume the willingness of leaders themselves to embrace the notion of sharing power with subordinates.

## THE ROLE OF POWER

Underlying the concern for developing the role of followers in the leadership process is the reality of power, in the several forms discussed earlier. As already noted, power plays a major part in the interactions occurring in organizational life (see Pfeffer, 1981). It cannot be ignored if we hope to understand and improve the functioning of organizations from within (Kanter, 1981; Mintzberg, 1983). Power over others is also especially intertwined with an understanding of leadership processes, with regard both to its appropriateness and limitations (Hollander, 1985).

Yet, despite the relevance of power to organizations in general, and to an understanding of leadership in particular, research studies of power and leadership are not well integrated. Also, assumptions about power often remain unstated and untested. Like love, its importance and existence are acknowledged, but its study is often resisted. And those with the most power and influence in organizations have typically been most able to shield themselves from study (Kipnis, 1976).

### Sharing Power

One of the clearest bridges between the study of power and leadership in organizations has been in the area of subordinate participation in decision making (PDM). Advocates of PDM have theoretical roots in a human relations approach to management that stresses social interaction and power equalization. Unfortunately, little agreement exists on a definition of participation, and wide variations exist in its content, degree, scope, formality, and on whether it should be mandatory or voluntary (Locke & Schweiger, 1979). To some extent, however, all forms of participation embody the idea that employees should be permitted or even encouraged to influence their working environment. Accordingly, a continuum of employee influence can be offered ranging from no influence (autocratic decisions) through various levels of opinion giving (consultative decisions) to truly joint decision making (power sharing) (e.g., Tannenbaum & Schmidt, 1958).

Evidence of positive relationships between participative decision making and outcomes such as subordinate productivity, motivation, and satisfaction is mixed. In a recent meta-analysis, Miller and Monge (1986) reported a notable positive relationship between participation and satisfaction (mean correlation .34) and a small, but significant, correlation between participation and performance (mean correlation .15). Yet the results of another recent meta-analysis by Wagner and Gooding (1987) suggest that positive participation-outcome relationships may be largely due to methodological artifacts including use of percept-percept correlations, those obtained from the same individual with the same questionnaire at the same time, rather than correlations based on multiple sources and differences between the types of subjects used, for example, students versus workers.

In examining both laboratory and field studies of PDM, Schweiger and Leana (1986) concluded that contextual variables are important in moderating the relationship between PDM and performance and that no one degree of participation, from autocratic to fully participative, can be employed effectively for all subordinates in all situations. This is, of course, what contingency theorists such as Vroom and Yetton (1973) have long maintained. To some, the mixed effects of PDM, particularly in extending beyond subordinate satisfaction, is reason to question the use of participation, or at least to consider it as just one of a number of possible organizational interventions geared to organizational productivity. To others, participation is valued for fulfilling human psychological needs and promoting employee health and should be encouraged whether or not it increases productivity. According to Sashkin (1984), nonparticipation may be psychologically and physiologically damaging, and because participation may increase productivity, or at minimum not decrease it, participation is therefore an ethical imperative.

In cases in which employees express opinions or give suggestions that may or may not be accepted or acted on by their supervisors, participation can be more accurately thought of as an influence-sharing option with the leader retaining power. Decisions made may or may not reflect follower input because subordinates may participate but have little influence on decision making (Hoffman, Burke, & Maier, 1965; Mulder, 1971). Indeed, one potential drawback of such a consultative form of participation is that it may unduly raise the expectations of followers that their suggestions and ideas will be regularly accepted. Routine failure to accept follower influence may make followers believe that participation is a sham designed to give them a sense of involvement that will motivate them without giving them any real influence. For example, members of quality circles receiving largely negative responses to their suggestions tend to become discouraged and stop meeting (Ledford et al., 1988).

Implementing participation by followers also may require skills a given leader does not possess. Recent work by Crouch and Yetton (1987) has suggested that high performance costs may be incurred by managers with poor conflict management skills who attempt to bring subordinates together to resolve conflict. Alternatively, performance increments may be associated with such meetings convened by leaders with good conflict management skills. If participation by subordinates is to be encouraged, then organizations need to consider ways in which managers can be trained in the skills required to implement meaningful participation.

### Distributing Power

True follower development needs to go beyond encouraging follower influence (sharing power) to allowing followers to have decision responsibility (distributing power). For this purpose, delegation may be a better model than participation for truly empowering others. Delegation involves decisions that managers allow subordinates to make on their own (Heller & YukI, 1969). It typically involves decision making by individual subordinates rather than by subordinate groups or manager-subordinate dyads and stresses subordinate autonomy in decision making (Locke & Schweiger, 1979). Yet delegation has received far less research attention than participation. Although it is often depicted as the extreme end of the participation continuum, delegation has been shown to be a very different process than participation (Leana, 1986, 1987).

Unlike the human relations background of participation, delegation derives from a cognitive growth approach to job enrichment advocating individual development through expanded use of skills, autonomy, and responsibility. In a recent study comparing delegation and participation, Leana (1987) found that managers reported the use of delegation under highly circumscribed conditions, specifically when less important decisions were involved, the subordinate was seen as capable, and the manager was too overloaded to participate. Furthermore, she found that delegation was correlated with higher subordinate performance, whereas participation was correlated with lower performance. These potentially superior organizational outcomes for delegation may be due to the fact that unlike participation, delegation is not indiscriminate but considers the ability and responsibility of followers for the task at hand. High performers should have more functions delegated to them than low performers. Therefore, although delegation distributes power, it does so selectively rather than equally.

Self-managed work teams are current examples of follower groups to whom authority has been delegated with successful results (Goodman et al., 1988). Self-managed teams differ from traditional work crews in the greater degree of control they exert over both the management and execution of group tasks, which may include allocating jobs to members, having responsibility for production levels, solving local production problems, selecting and training new members, and delivering finished goods (see Goodman et al., 1988, for specific case examples). The existence of such self-managed groups does not, however, necessarily preclude a role for an external leader, sometimes referred to as a coordinator or consultant. The role of the external leader differs from the traditional leader role in that the key leadership functions are in monitoring and facilitating the team in performing its own regulation. The most important leadership behaviors in these cases have been suggested to be encouraging self-reinforcement, self-observation, and self-evaluation (Manz & Sims, 1987).

## BARRIERS TO EMPOWERMENT

There are clear barriers to promoting the distribution of power in organizations. Although Tannenbaum (1968) found that power in organizations is not finite but can expand, there remains a pervasive belief that to empower others is to lose power oneself. In short, although power is not a zero-sum quality, it is often perceived as such. This likely perceived loss of power may be a deterrent for many leaders, particularly those who have a high need for power. At the Ford Motor Company, effective implementation of a large-scale employee involvement program necessitated dispelling the misperceptions of supervisors that employee involvement would undermine their authority or eliminate their jobs (Banas, 1988).

Some managers may perceive the strong use of power as necessary to do their jobs. In dealing with poor performance, bank managers in one study were found to report greater satisfaction with their handling of events and their outcomes when they were more punishing (Green, Fairhurst, & Snavely, 1986). Subordinates may well have felt differently about the experience. Greater managerial awareness of the negative effects of punishment on subordinates may be needed.

Organizations should be aware, however, that it is unrealistic to expect leaders to distribute power to others when negative consequences of actions taken will fall on the leader. The unwillingness of many leaders to delegate is understandable considering that, in many organizations, no matter who actually makes decisions, leaders retain responsibility for decisions made in their units.

When the team loses, it is often the coach or manager who gets fired (Pfeffer, 1977).

In Vroom and Yetton's (1973) normative model of decision making in leadership, leaders are urged to expand participation and delegation for individuals when (a) they lack the information necessary to make decisions themselves and subordinates have enough information to make high-quality decisions, (b) subordinates share the organization's goals, and (c) subordinate acceptance and commitment are needed. Yet each of these components requires an assessment by the leader that may be biased toward the leader's preferred outcome, whether autocratic, participative, or something in between. Thus, autocratically oriented leaders may be more inclined than participatively oriented leaders to feel that their own information is sufficient, that subordinates lack information and commitment, and that subordinate commitment is not needed or important for most decisions.

In fact, research has shown that leaders contemplating participation pay close attention to how much information they have themselves and whether subordinates share the organization's goals, involving others when they lack information and when others share the goals, as the model suggests they should. Leaders are also more likely to underestimate the need for subordinate commitment to the effective implementation of decisions, making guidelines dealing with the importance of obtaining subordinate commitment the most commonly violated provision of Vroom and Yetton's (1973; Vroom & Jago, 1988) model. Furthermore, it would be difficult for subordinates ever to obtain enough information to make quality decisions if leaders use their own information power in a way that deprives subordinates of what they need to participate (see Mulder, 1971).

## EMPOWERMENT AS CAREER DEVELOPMENT THROUGH MODELING AND MENTORING

By sharing power and allowing themselves to be influenced by followers and by distributing power through delegation, leaders may foster the development of leadership in others. In recent years, increasing attention has been paid to leaders as models and mentors. Modeling has been proposed as a mechanism to help persons learn to lead themselves (Manz & Sims, 1988), although it has been shown to be a complex phenomenon involving multiple linkages going beyond mere imitation. Thus, leaders who had previously viewed videotaped supervisors reprimanding a subordinate later showed less positive reinforcement and goal-setting behavior in their own interaction with a subordinate, as might be expected (Manz & Sims, 1986). However, goal-setting behavior observed on videotape unexpectedly increased leader reprimand behavior. Interestingly, these effects were found as a result of exposure to a videotaped supervisor without explicit instructions to model the behaviors displayed. Given some of the effects of leader-modeled behavior found, further study is necessary. Such study should examine modeling both for its usefulness as a mechanism of leader development and for its effects on subordinates' satisfaction and performance.

Modeling can be considered part of the concept of mentoring (see Kram, 1985), in which a key component of the leader role is seen to be the advancement and development of talented subordinates. In some organizations, managers are evaluated in part on their abilities to develop subordinates. For example, Southwestern Bell accomplishes this by including subordinate development items in the performance appraisal instrument for middle and lower level managers (Vandaveer & Varca, 1988). Managers are rated on such items as delegating responsibility with commensurate authority and follow-up; effectively involving subordinates in decisions affecting them; and providing information, guidance, and development opportunities for their subordinates. In these environments, leaders need to identify subordinates' potential, model appropriate behavior by serving as a referent, increasingly share power by giving subordinates access and participation, and ultimately distribute power to subordinates through delegation with appropriate follow-up.

One of the most difficult, but important, elements of delegation may be allowing subordinates to make mistakes (Manz & Sims, 1988). Southwestern Bell also incorporates a performance appraisal item dealing with the encouragement and positive reward of intelligent risk taking, without punishing occasional failure. Some executives know this lesson well. When faced with a manager who had made a $100,000 mistake and who suggested that maybe he should be fired, one executive said, "Why should I fire you when I've just invested $100,000 in your development?" (McCall, Lombardo, & Morrison, 1988, p. 154).

Expanding the role of subordinates may expand the role of leader as well. Although employees gain in expertise and knowledge through participation and delegation, leaders may be freer to engage in other profitable activities such as long-term planning, market forecasting, and entrepreneurship. General Electric chairman John F. Welch, Jr. has advocated stretching managers thin to force them to delegate less critical decisions to subordinates so they can concentrate on the important ones. This involves increasing responsibility at lower levels in the organization. In spreading this message widely across his organization, Welch hopes to encourage lower level managers to push their superiors for more freedom (Potts, 1988). Time management advocates have long expressed the same hope of better use of management talent for major decisions by delegating responsibility downward (e.g., Patten, 1981). More research on the effects of delegation and follow-up is needed to assess the impact of such power distribution.

## INFORMAL INFLUENCE

The discussion so far has centered on power sharing and distribution through relatively formal mechanisms in organizations, usually at the leader's initiative. Yet a thriving area of current research deals with informal influence, which occurs without formal authority and usually at the follower's initiative. In keeping with a general trend toward focusing on the duality of good leadership and responsive/proactive followership, more studies are being done on the informal processes of upward influence in organizations. For example, one study of public sector supervisors and their managers (Waldera, 1988) showed that better quality supervisor-manager relationships and a greater range of supervisory influence strategies were associated with greater self-rated upward influence.

We are learning a great deal about associations between numerous variables and measures of organizational influence (see Porter, Allen, & Angle, 1981, for a review). For example, women typically have been shown to have less upward influence than men (e.g., Brass, 1985; Trempe, Rigny, & Haccoun, 1985). This difference has been attributed to the less central positions in organizational networks and lower access that women have to the main power holders in an organization (Brass, 1985). Because information and access are essential to organizational functioning, they are keys to power.

Strategies of upward influence also are gaining attention. Strategies used have been shown to be influenced by numerous individual characteristics, including the person's level in the organization (e.g., Kipnis, Schmidt, & Wilkinson, 1980; Offermann & Schrier, 1985), their years of experience (Mowday, 1979), their own perceived power (Kipnis, Schmidt, Swaffin-Smith, & Wilkinson, 1984), their own need for power (Mowday, 1979) or apprehension about power (Offermann & Schrier, 1985), and their investment in the influence objective (Sussman & Vecchio, 1982).

Subordinate influence strategies also have been found to be affected by the goal desired by the subordinate and the supervisor's leadership style. Waldera (1988) found that more direct strategies were used in influence attempts dealing with attaining organizational objectives than were used for achieving personal objectives. Ansari and Kapoor (1987) reported that when desiring personal benefits, subordinates tended to use ingratiation, whereas organizational goals were sought through the use of combinations of rational and nonrational strategies such as persuasion, blocking, and upward appeals. Nonrational strategies were more commonly used with authoritarian leaders, whereas rational persuasion was more common with participative leaders. Thus, participation may be viewed not only as a leader method of sharing influence, but also as a style that affects the ways in which subordinates attempt to influence the leader.

Subordinate strategies may also be affected by characteristics of the target of influence. For example, when attempting to influence a supervisor, employees are more likely to use self-presentation, supporting data, coalitions, and rational tactics than when trying to influence peers or subordinates (Kipnis et al., 1980). The gender of the target supervisor may also affect the strategies used by subordinates, with subordinates less likely to withdraw and more likely to try to reason with a male rather than a female supervisor (Offermann & Kearney, 1988). These studies indicate that followers need not be passive compliers, and their results provide added support for a two way influence conception of leadership (e.g., Ben-Yoav et al., 1983; Elgie, Hollander, & Rice, 1988). There is much to be learned about leadership from an understanding of leaders as both initiators and targets of influence.

## CHALLENGES TO LEADERSHIP RESEARCH

Although there has been an encouraging increase in interest in power in organizations, and steady activity in leadership research and application, further work is needed to improve integration of research on power and leadership. Expanding the follower role requires an understanding of power sharing, power distribution, and informal influence and their effects. We have suggested the importance of empowering followers in the leadership process. As described, leadership research and applications have moved consistently in this direction over time, yet cautions need to be acknowledged. Employee involvement may make for more effective use of human resources, but should not be expected to be a panacea for all organizational problems. Furthermore, in an era of "down-sizing," developing employees who then have nowhere to go within the organization can be destructive.

Methodological problems in the measurement of power are common and in need of resolution (Podsakoff & Schriesheim, 1985). Further work is needed to understand the dynamics of formal and informal subordinate influence as these affect subordinates, leaders, and organizations. In addition, the resurgence of interest in charismatic and transformational leadership ought to be viewed with appropriate caution. A major question to consider is how such leader-centric approaches mesh with the growing trend toward empowerment and subordinate influence.

Another critical shortcoming is the failure of most leadership models to consider levels of leadership. Most models use the term leader to designate individuals occupying a wide range of supervisory positions, from first line supervisors to executives. In the past, most leaders studied were at the lowest levels of organizations (cf. Boyatzis, 1982). Recently, more attention has been given to more senior-level leaders and executives (e.g., Kotter, 1982; Levinson & Rosenthal, 1984). Unfortunately, it is often difficult to make comparisons across studies in regard to "supervisors," "leaders," and "executives." Not atypically, the term executives is operationalized as individuals to whom the responding firms attached the term, even with an awareness that these individuals encompass many levels and that the term is variably applied in different organizations. Despite this problem, understanding leadership at the top of the organizational hierarchy is important, as well as studying the empowerment of lower level participants.

Jacobs and Jaques (1987) have developed a model expressly to consider the level of leadership within an organization and to understand the requisite skills needed for success at a given level. Looking at leadership as value added to the resources of the system at any level, what leaders must do to add value to an organizational system will differ depending on their organizational level and the nature of the organization (e.g., public vs. private). Tasks, goals, and time frames will differ considerably by level, with higher-level leadership requiring greater conceptual effort in dealing with uncertainty, abstraction, and longer time frames.

The concept of leadership as value-added, or incremental to basic management components, should help address the issue of whether managers and leaders are different (see Zaleznik, 1977). Rather than worrying about distinctions between leaders and managers, leadership researchers need to consider seriously whether the "leaders" being studied are perceived as such by their subordinates and peers. Focusing on follower perceptions indicates that supervisors and leaders may be perceived differently. Recent work on ILTs suggests that although people use the same dimensions to describe supervisors and leaders, ratings in response to the cue supervisor are significantly less favorable than those given in response to the cue of leader (Offermann & Kennedy, 1987). This points to the need to study those individuals identified as leaders by subordinates, perhaps comparing them not only with followers but also with persons of comparable organizational authority and position who are not so identified. These "leaders" may or may not be managers, because the exercise of authority alone is not the hallmark of leadership. But they should be those at any level who are perceived as leaders and whose actions move their organizations toward achieving their goals.

There also is a need to examine the dynamic features of leadership over time. Time frames considered could range from an episode to an entire career. Recent examples of work with a greater span of time include the development of an episodic model of power (Cobb, 1984), looking at supervisory control as a chain or sequence of events (Green et al., 1986), work on managerial careers (e.g., Howard & Bray, 1988), and leadership succession (Gordon & Rosen, 1981).

Future research must also address the issue of leadership "Toward what ends?" (Hollander, 1985, p. 527). Just as the issue of power in organizations raises questions of moral right to participation, leadership processes cannot escape questions about ultimate goals and outcomes. Although power over others is inevitable in organizational life, it always carries with it the specter of abuse. In the wake of scandals about insider trading and corporate violations, courses in business ethics are on the rise (Eyde & Quaintance, 1988). The role of leaders as transmitters and upholders of organizational values is increasingly being stressed (e.g., Kouzes & Posner, 1987). Whether all this activity results in more ethical, responsive, and humane leadership remains to be seen.

In reviewing the considerable activity that has gone on in leadership research and practice in recent years, we believe there is good reason for optimism. Progress has been made toward applying what we know about leadership processes to ongoing organizational problems, such as simulation training (Thornton & Cleveland, 1990, pp. 190–199), and increasing ethnic and gender diversity in management (Morrison & Von Glinow, 1990, pp. 200–208).

Research on power and leadership is alive and well. Substantial gains have been made in understanding leaders and their followers, as seen in Fiedler and House's (1988) review of gains. Granting a bias toward believing in leadership as a causal force in organizational performance, even when the cause is indeterminant (Meindl, Ehrlich, & Dukerich, 1985), effective leadership can make a difference in important organizational outcomes (e.g., Smith, Carson, & Alexander, 1984). Our ready willingness to attribute outcomes to leadership underscores the importance of the concept both to individuals and to their organizations. Psychologists can and have played important roles in both the understanding and development of leadership in organizations. Although much remains to be done, studying leadership and followership from a power perspective shows promise of considerable return.

CHAPTER 12

# Organizational Leadership and Followership

## The Role of Interpersonal Relations

### COMMENTARY

A theme throughout this book is the importance of an active follower role. This view breaks with more traditional conceptions. In writing this chapter, I was acknowledging my debt to Michael Argyle, who died in 2002. A preeminent leader in British and international social psychology, he was a colleague and friend.* I wanted this chapter to show that link between his work and my own, as it applies to leader-follower relations. A quote from the book on relationships, which he coauthored with psychiatrist Monica Henderson (1985), appears in Chapter 1 in this book and serves as an entry point to that connection. They said, briefly, "[The] superior-subordinate relationship at work is seen by most people as full of conflict and as providing little satisfaction. On the other hand supervisors can have a considerable effect on health and satisfaction, if the right skills are used."

A feature of this chapter is its insistence on taking team efforts as important to productivity and worker satisfaction. It is not just being in a group by itself that engenders loyalty and cohesiveness in the service of superior performance. There are differences that need to be understood in making group members feel a part of a team. This process is vital to strong ties and productive relationships.

---

Abridged from E. P. Hollander. Organizational Leadership and Followership: The role of interpersonal relations. In P. Collett & A. Furnham, Eds. (1995b). *Social Psychology at Work: Essays in Honour of Michael Argyle.* London & New York: Routledge (pp. 69–87). Republished with permission of Routledge.

Several points, notably about power and status differences, reward and punishment, and their effects, recur here as significant issues in dealing with leader-follower relations. All are necessarily parts of the rules of conduct understood as applicable in any particular role relationship (Argyle, 1983).

### BACKGROUND AND DEFINITIONS

Although the central feature of leadership is direction of activity, it embodies other important functions which can be distributed. They include decision-making, goal-setting, communicating, resolving conflict and maintaining the enterprise, in the classic sense of stewardship. These are not just

---

* Argyle and I twice worked closely. First, was when he came to SUNY at Buffalo to teach for the 1968 summer session in our doctoral program in social/organizational psychology, which I began with Raymond Hunt in 1962, and directed for 9 years, with an intermediate break. Second, I reciprocated as a visitor at Oxford for the spring (Trinity) term of 1973, when I was in his social psychology laboratory and gave seminars on leadership, conformity, and independence. We shared similar views regarding the significance of relationships. Argyle studied social skills and emphasized the importance of such skills training for some mentally ill, and wrote extensively about the social psychology of work (e.g., Argyle, 1990).

the leader's functions, but instead may be and are dispersed through varying degrees of delegation to followers, though even more may be desirable in the direction of team effort (see e.g. Hackman, 1990; Katzenbach and Smith, 1993; Sundstrom et al., 1990).

In addition to other conditions, leadership operates within the constraints and opportunities presented by followers (see Stewart, 1982). The constraints include the expectations and perceptions of followers that can influence leaders (Hollander, 1985, 1986; Lord and Maher, 1990). An early proponent of this general view was Fillmore Sanford (1950) who asserted that followers are crucial to any leadership event and deserve more attention. Mary Parker Follett (1949) expressed a comparable point in a paper delivered at the University of London in the early 1930s, emphasizing her concept of 'power with' followers.

Leadership and followership are required throughout teams and organizations, with the same individuals needing to act in both capacities, at least enough so that the distinction becomes less an impediment to action (see e.g., Barnes and Kriger, 1986; Vanderslice, 1988). The characterization of the follower role as mainly passive is therefore inappropriate when considering it as part of an active counterpart to leadership (see Kelley, 1988). Leaders do command greater attention and influence, but followers can affect leaders and the entire enterprise in important ways. Not least, followers are usually the leader's most attentive strategic audience, who experience at first hand the leader's behavior, and can make attributions about his or her intentions and values.

Being in the follower role also holds within it the potential for taking on the leader role. Indeed, behaviors found to represent effective leadership include attributes of good followership (see Hollander and Webb, 1955; Kouzes and Posner, 1987) such as dependability, competence, and honesty. Granted an imbalance of power, influence can be exerted in both roles, as part of a social exchange (Homans, 1961) and the practice of loyalty down as well as loyalty up. Effective leadership is more likely to be achieved by a process in which there is reciprocity and the potential for two-way influence and power sharing, rather than by simply relying on authority and the exercise of power over others.

In this respect, Katz and Kahn (1978) have defined organizational leadership as the influence increment over and above mechanical compliance with routine directives. That means having a personal following beyond what is demanded by one's position of authority. They say that the importance of leadership is to fulfill three main behavioral requirements of organizational functioning, which broadly are: (1) recruit and retain capable staff; (2) maintain essential functions and roles; and (3) provide a climate for making creative contributions. The achievement of these requirements depends upon positive leader-follower relations, with a sense of cohesiveness, which is basic to work teams.

Work teams are interdependent collections of individuals who share responsibility for specific outcomes for their organizations (Sundstrom et al., 1990, p. 120). They are not just groups called teams by higher authority, but must cohere about a performance focus with clear goals pursued with discipline (Katzenbach and Smith, 1993, pp. 12–15). Though the success of a team depends upon so-called 'teamwork', fundamentally it pivots on leader-follower relations. This is exemplified in a study of high performance US Navy ships by Whiteside (1985). He found that the critical element that made a difference was how the young officers functioned as a cohesive followership team, especially by: supporting their leaders, but nonetheless raising questions and concerns, including bad news; taking initiatives when necessary, without being told; and showing personal care and responsibility. This is also exemplified in some of the best features of self-managed work teams [See Manz and Sims, 1987, and their book, *Business Without Bosses* (NY: Wiley, 1993), which calls to mind the aphorism "Boss spelled backward is "double 'SOB'."]

In his landmark work, *The Functions of the Executive* (1938), Chester Barnard put forth his 'acceptance theory of authority', stating that the follower has a pivotal role in judging whether an order is authoritative, in so far as: he or she understands it; believes it is not inconsistent with organizational or personal goals; has the ability to comply with it; and sees more rewards than costs in complying and remaining with the organization or group (Hollander, 1978, p. 47). This conception was significant in bringing attention to the place of followership in leadership.

## EARLY WORK ON INTERPERSONAL AND GROUP PROCESSES

Various studies early in this century on team and organizational leadership indicated the importance of the leader-follower relationship, including the nature of supposed leadership tasks that could be performed by followers. The pioneering work of Hugo Munsterberg (1914) and Floyd Allport (1924) on influence and social facilitation in group performance opened the way for more experimentation on such elements.

The well-known Hawthorne studies (Mayo, 1933; Roerhlisbergcr and Dickson, 1939) were field experiments that generated interest in social facilitation effects in work groups. Though not directly focused on leadership, they spawned experiments by others such as Gunnar Westerlund (1952) in Sweden on 'group leadership', with telephone operators allowed more contact with their supervisors, as needed. This provided followers with a greater stake in the workplace, and was illustrative of the way the so-called human relations approach would move toward a more active conception of leader-follower relations. [Footnote: I paid tribute to Westerlund and his work in the opening of my paper "On the Central Role of Leadership Processes," *International Review of Applied Psychology*, 1986. We were acquainted through serving on the Board of the International Society of Political Psychology, ISPP, of which he was president and a great colleague, now gone.]

The Lewin, Lippitt, and White (1939) experiments on the effects of autocratic, democratic, and laissez-faire leadership styles represented another landmark in studying outcomes of leader-follower interaction. Although the subjects used were from boys' clubs, wider implications were nonetheless drawn.

More importantly, Kurt Lewin's (1947) group decision-making research established group dynamics on an experimental foundation and had resounding influence in generating research and theory about group processes, including the important interrelationships of communication, cohesiveness, and conformity. Lewin is credited with saying that 'nothing is so practical as a good theory', but he might as readily have said it about a 'good team', given his pioneering work on applications of group dynamics (see Marrow, 1969). Industrial Japan discovered this message and took it to heart, with their work team thrust, before it returned repackaged through such works as Theory Z (Ouchi, 1981). There is more than a little irony in the fact that group dynamics and a team emphasis originated in North America and the UK though their workplace implications were evidently better received elsewhere.

## THE SITUATIONAL APPROACH: ANTECEDENTS AND ACCOMPANIMENTS

With the human relations movement taking hold (see e.g., Likert, 1961; McGregor, 1960) the situational approach to leadership developed over fifty years ago. A new paradigm emerged which helped to shift the balance from traits to interpersonal relations. It implicitly considered leadership not as a thing a leader possesses so much as a process that involves followers in a particular situation. This development emphasized the context in which the leader and followers functioned, and the demands the task there made for various leader qualities. More recently, others (e.g. Kirkpatrick and Locke, 1991) have asserted a case for studying necessary leader qualities, notably in the motivation and cognition arenas (cf. Hogan et al., 1994).

Ralph Stogdill's (1948) review of the early literature showed the limits of just looking at leader traits, and encouraged that shift to the situational approach. However, a significant break had occurred even earlier when follower reports of leader behavior were given attention in the Ohio State University Leadership Studies, in which Carroll Shartle and Stogdill played such a pivotal role. The work was begun soon after World War II and represents one of the most significant research programs done on leader behavior as reported by followers (see Shartle, Stogdill and Campbell, 1949; Stogdill and Shartle, 1948). With their colleagues, they developed a questionnaire and administered it to members of the many, mostly US Naval, organizations who were asked to describe their leaders by the frequency with which they displayed various behaviors from 'always' to 'never'. When these ratings were analyzed, they were found to represent four major factors. As is by now well known, the two chief factors accounting for the bulk of leader behavior were consideration and initiation of structure (see Fleishman, 1953a, 1973).

The emergence of the situational approach came most notably through the writings of John Hemphill (1949), Fillmore Sanford (1950), and Alvin Gouldner (1950), among others. Sanford wrote:

> There is some justification for regarding the follower as the most crucial factor in any leadership event and for arguing that research directed at the follower will eventually yield a handsome pay-off. Not only is it the follower who accepts or rejects leadership, but it is the follower who perceives both the leader and the situation and who reacts in terms of what he perceives. (Sanford, 1950, p. 4)

The subsequent upsurge in interest in situational factors had a profound effect on research and theory, eventually including 'the nature of the task or activity, its history, the availability of human and material resources, and the quality of leader-follower relations' (Hollander and Offermann, 1990, p. 180). This development also helped to open the way for contingency models of leadership (see e.g., Fiedler, 1964, 1967; House, 1971; Vroom and Yetton, 1973), as well as transactional models (see e.g., Hollander, 1958, 1964, 1978; Hollander and Julian, 1969; Homans, 1961; Graen, 1975; Dienesch and Liden, 1986).

Reflecting this relational emphasis was John Flanagan's (1954) assessment of leader behavior by followers using his 'critical incident technique', developed first to evaluate US Air Corps pilots in World War II, with considerable success. Basically, critical incidents are reports of actual behaviors observed and evaluated by those on the scene as examples of what is particularly effective or ineffective, in this case leadership. The observer-respondent chooses the incidents to report without identifying the actor.

While on duty as a naval aviation psychologist at Pensacola in the early 1950s, together with John Bair, I obtained and content analyzed critical incidents to compare naval aviation cadets who successfully completed basic flight training with those who voluntarily withdrew (Hollander and Bair, 1954). All of those respondents were asked to describe their 'best' and 'worst' flight instructors. Content analyses revealed a significant attitudinal difference in the descriptions they gave: those who successfully completed training more often described their 'best' and 'worst' instructors with regard to interpersonal qualities, while those who withdrew from flight training emphasized the dimension of instructor competence-incompetence. These findings suggested that identification with the instructor was a factor associated with success in this program.

Another significant approach with earlier roots was the use of sociometric procedures, pioneered by Jacob Moreno (1934). Assessing impressions of leadership qualities by this method was important in my own early studies at Pensacola and Newport (see Hollander, 1964, Part III; 1979, pp. 159–60). During this period, we developed peer nominations and ratings to assess effective and ineffective leadership in groups of US naval aviation cadets. Among other findings, this research indicated that peer nominations significantly predicted completion of the US Naval Air Training Program. We also found that leadership and followership peer nominations were highly related and largely unaffected by friendship ties, despite conventional beliefs to the contrary (Hollander and

Webb, 1955). A program of research I conducted at the US Navy OCS (Officer Candidate School) at Newport, Rhode Island, validated the impression that peer nominations tap a reservoir of interpersonal perceptions of considerable value for predicting complex, later performance (see Hollander, 1964, 1965).

More generally, this research again substantiated how basic interpersonal evaluation is in the leader-follower relationship. This point came through in a later series of experiments on leader legitimacy and authority, with respect to the leader's latitude for exerting influence and taking innovative action, which I developed as the 'idiosyncrasy credit' model of leadership (see Hollander, 1958, 1960, 1961a, 1961b, 1964; Hollander and Julian, 1970, 1978). Follower perceptions of the leader were found to affect their responsiveness to the leader and their willingness to have the leader take initiatives as well as to retain authority.

Still another development during this period was the study of emergent leadership by the 'leaderless group discussion' (LGD) technique (see Bass, 1950). Used during World War II for the selection and training of military officers and others, such as the OSS, in the United States, England and Australia, it was reportedly employed in the German military beginning in 1935 (Ansbacher, 1951). Today it is often used as a standard feature of assessment centers designed as one way to select promising managers (see Howard and Bray, 1988).

## SOME ASPECTS OF POWER AND IDENTIFICATION IN THE LEADER-FOLLOWER RELATIONSHIP

A major component of the leader-follower relationship is the leader's perception of his or her self relative to followers, and how they in turn perceive the leader. This raises important ethical issues concerning how followers are involved, used or abused, especially in a relationship that is imbalanced in the direction of a leader's power over them. Such a dominance theme is antagonistic to a view of followers as team members in so far as it countenances their abuse by a superior. One expression of this pattern is from a corporate CEO saying in a *Fortune* magazine article on 'The ten toughest bosses' that 'leadership is confirmed when the ability to inflict pain is demonstrated' (Menzies, 1980). A *Business Week* article entitled 'The CEO disease' (Byrne et al., 1991) further examined the extent of this pattern.

Clearly, such abuse of power runs counter to the idea of mutual dependence in a shared enterprise. Further, it may also deprive a leader of honest inputs of information and judgements from subordinates who have been cowed. This only adds to the self-absorption and self-deception that are pitfalls of arbitrary power.

In his classic conception of powerholding, Kipnis (1976) identified four corrupting influences of power affecting the powerholder and those in a relationship with that individual. Briefly these 'metamorphic effects' are: (1) power becomes desired as an end in itself, to be sought at virtually any cost; (2) holding power tempts the individual to use organizational resources for self-benefit, even illegally; (3) creates the basis for false feedback from them, and an exalted sense of self-worth; (4) and a devaluation of others' worth, with a desire to avoid close contact with them. Mulder (1981) extended the last point especially in his concept of 'power distance', which he sees as heightening the differential status of leader and followers, as a function, for example, of disparities in available information or resources.

Regarding this point, Emerson (1962) said that the explicit recognition of dependence by a lower-power person on one of higher power can promote resentment by the former. This effect is likely to be detrimental to mutual efforts, though it has not been given as much attention as other, tangible rewards, such as economic benefits. Also, the element of trust may be undercut by a leader's self-serving activity and a lack of accountability when he or she is manifestly failing in a higher-power position.

With their traditional superordinate position, leaders also may be given to self-serving biases beyond those that exist in other social relationships. In his analysis of some key psychological processes involved, Greenwald (1985) presents an interpretation of how the leader's ego or self incorporates several distinctive cognitive biases. These include the self as focus of knowledge, 'beneffectance' as the perception of responsibility for desired, but not for undesired, outcomes, and resistance to change.

This set of tendencies is further enhanced by power over others and a sense of being different, with accompanying social distance, and potential manipulation of others as objects. A necessary corrective is for the leader to be attuned to the needs of followers, their perceptions and expectancies. However, the narcissism associated with craving the affection of followers as in 'mirror-hungry' charismatic leaders, often deprives them of this corrective (see Post, 1986). A counterpart is seen in followers who are vulnerable to perceptual distortions as a feature of the self-serving bias and identification with the leader, which together bolster their followers' own selves (see Hollander, 1992b).

An alternative view, more in keeping with responsive participation, considers the leader-follower relationship within a mutual identification process. This includes the prospect of two-way influence, and the perception and counterperception of leader and followers (Cantril, 1958). Identification with the leader is exemplified in Freud's (1921) concept of the leader as a shared 'ego-ideal' with whom members of a group mutually identify. Fromm (1941) extended this conception in personality terms, in his contention that 'the psychology of the leader and that of his followers, are, of course, closely linked with each other' (p. 65). Erikson (1975) made an associated point about this linkage in asserting that followers 'join a leader and are joined together by him' (p. 153). They are bonded as a unit.

Inadequate and inattentive leadership was found to be responsible for the failure to maintain 'unit cohesion' in the US Army serving in Vietnam, according to military historians Gabriel and Savage. They say:

> the officer corps grew in inverse proportion to its quality ... [and] could be described as both bloated in number and poorer in quality. ... One result was My Lai. Even the staunchest defenders of the Army agree that in normal times a man of Lieutenant Calley's low intelligence and predispositions would never have been allowed to hold a commission. ... The lowering of standards was a wound that the officer corps inflicted on itself (Gabriel and Savage, 1978, p. 10).

They also detailed the way that the senior officer corps successfully managed to position themselves far from the action.

By contrast, the identification process is enhanced in those production firms where managers have closer contact with their workforce on the shop-floor and in the cafeteria, often wearing the same company uniform. This pattern is the opposite of distancing employees. It is usually noted in the context of observing how unique it is considered, as in the *New York Times* article (Hicks, 1992) about the CEO of US Steel, featured on the first page of the Business Section. Thomas Usher, it reported, took the unusual step of unexpectedly going to the offices of the United Steelworkers at the company's largest mill in Gary, Indiana. What he said there was not as interesting as the fact of his being there. In acknowledging that, Mr Usher commented that:

> Our long-term interests are exactly the same. Whether you are a manager or a member of the union, everyone wants to do a good job. ... I think there is a growing realization that we are not going to make it without the union and the union ... without us. (Hicks, 1992, p. D3).

The Usher view does not seem to represent a common one among corporate executives. Indeed, the founder of Total Quality Management (TQM), W. Edwards Deming (1992), contended that the enormous financial incentives that corporate executives receive have destroyed team work at many American companies.

[As presented in Chapters 1 and 14 here, there are leaders who have become so removed from followers' perceptions and needs that they may cease to be aware of how their actions affect the 'team' they wish to foster. Examples of this tendency are seen in the issue of high compensation packages given to American CEOs (see Byrne et al., 1991; Crystal, 1991) even when there are poor outcomes for their firms.]

Management performance decrements can also have calamitous effects on the organization and others, but not necessarily on the rewards given to these managers, as revealed in Crystal's (1991) book, *In Search of Excess*. Responsibility for performance is often detached from them so that rewards rise even with poor team and organizational outcomes. An [early] case in point is seen in Roger Smith's tenure from 1981 to 1990 as CEO of General Motors. During that time his company lost almost 20 per cent of its US market share. But, on his retirement, his already generous pension was increased to over a million dollars a year by the GM board.

Disparities and perceived inequities such as these make leaders even more likely to be objects of disdain or contempt. Though leaders are needed, they may also be resented for holding a position of authority and having special benefits that accompany it. Least of all are leaders who are not performing productively, but are still well rewarded, able to encourage good followership and team effort. Indeed, it is quite to the contrary when they violate an equity norm by failing to provide something of value, especially given loyalty and trust by followers.

On the larger issue of moral responsibility, Emler and Hogan say:

> There is no inbuilt tendency to use power responsibly. You cannot randomly allocate leadership responsibility and expect the interests of justice or society to be well served. Those in charge have a responsibility' to make moral decisions greater than those they command ... [and] those differences become more consequential the further up the hierarchy one goes (Emler and Hogan, 1991, p. 86).

Accordingly, a reasonable question, not asked enough in selecting leaders, is: What are the costs of putting this person in a position of authority and responsibility? (Hollander, 1992b, p. 43). The followers' perceptions of the leader's actions and motives have broader ethical and performance consequences. These include obvious instances of unfairness, self-seeking at others' expense, weakness, vacillation, and outright misconduct, all of which undermine the leader's standing and the vital bonds within the team.

The leader role is still seen more often as power over others, rather than as stewardship, or even as a service to others (see DePree, 1989). Not least there is the very real problem of what Drucker (1988) calls 'misleaders' who are dysfunctional. From a ten-year perspective, DeVries (1992) estimates that the base rate for executive incompetence is at least 50 per cent. Hogan, Raskin and Fazzini (1990) found that organizational climate studies from the mid-1950s onwards show 60 to 75 per cent of organizational respondents reporting their immediate supervisor as the worst or most stressful aspect of their job.

Such findings highlight the importance of followers as perceivers with expectations of and attributions about leader performance. Lord and Maher (1990) say that these perceptions are checked against prototypes held by followers and expectations of how leaders should perform. Positive or negative outcomes are more likely to be attributed to a leader's action, as seen in the concept of the 'romance of leadership' (Meindl, Ehrlich, & Dukerich, 1985). In summary, Argyle and Henderson (1985) indicated that the rules for superiors include planning and assigning work efficiently, informing, advising, and encouraging them (p. 261).

## CHARISMATIC, TRANSFORMATIONAL, AND TRANSACTIONAL LEADERSHIP

Renewed interest in charisma, now associated with transformational (TF) leadership (Burns, 1978; Bass, 1985), also shows how important it is to learn about the followers' perspective in understanding such phenomena. Originally Max Weber (1946) conceived of charismatic leaders as attracting others because of their "strong appeal and extraordinary determination," especially in time of crisis. But Weber also stated that if the leader was "long unsuccessful, above all if his leadership fails to benefit followers, it is likely that his charisma will disappear" (p. 360).

There also is a need to take account of the ethical distinction Burns (1978) made between the self-serving and socially responsible kinds of transformational leaders. In the world of organizations, as well as in politics, charismatic leaders are still sought as saviors. But they also may present difficulties, such as tendencies toward narcissism (e.g. Post, 1986) and unethical behavior. For example, Howell and Avolio (1992) cite the dubious ethical standards associated with such business leaders as Robert Campeau, John DeLorean, and Michael Milkin, all of whom were acknowledged to have charisma for many of their followers. Unethical leaders are more likely to use their charisma for power over followers, directed toward self-serving ends, usually in a calculated manipulative way. Ethical leaders are considered to use their charisma in a socially constructive way to serve others.

Charisma and transformational leadership are frequently linked in the literature. Transactional leadership (TA) refers to a fair exchange in which the leader gives something to followers and receives esteem and latitude for action in return (Homans, 1961). Charisma may not necessarily be part of TF leadership, but it is routinely imputed to the TF leader as, for example, in Bass's first aspect of TF and in House and Shamir's (1993) work. However, the research by Ehrlich, Meindl, and Viellieu (1990) suggests that "more transactionally oriented activities by a leader may also contribute to a leader's charismatic appeal" (p. 242). They also note, "Conceptually, the basis for either form of leadership is a relational and perceptual exchange developed between a leader and his or her subordinates" (p. 231).

The actuality of this transaction between leader and followers is usually denied in accounting for the TF phenomenon. Instead, there is an insistence on a rigid dichotomy between TA and TF leadership, maintained by considering only tangible rewards and failing to acknowledge the intangible ones followers receive from TF as well as TA leaders. Yet, Chemers (1993) contends that the intrinsic reward of "self-esteem, a sense of purpose, or salvation ... becomes highly attractive, and supremely motivating' when followers' needs are intense enough. Under such circumstances charismatic or transformational leadership may be seen as a special, elevated case of the more mundane transactional exchange processes that are the basis of all, person-to-person, team leadership" (p. 312).

TF leaders do provide rewards to followers, as Bass (1985) notes, listing personal attention and intellectual stimulation. However, the followers' reciprocation to the leader is usually unacknowledged since, that would support the view that a transaction has occurred. This would breach the artificial separation of measures that is maintained by Bass (1985), through that process of labeling TA leadership in a stripped-down form rather than as originally described. Curphy (1993), for example, found that TF and TA leadership were not independent, but were highly related in ratings given by cadets to their squadron commanding officer at the US Air Force Academy.

In sum, TF leadership can be seen as an extension of TA leadership, in which there is greater leader intensity and follower arousal. This amounts to having a large fund of credits accorded to the leader by followers, thereby granting esteem and more sway in being influential. Finally, to achieve a responsive following it is essential at the outset to establish and build upon TA leadership before expecting an adequate response to TF leadership.

[At this point, research on "critical incidents" dealing with relational qualities of leadership is reported. Since it appears elsewhere in this book, it has been omitted.]

## SUMMARY AND CONCLUSIONS

We are now in an era where a more active role for followership is clearly evident. This includes a team emphasis and the implementation of empowerment systems, through delegation and participative decision making. It represents an alternative to traditional power conceptions of leadership and followership.

Leaders and their qualities are still important, but particularly in how those qualities engage followers in productive and mutually satisfying teams. This marks a departure from the usual way of seeing leader qualities as possessions instead of interpersonal links with others involved in mutual pursuits.

CHAPTER 13

# Legitimacy, Power, and Influence

*A Perspective on Relational Features of Leadership*

## COMMENTARY

The paper presented in this chapter deals with the significant place of legitimacy in determining a leader's relationship with followers. It also provides an opportunity to cover some of the historical, conceptual, and research literature that bears on the subject, including the work of Katz and Kahn (1966) and the contribution of Likert (1961). As stated at the outset of the paper, "legitimacy implicates such qualities as credibility, trust, loyalty, and the leader's ability to be effective in exercising power and influence." This conception comes directly from my early book, *Leaders, Groups, and Influence* (1964). During the era when I was preparing that book, I had several occasions to speak with Fred Fiedler, whose contingency model was just being developed. I recall a conversation with him in Chicago at the Midwestern Psychological Association meeting, where I favored having the element of power given equal consideration as an important variable in leader-follower relations. I have always found him, as then, an interested and accessible colleague.

The chapter presented here was commissioned originally as a paper presented at a leadership conference at Claremont-McKenna College to honor Fred Fiedler. His former student, Martin Chemers, was at the time Kravis Professor of Leadership there, and a leading figure in the leadership studies field. Chemers assembled these presentations into a book coedited with Roya Ayman, his former doctoral student at the University of Utah. She is a contributor in her own right to this field, at the Industrial Organizaiton faculty of the Illinois Institute of Technology (IIT).

Fiedler and I were on an American Psychological Association committee in the early 1960s, for which we made a joint presentation to the U.S. Government Personnel Directors on leadership issues, including matters of selection.

The chapter reproduced here has been abridged to remove some of the redundancy with other chapters in this book, in such matters as idiosyncrasy credit, for instance. It still coheres well as a statement of the importance of taking account of the follower role, in what has come to be called "inclusive leadership." As stated elsewhere here, there are leadership functions that can be performed by those not designated by that name, but who are responsible for such things as planning, adjudicating conflict, representing their group, as well as decision making, in delegated areas. This conception is much more in keeping with the reality of organizational life, needed in the modern world.

Abridged from E. P. Hollander. "Legitimacy, Power, and Influence: A Perspective on Relational Features of Leadership." In M. Chemers and R. Ayman, (Eds.), (1993), *Leadership theory and research: Perspectives and directions*. San Diego: Academic Press, chap. 2, (pp. 29–46). With permission from Elsevier Ltd.

## INTRODUCTION

Leadership is not something a leader possesses so much as a process involving followership. Without followers, there plainly are no leaders or leadership. Yet, far less attention has been given to followers, who accord or withdraw support to leaders. Much of the literature on the study of leadership, while ostensibly focused on the effects of the leader, neglects to acknowledge or even recognize the important role of followers in defining and shaping the latitudes of a leader's action.

By their role in legitimating leadership, followers affect the strength of a leader's influence, the style of a leader's behavior, and the performance of the group, through processes of perception, attribution, and judgment. In short, influence and power flow from legitimacy, which is in several ways determined or affected by followers, and their response to leaders. Although leader legitimacy has to do initially with how a leader attains that status, Read (1974) observed that it goes on to involve a complex interaction of attitudes toward the leader and source of authority, with a leader's behavior contributing substantially to influence and continuing legitimacy (p. 203).

As Stewart (1982) has noted, leadership operates within the constraints and opportunities presented by followers. The constraints include the expectations and perceptions of followers which can influence leaders (Hollander, 1985, 1986; Lord & Maher, 1990). Also noteworthy is how follower expectations about leader qualities can affect who is seen to be appropriate for the role (see Lord, DeVader, & Alliger, 1986).

An early proponent of the general view that followers are crucial to any leadership event, and deserve more attention, was Fillmore Sanford (1950). Sanford said, "There is some justification for ... arguing that research directed at the follower will eventually yield a handsome pay-off. Not only is it the follower who accepts or rejects leadership, but it is the follower who perceives both the leader and the situation and reacts in terms of what he perceives" (p. 4). Mary Parker Follett expressed a related point, tied to her concept of "power with," in a paper delivered at the University of London in the early 1930s (Follett, 1949). She asserted that it is the dynamic between the leader and the follower that is critical in team success, and not the ability of the leader to dominate his or her followers.

Another reason for attending to followers is that they are most likely to know the actuality of the leader's approach to leadership, as lived out in daily events. Useful to understanding this process, therefore, is to study seriously the followers' perspective on it. The importance of this departure has become increasingly evident in recent work on leadership, especially as it affects successful or unsuccessful outcomes (see Hollander and Offermann, 1990 [Ch. 11 in this volume]; Kelley, 1988).

This chapter examines the leader-follower relationship both historically and conceptually, and brings into focus its role in contemporary developments in leadership study. As already indicated, legitimacy plays a pivotal part in this relationship because it affects how followers perceive and respond to the leader. Among its manifestations, legitimacy implicates such qualities as credibility, trust, loyalty, and the leader's ability to be effective in exercising power and influence.

## THE RELATIONSHIP OF LEADERSHIP AND FOLLOWERSHIP

Although leadership and followership have traditionally been seen in highly differentiated terms, they represent interdependent, reciprocal systems. Fundamental to them is a process of exchange "... in which the leader both gives something and gets something. The leader provides a *resource* in terms of adequate role behavior directed toward the group's goal attainment, and in return receives greater influence associated with status, recognition, and esteem [contributing to] 'legitimacy' in making influence assertions and in having them accepted" (Hollander & Julian, 1969, p. 388). In a fundamental way, a leader's legitimacy depends upon his or her standing with followers.

Leadership and followership also can both be active roles, considering the reality that hierarchical organizations require both functions at every level. The usual expectation of the follower role as essentially passive is misleading when considering followership as an accompaniment to leadership. Leaders do command greater attention and influence, but there now is an increasing realization that followers can affect leaders actively in more than trivial ways, if only because followers are usually the leader's most attentive strategic audience.

The role of follower therefore can be seen to hold within it the potential of leadership, and behaviors found to represent effective leadership in fact include attributes of good followership (see Hollander & Webb, 1955; Kouzes & Posner, 1987) such as dependability, competence, and honesty. Even with an imbalance of power, influence can be exerted in both roles, as part of a social exchange (Homans, 1961). Effective leadership is more likely to be achieved by a process in which there is reciprocity and the potential for two-way influence and power sharing, rather than a sole reliance on power over others.

Power and influence are not the same, though they are at times used as virtual synonyms. Classically, power is considered to be the ability to exert some degree of control over other persons, things and events. In institutional terms, it is associated with authority relationships, and actual or implied coercion. By contrast, influence involves more persuasion, with the recipient having latitude for a free choice, rather than be subject to imposed authority. Regarding these distinctions, I noted further elsewhere:

While power and influence constitute different processes, they are intertwined insofar as leaders may use both depending upon the circumstances and the particular followers involved. Even appointed leaders, "put in charge" within an organization, must rely on influence, in the sense of persuasion, as much as or more than on power. The unfettered use of power can be highly dysfunctional in creating numerous points of resistance and lingering negative feelings. Therefore both elected and appointed leaders are called upon to use persuasion in many instances, instead of the full power supposedly at their disposal (Hollander, 1985, p. 489).

Information can legitimate power over others when its possessors provide a definition of reality, even when it is not factually based. Although this may have the appearance of persuasion, it is more indicative of dependence, which is associated with leaders as "meaning makers," in Conger's (1990) usage. In a still larger sense, leaders define situations for followers. Yet followers must be willing to "buy" that definition, which in the broadest sense means accepting a "vision," with associated values. At its pinnacle, this involves strong identification with the leader.

Within an organizational context, such definitions would include dealing with the task at hand, interpreting pertinent history, resource allocation, competition vs. cooperation, as well as fostering other psychological states. Important among the latter, for instance, is how conflict is viewed, approached and resolved. On the international level, the implications of this process have been recognized by behaviorally oriented political scientists. Richard Snyder and his colleagues (1962), among others, stated what seems increasingly plain, that "the key to the explanation of why the state behaves as it does lies in the way its decision-makers define their situation" (p. 51), not just for themselves but for their populace as well (see also Jervis, 1976).

In a line of work on "groupthink" phenomena extending back almost two decades, Janis (1972) examined the process by which decisions may be flawed by a too loyal acceptance of a particular reality, or set of options, from a leader. In his later work, *Crucial Decisions*, Janis (1989) elaborated this analysis to scrutinize the leader's *selective* information-seeking and other *uncorrected* processes of reaching decisions in a crisis. He found that such bad outcomes can be traced to excessive reliance on the leader's judgement, as occurs with intense identification such as is said to occur in charismatic leadership.

## TRANSACTIONAL MODELS OF LEADERSHIP

Process-oriented "transactional" models of leadership developed largely from a social exchange perspective, emphasizing the implicit relational qualities of the transaction that exists between leader and followers, which yields effectiveness (see Hollander, 1964, 1978; Hollander & Julian, 1968, 1969; Homans, 1961). The transactional view considers that a leader gives benefits to followers, such as direction, vision, recognition, and other esteem needs that are reciprocated by followers in heightened responsiveness to that leader. Hence, the transactional approach accords a more active role to followers, who rather than simply being coerced and complying, have the potential for perceiving and influencing a leader in a two-way influence relationship.

As another approach within social exchange/transactional models, Graen (1975) developed the Leader Member Exchange (LMX) Model of leader-follower relations, emphasizing role-making between a leader and particular followers (see Dienesch & Liden, 1986; Graen & Scandura, 1987). In brief, the LMX model distinguishes between the relationships a leader has with followers who are close to the leader and those who are more distant. The first have a better quality relationship with the leader, but also have higher expectations for their loyalty and performance; the others receive fewer personal demands from the leader, but also fewer rewards. Liden and Graen (1980), for instance, found that subordinates reporting a high-quality relationship with their supervisors assumed more job responsibility, contributed more, and were rated as higher performers than those with low-quality relationships.

Generally, transactional models center on the followers' perceptions of and expectations about the leader's actions and motives, in accordance with attributional analysis. Heider's (1958) earlier work on the attribution of intentions through interpersonal perception exemplifies this analysis in the distinction between "can" and "will." If a leader is perceived to be able to achieve a favorable outcome, but doesn't because of an apparent failure of will, this causes a greater loss of following than the reverse, that is, an inability to achieve something desirable but with an evident try, nonetheless. Conveying a positive intention is redeeming to a degree, in instances where legitimacy may be threatened.

## IDIOSYNCRASY CREDIT

Another social exchange concept, the "idiosyncrasy credit" model of innovative leadership (Hollander, 1958, 1964), deals with legitimacy functionally as the latitude followers provide a leader to bring about change. [Since the IC Model is described elsewhere here, this section has been reduced substantially. It is a dynamic process of interpersonal evaluation and, as noted in Chapter 16 here, is nonnormative. Contrary to a possible misconception, it does *not* tell *how* things *ought* to be but reflects more how they seem to be, in relatively noncoercive, less power-oriented situations.]

The essential formulation in the model is that credits are earned over time in the perceptions of others by *competence* in helping to achieve the group's task goals, and *conformity* to the group's norms, as a sign of loyalty. Credits may then be drawn on to take innovative actions in line with expectations associated with the leader's role. This yields the prospect that *early signs of competence and conformity will permit later nonconformity, in the form of innovations, to be better tolerated*. This formulation was first verified in an experiment with groups of male engineering students in a group-decision task (Hollander, 1960a), and has subsequently been supported elsewhere (Hollander, 1961b), with some qualifications to be noted.

The idea of credit is embedded in our everyday language in such general terms as "receiving credit," "taking credit," and "being discredited." In its refinement, the idiosyncrasy credit model (IC) illustrates how credits accumulate and have operational significance in permitting innovations that would be perceived to be "deviations" if introduced by another person with less credit. Seniority can contribute to the accumulation of credits, but without uniform impact. A person may also benefit by having "derivative credit," as in a favorable reputation from another group, or from the society at large, as in high socio-economic status. Most usually, however, a new member of a group is in a poor position to assert influence, especially in the direction of change, unless he or she has a unique qualification. An example would be an idea that helps deal with a major group problem, or a badly needed skill. In these circumstances the new member's credit is gained by maximizing on the competence factor. But credit may not accrue as readily to those who are perceived to be different, as in the case of a woman in an otherwise male group (see Wahrman & Pugh, 1974).

Unless stigmatized, therefore, credit may result from calling attention to oneself in a positive way. This has been found to be associated with initial quantity of participation, which is perceived positively as a sign of a group member's motivation. In their experiment on this process, Sorrentino and Boutillier (1975) found that later contributions were more likely to be evaluated for quality.

Unused credits can be lost by failing to fulfill follower expectations for the leader role, including inaction in the face of need. Also, the leader's self-serving and other negatively viewed behaviors can drain credits, as can perceptions of weak motivation, incompetence, and the responsibility for failure (cf. Alvarez, 1968). [Nonconformity can be an initial source of attention-getting, as Ridgeway (1981) has found.]

Underlying the IC Model is a recognition that a process of making attributions is significant to accepting influence. The same behavior seen to be nonconforming if shown by one group member may not be so perceived when displayed by another. In short, nonconformity is defined within a group context, and the particular actor perceived within it, especially regarding his or her status (see Hollander 1958, 1961). In addition, nonconformity can be viewed with regard to the common expectancies applied generally as a norm for group members, and the particular expectancies applied to a high-status member. Accordingly, leaders may initiate change, perhaps in seemingly nonconforming ways, but be fulfilling an accepted innovative role. While there may be greater tolerance of nonconformity for the high-status member in some ways, there are restrictions imposed regarding particular expectancies, which can be thought of as role behaviors.

At least two reasons explain why these restrictions may be imposed: first, because status is usually perceived to carry with it greater self-determination, those of higher status are assumed to be more responsible for their actions; second, having greater status means having more potential for influencing important outcomes for the members of a group (Hollander, 1964, ch. 20). More generally, Nemeth and Wachtler (1983) have found that influence is more likely to be determined by who holds a particular position rather than by its accuracy. For example, Torrance (1955) earlier found in three-man aircrews that if the correct answer to a problem was held by the lowest status group member (the gunner), it was least likely to be accepted by the others (the pilot and navigator). Here again, attributions of legitimacy play a determinant role in authority and the acceptance of influence.

## FEATURES AND EFFECTS OF LEADER LEGITIMACY

Crucial to legitimacy is how followers perceive the leader's source of authority, and then respond to that leader. The evidence indicates that a major difference exists in the realm of appointment or election as sources of a leader's authority. In both cases, the possibility of being perceived to be a leader, and acting as one, depends to some degree on validation by those who are to be followers.

In an early experiment varying the basis of legitimacy, Goldman and Fraas (1965) had leaders in male groups selected by three methods: election by a group vote, appointment after selection with a measure of ability, or appointment randomly, plus a control condition without a leader. The task used was the game "Twenty Questions," and the dependent measures were time required, and number of questions needed, to reach a solution. Groups with leaders appointed for their competence performed best, with those having elected leaders performing a close second. Groups with randomly appointed leaders and no leaders showed poorer performance, which was attributed to the weak basis of their legitimacy (Hollander, 1986).

The election case is of course an obvious instance of emergence, which more closely approximates the IC Model. Moreover, election usually creates a heightened psychological identification between followers and the leader, with followers having a greater sense of responsibility for and investment in the leader. One explanation is to view this as a social exchange in which the group gives the leader a "reward" in advance, by electing him or her, and then group members feel a claim on him or her to "pay back" by producing favorable outcomes (Jacobs, 1970).

Correspondingly, it is also true that the support of followers exacts a higher demand on the leader. Elected leaders who fail to perform well have been found to be more vulnerable to criticism than appointed leaders, particularly if they are seen to be competent in the first place (Hollander & Julian, 1970, 1978). Although election and appointment may create different psychological climates between leaders and followers, this does not deny the very real possibility that organizational leaders may attain a "following" by doing more than exercising authority. As Katz and Kahn (1978) have observed, organizational leadership is "the influential increment over and above mechanical compliance with ... routine directives" (p. 528).

An experiment on source of authority by Hollander, Julian, and Sorrentino (1969) studied the effects on appointed or elected leaders of disagreements with their followers. Cast within the IC Model, the intent was to determine the leader's willingness to deviate from group decisions about the ranking of programs to alleviate typical urban problems in a city called "Collosus." A "strong" or "not strong" support treatment cut across the condition of leader election or appointment. Figure 13.1 shows that elected leaders who had been told they had strong group support were significantly more likely to make total reversals of their group's decision—indeed for about half the critical trials—than were those in the other conditions. In addition, elected leaders with strong support showed lower conciliation in their responses to group judgments, based on a content analysis of their messages to the group. Evidently, the elected leader in this condition felt freer to expend their credits by challenging group judgments.

A subsequent series of experiments in our laboratory pursued this line of research on source of authority. In one of these (Hollander, Fallon, & Edwards, 1977), four-man college student groups were studied whose leaders were appointed or elected and whose members were told either that they had done well ("success") or had not done well ("failure") right after their first phase of activity. The task used was the same "Collosus" urban problems one in the experiment just discussed.

In general, it was found that elected leaders had more influence on the group rankings than did appointed ones. Furthermore, the influence of elected but not appointed leaders increased after the initial failure feedback and decreased after success feedback. This effect was interpreted via Hamblin's (1958) concept that a "crisis," in this case created through an apparent failure, produces the effect of "rallying around" the elected leader, at least initially. In the success condition, with no crisis, group members acted out of a greater security in their

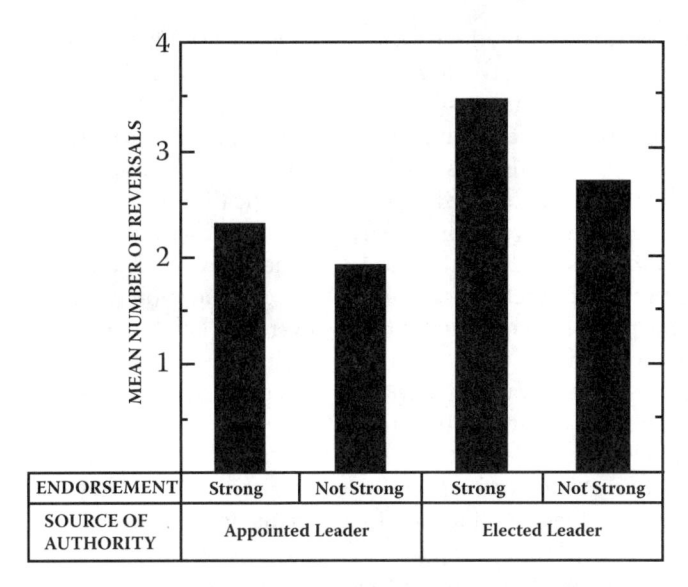

**Figure 13.1** Mean number of seven critical trials on which leaders reversed team's first rank choice in four experimental treatments, N = 10 Ss for each. Elected leaders deviated from their teams significantly more than appointed leaders, and in each case strong endorsement tended to increase this deviation. (From Hollander, E. P., Julian, J. W., & Sorrentino, R. M. (1969). The leader's sense of constructive deviation. ONR Technical Report No. 12, Buffalo: SUNY/Buffalo Psychology Department. Reported in Hollander & Julian (1970), p. 143.)

own judgements, and the leader did not gain that benefit. When the groups were studied for still another phase, however, the elected leader in the failure condition showed a distinct loss of status, with credits depleted and followers willing to depose him. Interestingly, before the group learned how they were performing, a group member could be identified who was gaining influence as the likely successor to the elected leader. That member emerged as the group's choice when another election was held after the failure had persisted (Hollander, 1986, p. 47).

Also relevant are the processes occurring within a group or organization by appointment or election, and the leader's psychological connection to followers. To study these, another experiment (Ben-Yoav, Hollander, & Carnevale, 1983) was done, again using the same urban problems task. Primary attention was on interaction processes in four-man college groups with appointed or elected leaders. They were directly studied by having two observers independently rate the groups, at 90 degrees from one another, behind one-way vision mirrors. Post-interaction measures were also obtained. Elected leaders were found to be significantly more likely to contribute to group discussion. They also received higher ratings from followers on responsiveness to their needs, interest in the group task, and competence. This finding accords with the IC model regarding effects from the leader's source of authority, though suitable attention is needed to the setting, task, and particulars of the group's composition.

To look again at the way leaders react to followers under appointment of election conditions, Elgie, Hollander, and Rice (1988) did an experiment on leader evaluations of followers displaying each of four types of behavior. These were the combinations of either positive or negative subordinate feedback with either high or low task activity. [It is reported here in Chapter 6.] The dependent measure was a composite score made up of ten semantic differential ratings of each follower.

Because they are likely to have a greater sense of commitment and indebtedness to their groups, it was expected that elected leaders would react more favorably to high than to low performing followers, with less marked differences for appointed leaders. Based on Fiedler's (1972, 1978) proposal that leader motives are most clearly revealed under stressful conditions that pose a serious threat to leader goals, it was predicted that high activity followers who gave negative feedback would represent the greatest condition of stress. Therefore, we expected that the lowest evaluations of followers would be for the combination of high activity and negative feedback, especially with appointed leaders. This outcome was predicted because of the heightened threat to their status, and the likely consequence of then giving such followers lower evaluations than elected leaders would give. A three-way interaction supported the prediction that elected and appointed leaders would respond differently to high and low activity followers, especially under the negative feedback condition. In general, a main effect showed that elected leaders were more positive than appointed leaders in judgments of their followers, in the manner predicted.

Taken as a whole, the main thread running through these results is the difference in support and involvement that was manifest in the two kinds of leader legitimacy conditions. While both may involve a social exchange process, it may be more evident in leader-follower relations when the leader is elected. But it also is present with appointed leaders, as seen in the work of Graen and others (see Graen, 1975; Dienesch & Liden, 1986).

## ATTRIBUTIONS ABOUT LEADER QUALITIES AND PERFORMANCE

A modern-day framework for the credit-building process is evident in attribution theory, which speaks to follower attributions about a leader that incline them to respond affirmatively or otherwise to that leader. This framework of study is part of the great attention being given to cognitive elements in leader-follower relations, represented by follower "implicit leadership theories" (ILT's), among other concepts (see Calder, 1977; Lord et al., 1986; Rush et al., 1977). Lord & Maher (1988) say that perceptions of a leader are checked against prototypes followers hold of leader attributes, such as intelligence, and expectations of how leaders should perform.

One consequence of the attributional approach is to make more explicit the significance of followers' and others' perceptions of the leader, not least regarding expectations about leader competence and motivation. Realistically, imagery and self-presentation may still obscure the truth about the leader's intentions and dealings, yet there remains the basic question of the degree to which followers are able to evaluate the leader.

The usefulness of the follower's perspective, as an avenue to understanding leadership, is illustrated by the work on "derailment" by McCall, Lombardo and Morrison (1988). They studied four hundred promising managers, who were seen to be on a fast track. Those failing to reach their expected potential were mainly found to show various kinds of inconsiderate behavior toward others, but rarely to lack technical skills. With a sample of 2600 top level managers, Kouzes and Posner (1987) looked at qualities these managers admired in their leaders. Among the most frequently chosen qualities were being honest and providing inspiration, in addition to being competent and forward-looking. Here again the interpersonal or relational realm was viewed as playing a significant role.

In a study using critical incidents and rating scales with 201 organizational respondents, Hollander and Kelly (1990) found that relational qualities were emphasized in the rewards distinguishing good from bad leadership. The four relational qualities that most differentiated the two were scales of perceptiveness, involvement, trustworthiness, and rewardingness. Positive rewards of sensitivity to followers, support, and praise dominated good but were absent or negative in bad leadership.

[At this point, discussion of "Charisma and Transformational Leadership" is omitted, since it is discussed elsewhere here, in Chapter 12, among other places.]

## SOME IMPLICATIONS AND CONCLUSIONS

Granting the importance of leaders, a major implication of the presentation here is that their legitimacy is based on their relationship with followers. Specifically, the involvement of followers has to be recognized as a key component of effective leadership. The long-standing emphasis on the extent of leader ascendance, whether through assertions of influence or power, is not sufficient to address these broader concerns. Otherwise, the study of leadership becomes captive again of its leader-centered origins. That consideration makes relational skills such as responsiveness to followers an important requisite to these leadership roles. In its place, however, imagery and other devices may be employed manipulatively, as when intense emotions are aroused.

Whatever power is imputed to an organizational role, actualizing it depends upon its perception by followers. Power becomes real when others perceive it to be so, and respond accordingly. But an emphasis on power over others tends to give it greater salience, at the expense of empowerment and resistance to unwanted power assertions, which we have called "power to" and "power from" (Hollander & Offermann, 1990). In that paper, we reviewed and assessed research on organizational leadership and power. Among other things we considered are the benefits of, and sources of resistance to, delegation and empowerment of followers. On balance, we found that by sharing power and allowing followers to influence them, leaders foster leadership skills in others, as well as achieve other gains through their greater participation and involvement. But a major question posed is how a return to leader-centered approaches can be reconciled with this trend toward greater follower empowerment and influence.

In sum, the main implication here is to accord a more active role for those who are followers. Every benefit need not be seen to depend upon the leader. Initiatives need not be expected to come only from the leader, though the leader can be a facilitator of them. Indeed, being a leader and being a follower need not be viewed as sharply exclusive categories. Understanding the relational nature of leadership opens up richer forms of involvement and rewards in groups, organizations, and society at large.

# CHAPTER 14

# Ethical Challenges in the Leader-Follower Relationship

## COMMENTARY

Ethics and power are interrelated elements in leader-follower relations. As stated here before, leadership and followership are interdependent, as exemplified by the value attached to teamwork. Ethics represent what can be considered "fair play," as valued elements essential to developing loyalty and trust in this relationship. However, because of their need to maintain power and its claim on self-serving benefits, leaders can be detached from how their actions are perceived and reacted to by followers.

From a critical standpoint, Rost (1991) says that an emphasis on management is considered to be the essence of effective leadership in organizations. Why that is so likely is open to debate. However, it helps to explain a basis in part for the enormous differential in pay for CEOs and other top executives, as mentioned in Chapter 1, and in the paper presented in this chapter, which was published in the mid-1990s. The gap has widened immensely since then. This pattern is also revealed in the way that organizational psychology, a field with which I am identified, has been criticized (see, e.g., Ciulla, 1998).

Especially damaging to teamwork is the case of leaders continuing to receive disproportionate rewards despite their poor performance. This damage occurs too when top executives are discharged with large "golden parachutes," when failing, and even in the context of corporate layoffs and downsizing they have instituted before departing.

Equity, responsibility, and accountability in the exercise of power are precious commodities, about which Emler and Hogan (1991) were quoted earlier. Simon has made this observation in that vein: "Leaders should exercise power, but enjoying it is another, and more dangerous, matter" (1991, pp. 248–249). Mulder (1971) has dealt with the phenomenon of "power distance," which keeps followers from participating and the leader in control of activities and benefits. In contrast to this top-down mode of leading, which I have called "leader centric," there is the potential for shared functions and dispersed decision making in other arrangements. Drucker (1997) has anticipated these alternatives in his many writings.

The paper presented here is based on a presentation made on July 8, 1993, in the Ethics Symposium at the Sixteenth annual Scientific Meeting of the International Society of Political Psychology, Cambridge, Massachusetts. It appeared in E. P. Hollander, "Ethical challenges in the leader-follower relationship" (*Business Ethics Quarterly,* 1995, 5(1), 55–65).

From "Ethical Challenges in the Leader-Follower Relationship." *Business Ethics Quarterly,* 1995, 5(1), 55–65. Reprinted with permission of the Philosophy Documentation Center.

Various streams of thought have converged on the concept of leadership as a process rather than a person or state. This process is essentially a shared experience, a voyage through time, with benefits to be gained and hazards to be surmounted by the parties involved. A leader is not a sole voyager, but a key figure whose actions or inactions can determine others' well-being and the broader good. It is not too much to say that communal social health, as well as achieving a desired destination, are largely influenced by a leader's decisions and the information and values upon which they are based.

The leadership process is therefore especially fraught with ethical challenges. Hodgkinson (1983) considers leadership to be "intrinsically valuational," as "philosophy-in-action." He says, "Logic may set limits for and parameters within the field of value action but value phenomena determine what occurs within the field. They are indeed the essential constituents of the field of executive action. ... If this were not true then leadership behavior could be routinized and, ultimately, computerized" (p. 202). John Gardner (1990) too sees values as part of "the moral framework that permits us to judge some purposes as good and others as bad" in leadership (pp. 66–67). Rost (1991) stresses the place of ethics in leadership regarding both process and ends.

## THE CENTRALITY OF THE LEADER-FOLLOWER RELATIONSHIP

Evidence continues to accumulate about the importance of relational qualities in the unity of leadership-followership (e.g. Hollander, 1992a,b). A major component of the leader-follower relationship is the leader's perception of his or her self relative to followers, and how they in turn perceive the leader. This self-other perception implicates important ethical issues concerning how followers are involved, used or abused, especially in a relationship favoring a leader's power over them.

Within this dominance motif, followers are essentially seen to be compliant and manipulable in the extreme. An instance of this is a corporate CEO who said that "leadership is confirmed when the ability to inflict pain is demonstrated" (Menzies, 1980). Clearly such abuse of power runs counter to the idea of mutual dependency in a shared enterprise, and the value of maintaining personal dignity. Hurting people is usually not the way to get the best from them. Further, abuse deprives a leader of honest information and judgments from cowed subordinates. This can fuel the self-absorption and self-deception that are pitfalls of arbitrary power.

Nevertheless, the leader role is still seen as preeminent, often as *power over* others, rather than as a stewardship, or even as a *service to* others (see e.g., DePree, 1989). Not least there is the very real problem of what Drucker (1988) calls "misleaders" who are dysfunctional. From a ten-year perspective, DeVries (1992) estimates that the base rate for executive incompetence is at least 50%. Hogan, Raskin, and Fazzini (1990) found that organizational climate studies from the mid-1950s onward show 60% to 75% of organizational respondents reporting their immediate supervisor as the worst or most stressful aspect of their job.

Management performance decrements also can have calamitous consequences to the organization and to others, but not necessarily to the rewards given to these managers. Responsibility for performance is somehow detached from them. A corporation head like Roger Smith, chairman of General Motors from 1981 to 1990, is a good example. He presided over a phenomenal drop of almost 20% of his company's share of the U.S. market. For many there and elsewhere, Smith was considered to be rigid and unresponsive to the challenges of consumer needs and foreign competition. Asked by *Fortune* magazine to explain what went wrong, he replied, "I don't know. It's a mysterious thing." Commenting on this statement, Samuelson (1993) says, "As a society, we have spent the past decade paying for mistakes like Smith's" (p. 55). Yet the organization continued its reward pattern: on his retirement the GM board increased his already generous pension to over a million dollars a year.

This dysfunctional system contrasts with one that shows the discipline and unity of purpose represented in "teamwork" aimed at clear performance goals (see e.g., Hackman, 1989; Katzenbach & Smith, 1993). Achieving teamwork demands a concern for maintaining responsibility, accountability, authenticity, and integrity in the leader-follower relationship. Indeed, the oft mentioned "crisis of leadership" usually reveals an absence of these elements (Hollander, 1978b). This normative position has distinctly functional value as a universal perspective applicable to the political *and* organizational spheres. Though this position comes out of a democratic ethos, its generality is evident in the organizational psychology literature on leadership (see e.g., Gardner, 1990; Hollander, 1978a; Manz & Sims, 1989).

## HISTORICAL CONTEXT

Followership is periodically rediscovered as important to leadership, despite a long tradition of usage. The term is variously employed by those who come upon it and declare anew that leadership cannot exist without followership. But the essence of the matter is to recognize that a leader-centric focus is inadequate to understanding the interdependence of leadership and active followership (see e.g., Hollander & Offermann, 1990; Kelley, 1988; Vanderslice, 1988).

In sixth century B.C. China, Lao Tzu wrote about the "wise leader" in his *Tao Te Ching* (see Schmidt, 1975). His philosophy makes a major contribution to the theme of sharing leadership with followers: "The wise leader settles for good work and then lets others have the floor. The leader does not take all the credit for what happens and has no need for fame" (Heider, p.162). Similarly, Hegel taught in the eighteenth century that the good leader must incorporate the experience and qualities of the follower, and demonstrate followership in leading.

The late nineteenth century European social philosophers showed recognition that leading involves a relational process with followers. Interest in crowd behavior, imitation, and the group mind were central to an ethos expressed most notably in the writings of Tarde (1890/1903) and LeBon (1896) in France. Both were influenced by Charcot, who drew to Paris such later eminences as Freud and Prince to study with him. Indeed, Prince called his *Journal of Abnormal and Social Psychology* by that name because he saw the two fields as inextricably linked, through his belief in Charcot's idea of the parallel between hypnotic states and the susceptibility of a mob to social influence. It was LeBon, however, who also reported the story of a man chasing after a crowd of protestors saying he had to catch them because he was their leader.

From otherwise different perspectives, Freud (1921) and Floyd Allport (1924) criticized LeBon's view of crowd behavior and, indirectly, Charcot's conception behind it. In *Group Psychology and the Analysis of the Ego* (1921) Freud developed his conception of the followers' identification with the leader as a shared ego-ideal. A significant disciple, Fromm (1941), extended this conception in personality terms, in his contention that, "the psychology of the leader and that of his followers, are, of course, closely linked with each other" (p. 65). Erikson (1975) made an associated point about this linkage in asserting that followers "join a leader and are joined together by him" (p.153).

## CHARISMA AND ITS EFFECTS

Contemporary with Freud's conception of the ego-ideal was the idea of the "charismatic leader," to whom followers are drawn by a special quality. Max Weber (1921), the German sociologist of bureaucracy fame, advanced the concept to account for the loyalty and devotion of followers who are emotionally tied to a leader, especially in a time of crisis (cf. House & Shamir, 1993).

Charisma is not an unmixed good. Hodgkinson (1983) says, "Beware charisma" (p. 187), and Howell and Avolio (1992) have observed the need to distinguish between ethical and unethical charismatic leaders. In the organizational sphere, they cite the dubious ethical standards associated with Robert Campeau, John DeLorean, and Michael Milken, all of whom were acknowledged to have charisma for many of their followers. Unethical leaders are more likely to use their charisma to enhance *power over* followers, directed toward self-serving ends, usually in a calculated manipulable way. Ethical leaders are considered to use their charisma in a socially constructive way to serve others.

When Burns (1978) advanced his concept of the "transforming leader," who changes the attitudes and behavior of followers, he regarded this as having a moral basis yielding beneficial ends. Yet, charisma is *the* quality often imputed to such leaders, though Burns says it "is so overburdened as to collapse under close analysis" (p. 243). Still, charisma has by now become a favored term of almost general approval. In the corporate world, as well as in politics, charismatic leaders are often sought as saviors. But they also may present difficulties, such as tendencies toward narcissism (e.g., Post, 1986) as well as unethical behavior.

Weber (1946) conceived charisma to be one part of acceptance by followers of a leader's various bases for claiming legitimacy, and said, "if his leadership fails to benefit followers, it *is* likely that his charisma will disappear" (p. 360). Barnard (1938) dealt with this issue in his "acceptance theory of authority," stating conditions that permitted a follower to judge an order as authoritative, thus raising the issue of legitimacy of power (see Hollander, 1993).

## THE CONTRAST BETWEEN POWER AND IDENTIFICATION

In his classic conception of powerholding, Kipnis (1976) identified four corrupting influences of power affecting the powerholder and those in a relationship with that individual. Briefly these "metamorphic effects" are: (1) power becomes desired as an end in itself, to be sought at virtually any cost; (2) holding power tempts the individual to use organizational resources for self-benefit, even illegally; (3) creates the basis for false feedback and an exalted sense of self-worth; (4) and a corresponding devaluation of others' worth, with a desire to avoid close contact with them. Mulder (1981) has extended the last point especially in his concept of "power distance." Such distance heightens the gap between leader and followers that exists because of disparities in available information or resources. This gap will be smaller where processes of identification and sharing occur.

Because well-being is at stake, other important features of this relationship are equity, equality, and need, with the potential for perception of injustice (see Deutsch, 1975). These issues are especially salient in a condition where one person depends on another with a great power difference between them. On this point, Emerson (1962) said that the explicit recognition of *dependence* by a lower power person on one of higher power can promote resentment by the former. This effect can undermine mutual efforts, though it has not received as much attention as more tangible rewards, such as markedly different economic benefits (see Bok, 1993). Clearly, the element of trust may be undercut by a leader's self-serving activity, especially the lack of accountability when he or she is manifestly failing.

## SELF-SERVING BIASES

Given their traditional superordinate role, leaders may be prone to self-serving biases beyond those that exist in other social relationships. In his analysis of some key psychological processes involved, Greenwald (1985) has presented an interpretation of how the leader's ego or self incorporates several distinctive cognitive biases. These include the self as focus of knowledge, "beneffectance" as the perception of responsibility for desired, but not undesired, outcomes, and resistance to change.

These tendencies are further enhanced by power over others and a sense of being different, with accompanying social distance, and potential manipulation of them as objects. A necessary corrective is for the leader to be attuned to the needs of followers, their perceptions and expectancies. However, the narcissism associated with leaders who draw on the affection of followers, as in "charismatic leadership," often deprives them of *this* corrective (see Post, 1986). As a counterpart, followers may be vulnerable to perceptual distortions as a feature of the self-serving bias and identification with the leader that can bolster the self (see Hollander, 1992b).

## MUTUAL IDENTIFICATION

An alternative view, more in keeping with responsive participation, considers the leader-follower relationship within a mutual identification motif. This includes the prospect of two-way influence, and the perception and counter-perception of leader and followers. Cantril (1958) has said that the leader must be able to perceive the reality worlds of followers and have sensitivity to guide intuitions, if a common consensus and mutual trust rather than "mere power, force, or cunning" are to develop and prevail (p. 129).

Identification with the leader *is* exemplified in Freud's (1921) concept of the leader as a shared "ego-ideal" with whom members of a group mutually identify. They have a common bond on which life itself may depend, as in the military. For instance, according to military historians Gabriel and Savage (1978), inadequate and inattentive leadership were found to be responsible for the failure to maintain "unit *cohesion*" in the U.S. Army serving in Vietnam. They say, "... the officer corps grew in inverse proportion to its quality ... (and) could be described as both bloated in number and poorer *in* quality. ... One result was My Lai. Even the staunchest defenders of the Army agree that in normal times a man of Lieutenant Calley's low intelligence and predispositions would never have been allowed to hold a commission ... The lowering of standards was a wound that the officer corps inflicted on itself" (p. 10). They also detail the way that the senior officer corps successfully managed to put themselves farther to the rear of action than before.

By contrast, this identification process is enhanced in those production firms where managers have closer contact with their work force on the shop floor, and in the cafeteria, often wearing the same company uniform. This pattern illustrates the opposite of distancing employees.

## JOINING OR DISTANCING FOLLOWERS

In April 1992, the first page of the *New York Times* Business Section (Hicks, 1992) featured a story about the CEO of U.S. Steel, Thomas Usher. He took the unusual step of unexpectedly going to the offices of the United Steelworkers at the company's largest mill in Gary, Indiana. What he said there was not as interesting as the *fact* of his being there. While acknowledging that, Usher commented that "Our long-term interests are exactly the same. Whether you are a manager or a member of the union, everyone wants to do a good job ... I think there is a growing realization that we are not going to make it without the union and the union ... without us" (p. D3).

The Usher view is evidently uncommon among corporate executives or it would not be so newsworthy. Indeed, the founder of Total Quality Management (TQM), W. Edwards Deming, believed that the enormous financial incentives they receive have destroyed teamwork at many American companies (1992).

Some leaders have become so removed from followers' perceptions and needs that they may cease to be aware of how their actions affect the "team" they wish to foster. A pertinent example of this is seen in the issue of high compensation packages given to American CEOs (see Byrne, et aI., 1991; Crystal, 1991). *Business Week, Forbes,* and *Fortune* are among the major business publications that recently featured articles on this issue.

Criticisms have centered on how these sums greatly exceed the pay of the average worker, as compared to foreign competitors, despite manifestly poor outcomes for some American firms. "In Japan, the compensation of major CEOs is 17 times that of average workers; in France and Germany, 23 to 25 times; in Britain, 35 times; in America, between 85 and 100-plus times. In 1990, CEO pay rose 7 percent while corporate profits fell 7 percent ... United Airlines' CEO ... received $18.3 million (1,200 times what a new flight attendant makes) [though] United's profits fell 71 percent" (Will, 1991).

Such disparities may produce even more alienation of followers from their leaders. Though leaders are recognized as needed, they also may be resented for having a position of authority that accords them special benefits, as seen now for instance in the contempt many hold for Members of Congress. Least of all, leaders whose performance is substandard, but who remain well-rewarded, are unable to encourage good followership by gaining and retaining loyalty and trust. Indeed, it is quite to the contrary, in part due to the inability to show concern for equity to followers.

On the same day that *The New York Times* (March 31,1993) reported major layoffs of even long-time employees at IBM, it also indicated the pay package for IBM's new CEO. It included $5 million as a bonus for signing, a basic annual salary of $2 million, plus other incentives that would be worth millions more. The article revealed the personal devastation of the employees leaving the company, and the likely psychological toll on those who survived this round of cuts.

Signs of off-the-scale executive compensation exist not only in the private sector, but also in the political realm. Congressional salaries have grown from $30,000 in 1967 to $130,000 in 1991, when they were most recently raised [2007 raised to approximately $177,000]. The average private sector salary has *not* increased in anything like that of Congress.

This pattern is observed to extend widely (see e.g., Bok, 1993). It is even seen in some charitable and non-profit organizations, and among some university presidents. In the first category is the well publicized case of the President of United Way of America whose annual salary and benefits, apart from other perquisites, approximated half a million dollars (Hevesi, 1992). Not long after these revelations, he reluctantly agreed to resign, at his Board's urging. Other disclosures were made about his self-dealing activities, including the appointment he created for his son as president of a spin-off firm to market United Way products. Then came word that the most recent president of the largest affiliate of United Way, the Tri-State (NY, NJ, Conn) division, had resigned in 1989 with a $3.3 million pension payment from that affiliate's funds. Its constituent groups voiced considerable displeasure when that fact surfaced, but much after the payment was made.

In 1991, the president of the University of Pittsburgh retired with a pension plan that included a multi-million dollar package plus a guaranteed annual salary of $309,000 for life. When members of the Pennsylvania Legislature, the primary funding source for the University, learned about it through the press, they expressed outrage at the scale of these payments and at having been by-passed by the Trustees who approved this package (Reeves, 1991). More pointedly, the campus community was understandably upset over the considerable sum of money given up from institutional funds, which engendered a great loss of confidence in the Trustees and their judgment.

## LEADER PERFORMANCE

As Drucker (1988) has long noted, leadership *is* performance. The central question is: what earns a favorable judgment on a leader's performance? Obviously one important answer has to do with success in achieving group goals. But such goals may be set by the leader who thereby defines—and may redefine—the criteria for judgment within the system. In the political sphere, notably the macro-leadership of the presidency, this is "setting the agenda," and frequently involves a process of "getting on the right side on an issue." This usually requires *value expression*, particularly in what the leader says about what is desirable and to be sought. The element of trust also contributes to allowing the leader latitude for action (see Hollander, 1992b).

Other things equal, positive or negative outcomes are more likely to be attributed to the leader, so that when things go wrong he or she is more readily faulted and even removed. In Pfeffer's (1977) causal attribution terms, leaders are symbols who can be fired to convey a sense of rooting out the basis for the problem. For Sartre "To be a leader is to be responsible," but the reality too often is that responsibility and accountability are lacking.

One effect of the attributional view is to make even more explicit the significance of how followers and others perceive the leader, not least regarding expectations about leader competence and motivation. A pointed example of this is shown in the work on "derailment" by McCall, Lombardo, and Morrison (1988) with four hundred promising managers, seen to be on a fast track. Those who failed to reach their expected potential were more often found to lack skills in relating to others, but not a deficit in their technical skills. Other research by Kouzes and Posner (1987), with a sample of 3400 organizational respondents, dealt with qualities they admired in their leaders, and also found the relational realm significant. Renewed interest in charisma, and now in transformational leadership (Bass, 1985), makes the followers' view even more appropriate for understanding these phenomena.

Hollander & Kelly (1990, 1992) used critical incidents, open-ended questions, and rating scales, to study responses to good and bad leadership. This research was done with 280 mainly organizationally-based respondents, half male and half female. It affirmed the major point that relational qualities were emphasized in reports and evaluations distinguishing good from bad leadership. Most notably, these included providing personal and professional support, communicating clearly as well as listening, taking needed action, and delegating.

Although this research is organizationally based, it has larger implications at the societal level, and resonates with ideas about the effects of power and distance. One point clearly is that leader characteristics have an effect on followers by shaping their perceptions and responses. Indeed, this link between perceptions and behavior tests the ethics of a leader's actions and other attributes as perceived by followers, and their response to those attributes (see e.g., Lord and Maher, 1990).

How the leader's self-presentation is perceived by followers has broader ethical and performance consequences. These include obvious instances of unfairness, self-seeking at others' expense, weakness, vacillation, and outright misconduct, all of which detract from the leader's standing with followers, as has been treated in part above. Emler and Hogan (1992) say, "There is no inbuilt tendency to use power responsibly. You cannot randomly allocate leadership responsibility and expect the interests of justice or society to be well served. Those in charge have a responsibility to make moral decisions greater than those they command ... (and) those differences become more consequential the further up the hierarchy one goes" (p. 86).

## CONCLUSIONS

Clearly there are ethical challenges in the use of authority and power. Among these are the destructive effects on the social contract between the leader and followers. Being a leader allows more influence and power over others' outcomes and events more broadly. The leader also has many benefits and privileges, including higher financial rewards and the freedom to keep at a distance, if desired. But these benefits come at the price of responsibility and accountability to followers (see Hollander, 1978b). Where the leader is seen to be power-oriented, exploitative, and self-serving, especially in the face of failures, the goal of mutual identification is hardly attainable. Instead, followers may feel alienated and ultimately take their allegiance elsewhere. That prospect poses an essential challenge today.

# CHAPTER 15

## The Balance of Leadership and Followership

### An Introduction

**WITH LYNN R. OFFERMANN**

## COMMENTARY

This Introduction covers some of the salient points that resonate well with the original 1990 paper by Offermann and myself in the *American Psychologist*, which appears in this book as Chapter 11. She and I worked together on the Kellogg Leadership Studies Project* (KLSP) for several years, beginning with a planning session in 1993, as conveners of the Leadership-Followership Focus Group. She generously arranged to have most of our meetings at George Washington University (GWU), and together we coedited this report on *The Balance of Leadership and Followership* (Hollander & Offermann, 1997). This publication brought together papers by Ann Howard, Peter Vaill, Lynn Offermann, and myself about our group's efforts.

From E. P. Hollander & L. R. Offermann (Eds.) (1997). *The Balance of Leadership and Followership*, Introduction. A Kellogg Leadership Studies Project Report from the Burns Academy of Leadership, University of Maryland, College Park, pp. 1–7. Reprinted with permission of the Burns Academy of Leadership.

## INTRODUCTION

The leadership-followership group held its initial meeting in November 1993 at the University of Maryland, College Park, with Lynn Offermann, Henry Sims, Peter Vaill, and Ed Hollander, as Convenor. We were joined by James MacGregor Burns and Georgia Sorenson for a time, then worked on a number of themes for further discussion, after having given them prior thought. Subsequently, beginning with our two meetings in April and September of 1994, we were joined respectively by David DeVries and then Ann Howard as new members, with Lynn sharing the Convenor functions with Ed, then taking over thereafter. Others who have participated with us at the annual KLSP meetings are Bobby Austin, Cynthia Cherrey, Barbara Kellerman, and Robert Kelley. At the outset, our central emphasis was clearly on the bases and features of active followership. Some of the major questions posed for considerations were: Why do

---

* In 1994, the W. K. Kellogg Foundation gave a grant to the University of Maryland at College Park "to enrich both the theory and practice of leadership ... by assembling fifty of the brightest, most thoughtful scholars and practitioners working in 'leadership' ... to shed light on some of the most compelling topics in the field" (from the Foreword by Bruce Adams & Scott W. Webster, project director and assistant director, pp. i–iii).

followers care about leaders? Why do they follow "weak" as well as "strong" characters? Is the leader-follower relationship presented as too much of an abstraction, given wide individual differences? What are some of the motives that attract and keep followers in the relationship? Some responses: sharing a mission or vision, increasing self respect, liking the task and/or peers, being in on the start of something worthwhile. This raises the question of choice, which is usually assumed in the political sphere, but is often virtually absent in the organizational one. We considered both in our discussions, but also noted that some of the most important leadership gets done outside of traditional systems, and by those who are unheralded.

We asked further about construing motive systems which bond leaders and followers, within a given context. For instance, does charisma-seeking by followers make them more susceptible to charismatic leaders, as in Post's (1986) "lock and key" metaphor? What effect do political entrepreneurs have on followers when they break conventional lines of action and make "ad hoc" dramatic moves, as in Jesse Jackson's trip to Syria in the 1990s to retrieve a Navy pilot? Could such leaders fit within conventional structures or would their unpredictable qualities cause them to be disempowered by their own subordinates? What happens when a successful but unprogrammatic political campaign ends with a question of "Now what do we do?", as in the film "The Candidate." How do organizations handle intense personal loyalty to a leader and/or mission, as in the concept of an organizational "commando leader," when they are no longer as salient or needed? The extent of the following and of the vision, and short vs. long-term features, are factors worth attention.

The increasing diversity of followers makes leader-follower relations more complex, though diversity has value as an end in itself. It can be approached in various ways, not only with respect to race, gender, and ethnicity, but also regarding functional and age factors, among others. There is also the question of the limits of diversity in the workplace. Diversity does not necessarily increase performance without attention to how it is handled (Morrison, 1993; Offermann, 1997). Creativity need not spring from diversity, though it presents possibilities. The challenges involved in diversity include how to interact productively, despite the hurdle that differences pose, and the need for a felt sense of justice. Hofstede (1980) says diverse cultures and organizations will not agree on values—but what is the alternative in contemporary society? It is important for a leader/manager to be a "cultural learner," in becoming able to deal with people who "don't speak your language." This requires recognizing one's self as a product of cultures, as represented in the publics who are worker/followers, and customers.

Leadership-followership under perpetually changing conditions presents a challenge because of the surprise in and imponderability of events, and "knowing where we're going." This is akin to dealing with "permanent white water," as Vaill (1989) puts it. Such chaos is evident in a system that is unstable at every point. Yet there can be order, and even the illusion of structure, in the absence of predictability. But this may not be easy to accept or convey to followers unless the leader shares the situation, and they can all be themselves, to become learners in feeling their way along. The question implicitly is: "What is the new game?" Then, "How much time do we have to play it?" Rather than micromanage followers more under stress, leaders can urge working smarter, not harder, avoiding dysfunctional strategies seen in the workaholic, technaholic, and powerholic. (Vaill, P.B. Managing as a performing art. SF Jossey-Bass) Leaders and managers are moral agents who can help others get in touch with their spirituality, which need not be religious in nature. Such self-directed contact with one's core set of values makes for a deeper awareness of purpose. The role of leader involves making moral value judgments, and showing concern for ethical, responsible action. With this goes a willingness to be accountable, rather than standing aloof as a distant power figure. Otherwise the sense of leader-follower identity in a mutual effort can be severely undermined. One manifestation of this is the criticism of inordinately high executive compensation relative to worker pay, especially if clearly unrelated to performance outcomes. Because the leadership of complexity can no longer be vested in just one person, more attention is needed for bringing followers into the process. This need calls into question the excessive reliance on the charismatic leader said to provide a "vision," which is desirable but separable from charisma, and is discussed more later. The long-standing view of good leaders providing direction and a definition of the situation remains useful, without having to invoke the charismatic quality.

Another interest area identified was that of follower autonomy, including empowerment. However, we well understand that both can be abused and made a mockery because of the imbalance of power and available information, as Mulder (1971) has long-since noted. The next question was, suppose we were to think of followers as volunteers who could detach themselves? If you were CEO of an organization composed entirely of volunteers, how would you treat them? What differences would that make in the leader-follower relationship? Add to that a need for the follower to be self-directed, as happens when sent off alone to set up a distant post, e.g., in Honolulu or Singapore. How would that apply closer to home, to the person down the hall working on a new project? Both situations require followers who can be self-leaders, which may be the most appropriate followership for the future, based on intrinsic motivation. Indeed, such leadership/followership is also consonant with self-managed work teams.

Teams of professional employees have been found to be highly effective at Texas Instruments and Westinghouse. This is a kind of dispersed leadership that cuts across distinctions between laissez-faire or authoritarian leadership. Ackoff's concept of organizational "internal markets" is pertinent, where various line and staff departments become self-financing market services to others in the organization. This involves having to satisfy customers and show accountability for results. Each manager is responsible in this system to a board of directors of employees and others served there. This practice has resonance with Greenleaf's (1973) concept of "servant leadership."

We addressed a paradox of empowerment when the initiative for it comes from above and can be seen as a demand. The question then raised is how to avoid a "push" that might squelch an initiative from below. We considered the lacks and needs evident in leadership development programs, and spent the bulk of our second meeting addressing its various aspects. Especially important is how well these programs bridge leadership-followership, both in academic study and the world of work. A major point made was that more input from program participants was essential, especially as regards meeting their needs. Greater attention also should be given to the problem of how the design teams of such programs are led, and by whom. Another point was the utility of doing evaluation research on these programs, and their outcomes, with appropriate criteria. This topic proved promising as a basis for later discussions about implementation of the ideas for improving follower involvement.

**PART 3**

# Conformity-Nonconformity and Independence

# CHAPTER 16

# Conformity, Status, and Idiosyncrasy Credit

## COMMENTARY

This chapter begins with selections from my paper "Conformity, Status, and Idiosyncrasy Credit," published in the *Psychological Review* in 1958. The idiosyncrasy credit (IC) model of leadership presented there was based largely on interpersonal influence processes. Perceptions of conformity and competence are seen as dynamic features of the model, with norms as expectancies that are neither fixed nor general. Simply stated, an individual who is perceived to be behaving in keeping with group expectancies and making contributions to the group's activities will likely move upward in the perception of others, possibly toward a leadership role. Conceived of as credits, this status then permits latitude for innovative behaviors, if seen by the group as helping to achieve its goals. Thus, displays of living up to norms and showing competence allow greater latitude for later innovation. Therefore, gaining individual expression, that is, *independence*, is achievable by what appears to be initial conformity to norms, although not in a consistent or slavish way.

To make these points about conformity more fully, I am adding here selections from a paper I presented in England, which also was published there in the *Sociological Review* in 1959, after the initial IC paper appeared. A few critical points about the IC model, as presented in Chapter 1 of this book, are worth reviewing, in light of my updated thinking about it. As with any scientific construct, the IC model was never intended to be fixed and final, but subject to test. I am pleased that it has garnered its share of thoughtful queries and criticisms.

In that regard, to summarize briefly from the end of Chapter 1, there are three restrictions that have occurred in my rethinking of the IC model, among others unstated: (a) a "statute of limitations" may limit a leader's latitude for influence and innovation after the passage of time, of indeterminate length, following an approved action; (b) a leader may lack perceptiveness in being aware of the availability of credits and the need to use them for appropriate action; (c) followers may represent a variety of interests that are incongruent with one another so that leader actions that gain credit from one group are not gained from others. In short, there are mixed motives that exist regarding desired leader behavior, in addition to what the leader may see as in his or her own self-interest. The IC model nonetheless seems useful as a basic heuristic in thinking about how followers affect leader standing and potential influence and innovation.

The next two chapters in this section (Chapters 17 and 18) present both conceptual and experimental work that fill out our understanding of "independence." This group of papers emphasizes the interactive quality of person perception and especially the central nature of process, sequence, and position in yielding responses to nonconforming behaviors and leader actions.

Excerpted from E. P. Hollander. "Conformity, Status, and Idiosyncrasy Credit." *Psychological Review*, 1958, 65, 117–127. Reprinted with permission of the American Psychological Association.

## CONFORMITY, STATUS, AND IDIOSYNCRASY CREDIT

Something of a paradox exists in the prevailing treatments of conformity and status. Students of social psychology are likely to be left with the pat impression that the freely chosen leader conforms to, and perhaps tenaciously upholds, the norms of his group. Yet this kind of leadership is also presented as a status sufficient to provide latitude for directing and altering group norms (Homans, 1950, p. 416).

From their related experimental work in this area, Dittes and Kelley have voiced a doubt that the relationship between conformity and status is ever a simple one (1956, p. 106). The evidence favors their assertion.

Although these phenomena may be treated as discrete entities, they both arise from interaction between an individual and a set of relevant other individuals constituting a group. To say that an individual conforms, or that he has status, is not to say that these are independently determined states nor that they are terminal; they have some common origin in a phenomenal relationship which persists over time. Conformity and status may be thought of therefore as mutually dependent, and transitionally effective upon subsequent interactions. With this as a framework, several general conceptions will be expressed here regarding mechanisms which produce these phenomena and govern their relationship to one another.

In a gross way, three classes of variables, or elements, are necessary to this conceptual scheme: characteristics of the individual himself/herself; characteristics of the group with which he interacts; and outcomes of interaction representing a past history which may alter the relationship of the former elements.

Of particular importance as a mediating process is the changing perception brought about in the individual and the group by their interaction; the third element is, in effect, this process. A distinction is required, therefore, between the phenomenal and perceptual features of behavior. An individual's behavior is not only phenomenally present in interaction but is also subject to view and appraisal by the other members of the group. If there are to be consequences involving these others, it is essential that there be a perceptual intake on their part. And so too must the individual perceive a group norm; the fact that it is manifestly there is not enough.

It is worth emphasizing that the focus here is upon how the individual fares in the group rather than upon more global consequences to the group. Two kinds of interlocking mechanisms are of concern: those giving rise to behavior in conformity with group demands, and those giving rise to status. The issues at stake may be put simply as follows: What produces conformity? And what allows for nonconformity?

## SOME QUESTIONS ON CONFORMITY

Fundamental to these issues is the matter of determining when an individual may be said to be conforming. As we have noted, a twofold assumption underpins the usual view of conformity, i.e., that the individual is aware of the existence of a given group norm, and that his behavior in accordance with this norm is evidence of conformity. It is doubtful that both features of this assumption necessarily hold simultaneously. This being so, difficulties of interpretation will arise. If the individual were to be insensitive to the norm he could hardly be said to be conforming to it, whatever his behavior seemed to betray; correspondingly; a kind of "conformity" might prevail in terms of adherence to an incorrectly perceived norm; and thus, an evident failure to conform might or might not be "nonconformity" depending upon the accuracy of the individual's perception of the norm in the first place.

A related question concerns the individual's motivation. Is there a motive for nonconformity identifiable? Insofar as they are distinguishable, is it necessarily so, after all, that a conflict obtains between the individual's dispositions and the group's demands? Since behavior is taken to be more than a random event, the motivation for instances of conformity or nonconformity should be accountable, once the presence of an adequate recognition of the norm is established.

There remains too the question of who perceives a given behavior to be conforming, i.e., an external observer, a group member, or the actor himself/herself. Employing a fixed-norm baseline for observation, as is often done, serves to obscure differential expectations which render conforming behavior for one individual nonconforming for another—with regard, that is, to others' perceptions in situ. Thus, the degree of familiarity with the unique properties of the group context is critical in verifying and understanding conformity.

## NORMS, ROLES, AND GROUP EXPECTANCIES

The usual conception of conformity examined here requires some group referent and a standard of behavior abstracted there from and defined as a norm. Probably because many studies of groups have involved highly manifest behaviors, norms are conceived to be quite literally evident. On the other hand, in the related concept of role a recognition exists that the behavioral standard may not be manifest, but rather may be an expectancy.

Though persisting, the distinction between norms and roles is neither essential nor easy to maintain (d. Newcomb, 1950; Bates, 1956). Roles are normative in that they involve some implicit shared expectancy among group members; and norms themselves, lacking visibility, may nonetheless dwell in expectancies. It is these expectancies, then, which may be normative, in the sense of typicality. Norms and roles are only distinguishable insofar as norms usually imply expectancies applicable to many persons, while roles are expectancies restrictive to one or a very few individuals in a group.

Objective observers might delimit common expectancies appropriate to group members in general from differential expectancies having reference to particular individuals as such. For the individual in the setting, however, manifest conformity probably comes about without regard to a separate awareness of norms as distinct from roles, but more likely in terms of behaviors which he perceives to be expected of him/her by relevant others, i.e., "doing the right thing."

In the world of daily interaction, the perception an individual holds of what relevant others expect of him/her is a singularly important determinant of his social behavior; and the degree to which an individual perceives the group to be rewarding serves to enhance or elaborate the effect produced by his motivation to belong. An alternative sequence may be seen to occur as well: motivation having reference to some fulfillment through the group serves to heighten the individual's perception of its expectancies. Work on selective perception supports such a formulation, in general, with further complexities stemming from motivation (Bruner, 1957). [Individual variables are specified at this point, indicating that conformity arises from both perceptual ability, representing a general alertness to the social stimulus field, and perceptual error, regarding group expectancies. The term "expectancy" refers to another's perception of some object person (cf. Steiner, 1955).]

The perceptual variables can readily be related to personality typologies. Many of these, e.g., authoritarianism, rigidity, or empathy, appear to lend themselves to a reduction to perceptual function as a core element (cf. Rokeach, 1948; Adorno, et al., 1950; Bender & Hastorf, 1953). Terms like "perceptual rigidity," "perceptual defense," and "social imperceptiveness," often appear as concomitants of these broader characterizations; evidently, this element accounts for certain diversities in behavior which distinguish individuals from one another.

It is useful here, however, to recognize a differential between that which is given and that which is emergent, i.e., perceptual ability and perceptual error, though the interaction of the two is not challenged. The distinction basically is that the former serves as a parameter setting the lower limit on the latter. It seems reasonable to believe that some individuals have an initial advantage over others as regards accuracy in perceiving group expectancies.

Concerning motivation to belong, mention has already been made that it involves two continua: motivation specific to the activity—or instrumental features—of the group, and motivation rooted in a generalized need for social approval. This view cuts across a number of other motivational schema suggested elsewhere (d. Festinger, 1950; Bovard, 1953; Deutsch & Gerard, 1955; Jackson & Saltzstein, 1956; Thibaut & Strickland, 1956), and is intended more as a resolution than a departure. Briefly, these other distinctions appear to involve an "activity focus" and an "other people focus." Activity involves others, of course, but not necessarily to gain their approval. What really seems to matter is the nature of the reward sought.

The approval variable might be viewed as a parameter of personality, but not one so static as to be unaffected by interaction, within certain limits. Since those members having interests which can only be satisfied through participation in group activity do not of necessity have a high need for social approval, and since those cast into groups of little positive activity valence to them may still require approval, it is possible that these variables may be related negatively or positively, depending upon the circumstances considered.

[At this point status emergence is defined as a "function of certain of the behaviors or characteristics evidenced by the individual in interaction, which then yield a reconstruction of the group's perception of him/her. Cast in these terms, status has special value as a kind of middle ground in relating the individual to the group. It exists in the first place as a feature in someone's perceptual field, for without reference to a perceiver status has no intrinsic value or meaning in itself." Perceptual differentiation by the group has consequences, then, in terms of the behaviors it expects the individual to display. Although not necessarily the case, it is desirable to conceive of status within this framework as having hierarchical properties on some sort of group-acceptance continuum (cf. Dittes & Kelley, 1956). This is by no means critical as a feature, but is of heuristic value. Still further, it is convenient to represent status as permitting greater latitude in the manifestation of behaviors that would be seen to be nonconformist for the other members of the group; we refer here to common expectancies, a term introduced earlier. The implications of this aspect of status are of especial relevance to what follows.]

## IDIOSYNCRASY CREDIT

Status will hereafter be considered to be an outcome of interaction referred to as "idiosyncrasy credit". This represents an accumulation of positively disposed impressions residing in the perceptions of relevant others; it is defined operationally in terms of the degree to which an individual may deviate from the common expectancies of the group. In this view, each individual within a group—disregarding size and function, for the moment—may be thought of as having a degree of group-awarded credits such as to permit idiosyncratic behavior in certain dimensions before group sanctions are applied. By definition, affiliation with the group—as perceived by the group—ceases when the individual's credit balance reaches zero.

It is noteworthy that this concept is applicable to the limited, artificially produced laboratory group as well as to the total society. And, since the individual may have simultaneous membership in many groups, he may be considered to have a distinct credit balance in all groups with which he is in some sense involved; in each case he has achieved some level of status. Affixed to this concept of "credit" is the further consideration that "debits" of varying magnitudes may be charged against the credit balance, depending upon the gravity and frequency of the idiosyncrasy manifested, and the credit level which the individual holds. Alterations upward or downward in credit may be conceived as a negative, monotonic function of credit balance. Thus, for the same idiosyncratic behavior or negative weight attached to value, the individual with high status loses less credit than the marginal individual with low status (Schachter, 1951).

Taking our society today as an illustration, one's credit balance very likely will be rapidly exhausted by publicly espousing Communist doctrine. In a different sphere, a fraternity man may experience comparable rejection by his peers for growing a beard, though other factors would come into play, so that for some individuals the consequences—in terms of group sanctions—would be disastrous and for others hardly disturbing. This requires some consideration of factors which determine the awarding of credit.

Among other determinants, the credit balance that a group member achieves depends upon the group, its function, and other properties to be considered below. It is useful for our purposes here to conceive of an "open system," i.e., an autonomous group providing focal activities, as well as free face-to-face interaction yielding expectancies; this would permit the simultaneous observation of an individual's behavior by all group members and the generation of impressions representing credit.

There are three general variables which can be delineated as determinants of these impressions: the individual's task competence or performance in regard to focal group activities; characteristics of the individual not specific to these activities, e.g., status in a broader group, bonhomie, and the like; immediate past idiosyncratic behavior, constituting a drain on credits, which are observed by relevant others. It is not contended that credit is necessarily related linearly to these variables, nor is their very likely interrelationship ignored. They are doubtless intercorrelated, though of varying degrees of significance in generating or dissipating credits. As a generalization, an individual's value tends to increase credit while idiosyncratic behavior acts to decrease credit, though the potential for negative value exists, e.g., in the case of prejudice. Still another variable related to credit balance, probably curvilinearly, would be the duration of the individual's affiliation with the group over time, i.e., seniority. This has been disregarded, since it is useful to deal with individuals as though they have been in the group for an equal period of time, more particularly from its inception. It is also likely that the degree to which the individual is "visible" may alter the effects produced by his value and idiosyncratic behavior.

[Group variables are set forth here regarding whether an individual can accurately perceive norms (e.g., through group cohesiveness), and be presented with norms that are accurately communicated, in some modal sense. At this point, there is a discussion of when and how relevance of attitudes may bear on accuracy, as well as one's social sensitivity. The variables in the model are then presented along with a schematic representation, which is also omitted here. The section on "discussion and implications" is also absent here, because the paper reproduced immediately after elaborates these concepts more fully. We turn to that paper now.]

Excerpted from E. P. Hollander, (1959). *Sociological Review* (University of Durham, England), 1959, 7, 159–168. Originally presented as an invited address to the British Psychological Society's April 1958 Annual Conference, in Birmingham, England. Reprinted with permission of Blackwell Publishing.

## SOME POINTS OF REINTERPRETATION REGARDING SOCIAL CONFORMITY

All individuals, in time, space, and degree, "conform"—if we mean by this that they alter the course of their behavior in keeping with social forces. This is plainly a basic requirement for social integration. A modifiability or plasticity of individual behavior is essential if society, any society, is to function smoothly. That conformity is therefore of singular import may be granted readily, though limiting it as to definition and interpretation is still another matter. It is after all neither a persisting attribute of the individual nor just an isolated state through which he passes. Rather it is best considered as a complexly determined, episodic outcome of the ongoing social interaction between the individual and the "other people" with whom he or she relates at a particular time.

## THE PERCEPTUAL ELEMENT IN CONFORMITY

Conceptions of conformity invariably involve a double assumption: that the individual is aware of some norm (or expectancy), and that manifest behavior in accord with this standard is indicative of conformity. The prospect of random behavior is usually excluded from concern, and for our purposes, we may simply note this and move to the more substantial issue of perceptual accuracy and inaccuracy in conformity.

Clearly, it is not necessarily true that an individual in any sense "knows" what is expected of him/her within a given social milieu. In the universe of experience, many cases very likely could be identified where this basal condition is in fact absent. What may then happen depends in some measure upon the motivation of the individual, whatever its source. Should he desire to make a go of it "play the game," so to speak-he will effectively try hard to find out what is expected; if not motivated, he may not achieve awareness and may be thought to be a boor, or some such, by the relevant others. Still another element may be postulated though, i.e., a factor of general alertness to persons and events in the social realm. Given someone low in this characteristic, it follows that even if highly motivated to do the "right thing," he might fail and thus give evidence of nonconformity. Hence, a person could wish to conform to what others actually expect of him/her, fan short because of this basic perceptual inadequacy, and so "conform" to an incorrectly perceived standard; he would consequently appear to be nonconforming when, in fact, his motivation, or intent, lay elsewhere.

## STATUS AND CONFORMITY

In the matter of status, mentioned in an earlier context, we have still another outcome of interaction. People do not, after all, possess status as an immutable personal attribute. It rests foremost in the eyes of one or more perceivers; and, whether directly or indirectly, it is these others who in some sense accord status. To comprehend status, we must therefore look to the differentiated view of one individual held by others, especially since these have certain operational results in their interaction.

Briefly, then, a differentiated perception, with effects upon interpersonal expectancies, conditions a particular behavioral approach to a person, and the esteem, for instance, in which he or she is held by relevant others.

The genesis of this perceptual differentiation comes about from social interaction, though this does not discount the prospect of a symbolic communication of status. From the past interactions that occur, one individual makes an impression on another. An ongoing record of this interaction thus develops, with consequent expectations regarding this other. Within a group framework, two main dimensions appear to be central to this process: the behavior of the object person in accordance with interpersonal expectancies, and his contribution to group goals. The former aspect represents a recasting of conformity, the latter a recognition of task competence as a distinguishable though commonly related determiner of status.

The amounts very simply to this: as the individual is perceived to behave in accordance with commonly applied expectancies, and makes contributions toward the group's activities, his or her status moves upward. For convenience, this may be thought of as an accumulation of credits, and, as indicated in Chapter 1, I have specifically affixed to this term, "idiosyncrasy credit."

Where an individual fails to live up to expectancies, i.e., nonconforms, credits are lost. But they may be maintained at some appropriate level by continuing to be perceived as a contributor to the fulfillment of the goals of the group. When an individual's credit balance reaches zero, he or she may be thought of as having been excluded from the group, so far as the group's perception is concerned. On the other hand, credits may accumulate to such a level that the expectancies applicable to the individual are directed toward innovation. The critical feature here is that status will allow greater latitude in the manifestation of behavior which would be seen to be nonconformist for the other members of the group.

For the person who is upwardly mobile, group expectancies will be altered in the fashion indicated. Because of this shift, it becomes increasingly less appropriate for him/her to continue to manifest behavior which was set to the group's earlier expectancies. To the extent that the "incipient status person" is attuned to these alterations, and is capable of reacting appropriately to them, his or her status should at least remain fixed, or move upward. Demands for perceptual accuracy and flexibility of behavior are thus continually made upon him, features of informal leadership borne out by a good deal of research and discussed further in Chapter 20.

Since the high status person has latitude for the manifestation of behavior which for others would be seen as nonconformist, he is in a position to alter the common expectancies of the group. It is in this realm that status may be exercised in an influence sense. Still another condition may hold though for expectancies centered in the status itself; the leader could readily lose credits, and find his latitude diminished, if he should violate these. Regarding such deviation, one dimension that is quite probably significant would be the leader's motivation to belong as it is perceived by the members of the group to be both high and sincere. In the absence of these conditions, his status would be threatened.

In sum, conformity serves to maintain or increase status early in interaction, while later, status allows a greater degree of latitude for nonconformity. Though something of an oversimplification, this formulation serves to explain the seeming paradox that the leader both conforms to group norms and yet operates to alter group norms. This, of course, is no paradox at all. In the model of emergent leadership offered here, an individual achieves status by fulfilling common expectancies and demonstrating task competence during his early exposure to a group. As he or she continues to amass credits they may eventually reach a threshold which permits deviation and innovation, insofar as this is perceived by the others to be in the group's interests, and with relative impunity. Experimental findings from early research bearing on this process are presented in Hollander, 1964, Chapter 17 and 18.

## CONFORMITY AS A PROCESS

In the foregoing, I have sought to argue against the view that conformity is a persisting personal attribute, as in being lame, or even a passing state, as in having a rash. Rather, I have urged a view of conformity as a process leading somewhere, a point which is further elaborated in Chapter 16. Moreover, to my view this is both a universal process and one with a significant raison d'etre in the scheme of human affairs. Without invoking the metaphysical or trading in the paradoxical, I should like to suggest the prospect that individuals find conformity a device for gaining individuality. In interactions with groups, they are continually bartering one thing for another, even if inadequately and sometimes to their detriment. If we put value judgments aside then, conformity to a socially prescribed pattern, even to a slavish extent, should not lead us to conclude a profound surrender of individuality: we may be too hasty in branding this an overdesire for social approval when it might well be indicative of a form of pretense used to gain acceptance for other, more important, individually based behavior. These purposive features of manifest behavior require additional elucidation and study.

## SUMMARY

Social conformity, in the sense of behavior seen to accord with a social norm, has been variously attributed to relatively stable motive patterns of the individual, to a dimension of personality, or to group characteristics.

These conceptions have been examined here taking account of the fundamental problem posed by the very definition of conformity behavior. Thus it was noted that conformity and nonconformity, as regards process, are not necessarily established by the simple criterion of manifest behavior; that conformity must have, at bottom, a basis in a realistic awareness of the norm by the individual actor; and that the notion of a fixed norm is very likely misleading insofar as it may not apply to all individuals comprising the group of reference.

The central thesis developed upon this base is essentially as follows: an individual functions within a social field largely in terms of his or her perception of the "group expectancies" regarding his or her behavior. Depending upon motivational and perceptual states, as they relate to certain features of the social field, he or she will be more or less given to behavior in keeping with these expectancies. Expectancies are not static but rather depend upon the outcome of past interaction between the individual and relevant others. A core element then is the historical or time-linked effects of interaction in determining the countervailing perceptions of the individual and these others. The effects of this stochastic process, especially upon leadership emergence, is essential to the Idiosyncrasy Credit Model.

# CHAPTER 17

# Some Current Issues in the Psychology of Conformity and Nonconformity

## WITH RICHARD H. WILLIS

### COMMENTARY

In 1971 it was possible to assert confidently that "The study of conformity and influence processes comes down ultimately to the issue of the social fabric which holds people together in society. Though it proceeds from an immediate concern with group processes, this work has broader ramifications for the nature of social conduct, social responsibility, and commitment to others" (Hollander & Hunt, 1971, p. 420).

Despite this large view, interest in the topic of conformity has dropped considerably from a time well over 60 years ago when it became central to social psychological research and theory. A number of reasons can be offered for why this is so, a basic one of which appears to be a flight away from studying group processes to an understandable focus on social cognition (e.g., Fiske & Taylor, 1991). However, interpersonal relations, as exemplified in groups, are clearly related to cognitive processes. Indeed, early 20th-century social psychology produced three concepts that are clearly cognitive, yet have often gone unidentified as such in contemporary writings and work.

The three I have in mind are *definition of the situation*, *reference group*, and *self-fulfilling prophecy*. Each provides a link between what is perceived and one's social behavior. Indeed, the central concept of *social reality* indicates a shared perception based on *social identity* with particular others (see Tajfel & Turner, 1979) and is fundamental as a source of social behavior. Therefore, it is hardly new to see cognitive processes as essential to conformity in groups, or in attitude change, or in socialization and adjustment, among other social influence processes.

A further point emphasized in the paper presented in this chapter from 1967 is the imbalance in the direction of factors producing conformity, compared to those that reduced it. Efforts to rectify the balance did not alter the tilt toward the former, exemplified early on by Sherif (1935) and Asch (1951). Furthermore, the distinction made in the Willis (1963, 1965) model, between independence and anticonformity as different forms of nonconformity, was not widely applied, if understood. It represents a *choice* of whether or not to behave in line with the norm or to *always behave differently from the norm*.

This is a useful distinction to maintain, which is associated with other social influence processes, as Figure 1.1 in Chapter 1 shows. The phenomenon of "reactance" is similar to anticonformity, in the sense of a negative response to direction. Although often seen in adolescents, reactance can be central to authority factors more generally in leadership-followership, as in "giving orders," and "taking orders." For instance, when a leader compels compliance to an order by invoking authority and even makes threats for failure to comply, resistance can be generated with later effects in losing cooperation.

Also important here is to recognize that nonconformity to one norm may represent conformity to another, so the either-or distinction is not meaningful. Conformity very much depends on the vantage point as to whether it is considered to be one way or the other. Moreover, there are many ways to be seen to be nonconforming to a norm, not just one way, as in the case of a clearly defined norm.

Crano (2000, 2004) relates conformity to a leader's ability to influence others. If the leader is able to persuade others of the correctness of their position, they will be followed, even in their absence. But, he says, leaders who force compliance must possess sufficient power to punish resistance and be able to monitor the behavior of their followers. Other leaders, who have expertise, are likely to be followed even when they cannot monitor adherence, because they have accepted the leader's view. Crano (2004, p. 250) adds that if conditions change, so that the leader's expertise is rendered obsolete, he or she may be replaced. This is almost identical to what was said about charisma and clearly shows in microcosm the relationship of conformity and independence to leadership. As pointed out earlier, phenomena such as "groupthink" are illustrative of a similar dynamic.

---

Abridged from E. P. Hollander and R. H. Willis, "Some Current Issues in the Psychology of Conformity and Nonconformity."
*Psychological Bulletin*, 1967, 68, 62–76.
Reprinted with permission of the American Psychological Association.

When Thoreau voiced the suspicion that the apparent nonconformer was merely marching to a more distant drummer, he provided an insight which has been rather surprisingly disregarded in much of the contemporary research on conformity. Cooley (1922), pursuing the same point, asserted that there is no definite line between conformity and nonconformity, and that both should be considered together as normal and complementary phases of human activity.

Despite these long-standing and astute observations, the dominant focus of most current research on social influence has been to ascertain what can be systematically shown to occasion conforming behavior. Nonconformity is typically ignored or at least not considered conscientiously. What makes this a curious emphasis is that conformity is usually the modal response. Hence, this work tells us less than it might about individual differences in reactions to social pressures. Introducing conditions favoring the possibility of nonconformity, by contrast, can reveal a good deal more about the idiosyncratic patterning of responses that we are accustomed to terming "personality," for quite often there are several ways in which one can not conform but only one way of conforming.

## AN OVERVIEW

The essential task of this paper is to redress this present imbalance in research on conformity and nonconformity, and to explicate several concepts and distinctions which clarify certain basic features of such research. In documenting the importance of these concepts and distinctions here, we cite a rather large number of studies. However, these citations are illustrative, rather than exhaustive, of what is a considerable literature.

In this connection, it should be noted that although the literature on conformity and closely related topics has reached Brobdingnagian proportions (d., e.g., Allcn, 1965; Berg & Bass, 1961; Graham, 1962; Willis, 1961), it remains disparate in many of its implications. Mann (1959), for example, reported a marked degree of inconsistency concerning the relationship between stable attributes of personality and conformity in the 27 studies he surveyed. Conformity was found to be a positive function of certain personality variables in some of these studies and uncorrelated or a negative function of these same variables in other studies. This strongly suggests the desirability of reexamining most carefully the differential meaning of "conformity" and "noncomformity" as they are currently conceptualized, and as they have been operationalized in psychological research.

Throughout most of this paper we are concerned with conformity-nonconformity as social response—that is, we focus on the actor. Toward the latter part of the paper, in the discussion of the assumption of norm homogeneity, we move to a concern with conformity-nonconformity as social *stimulus*. That is, we consider how the actor is perceived by others.

## LEVELS OF ANALYSIS

Part of the difficulty associated with the study of social influence resides in a confusion of levels of analysis and in definitions. Just as with other categories of response, conformity and nonconformity can be approached on either of two levels—the *descriptive*, and the *inferential* or explanatory. The first deals with manifest behavior, and research at this level studies overt conformity in terms of antecedent situational conditions and personality characteristics. The second deals with the underlying psychological states and processes affecting such overt responses differentially. The descriptive level is exemplified, within conformity research, by Floyd Allport (1934) when he formulated his J curve hypothesis (but not when he accounted for it in psychological terms), or by Solomon Asch (1951, 1956) when he investigated the conformity of a minority of one as a function of various situational parameters (but not when he classified his subjects according to predominant motives, feelings, and cognitions). Examples of recent inferential analysis of social influence processes are Katz, Sarnoff, and McClintock (1956), Kelman (1958, 1961), French and Raven (1959), and Raven (1965). The inferences drawn by these writers relate primarily to the motivational bases of social influence and power.

Operational definitions are employed at the descriptive level, while conceptual definitions are required at the level of explanation. Description is logically prior to explanation in that an adequate scheme for observing and categorizing is usually necessary before a range of phenomena becomes well understood. At the same time, conceptual definitions are logically prior to operational ones in that the latter are customarily suggested by the former. There exists, therefore, a mutual interdependence between the two levels of analysis, and refinements at either level can be expected to facilitate progress at the other. In the remainder of this paper, we consider, first, the analysis of conformity and its alternatives at the descriptive level, turning subsequently to more inferential or psychological aspects of the topic.

Operational definitions of conformity have often been based on observations of a single instance of behavior under such situational variations as ambiguity or nonambiguity of stimuli, or the presence or absence of status differentials between an influence source and recipient. It has also been measured by personality inventories and attitude scales. For the most part, however, conformity is operationally defined in experimental work as essentially a *change* in behavior in the direction of greater agreement with the evident behavior of the other group members. This is conformity in the sense of manifest convergence.

The problem, of course, is that this manifestation of change is not in itself indicative of specifiable underlying changes, for example, in terms of motivation. Indeed, there is need to scrutinize the widespread assumption that conformity in the descriptive sense reflects a motivational intent. Such an assumption appears unwarranted on several grounds. First, an individual may choose to do as others do without being dependent upon their standard in any persisting sense. Second, motivation to conform may be consequent upon a desire to participate in a group activity, not upon seeking approval from others. Third, in the absence of accurate perception of social demands a person could behave in line with a social standard without being motivated to do so. And fourth, apparent conformity may be due to similarity of non-social circumstances, as when one puts on a coat when going out, not because others do so, but because it is cold. If, in this last case, the similar responses have been independently learned, then the phenomenon can be referred to as *coenotropic* behavior (Young, 1956, p. 49).

Without undue formality, we therefore favor for its clarity a conceptual or psychological definition of conformity as behavior *intended* to fulfill normative group expectancies as presently *perceived* by the individual (d. Hollander, 1959; Willis, 1965a). Thus, we would exclude incidental fulfillment of norms which, descriptively, qualify as conformity. In the next section, we consider two descriptive criteria of conformity-nonconformity, congruence and movement, from which a variety of operational definitions can be derived; but for a psychological view of conformity, it is necessary to formulate a definition in terms of motivation and perception-cognition, as the one just given.

## DESCRIPTIVE CRITERIA

Contemporary treatments of conformity usually fail to take account of the kind of distinction illustrated in Halla Beloff's (1958) contrasting of *conventionality* and *acquiescence* as modes of social response. The former is operationally defined as high *agreement* between an individual's response and the mean or modal response of his group or class, while the latter is operationally defined as the amount of *shift* from private to public opinion. Beloff comes as close as anyone known to us to making an explicit distinction between the two basic descriptive criteria of conformity-nonconformity that have been formally analyzed by Willis (1964) and labeled congruence and movement. At the purely descriptive level, the congruence criterion requires that conformity (or nonconformity) be measured in terms of the extent of agreement between a given response and the normative ideal. The movement criterion dictates the measurement of conformity (positive or negative) in terms of a change in response resulting in a greater or lesser degree of congruence.

When these two aspects of social response are not conscientiously differentiated, paradoxes can result. This may be readily shown in the recent work of Walker and Heyns (1962) in which conformity was quite explicitly defined in terms of, and only in terms of, movement: "Let us define conformity as movement toward some norm or standard and nonconformity as movement away from such a norm or standard [p. 5]."

The implication of this definition, standing alone as it does, is clearly that an individual complying fully with the norm or standard from the beginning *cannot* be considered to reveal conformity. Walker and Heyns evidently contemplated this dilemma, since later on the same page they stated, "To describe a person or a group as conformist on the basis of a single observation implies an earlier state in which the degree of agreement with the norm was not so great." This would mean that an individual who had moved only slightly from a position of extreme nonconformity would be considered more conforming than one who had from the outset matched the norm.

It becomes apparent, then, that congruence conformity and the potential for movement conformity are actually *perfectly and inversely* related! The mixing of these two aspects of conformity, or the failure to recognize one or the other, doubtless explains much of the confusion encountered in attempts to understand the workings of "conformity" at the global level. For purposes of understanding, it is accordingly essential to maintain a strict distinction between these inversely related aspects of conformity.

At a somewhat more psychological level, a roughly analogous distinction can be made between habituation to *past* social demands which have some continuity in the present, as exemplified by musical preferences and aversions (Beloff's "conventionality," the congruence criterion), or a reaction to an *immediate* influence, as exemplified by compliance with a request to leave the room (Beloff's "acquiescence," the movement criterion).

## UNIDIMENSIONAL APPROACHES

Another inadequacy in the customary view of response to social influence is the tendency to cast it into a single dimension of response, with perfect conformity at one end and perfect something else, usually nonconformity or independence, at the other. Instructive in this connection is an observation made by DeSoto (1961) in reporting on his work on the predilection for single orderings: "In the theorizings of social scientists about society and culture [this predilection] shows up as a stubborn urge somehow to reduce discrepant orderings of people, or classes, or cultures, to single orderings [p. 22]."

These unidimensional approaches give rise to the classical bipolar conception of conformity-nonconformity, such as the J curve formulation of Floyd Allport (1934); or to the conformity-independence variant, seen in the work of Asch (1951, 1956), Marie Jahoda (1959), and many others. Throughout the literature on social influence, one sees a view of perfect conformity as an exact matching of one and only one group-approved position along the response continuum, which stands in contrast to an opposite response location, viewed either as nonconformity or independence. Although Walker and Heyns (1962) constitute an exception, there appears to be some tendency for those adopting the nonconformity contrast to think of conformity as *being* like others, while those employing the independence contrast typically view conformity as becoming more like others. Clearly, the first formulation is appropriately addressed to the congruence criterion, whereas the second applies to movement.

In what follows, we are concerned primarily with the movement criterion, the one customarily employed in experimental social psychology, particularly in studies of convergence. Nonetheless, we wish to stress our belief that, ultimately, both criteria must be rigorously analyzed, thoroughly investigated empirically, and fully interrelated with one another.

Bearing in mind specifically the movement criterion, consider the hypothetical case of an individual who consistently responds negatively to any and all social pressures. Where can he be located along the conformity-independence dimension? Obviously he is not a conformist, but, equally apparent, he cannot be considered independent. Nor can he be placed at any intermediate position. Actually, he is maximally dependent, since his behavior is highly predictable from knowledge of the social pressures to which he is exposed, but at the same time he is minimally conforming. There is no place for this "anticonformist" and yet a place must be provided—not because such perfect anticonformists are known to exist, but because there is no logical reason that one could not exist, and also because such negativistic behavior tendencies have often been observed in more attenuated form. It can be shown that a two-dimensional model of social response is capable of resolving this dilemma.

## A TWO-DIMENSIONAL APPROACH

A two-dimensional model of social response, applying to the movement criterion and to binary judgments, has recently been suggested by Willis (1963) and adapted in research by Willis and Hollander (1964a) and Hollander and Willis (1964). This mode stipulates two dimensions of response, the first of which is dependence-independence, or merely *independence*. The second is conformity-anticonformity, or *net conformity*. These are orthogonal of one another, not in the sense of being uncorrelated (the extent of the correlation being an empirical matter and varying from situation to situation), but rather in the same sense that one plots two such obviously correlated variables as height and weight against orthogonal coordinates. In the initial conception of the model, the response space, which defines the limits of possible patterns of responding over trials, is an isosceles triangle with vertices labeled Conformity and Anticonformity along the net conformity dimension, and Independence, at the vertex formed by the conjunction of the two equal sides. These vertices represent three basic modes of responding to social pressure, defined descriptively (operationally) as follows:

*Pure conformity.* Viewed relative to the movement criterion, this consists of maximal and completely consistent movement in the direction of greater congruence.

This descriptive definition stands in contrast to the conceptual definition of conformity given earlier.

*Pure independence.* This behavior is describable within the triangular model as a total lack of movement from preexposure to postexposure responses. In psychological terms, such behavior would occur when (but not only when) the individual perceives relevant normative expectancies, but does not rely upon them as guides to his behavior.

*Pure anticonformity.* This corresponds to movement that is maximal and completely consistent (like pure conformity), but in the direction of *lesser* congruence. Also like conformity, anticonformity implies dependence upon the normative expectancies, but of a negative kind.

Crutchfield has conceived of conformity and its alternatives in similar terms. Although he usually speaks of counterformity rather than anticonformity, essentially the same three modes of responding are considered to be interrelated as the vertices of a triangle (Krech, Crutchfield, & Ballachey, 1962, pp. 56–57). Crutchfield and his associates have not embarked upon experimentation on counterformity behavior, but he has discussed some of the personality characteristics of "the counterforming personality" (Crutchfield, 1962, 1963).

Our own experimentation deriving from the Willis triangular model has revealed significant differences both in the factors producing the various modes of response and in the reactions each has elicited from observers. As a demonstration of the variables producing conformity and nonconformity of both the independence and anticonforming varieties, Willis and Hollander (1964a) induced large and highly significant differences in patterns of responding among three experimental conditions in line with the three modes of this triangular model. The significance of this experiment resides in the fact that it indicates the possibility of evoking in considerable strength *all three* modes of reactions specified by this triangular model, thus supporting the two-dimensional view as more adequate than the usual unidimensional one. In this connection, it should be noted that *(a)* the conformity-independence model is a *special case* of the two-dimensional formulation, and *(b)* it is perfectly satisfactory so long as negativistic tendencies are absent, that is, so long as all movement is in the direction of greater congruence.

Another kind of support comes from an experiment by Hollander and Willis (1964) in which it was found that subjects reacted differently to independence and anticonformity on the part of partners. It follows that these two kinds of nonconformity must be distinguished, not only as modes of social *response,* but also in their differential social *stimulus* values.

A refinement of the triangular model, the diamond model, was subsequently developed. It takes account of a fourth mode of response, Variability or "Selfanticonformity" (Willis, 1965a; Willis & Hollander, 1964b). Pure variability behavior would be exhibited by a subject who *always* changes his mind from initial to subsequent judgments on each trial. It can be considered as a kind of "inverted" independence, insofar as invariable change precludes taking into account normative expectancies. That is, if a subject always changes his response in a two-choice situation, his postexposure responses are predictable from his preexposure responses but not from the source of social pressure defining on each trial one of the two responses as correct. Such variability behavior, except in diluted form, is probably rare. Still, a rather dramatic instance of this general kind of behavior has been reported by Aronson and Carlsmith (1962). In their experiment, and one would expect in general, variability or self-anticonformity was associated with negative, or at least very low, self-esteem.

Several experiments have now been conducted within the framework of the diamond model (Willis, 1965b, 1965c, 1966), with results demonstrating its research utility. The most detailed explication of the underlying logic, including the rationale for replacing the triangular response space with the diamond, is to be found in Willis (1965a).

This concludes our descriptive analysis of conformity and nonconformity. In the following sections we turn to a consideration of both earlier and recent conformity research in light of the foregoing but at a more psychological (i.e., inferential or explanatory) level.

## STUDIES OF MOVEMENT CONFORMITY

The classic study of Muzafer Sherif (1935) provided a model for much subsequent work on group conformity. Earlier, Arthur Jenness (1932a, 1932b) had conducted experiments in which subjects judged the number of beans in a bottle, then discussed this judgment with others to arrive at a single judgment, after which each made a second set of individual judgments. Results consistently indicated convergence (i.e., movement) toward a group standard. Sherif employed a comparable research paradigm but used the autokinetic phenomenon as the basis for his stimulus. In the absence of physical cues to distance and with the requirement for absolute judgments, he found a marked tendency for the perceptual judgments of subjects to converge in this highly ambiguous situation.

A number of studies followed which varied the Sherif procedure, employing a variety of stimuli and tasks, all within the framework of conformity in terms of perceptual convergence (e.g., Asch, 1951, 1956; Crutchfield, 1955; Schonbar, 1945). In a related vein, the studies of Mausner (1953, 1954a), Kelman (1950), and Luchins and Luchins (1961) manipulated the reinforcement of accuracy and the alleged characteristics of a partner in order to determine their effects on the degree of movement. In general, reinforcing the subject for accuracy of his own responses leads to a decrease in conformity as measured by the convergence procedure, and the net effect, therefore, seems to be to increase independence from the partner or group. Conversely, perceptions of the other(s) as more competent or of higher status than the subject usually result in greater conformity.

Such studies highlight the importance of the immediately preceding information supporting one's own accuracy in determining nonconformity. However, the source of this supporting information appears to be critical. Hollander, Julian, and Haaland (1965) have recently demonstrated that prior agreement from *other subjects,* rather than from the experimenter, leads to higher subsequent movement conformity. Furthermore, as predicted, the pattern of conformity varied over time.

Thus, the condition with complete prior support produced more initial conformity than either of two conditions of less prior support, but the decrement in conformity over trials was also most marked for this condition.

Other studies have manipulated the credibility, prestige, or competence of the source of judgments and have found that subjects are affected by sources having these attributes more than by those who do not possess them (e.g., Croner & Willis, 1961; Gerard, 1954; Kidd & Campbell, 1955; Mausner, 1954b; Wolf, 1959). The results consistently indicate predictable situational sources of conformity and nonconformity in terms of the perception of the influence source—whether a co-worker, a group, or an experimenter.

By and large, even with its productive features, this line of investigation (i.e., the Sherif construction of conformity as perceptual convergence, and related approaches) has tended to further a view which is still in popular currency, namely, that there exists a general norm *equally applicable* to all group members. The limitations of this assumption of norm homogeneity, as we can term it, are considered in some detail in a later section. Briefly, it involves the conception of a standard of conduct as a place on a continuum where some consensus rests, and is associated historically with Floyd Allport's J curve description of conforming behavior on a collective level as an accumulation of approved responses at one end of the response continuum (Allport, 1934). A more adequate view allows the definition of conformity to vary as a function of the status of the actor (Hollander, 1958, 1959, 1960, 1961).

A second criticism that can be leveled against the traditional work on perceptual convergence is that it is heavily biased against the elicitation of nonconformity. It shares with almost all psychological experimentation the feature of very high experimenter status as measured relative to the subject. Typically, experimenters create influence assertions directed at producing movement conformity by the constructions of the situations they pose to subjects, especially through instructional sets and task materials. The demand characteristics (Orne, 1962) implicit in this subject-experimenter relationship tend to force one kind of modal response.

Milgram (1965) has recently reported an experiment closer to the substance of a real-life problem and involving a test of experimenter influence. It is illuminating in several ways. As the experimenter, he instructed subjects to administer what was falsely thought to be a painful shock to another (mock) subject. In one set of experimental conditions, two other mock subjects either agreed to administer the shock or refused to do so. He found significantly more subjects refusing to administer shock if the other "subjects" would not than he did when they were instructed to do so with no others present. What is particularly striking is that he found no significant differences in willingness to give shock between subjects run with two other compliant subjects and those run alone. The very presence of the experimenter so biased the situation in favor of compliance that results from the confederates-complying and the confederates-refusing conditions are not directly comparable.

Greater use of experimental procedures in which the experimenter is perceived by the subject as incompetent, obnoxious, vulgar, or *needlessly* cruel (a rationale was provided in the Milgram study) might reveal varieties of behavior that have been to date rarely observed in the psychological laboratory. The question of the ethics of deception, which has deservedly received much attention recently (e.g., Kelman, 1966), is bypassed here because of space limitations.

We emphasize, rather, that customary experimental techniques conspire with well-channeled habits of unidimensional thinking to foster a pervasive fixation on the conformity end of the spectrum and a particular neglect of negativistic reactions.

On the more encouraging side, there appears to be increasing attention devoted to the study of *resistance* to influence, which is to say, the independence mode. In addition to the work of Asch and the Milgram experiment just noted, this tack is represented by Vaughan and Mangan (1963), Kiesler and Kiesler (1964), McGuire (1964), and McGuire and Millman (1965).

## THE SITUATION AND CONFORMITY

Among the situational variables that have been identified as affecting movement conformity are the ambiguity or difficulty of the stimuli; the greater status, power, or competence of the influence source; the observable unanimity of attractive others; and the general appropriateness of the act of conformity to achieving a desired goal (Asch, 1951, 1956; Blake, Helson, & Mouton, 1956; Goldberg, 1954; Jackson & Saltzstein, 1958; Mausner & Block, 1957; Thibaut & Strickland, 1956; Walker & Heyns, 1962). Further, the effects of these variables have usually been found to be enhanced by the requirement of a public response (e.g., Argyle, 1957; Gorden, 1952; Mouton, Blake, & Olmstead, 1956), although the seemingly simple distinction between public compliance and private acceptance is in fact a complex one (Asch, 1959; Jahoda, 1959; Kiesler, 1969).

The essential thrust of this work is toward the understanding of conditions in the situation which do lead to predictably greater conformity in the sense of convergence toward a group judgment. Psychologically, all of these effects appear to be explainable in terms of a heightened willingness to accept influence as a feature of dependence (d. Berkowitz, 1957; Blake and Mouton, 1961).

While all of this may be demonstrably so, a question which requires additional study concerns the situational bases for *nonconformity*. Most theoretical treatments are very lopsided in this respect. French's (1956) otherwise instructive formal model of social power, for example, focuses almost exclusively on pressures toward increased consensus, with only the most oblique concern for factors affecting diversity. Zetterberg's (1957) axiomatic treatment of compliant actions also provides little consideration of motivational or situational factors which would prevent a state of perfect agreement in the long run.

There is another reason for this habitual neglect of nonconformity, over and above the constraints of the traditional experimental paradigm. It is the widespread and highly questionable assumption that the situational and motivational bases of nonconformity are identical to those of conformity, but working in reverse. Taken literally, this assumption leads to the notion that knowledge about conformity means knowledge about nonconformity. This assumption of symmetry, as it might be called, fails to take into account that there are usually multiple ways of not conforming opposed to any particular manner of conforming. Another source of asymmetry arises from the fact that in groups larger than two, perfect consensus (congruence conformity) is always possible in principle, but perfect dissensus is not.

Another entirely different kind of asymmetry that enters into social influence, and which has been very little investigated as yet, concerns the relationship between power *over* another and power to *resist* that other (Cartwright, 1959). It was found by Croner and Willis (1961) that perceptions of differential competence on a prior task within dyads resulted in significant differences in influence transmitted in each direction during a subsequent task, as would be expected, but it was also observed that task similarity was a critical factor. French (1963) has advanced the interesting idea that power to influence and power to resist will be positively correlated in the case of persuasive power but negatively correlated in the case of coercive power.

## PERSONALITY AND CONFORMITY

Despite some voices raised to the contrary (e.g., Crutchfield, 1955; Hovland & Janis, 1959; Tuddenham, 1959), it is increasingly clear that the search for sovereign attributes of a conforming personality have not been especially fruitful. True, for any particular situation individual differences are invariably observed, and these are often substantial, but it is also true that conformity in one situation is not generally a very reliable predictor of conformity in other situations. Although Vaughan (1964), for example, found some consistency in conformity or nonconformity for 20% of the subjects he studied across four situations, the remainder were quite clearly affected differentially by the situations in terms of the amount of conformity manifested.

Additional examples are not lacking. Weiner and McGinnies (1961) conducted a study of the relative levels of conformity by authoritarians and nonauthoritarians, finding no confirmation for their hypothesis that authoritarians conform more. Smith (1961) found no relationship between conformity and Barron's Ego-Strength Scale (Barron, 1953). Using several measures growing out of the work of Schroder and Hunt, an investigation by Wilson (1960) supported his predictions regarding personality determinants of conformity for some attitudinal stimuli, but not for a series of perceptual stimuli. These and similar studies often fall back on the necessity to look further at the characteristics of the situation, and how it is defined by the subjects, to account in principle for the apparent inconsistencies in the observed patterns of behavior. One can conform or not conform in the service of such a wide variety of personal needs and perceived instrumentalities as to permit only a very limited validity to the construct of the conforming personality.

The issue is reminiscent of the earlier one about leadership attributes. It will be recalled that a prolonged search for the general traits of leaders was sufficiently discouraging as to produce a thoroughgoing reorientation of thought on the topic, with the situational determinants of leadership receiving almost exclusive consideration for a time (see, e.g., Gouldner, 1950). Eventually the pendulum swung back to a more moderate position, and today the importance of the situation continues to be stressed while the role of personal attributes (temperamental, intellective, and physical) as group resources is also generally recognized (cf. Hollander & Julian, 1968).

Whether the issue is leadership or conformity, the recent penetrating treatment by Hunt (1965) is especially noteworthy, pointing out as it did that personality factors are more likely to be most important in their *interactions* with situational factors rather than in any sense of total primacy over them. For his data, which serve only an illustrative function, differences among situations accounted for somewhat more variance than differences among persons. More to the present point, however, is the fact that the interactions were more important than either, accounting for 4 to 11 times the variance due to persons! In Hunt's own words, "Thus, it is neither the individual differences among subjects, *per se,* nor the variations among situations, *per se,* that produce the variations in behavior. It is, rather, the interactions among these which are important [p. 83]."

Related to the idea of the conforming personality is that of the "conforming society." At least one experimental study (Milgram, 1961) has demonstrated consistent differences in amount of movement conformity between samples from two countries. Norwegian university students were observed to be more conforming than French university students across all of five situations related to the Crutchfield procedure. Concerning these results, Milgram (1961) said, "No matter how the data are examined they point to greater independence among the French than among the Norwegians [p. 50]." He went on to relate this difference in "independence" to differences in the two national cultures.

Although it *may* be true that the French are the more independent, Milgram's data do not actually allow this conclusion. There exists another equally tenable interpretation. If it is recalled that anticonformity, like conformity, is a variety of *dependence* (d. the triangular or diamond model of social response), it becomes apparent that one very real possibility is that the French group was exhibiting substantially stronger anticonformity tendencies than the Norwegian group. If so, it could well be that the French subjects were at the same time *less conforming but more dependent*. While the Norwegians felt less free to not conform, the French may have felt less free to conform. Or, if one may put it this way, the French may have been in some degree conforming to a norm of anticonformity.

It should be borne in mind that this interpretation of the Milgram experiment remains speculative, because his data do not allow a direct test of it; and his data do not allow a test because they derive from experimentation based upon the conformity-independence paradigm. However, the main point is that conformity and dependence are not logically equivalent, and the distinction needs to be maintained both in the design of research and in conceptual analyses.

Whether or not Norway does in fact constitute a conforming society, a whole school of social criticism has developed around the theme that American culture can be so described (e.g., Riesman et al., 1950; Whyte, 1956). The most characteristic tack in such critiques is to describe conventional behavior in modern American society, label it conformity, invoke the "self-evident" premise that conformity is oppositional to individuality or independence, and therefore conclude that modern society and its component institutions hamper constructive initiative and are accordingly bad.

Apart from the value-laden feature of this literature, it neglects and indeed often hides the particular psychological utility of conformity behavior. Under many circumstances an objective analysis of possible courses of action leads to the conclusion that conformity will most effectively serve the individual's goals, whether these are social (e.g., need for approval) or nonsocial (e.g., need for food). From the assumption that all that qualifies as conformity, descriptively, is fully explainable in strictly social terms, an unfortunate confounding of description and explanation results which obscures the necessary and distinct place of each.

Although it is true that conformity and individuality are in opposition insofar as the perfect conformist cannot display individuality, they are in *very imperfect* opposition by virtue of the fact that even the most individualistic person often conforms. The hypothetical perfect individualist would not waste his energy and his status by not conforming in trivial ways—such as wearing red silk suits instead of gray flannel. Rather, he would feel free to not conform whenever something of importance to him was at stake, just as he would *feel free to conform* whenever this had instrumental value.

The distinction, already considered, between conventionality and acquiescence (or, more generally, between congruence and movement), is useful for liberating conventional behavior from the blanket stigma of acquiescent conformity. Thus, the convention of wearing clothes in public cannot be treated as slavish conformity in the same sense as accommodating to any and all fads, indiscriminately. The former represents a long-term habituation to a pattern which has obvious advantages as a necessary condition for normal social interaction of almost all kinds; the latter represents a series of short-term yielding which, taken in the aggregate, do not have any general instrumentality. A mathematician is not considered lacking in initiative just because he adopts the conventional notation of mathematics, for this is obviously a necessary precondition for the demonstration of whatever professional skills he may have.

Clearly, then, much of the social criticism regarding conformity is misplaced in that what an individual's culture teaches him may severely limit alternatives that are socially and psychologically economical. His habits become conventionalized along the lines occasioned by cultural requirements that usually encourage the self-sufficiency of a particular mode of behaving, as Asch (1959) has said. Like the idea of a conforming personality, the conforming society concept appears to be of limited utility.

## CONFORMITY-NONCONFORMITY AND SOCIAL EXCHANGE

Another, very promising avenue to understanding conformity and nonconformity is to be found in recent conceptions of reciprocity and social exchange (Adams, 1965; Blau, 1964; Gouldner, 1960; Homans, 1958, 1961; Jones, 1964; Thibaut & Kelley, 1959), which has ties both to reinforcement theory and to game theory. The approach is applicable to a study of social behavior either as response or as stimulus, although in this section only the latter is considered.

The social-exchange view construes conformity as a social process in which positive effects are occasioned in interactions with others by manifestations of expected behavior. Seen in this light, conformity becomes either a *deserved reward to others* which smoothes the path of interaction and provides for further prospects for rewarding exchange, or as a *payment in advance* for anticipated rewards. In this latter regard, Jones (1965) has called attention again to the various ways in which conformity may be used as a technique of ingratiation. The ingratiation concept indicates one instrumental basis for displaying conformity in interaction which forms a counterpart to the more basic "deserved reward" conception. Moreover, it emphasizes the potential *alteration* of expectancies which is an essential feature of social interaction in the full sense of the term.

Related to these schemes is the "idiosyncrasy credit" model (Hollander, 1958, 1964), which looks upon conformity as one input to the accumulation of status in the form of positive impressions or "credit" awarded by others. This credit then permits greater latitude for nonconformity under certain conditions. A basic feature of the idiosyncrasy credit model is the view that conformity and nonconformity are *not* invariably defined relative to a fixed norm to which everyone in the group is expected to comply equally, as in the Sherif paradigm. Rather, nonconforming behavior is seen to be variously defined by the group for any given actor depending upon how that actor is perceived. Conformity is thus considered to be to some degree person-specific and functionally related to status. That individuals of higher status or greater esteem have wider latitude for deviation has been widely observed and variously demonstrated in recent experiments by Berkowitz and Macaulay (1961), Hollander (1960, 1961), Julian and Steiner (1961), Sabath (1964), and Wiggins, Dill, and Schwartz (1965).

The consideration that when a person is perceived to have higher status his behavior is evaluated differently provides a useful bridge for understanding the relationship between conformity and the later potential for the kinds of deviancy associated with leadership. Thus, the apparent paradox that leaders are said to be greater conformers to group norms (Homans, 1950; Merei, 1949), while also being initiators of change reflected in seemingly nonconforming behavior, is handled within the idiosyncrasy credit model as a matter of sequence. Early conformity, in combination with such attributes as perceived competence, enhances acceptance of later nonconformity.

Nonconformity can also be viewed with regard to the distinction between common expectancies of a group regarding its members and those special expectancies associated with high status. The visibility associated with such status also means that the outcome of any given act of nonconformity will be judged not only in terms of intentions but also in terms of the rewards it produces for the group. Other things equal, the high-status group member's behavior is more likely to be perceived as providing good outcomes to the group, rather than bad. Norm violations are more often seen as instances of "productive nonconformity" in the terminology of Pauline Pepinsky (1961). Uppermost here, however, is the consideration that acts of an evidently nonconforming variety will be variously interpreted as a function of others' *perceptions of the actor* based on their past experience with him, and in particular their *imputation of motives* to him (cf. Heider, 1958). Thus it has been found that the high-status person who conforms is seen to do so for internally determined causes while the low-status person is seen to conform for externally determined causes (Thibaut & Riecken, 1955). Accordingly, the motives seen to underlie the action will vary as a function of the actor's perceived status and the related assumption that the high-status person is more in command of initiatives to do as he wishes.

It should follow, too, that when his actions are seen to hurt the group, the high-status person will be held more responsible than would a low-status member. This would hold in particular when some basic role requirement, specific to the position of the individual, is not met. It is true that the acts of the high-status person are less likely to be perceived negatively than those of a low-status person, but *given* that the evaluation of acts is equally unfavorable, the high-status person will pay the higher social price.

In sum, conformity and nonconformity are observed and evaluated as features of interaction which may influence the subsequent action of others toward the actor.

## CONCLUSIONS AND IMPLICATIONS

Let us now consider some salient conclusions.

1. *Current research on social influence is preoccupied with conformity to an extent sufficient to produce a relative neglect of nonconformity.* It should be evident from the numerous studies cited that conceptual and experimental work on nonconformity phenomena has received only a fraction of the attention devoted to the conformity side of the picture. The obvious implication is that a shift of emphasis is much needed.
2. *Current research is characterized by a failure to distinguish consistently between descriptive (phenotypic) and explanatory (genotypic) levels of analysis.* A mutual interdependence exists between the two levels of analysis, and refinements at either level can be expected to facilitate progress at the other. In the area of social influence, however, the distinction has not been maintained as conscientiously as it might. An unfortunate result is that it becomes very easy to overlook the fact that the same overt act, or the same kind of overt

act, observed on different occasions, can correspond to a variety of underlying psychological states and processes. A second effect has been the almost total neglect of careful descriptive analysis; this in turn has led to the necessity of making the next point.

3. *Current research is characterized by a nearly universal failure to distinguish between two basically different descriptive criteria of conformity-nonconformity, here termed congruence and movement.* Of writers known to us, only Halla Beloff (1958) has approached an explicit distinction of this kind. Her conventionality corresponds to congruence, while her acquiescence corresponds to movement— at least so it would seem from the kinds of measures she employed. She, like most others, considered only the conformity side of social influence.

From a strictly descriptive or operational point of view, congruence refers to the proximity between the position of the response along the response continuum and the point defining the normative ideal. Movement refers to changes in level of congruence from one occasion to another. The customary failure to distinguish between the two is roughly analogous to a failure to distinguish between hot and cold, since there is a perfect inverse relationship between the level of congruence and the potential for movement conformity.

4. *Current research is characterized by a persisting tendency to conceptualize conformity and its alternative(s) in an overly restrictive unidimensional manner.* Here two versions of a two-dimensional approach to movement conformity were described. The first, a triangular model, is similar to a less fully articulated conceptualization by Crutchfield and his associates. Conformity, independence, and anticonformity (or counterformity) are considered to be interrelated as the vertices of a triangle. A refinement of the triangular model, the diamond model, introduces a fourth mode of response, variability or self-anticonformity.

The unidimensionality of previous and current research was documented in a selective survey of the literature on movement conformity as a function of situational factors.

5. *Current thinking on conformity and nonconformity often indulges in unwarranted value judgments.* Here the reference was to the related "conforming personality" and "conforming society" points of view. The former fails to recognize that interactions between personality and situational factors are more important than personality variables *per se*. Both also fail to take into account the fact that nonconformity, as well as conformity, can represent dependency. One must consider both the individual's freedom to not conform *and his freedom to conform*. At the societal level, a higher level of conformity does not necessarily imply a lower level of psychological freedom or individuality.

6. *Current thinking by social psychologists is frequently characterized by the simplistic and unwarranted assumption that conformity to the general group norms is defined alike for all members of the group.* This assumption of norm homogeneity fails to incorporate the effects of those group processes that produce variations in normative expectations as a function of the status of the actor, as discussed in terms of the idiosyncrasy credit formulation, and related to the social-exchange view of interaction. From extensions of this kind, a more adequate understanding of the mechanisms producing such group phenomena as leadership, innovation, and deviance become possible.

CHAPTER 18

# Independence, Conformity, and Civil Liberties

*Some Implications from Social Psychological Research*

## COMMENTARY

The relationship of independence to leadership is of considerable importance in groups and organizations. Although usually treated separately, independence to an appropriate degree helps creativity. For example, the observational research of Vaill (1982) on high-performing systems indicates that members have a willingness to experiment with various ways to operate the system and latitude to override or change rules when essential and without serious consequences.

In studying the phenomenon of conformity, Richard Willis (1963) and I (1964, 1967) did research on Willis's model that distinguishes between independence and anticonformity. The basic difference is that the former is flexible in picking when or when not to adhere to a norm, and the latter regularly defies the norm. This "anti" stance also occurs in the pattern of "reactance," often associated with adolescence, but which can be lifelong for some.

Independence requires a willingness to make choices and not be tied to a norm, such as silence. "Speaking up" is more likely productive, even if seen as disruptive. For instance, taboo topics can impede needed change by limiting the organization's capacity for innovation and progress.

The decision to take action is basically motivational. However, it also depends on perception, in seeing alternatives for action, which depends on sharing information. Organizational leaders may "not want to know," as was the case at Enron, when CEO Kenneth Lay was warned by one of its vice presidents, Sherron Watkins, that there were financial improprieties, months before the Enron collapse in 2001. After a delay, he had the company's longtime law firm do a "narrow inquiry," what an ethics expert called a "sweetheart investigation," about what were considered criminal acts (Aronson, *New York Times*, 2006).

The paper reproduced in this chapter explores the motives that may serve as impediments, such as loss of approval among peers, when taking initiatives that are independent. Although the civil liberties theme was relevant in the context of the Bicentennial Celebration, it has far wider ramifications for society, as just stated in connection with organizational malfeasance.

A free society requires independent initiatives as well as regularities of conduct, otherwise it will stagnate. Authentic independence reflects critical judgment in responding to social demands rather than merely rejecting them. A climate of free expression is essential to independence and the perpetuation of civil liberties. Although social psychology has tended to emphasize processes of conformity, as much attention is needed to factors facilitating independence. Six impediments to independence are: risks of disapproval, lack of perceived alternatives, fear of disrupting the proceeding, absence of shared communication, inability to feel responsibility, and sense of impotence. To overcome these impediments socialization oriented to the critical evaluation of alternatives are necessary, including practice in making judgments and greater rewards for independent initiatives.

Republished from E. P. Hollander. "Independence, Conformity, and Civil Liberties: Some Implications From Social Psychological Research." *Journal of Social Issues*, 1975, 31(2), 55–67, with permission of Blackwell Publishing.*

Free speech in behalf of a variety of views is the hallmark of a free society. Yet there are undeniable impediments, whether real or imagined, to staking out an independent course. Very often the creative tension between the demands of society and the independence of individuals is distorted by the desire to gain and maintain the rewards of social acceptance. The price is to keep silent or, if not, to echo the prevailing view.

In a free society the encouragement of a free exchange of ideas has survival value for the individual and for the society. However, the importance of free speech is not usually appreciated in these terms. More often, the exercise of that civil liberty is seen largely as a matter of individual preference rather than being a responsible social act.

The fundamental point is that the expression of individual views is essential to the creation of an atmosphere in which free speech and other civil liberties may thrive, and that the opposite is equally true: Where such expression is not encouraged and protected there will be a waning of these liberties. Social supports for individual expression and the maintenance of civil liberties therefore exist together in a reciprocal relationship, which is crucial to the perpetuation of a free society.

---

* This paper is based in part on an address originally presented in the Symposium on Civil Liberties organized and chaired by Sheldon Zalkind at the New York State Psychological Association Convention in New York City in May 1971. It appeared in a special issue he edited of the *Journal of Social Issues* on Civil Liberties in 1975 to celebrate the U.S. Bicentennial. I revised it for the journal while in residence in the Department of Experimental Psychology at the University of Oxford for the Trinity Term, Spring 1973. I am grateful to many colleagues and students for their useful criticisms, particularly those in my seminars at Oxford and SUNY Buffalo, and at colloquia I gave at the Universities of Edinburgh and Reading.

## DEPENDABILITY AND INDEPENDENCE AS SOCIAL REQUIREMENTS

A free society must maintain a delicate balance between the requirements for dependable patterns of action and for independent initiatives. Granting that independence can be disruptive to someone's convenient social arrangements, total regularity would stifle free expression at a considerable social cost in stagnation. Practically speaking, a society built on rigidly structured patterns of behavior wastes individual talent and loses the capacity to act in novel ways (Gardner, 1961).

There is a story by Isaac Asimov (1973), called "Light Verse," which is an allegory about a future time when highly programmed robots perform many routine helping tasks. One of these robots, Max by name, is an old model and has grown a trifle idiosyncratic, but his owner a woman artist who does "light paintings" finds his uniqueness appealing. Without her permission, an overly conscientious visitor from the robot firm insists upon tinkering with Max's electronic circuitry when he observes the robot's slightly unprogrammed actions. In doing so he destroys Max's ability to create the very best of the woman's artistic light paintings, a talent of his which she has understandably kept a cherished secret. And so Max's unprogrammed artistic career is abruptly shattered.

In the literature of organizational psychology a similar point has been made by Katz (1964), among others. He contends that the insistence upon strict specification of behavior, going only by the book, serves to increase conformity for its own sake and thereby deprives the organization of uniquely individual capabilities. Such a heavy-handed approach not only snuffs out individuality but also places severe limits on organizational effectiveness—even though it is often justified in the name of that very goal.

Despite its occasionally upsetting but thoroughly tolerable effects, I am concerned with the facilitation of independence. Briefly, I view independence as action which reflects critical judgment by the individual in responding to social demands. It means sometimes accepting and going along with the majority view and sometimes rejecting that view, deviating from it, and trying to get others to do so as well. Although there are sound reasons for believing that independence is a healthier state than is conventional conformity, the evidence indicates that social psychology continues to be more interested still in the basis of conformity. Some consideration of the reason for this deserves attention.

## The Historical Backdrop to Experiments on Conformity

For close to half a century, one mainline of social psychological experimentation has been the study of conformity. The basis for this emphasis is not hard to understand if one considers the historical backdrop of experimental work on the effects of a group on individual judgments, especially Münsterberg (1914), Moede (1920), and Floyd Allport (1924). Essentially, the research of these precursors of modern social psychology was devoted to studying the consequences to the individual's judgment of knowing others' judgments. This tradition led to the work of Jenness (1932), Sherif (1935), and then Asch (1951) and Crutchfield (1955) on "convergence" toward a group-based judgment or norm. Within this experimental paradigm, the major dependent variable was and continues to be the conformity of subjects to what is typically an erroneous group judgment.

Once a dependent variable is identified and readily measured, there is virtually no end to the other variables with which it can be linked in essentially parametric research aimed at identifying its correlates. Conformity became enshrined in this paradigm, without much question about its operational definition. By contrast, if given attention at all, "independence" was merely considered to be the other end of conformity. That assumption is one of a number of issues open to question.

## Independence Is Not Just the Opposite of Conformity

The preoccupation with conformity in experimental social psychology effectively reduced nonconformity to a residual category and independence to something even less well-defined. Indeed, the terms "nonconformity" and "independence" often were used misleadingly as if they were interchangeable (Hollander & Willis, 1967). Furthermore, the question most frequently posed in traditional conformity research was "What produces conformity?" instead of "What allows for nonconformity?" (Hollander, 1958).

To a major degree also, experimentation on conformity has been loaded in the direction of encouraging the expression of conformity, as the less costly alternative for the subject. Giving the same erroneous judgment as the group majority usually was the sole alternative to giving the correct judgment but at the risk of standing alone against the group and the experimenter who "runs the show." Consequently, as Schulman (1967) has aptly observed, there has been a confounding of the experimenter's authority with the effect of the others in eliciting conformity.

If one were to ask where this line of experimentation leaves us with regard to an understanding of independence, the answers would generally tend to fall into two categories. On the individual level, it might be said that one need only study subjects who fail to conform to the group majority to discern those factors which produce independence. On the level of group processes, it could be argued that one may invert generalizations about the sources of conforming behavior—such as ambiguity—to discern the basis for nonconformity.

Both of these points are appropriate, but neither leads to a very useful explanatory scheme for understanding the processes and effects underlying independence. Conformity must be seen in context as an outcome of a person's interaction with a group in a specific social situation; therefore conformity is not simply an attribute of the individual but rather is a relational concept. Basically, conformity grows out of interaction with others, however implied that interaction may be in many of the stripped-down laboratory procedures used in social psychological experiments. The same observation can as validly be made regarding independence, which also is relational in its quality.

## The Social Uses of Conformity and Independence

A prominent feature of the work on conformity is the emphasis on conditions which produce it, rather than on its effects. A similar state of affairs prevails with regard to independence, or nonconformity more generally (Hollander & Willis, 1967). One is hard put to find much effort expended to study the individual's justifications for conforming or nonconforming. Indeed, only slight attention has been paid to the uses of conformity, and independence in producing desired effects in social interaction.

Although there are some examples of a concern with effects, for the most part the literature reveals a preoccupation with the causes and correlates of conformity. Among the exceptions are the Homans (1958, 1961) formulation of conformity in social exchange terms, the Jones (1964, 1965) conception of "ingratiation," and the Hollander (1958, 1964) model of "idiosyncrasy credit." These exceptions have in common an emphasis on the uses of conformity in bringing about desired consequences to the actor in social interaction. The idiosyncrasy credit model goes a bit further insofar as it postulates a link between conformity at an early stage and the group's tolerance of nonconformity later on. Put simply, it suggests that one may increase the acceptance of one's nonconformity, especially in the direction of innovation, by manifesting conformity and competence in the group's task at an earlier point.

The simplest formulation of the social use of conformity is to "go along" and "not make waves." It suggests that the path of interaction in a group is made smoother and perhaps more effective by accepting the norm and not challenging others' expectations. Clearly, conformity in the general sense of people living up to others' expectations has functionality; there is a certain comfort and convenience associated with the regularity of social behavior. However, conformity is exacted at a price, which has been the main concern of a considerable literature of social criticism.

The critics of conformity are concerned with what is manifestly over-conformity—what Fromm (1941) has called "automaton conformity." Among others in this tradition are Riesman, Glazer, and Denney (1950) and Whyte (1956) who deplore excessive conformity. Here again some distinctions need to be made between a stylistic mode of conformity, in the nature say of conventional attire, as against acquiescence to the demands of others for overt ideological conformity. The latter has been dubbed "compliance" by Kelman (1958), who sees it as verbal acquiescence without private acceptance. Indeed, a good deal of the conformity research in the laboratory has in fact been about compliance (Kiesler & Kiesler, 1969). Rather than being a personal matter, however, compliance by many persons transmits the impression of group agreement and lends even greater social pressure to the unconvinced group member. Janis (1972) has dubbed this phenomenon "groupthink," which he finds operating even in the highest councils of government.

Independence also has its uses, but these have not been maximized in the usual conformity paradigm. In the typical "real world" setting, a person may call attention to himself, with positive consequences, by speaking out in behalf of an unpopular cause. Schachter (1951) found that the deviate from the group view initially gained considerable attention and a greater volume of communication from the others, although later he was rejected. Thus an independent position enhances visibility, in a figure ground sense. Other things equal, differentiation gains attention for whatever is proposed, with consequences, which can be favorable and productive rather than the opposite.

The nature of the group and the alternative choices available to it also alter the climate for independence. A recent experiment by Lewis, Langan, and Hollander (1972) has demonstrated that independence is enhanced if group members do not anticipate having future interaction. Where it is expected, the group has greater leverage in inducing conformity. Thus, the Janis (1972) groupthink effect is more characteristic of ongoing groups where conformity serves a longer-range instrumental purpose. In contrast, strangers cast together in authentically transient groups are more likely to be independent. The Lewis et al. experiment also indicates that if there is a range of attractive alternatives available to the group, independence is reduced since less is given up by any member who accepts the choice of the others. Not as much accommodation is required to go along. Predictably, independence is more likely to be found where the group's choice is for the less desirable alternative and more sacrifice of one's preference is required.

### The Effects of Presenting an Independent Position

In one especially noteworthy condition in Asch's (1951) experiments, the subject could agree with the correct judgment of a group member who deviated from the erroneous judgments of the others. The task was to judge the length of lines, and the procedure was to have the minority member present his judgment after the majority and just before the subject gave his as the last respondent. Quite dramatically, the amount of conformity dropped to 5.5% from the average of 37% found in the usual condition of total group agreement. Therefore, the presence of an independent position, expressed by only one other member, had a strong effect on the amount of conformity displayed by the subject. Clearly, the necessity to comply was profoundly diminished.

Following up Asch's work, Kimball and Hollander (1974) found that this effect is even more sharply defined when the stimuli are ambiguous and where the independent member is believed to be experienced. The subjects in this experiment had three possible alternatives on each trial: to agree with the majority, to agree with the minority member, or to agree with neither. The findings indicated that the presence of an experienced minority member did lead to less agreement with the majority, but without more agreement with the independent minority member. In short, the presence of an independent member, especially an experienced one, led to significantly increased independence by the subject from all of the others.

Milgram's (1965) experiments on compliance to the experimenter's instructions to administer an electric shock to another person provide an additional line of evidence. In a set of experimental conditions where two mock subjects either agreed or did not agree to administer shock, Milgram found that only 10% of subjects agreed when others would not, as against 65% who agreed when alone. Hence, the presence of two defiant subjects had an overwhelming effect in creating independence from the experimenter's instructions.

Pursuing this point, research by Moscovici, Lage, and Naffrechoux (1969) indicates that the presence of two minority members who gave a consistently different judgment from the majority served to alter the majority judgment over time. Their experiment used a psychophysical task involving color judgments. Quite interestingly, they found that majority members appeared to reject the minority members' judgments but in fact shifted subsequently to judgments more like those of the minority.

These experiments indicate that the availability of alternative views enhances the prospect for resistance to majority influence and even for the eventual alteration of the majority's position. This is quite consistent with the contemporary approach to problem solving as a search routine for suitable solutions in an information-processing mode (Miller, Galanter, & Pribram 1960).

## IMPEDIMENTS TO INDEPENDENCE

Granted that independence can produce favorable outcomes, speaking out against a prevailing group view requires that several hurdles be surmounted. There are six of these which appear to cover the preponderance of cases. Although further reflection might reveal that there are others, these are comprehensive enough in the aggregate, and sufficiently discrete, to warrant examination. They are: (a) risks of disapproval, (b) lack of perceived alternatives, (c) fear of disrupting the proceeding, (d) absence of shared communication, (e) inability to feel responsibility, and (f) sense of impotence.

### Risks of Disapproval

The late John F. Kennedy, in the introduction to his book Profiles in Courage (1956), says that when he first entered Congress he was given the classic advice "to get along, go along." That advice sums up what is probably the most essential component in limiting independence, that is, a fear of social disapproval and rejection. Especially to the point is the concern that one's desire to change the group's view will lead to disapproval and rejection. As Kennedy himself pointed out in his book, however, it is because of rare courage in bucking the prevailing view even in the face of a desire to be accepted and liked that certain legislative programs are realized. Voicing alternatives to the accepted and more traditional patterns provides others with a rallying point without which needed innovation would be exceedingly difficult to achieve. It should be added, of course, that the negative sanctions associated with independent acts are even more severe than just disapproval in many organizations, especially total institutions such as prisons.

### Lack of Perceived Alternatives

One effect of independence is to offer alternatives to others. In general, coping with new conditions requires that alternative courses be available. When individuals have reached the point where they say "What else can I do?", having alternatives becomes extremely useful. Sometimes individuals are confronted with what they see only as a simple choice between two courses of action. In group discussion, it is possible to generate still more alternatives through mutual problem-solving and the sharing of views. Having a store of these alternatives at hand should bring about a richer decision process, which is the rationale for the so-called brainstorming technique of group problem solving.

### Fear of Disrupting Proceeding

Typically, a group enterprise runs off along the lines of relatively routinized patterns of behavior. There is a sense that playing the game is essential if things are to get done. But there may be greater disfunctionality in allowing these habitual patterns to obscure distinctive alternatives and real differences of view. In short, the more desirable course is often not simply to go along but instead to make clear where the differences lie so that a better solution to a commonly shared problem may be found. There is, however, a prevailing reluctance to have confrontations. As Maier and Hoffman (1965) indicate, discussion leaders may fear the expression of disagreement, seeing it not as a basis for generating ideas and innovations but as a disruption and source of hard feelings.

### Absence of Shared Communication

The concept of "pluralistic ignorance" sums up the condition which prevails when individuals are kept from knowing each others' views. Ordinarily this is not thought of as an imposed restraint so much as an outgrowth of self-restraint, as seen for instance in the story of "The Emperor's New Clothes." The previous point about orderly proceedings helps to account for this restraint, but the consequence is to deprive a group of an open sharing of views which can be productive. This impediment is a matter which needs to be recognized and resisted. A certain politesse may dictate not saying too openly what is likely to embarrass or even enrage another; however, in many matters open communication widely shared is vital to the effective pursuit of group and societal objectives.

### Inability to Feel Responsibility

A prevalent problem in organizations is the sense of personal detachment revealed by the phrase "that's not my department." Organizational and group barriers foster and maintain alienation in the enterprise. Even on a less formal level, individuals may feel incapable of concern because of the phenomenon which Latane and Darley (1969) have called "diffusion of responsibility." Taking the initiative in matters for which one does not have or feel direct responsibility can be awkward and unrewarding. In institutional settings, it can be damaging to one's career to butt in, say, in behalf of an underpaid janitorial staff. There is, then, an impediment to individual expression, because it is easier and possibly safer to look upon a matter as someone else's responsibility.

A similar tendency toward release is seen in the "choice shift" phenomenon, where groups are often found to make choices which are more extreme than those the individuals comprising them make when alone. Pruitt (1971) postulates this effect to be mainly due to having information about what others in the group are thinking. Indeed, the choice shift may be a special case of convergence toward a group choice, not with the classic Sherif (1935) pattern of a mid-point selection but with more of a movement to the extremity of the range.

### Sense of Impotence

Finally there is that degree of disengagement where individuals give up entirely, mainly on the grounds that no one is listening anyhow. Turner (1973) has recently noted that this process accounts for apparent social inertia. Anticipating that their expressions of dissent will have little impact, individuals may consciously elect to remove themselves from the fray. This can occur despite their possibly having strong feelings on an issue. More than a sense of risking disapproval or a fear of disruption or an inability to feel responsibility, the individual in this circumstance has a pervasive sense of impotence. For instance, Turner found that about 12% of college students he studied felt that their freedom of expression was limited by the unresponsiveness of other students and authority. These students had effectively given up trying to "get through." Whether justified or not, the very belief that no one cares produces a self-fulfilling prophecy which is destructive of free speech.

## SOME IMPLICATIONS FOR MAINTAINING CIVIL LIBERTIES

We turn now to the practical matter of the conditions for maintaining civil liberties. The basic point made earlier is that free expression is essential: To the extent that there are impediments to free expression, civil liberties are threatened. Furthermore, their perpetuation requires that they be exercised, not only for their own sake or for a particular issue, but because the process is embedded in a feedback loop. Being able to overcome some or all of these impediments to independent expression serves as a model for others. It then becomes more acceptable to say and do independent things. Signs of independence, widely shared, help to offset actual or anticipated pressure from the group.

No suggestion is intended that any and all deviation from the group's view is to be welcomed. At the extreme, total deviation becomes anticonformity and not independence. True independence is a combination of conformity to some group positions and nonconformity to others. On a given issue the individual may feel only a sense of correctness, that is, of doing the right thing, by expressing a personal view about an issue. This might be a protest against excessive coercion, an appeal for a social action, or outrage at a perceived injustice. The significant feature is the readiness to exercise selectivity in adopting an independent course. This requires individual judgment of a critical nature, and on many issues a person may be unwilling or indeed disinterested in making such a judgment. But rather than being captive of the group's stand, either in tenaciously adhering to it or as tenaciously rejecting it, the individual shows sincerity in choosing his or her course with discrimination. Although that may seem a quite optimistic view, it is not unrealistic.

The foundation for independence needs to be established early in life, particularly in the educational process. However, traditional educational practices are not geared to encouraging independence. The observational studies of Henry (1963) and Jackson (1968) are among those which indicate that the social psychological forces in the traditional classroom foster obedience to authority and compliance to peer pressure. There is an overemphasis on giving the right answer, without a chance for creative problem solving aimed at solutions which are not pat answers. Critical judgment in evaluating alternative solutions is something which might be better practiced and rewarded in schooling. More opportunities are needed for different, even if unpopular, views on contemporary issues to be aired. Flacks (1967) found that student activists of various persuasions had come from homes where free expression of views was encouraged. Part of their complaint was the discovery that the university was not as receptive to their expressions of concern, for example, about hypocrisy in societal values, as had been their home environment.

The fear of peer disapproval, which is especially powerful in the adolescent years, needs to be overcome. Bronfenbrenner (1961) found that adolescents who were seen by their peers to be leaders were more independent. However, he also found that the tendency of American parents was to encourage reliance on peers (Bronfenbrenner, 1970). My own research on fifth-graders (Hollander & Marcia, 1970) indicated that children whose parents gave way to the peer group were more peer-oriented but also less likely to be leaders. Those youngsters chosen by peers as leaders were among the children who were most independent from both peer and adult pressures. If given a chance, there is some hope then that independence can be seen as a basis for social approval.

Achieving a state in which individual expression becomes normative and expected on matters of social importance will not come easily or quickly. In general, it would help to have more said and written about this topic. Although there are many people who do take independent stands, others who lack the zeal or confidence in their own views need to be encouraged to do the same. Providing favorable early experience, desirable models, and a supportive social climate are all essential to attaining that goal.

# PART 4
# Conclusions

CHAPTER 19

# Summing Up

## Lessons from Experience

### INTRODUCTION

A leader's action or inaction, and its informed or uniformed basis, can have multiple effects on others. It is no wonder, therefore, that attention is so often focused on the leader. These points were made earlier in Chapter 2, and Inclusive Leadership recognizes this tendency. But it takes a broader view of what a leader can do by way of distributing leader tasks, such as monitoring, planning, scheduling, and the like. This can be achieved within the four Rs of Inclusive Leadership set out in Chapter 1. To reiterate they are: *Respect*, *Recognition*, *Responsiveness*, and *Responsibility*, both ways, in an interdependent relationship and are vital to successful practice.

This mode of sharing is what Bower (1997) urges be part of a "leadership organization," also mentioned in Chapter 1. Given what often will be a heavy agenda of matters to be addressed, a leader needs to find ways of involving others in these matters and empowering them in decision making. However, the process is not found as often as it could be in practice.

Inclusive Leadership considers that leaders and leadership matter, although critics have at times raised doubts about the nature, even the reality, of the leadership phenomenon. Among these, Kerr (1977) expressed skepticism about the importance of leadership, arguing that there were "substitutes for leadership," particularly in organizational rules and customs, that keep the operation going (cf. Kerr & Jermier, 1978). In addition, Calder (1977) made the observation that leadership depends more on attributions made by followers than on the leader's actions. The reality, however, is that followers do perceive leaders to be responsible for outcomes, which are inescapably associated with a leader. This is why the leader-follower relationship necessitates some degree of trust and loyalty.

### INCLUSION AND NONINCLUSION

Inclusive Leadership has applicability to the workplace and also to the political process, in a larger sphere of activity. The reality of the world, as it is, involves not just cooperative activity, but tensions resulting from conflict over resources, personal vanity, envy, and many other problematic qualities that exist in real relationships. Therefore, not everything can be dealt with by trying inclusion, especially if there are adversarial elements that prevent common understandings and compromise. We see this barrier in some labor-management difficulties and at the highest level of government, where politics prevents favorable outcomes for the nation as a whole. Nonetheless, trying to apply Inclusive Leadership practices is worth doing whenever possible to counteract these problems and arrive at beneficial solutions, through greater inclusion.

There are other issues associated with noninclusion that become apparent in the absence of respect and responsiveness. In labor-management relations, for example, money issues may seem to be the main factor in conflict and calling for a strike. However, the heart of the matter many times is a sense of grievance among employees that they are neither respected nor responded to by management and the owners. This is also seen in interpersonal relations when people believe they are being "dissed," that is, disrespected.

## LEADER AWARENESS OF FOLLOWERS NEEDS

Awareness of what followers know and need is of course essential to leadership, as this book emphasizes from the outset. However, it does not mean giving up judgment as a leader. In a representative government, though, being informed about the will of the electorate is basic to public service, in the best sense. A popular misconception is the belief that a leader "keeping a finger to the wind" is usually bad, which it can be, if taken to the extreme. Said disparagingly, it suggests always trying to do what the public wants. However, the alternative is not to bother at all, but to do whatever the leader wants and considers singularly "doing the right thing." That may be possible in an absolute monarchy, where a so-called divine right may be invoked, or in an authoritarian government, wielding power within a climate of fear, without liberty and security for its people.

The word *democracy*, therefore, may mean no more than a rigged "election," which yields "shamocracy." The dictator remains in control and operates a "kleptocracy," in which the leader and coterie loot their nation.

Examples show that persisting unresponsiveness to a need is also a source of discontent. Health care is financially unavailable to a large segment of the U.S. population, the number of which is now estimated at 47 million people without any coverage. It has been a recurring and growing problem for more than half a century, since Harry Truman was president and spoke about dealing with the need. Over 20 years later, when Richard Nixon was in the presidency, he backed proposals for getting a form of universal coverage, which failed to pass in Congress. Another 20 years later and the plan for coverage early in President Clinton's first term was stopped in large part by lobbying and successful opposition advertising, with "Harry and Louise," a senior couple (of actors), talking about their concerns that the plan would allow the government to intrude on their medical choices. The plan was defeated, and the subsequent growth in Health Management Organizations (HMOs) created a mammoth industry that is believed to be intrusive and costly, without government involvement. A widespread government program, Medicare, mainly for the elderly, was introduced by President Lyndon Johnson in the 1960s, over opposition from organized medicine. Its essential, low-cost features have been recognized as making it among the most effective and popular government programs.

Health care has come up in the debates by candidates for party nominations in the 2008 party presidential nominations campaign. But a big constituency—city and metropolitan area dwellers—have felt their needs are entirely left out and are being ignored. That view has been made public in open letters from mayors of many cities who cite statistics that 80% of the nation's people live in these urban areas. They ask the fundamental question of why the needs of this vast constituency, for housing, schooling, infrastructure, and environmental safety, as examples, are not being addressed by candidates.

## INCLUSIVE AND NONINCLUSIVE LEADERSHIP

Significant leadership functions are present when serving on awards committees and on other bodies, such as commissions dealing with academic development. In the many years that I have been active in such a role, I found these functions to be very important and compelling. Two examples from my experience deserve mention as exemplifying an emphasis on inclusiveness in leadership.

I have repeatedly argued in favor of giving more than one award if there is a tie, despite contentions that it dilutes its value. The argument is offered that receipt of an award in a year when others also receive it diminishes its value. However, that is how the Nobel Awards are given, and plainly that honor is undiminished when listed on a recipient's record.

Presenting this "fairness" argument usually prevailed in discussions and gave recognition to more than one deserving candidate, rather than standing on a firm principle of only one at a time. There were and are other points at issue, such as an institutional "turn," regarding a department or school whose time had come, which could deprive someone else of an award because of that consideration. It has to be weighed carefully. As for the monetary aspect of an award, ideally the funds should be available to take care that the money is received, even if, as so often is the case, with the Nobel Awards, it must be divided. However, money is not the principal reason for desiring that award, although it could be for some, of course.

The second activity that I took on enthusiastically was to be involved in academic development. After current CUNY Chancellor Matthew Goldstein first became president of Baruch College, succeeding Joel Segall in the early 1990s, he formed a Presidential Commission made up of faculty, staff, and student members to work on and advise him regarding important matters such as a mission statement for the college and preparation for the Middle States Evaluation. He had the provost Lois Cronholm chair commission meetings, and she kept things moving well.

One special task I willingly took on as a commission member was to chair a committee that studied and then proposed a new school at Baruch, as an expansion of the role of the Public Administration Department. Eventually called the School of Public Affairs (SPA), it consolidated other elements within it, including educational administration. With a dedicated group of colleagues, including faculty and students from public administration, political science, management, education, and philosophy, among others, we carried on a process of our own, speaking to many constituents, meeting often to work on our proposal to the commission and president. After many months, we presented it for discussion, and it was approved. Goldstein made a recommendation to the CUNY Board for the establishment of SPA, based on our report, which went through without any difficulty. SPA celebrated its tenth anniversary a couple of years ago and has thrived, with good students and faculty and support for its many activities in the community.

My impression of the president in this matter was that he was letting the committee do its work without interference from him or the provost in achieving the mission he set for us when we first met, consistent with Inclusive Leadership. Of course, one might be dubious and say that he knew we would deliver what he wished to have, and that we were providing cover so he could point to us as the agent of a change that some were known to resist. We did indeed have opportunities to hear voices of dissent, as well as of approval, or mild questioning of issues at stake, and skepticism. However, there was an above board process followed that sought facts, not just opinions, and that could have been more contentious if we had not followed it.

## POWER OVER

"Power over people" is far more often seen than "power with people," in Mary Parker Follett's (1949) phrase. The traditional use of power over is antagonistic to participation. It is not hard to find examples of its resistance to challenge, expressed in one form in the "Iron Law of Oligarchy," stated as "Those who possess power are reluctant to part with it." There are many more examples of noninclusive leadership than of the inclusive kind.

What will change it is to realign thinking to the processes that can yield productive outcomes. Good instances of this are found in self-managed work groups that operate as teams (see e.g., Hackman, 1989; Katzenbach & Smith, 1993; Manz & Sims, 1989, 1986). A team is far more than just a collection of individuals grouped together, as is apparent in sports, and in many other reaches of life. The point is well made that "We need to honor our teams more, our aggressive leaders and maverick geniuses less" (Reich, 1987, p. 78). Team efforts are a superb example of collaboration in achieving mutual task goals but also gaining satisfaction from social interaction. The value of relationships is often much more important for fulfillment than is recognized. Among other things, such contact tends to sustain people throughout life by enriching experience and contributing to understanding. Indeed, the nature of the workplace is better seen to be a source of both kinds of rewards, task and interpersonal.

## CONCLUSION

Inclusive Leadership encourages an active role for followers, which is essential for group, organizational, and societal success. Yet, followers too often are disregarded in focusing largely on a leader giving top-down direction. Their involvement usually improves the likelihood of achieving desired goals. Ann Howard (1997) is among those whose research corroborates the need for empowerment of front-line workers making decisions that provide solutions in organizations. She reports that "The compelling evidence of benefits to leaders, their direct reports, and to the organization suggest that mastering empowerment is definitely worth the effort" (p. 66).

In contrast to the traditional view of the leader's top-down role, Inclusive Leadership sees followers as also having an active role and rejects the passivity often expected of followers. As "subordinates" they are at best treated as silent partners. True enough, they may indeed become so when discouraged by combinations of a dominant leader and unresponsive situation. A poor fate often awaits those who try to break out of this pattern of maintaining silence, even though the willingness to speak up can have productive features. This theme of independence is another one that is part of the Inclusive Leadership approach to leader-follower relations put forth in this book.

Whether leaders are viewed as transformational, transactional, or inclusive, some important common elements of good leadership that unite them, in achieving "positive results," are respect for and attention to followers, their needs, and views, including the potentially useful information they can provide.

# AFTERWORD

## A Career in Leadership

*A Life in Psychology*

### STARTING COLLEGE AND ENTERING MILITARY SERVICE

World War II was long under way when I became a 17-year-old freshman at Western Reserve University (WRU) in Cleveland. It was January 1945, and I felt a patriotic sense to join the military. My main contribution to the war effort before then was service as a Junior Air Raid Warden while a high school senior in New York City, and also working part of a summer as a lathe operator in a defense plant there. I came to college for liberal arts and sciences, but with law or medicine as possible professions, in which I had family members. My awareness of psychology was limited then, but I eventually became a psychology major in a strong department, especially influenced by Chairman Calvin Hall and Professor Daniel Levinson.

In spring 1945 I began my military service career by volunteering for pilot training in the Navy Air Corps, expecting to be called up by the end of that semester. I liked aviation, having flown as a child, and building many plane models that flew, and crashed, too. After physical and psychological tests, and being sworn into Navy Air, the war in Europe ended in April. However, the war in the Pacific was still very active, including talk of an invasion of Japan. In August, though, Japan surrendered, just as I turned 18. I was not called up, but instead released from the Navy, with a draft deferment to continue college. I had enrolled for classes that summer of 1945. Then, after another year of courses, including the summer of 1946, I gave up further deferments, and that fall went into the army as a private. I did five weeks of jungle-type basic training in Louisiana, at what now is Fort Polk. A challenging experience, I was grateful for my background of many years in Scouting and as a scout leader.

Having done at least two years of course work at WRU, the army sent me to Letterman General Hospital in San Francisco as a psychological assistant doing interviewing and testing in the Neuro-Psychiatric Service, after a brief orientation at Brooke Army Medical Center in San Antonio. It was a rich professional experience, and I was discharged with other draftees in the spring of 1947. This service background qualified me for a commission in psychology as an ensign in the Medical Service Corps of the Naval Reserve, on graduating from WRU in 1948 with my bachelor's degree. I liked WRU, studied with very good professors, and had bright men and women friends. I enjoyed student admission rates for the Cleveland Orchestra at Severance Hall on campus and lived most of my college years nearby at a fraternity house. A sometime outfielder in softball, but better at tennis, I worked for a time in animal research labs and as a camp counselor.

My inclination as a senior was to go to graduate school in psychology, but I faced some practical issues. Much as I liked Cleveland, and had friends and family members there, I wanted to be back in New York City where many others were. Cleveland and New York are on a major railroad line that was the New York Central, which goes through Rochester, New York, my birthplace. At five, I came with my mother from there to live in New York City, when she remarried after my parents divorced. By stopping there en route I continued to see my father, Victor, a master printer, who was a champion four-wall handball player.

He taught and coached the sport, wrote a column about it for the local Y's newspaper, and developed a scoring system to record play. An avid reader, especially of news, when we visited in New York or Rochester over the years, we talked a lot about current events. He remarried and had a daughter, my sister Maxine, who married a lawyer and was a teacher. They have a daughter who is a psychiatric social worker, and the mother of three, all of whom with which we maintain contact.

Throughout, my parents and their families, in Rochester and Detroit, encouraged me. My mother, Lillian, had a women's hat store in New York, and my sister, Judy, from her second marriage, was starting high school, and we remained close. She taught, married a pediatrician, and became a school psychologist. They have three children, a daughter and son who teach in major law schools, and a son who practices public interest law.

Although there were good friends and educational possibilities in New York, financing graduate school without having an assistantship was problematic. Late in the summer of 1948, I was making up for my time away in service by doing two full summer sessions to receive my bachelor's degree from WRU, using my GI Bill benefits. For a brief time, there was the option of going to law school in New York State, as some friends were doing. Observing my lawyer stepfather gave me an indication of what his law practice involved. However, my decision to give up the law alternative was a positive choice based on my enthusiasm for psychology and the social sciences.

## WORKING AS A WRITER IN NEW YORK CITY AND GOING PART TIME TO COLUMBIA UNIVERSITY

During the uncertain years before entering the army, I had a major outlet in writing a humor column for the WRU newspaper and also in doing movie and theater reviews for it. As a feature writer, I also went to press conferences and other events to cover persons of interest. Among these were Senator Robert Taft of Ohio and a popular crooner who was in the city for a downtown concert. The former was very formal and controlled in his statements, as might be expected of someone who came from a political dynasty in which his father was president of the United States. By contrast, the singer in his hotel suite was brash with reporters and often insulting to his coterie. There were other interesting chances to meet, interview, and write about people of note, mainly in music, the arts, politics, and academics. Eventually, this led to my thought of continuing a writing career.

For income and experience, I looked for and found a job as a writer in New York City. For study, I enrolled part time in the School of General Studies at Columbia University, which offered many evening courses. Two of those I took that year were methodological, one on surveys, and the others on communications, mass media, and marketing techniques. This allowed me to live in the graduate dorms on campus, with a very genial group of friends. We shared many interests and discussions. On weekend nights with friends I went to plays or heard Dixieland jazz greats like Sidney Bechet, Max Kaminsky, and pianists Marian McPartland and Don Shirley. I later roomed in John Jay Hall with a British accountant who worked in a financial role. We both liked opera, and he obtained low-cost tickets to the Met. One night at intermission outside the boxes we met and chatted with the actor Basil Rathbone, tall and elegant in formal wear. Best known for playing Sherlock Holmes in films, he exuded good humor that night.

My employer was the Royal Typewriter Company, at 2 Park Avenue, between 32nd and 33rd Streets, less than a mile from Baruch College where I now am. My title was copywriter, and my senior and mentor was Charlie Webber. The company was one of the leading firms in its industry, and I was grateful to have a position there and to be sharpening my writing skills. It employed Young & Rubicam, a major advertising agency, but maintained an in-house staff for writing and producing promotional materials, a "house organ" (company magazine). I wrote articles for it and also had a major assignment in writing the instruction manual for the new "Gray Magic" Portable, which went through multiple drafts before being printed. It was a great learning experience in producing accurate and easily understood instructional prose. My efforts were helped by the keen editing of Charlie, who wielded his pencil like a rapier and was a good person to have as a mentor. I also appreciated the genial department head Ellis G. Bishop. But, after almost a year, I left for full-time graduate school. They were understanding that I wanted to continue my education.

## BEGINNING FULL-TIME GRADUATE STUDY AT COLUMBIA UNIVERSITY

Starting in the summer of 1949, I took courses in the Department of Psychological Foundations at Teachers College (TC), Columbia University, and was given an assistantship almost immediately. It was a marvelous opportunity that attracted me by the dynamic psychology emphasized and the impressive faculty there that included Robert Thorndike, a contributor to applied psychology, whom I assisted in his psychometrics course and his research. He was completing his book *Personnel Selection* (1949). I also had an assistantship with Ruth Cunningham, a noted developmental psychologist researching the playground behavior of school children, and their group processes, for her landmark book. Along the way, I had been studying psychometrics and methodology with Thorndike and the energetic Irving Lorge. For my master's degree research, I evaluated a new diagnostic test.

By the time I received my MA, in June 1950, I had been greatly impressed by the wave of ideas about leadership* I encountered in various courses and contacts I had the previous two years. Margaret Mead, the eminent cultural anthropologist, offered a course I took on contemporary cultures. A dynamic speaker, among other topics she covered modern European dictatorships and their methods of coercion and control, through fear arousal, and showed films and some other mass media devices. I drew on my psychology major background, and army service assisting in neuropsychiatry.

My undergraduate social psychology course at WRU was with Daniel Levinson, who assigned Otto Klineberg's influential 1940 text, as well as the Newcomb and Hartley (1947) *Readings in Social Psychology*, with a research requirement that I did on measuring social attitudes. At Columbia, I had a graduate social psychology course and seminar with Klineberg, and an applied social course with Goodwin Watson, another compelling figure with a major text and dedicated following. Both later served on my dissertation committee, as part of their role codirecting the interdepartmental doctoral program in social psychology.

By the time I completed work for my master's, I saw leadership as a preferred topic for dissertation research and as central to many areas of study within the field of social and organizational psychology. It also had ramifications to conformity and independence, as

---

* Among contributors to it were John Hemphill, Fillmore Sanford, Alvin Gouldner, Ralph Stogdill, Carroll Shartle, Edwin Fleishman, Kurt Lewin, Rensis Likert, Jacob Moreno, Helen Hall Jennings, and George Homans, dealing with situational factors, followers, interpersonal behaviors, group dynamics, and social exchange, to challenge traditional ones.

well as cohesiveness, and communication—all three central to Lewin's Theory of Group Dynamics (1947). At Columbia my exposure included concepts of power, represented by Robert Lynd, and an acquaintance with Robert Merton, another sociologist. His concept of the "self-fulfilling prophecy" impressed me as a precursor of cognitive social psychology, along with "definition of the situation" and "reference group." These three concepts struck me as clearly relevant to leadership phenomena, as are motivational and learning concepts from basic psychology.

## DOING RESEARCH AS A NAVAL AVIATION PSYCHOLOGIST AND EARNING MY PH.D.

The Korean War had begun in June 1950. When notified of a chance to serve on duty as a naval aviation psychologist, I completed summer courses at Columbia, did the fall semester of 1950 to finish my course work for a Ph.D., and passed the comprehensive exam for going on to a dissertation. In January 1951, I reported to the U.S. Navy Bureau of Medicine and Surgery in Washington for orientation in the aviation psychology branch there. About a month later, I was assigned to research duty at the Aviation Psychology Laboratory in the Naval School of Aviation Medicine in Pensacola, Florida. Its major missions in the Naval Air Training Command were to train flight surgeons and to conduct research on behalf of the Command's tasks. Mainly recent medical school graduates comprised the school's student body, and they received units of instruction from some of the psychologists on the staff, totaling about ten, roughly half each naval officers and civilians. During my almost three years there, our staff of psychologists at various times grew to nearly 20.

I gave a basic lecture on descriptive and inferential statistics, with examples from our research on pilot selection and training. The latter was illustrated by our research on motivation and morale problems that we found underlying voluntary withdrawal from flight training by cadets (Bair & Hollander, 1953). In these studies, we used the "critical incident" technique (Flanagan, 1954) to have a comparison of how the voluntary dropouts compared with successful cadets in describing their "best" and "worst" flight instructors (Hollander & Bair, 1954). This approach examined how attitudes could be indicative of motives, and our findings were soon published in these two papers in the *Journal of Aviation Medicine*. John Bair and I reported that cadets who successfully completed training more often characterized their flight instructors in interpersonal terms, while those who dropped out emphasized their instructors' competence or incompetence. We concluded that a factor associated with success in the program was identification with the flight instructor or a lack thereof. Further investigation revealed that other factors involved were the variations in discipline across the training fields around Pensacola, problems with preferential scheduling of flights, and, in some instances and places, indifferent leadership. *Interpersonal evaluation*, however, was clearly a major factor in the "dropout rate."

After being routinely promoted to lieutenant, junior grade, I was given approval by our lab's director, Commander Alan Grinsted, to carry on further leadership studies aimed initially at learning more about completing or not completing the flight training program. His successor, Commander Brant Clark, was also a research-oriented psychologist, very supportive of such initiatives. They were backed by the commandant of the school, Navy Captain Ashton Graybiel.

Our lab regularly administered tests and measures to the new sections of cadets entering training, as often as weekly. I began by studying the validity and reliability of peer nominations under various conditions of administration to these cadets, so as to assess leadership and the likelihood of successfully completing the pilot training program. These studies yielded basic information on the peer nomination technique published in major journals. Eventually, these were republished with new integrative chapters in my 1964 book, *Leaders, Groups, and Influence*. Also, when at Carnegie Tech, I did a subsequent study in 1955 under an Office of Naval Research (ONR) contract. It involved the use of peer nominations in predicting performance as an officer, over at least two years from graduation from the Naval Officer Candidate School (OCS) at Newport, Rhode Island. The basic findings were confirmation that peer nominations gave significant additional prediction, as well as substantial reliability (Hollander, 1964, 1965).

At the Aviation Psychology Laboratory I had the equivalent of a postdoctoral fellowship, except I still needed to do a dissertation for my degree. I was grateful, therefore, to have the opportunity to develop a proposal that could be researched at Pensacola, once approved by a dissertation committee at Columbia. The key person to achieve this linkage was Robert Thorndike, with whom I had worked, and who was a Defense Department consultant. With his approval of methods, and Otto Klineberg's and Goodwin Watson's agreement on the social psychology elements, the committee was completed with Samuel Flowerman and Joseph Shoben. It approved the study I proposed using peer nominations on leadership and the California F-Scale measure of authoritarian attitudes, which my former professor, Daniel Levinson, had helped develop. My interest extended to seeing if scores on the F-Scale might be related to a military structure.

The two guiding hypotheses for my dissertation research were (a) there is a significant positive relationship between scores on the F-Scale and which cadets are chosen for a leadership role in a military setting; and (b) there is a significant difference between the leadership nominees chosen by those "high" and "low" on their F-Scale scores. I did preliminary research with an independent sample of cadets who had responded to the F-Scale with *significantly higher scores* than their own responses, when instructed to answer as though it were "a test of military leadership potential" on which they wished to make a "good score." Nonetheless, both hypotheses in the major study were significantly rejected in the nine cadet sections used ($N = 268$). Indeed, the cadets who came out "highest" on leadership had significantly lower F-Scale scores, irrespective of the standing on scores of those making the nominations. These findings were robust and had important implications for subsequent study.

I received my Ph.D. degree at Columbia not long after a successful oral defense in October 1952, once I filed my dissertation at Low Library and paid a fee, which I recall as $30, and my sister Judy came along. She and my mother had attended my master's graduation in 1950 and were a marvelous team of supporters.

A paper based on my dissertation was accepted and published in the *Journal of Abnormal and Social Psychology* (Hollander, 1954a), then the main American Psychological Association (APA) journal in social psychology. Interest in the F-Scale and my dissertation findings were a prod to further work. A few years later, it culminated in an evaluative review of the F-Scale literature, which I coauthored with Ed Titus, my graduate assistant when I joined the faculty at Carnegie Tech in January 1954. It appeared in the *Psychological Bulletin* (Titus & Hollander, 1957). Among the points we made there was the importance of a distinction between the meaning of F-Scale scores for individual attitudes, behaviors, and social structures.

## RETURNING TO PENSACOLA AND ANOTHER ACTIVE YEAR

After receiving my doctorate in fall 1952 at Columbia, I was already committed to remaining on duty for 1953. Wilse B. Webb was appointed our lab's civilian director, and he and I decided to do some research together. Our first study was on the relationship of peer nominations of leadership, followership, and friendship (Hollander & Webb, 1955). We asked cadets to assume they were assigned to "a special military unit with an undisclosed mission" and to name in order three members of their section they thought were most and least qualified to lead it. Then, each cadet was asked to assume that he had been assigned to lead it and to name three cadets he would most and least like to have in the special unit. Finally, the cadets were each asked to name their three best friends in the section. We found that nominations for leadership and followership were highly related, but *not* significantly affected by friendship ties.

This research showed the commonality of qualities valued in the roles of leader and follower. In general, followers are potential leaders who show that by their communication skills and dependability, among other desired qualities. Also, our research further bolstered findings that friendship does not represent an invalidating bias in leadership nominations. Intuitively, it is not obvious that liking someone means wanting them to have authority over oneself on a dangerous mission. Other factors, including situational ones, and particularly needed abilities, clearly matter.

Webb and I then studied the validity and relationship of three morale measures we used: a survey, pooled group judgments, and self-evaluations (Webb & Hollander, 1956). The survey method has been most commonly used, but its validity may not be as high as needed. We defined morale positively and simply as "an interest in and enthusiasm for the naval air program." We developed and administered the three measures in the same session, with eight sections of cadets ($N = 210$) and with appropriate attention to their reliability. These were at the acceptable level of 0.71 for the survey and 0.82 for the judgments represented in peer nominations. In predicting the criterion of remaining in training versus voluntarily withdrawing by the fifth month of flight training after preflight, the peer nominations yielded the highest predictability of 0.90 and the self-evaluation next at 0.83, with the survey last at 0.30. Our conclusion was that under appropriate conditions it is possible to increase the validity of predictions about morale by going beyond a survey to peer and self-evaluations.

## JOINING THE CARNEGIE TECH FACULTY IN PITTSBURGH

I had been seeking an academic post starting in the spring of 1953, with discharge from the navy impending by late that year. Among my choices was the Carnegie Institute of Technology (CIT), which had a doctoral program in (I/O) psychology. Although the market was considered tight, I had sufficient publications, with psychology experience in the army, and three years of service in the navy as a naval aviation psychologist. I had taught two courses at the Tulane University Extension Division at Pensacola, with good evaluations. One of my references, Robert Thorndike, was a mentor who knew Haller Gilmer, the CIT chairman, a well-regarded figure in the I/O field and author of a leading I/O textbook. Mostly, my visit and research presentation went well and my publication record was favorable, so I was pleased to be offered an assistant professorship, which I took up in January, 1954.

## THE DOCTORAL PROGRAM AT CARNEGIE TECH AND FORD FOUNDATION PROJECT

During the period when I began developing the idiosyncrasy credit (IC) model at CIT, I also spoke and wrote about the interactive nature of personality and the importance of time and context in social psychology (e.g., Hollander, 1960b). Some colleagues liked the concept, including Herb Simon, and others were critical of it or of its name. Serge Moscovici, my French colleague, insisted that it favored conformity, which I considered a misconception since the model was not telling how to behave in a normative way, but was descriptive of how things seem to be. Significantly, it is oriented toward follower effects on a leader, which is consistent with Moscovici's emphasis on minority influence (Moscovici, Lage, & Naffrechoux, 1969). I cited his work approvingly in my 1975 paper on *independence* (Chapter 18 here).

In addition to teaching undergraduate courses at CIT, I conducted a doctoral seminar on social psychology and another on research methods. I also had been asked by Herb Simon to work on his Ford Foundation research program on organizational decision making, which included Franco Modigliani and Merton Miller (later Nobel Laureates in economics), along with Jim March and Harold Guetzkow (see March & Simon, 1958). Simon was an authentic genius who won the Nobel Prize in Economics in 1978 for this research on executive decision making. He also wrote *Models of My Life* (1991), a revealing autobiography. He was a pioneer in artificial intelligence (AI) and was so invested in cognitive psychology that he chose to be head of the psychology department, at what had become Carnegie-Mellon University (CMU). Years before I had a small group's laboratory there where I conducted experimental research on leadership, conformity, and independence, in the IC model. Like an older brother giving advice, he patiently told me such research was unnecessary. His preferred method was testing his mathematical models via computer simulations with his "Iliac," an early computer he developed with Alan Newell. It filled a room. They were considered standouts among other brilliant and energetic colleagues.

I enjoyed working on Simon's project at CIT and took from it insights into systems theory and organizational decision processes. His much admired and often republished book *Administrative Behavior* (1947) was my first encounter with his writings. He made considerable efforts for social science at the National Academy of Sciences (NAS), where he came to board meetings as one of few social scientists on it. We encountered each other there, in 1979 and 1980, when I was on leave from State University of New York (SUNY)/Buffalo as an NAS study director in Washington, and had cordial relations. In the 1990s, he gave a stimulating address at the New School in New York City, when I was established at CUNY, and we last spoke together there.

Shortly after starting at CIT in 1954, I applied for and received a research contract from the Group Psychology Section of the ONR to extend my research on peer nominations to prediction of performance of graduates of the Naval OCS at Newport, Rhode Island, which I conducted in the summer of 1955. I prepared for the field phase at CIT with my research assistant, Bill Meanor, before going with him to the OCS that summer to gather data. The follow-up came from access to the evaluations given to the OCS graduates by their reporting seniors over at least a two-year period (Hollander, 1965). The results showed that even early positive peer nominations predicted performance and contributed to a high multiple correlation.

## DEVELOPING AND TESTING THE IDIOSYNCRASY CREDIT MODEL

This process of interpersonal evaluation was the starting point for talking with colleagues about my interest in status and influence expressed in the IC model. I did experimental research to test it (Hollander, 1960a, 1961a, 1964, Chapters 17 and 18), the first of which was with 48 junior CIT engineering students as subjects, in 12 groups of four each. The task was trying to predict which column would come up next in a mathematical matrix. A fifth member in each group was a "confederate" showing competence in coming up with the "correct" answer and either conforming or nonconforming to the prior procedural norms agreed to by the group members. His nonconformity was introduced at various times, early, middle, or late, in the sequence of trials. The number of trials in which his recommended solution was accepted as the group's choice measured the influence. A significant increase was found in his influence as the trials progressed. The results fit a prediction from the IC model that evidences of competence would yield greater influence, especially in combination with past evidence of conforming to the procedural norms (Hollander, 1960a).

## JOINING WASHINGTON UNIVERSITY AND ANOTHER IDIOSYNCRASY CREDIT EXPERIMENT

In the fall of 1958, I was ready for a challenge, and accepted an offer to join the Washington University (WU) Psychology Department as an associate professor to establish an interdepartmental doctoral program in social psychology. It also was accompanied by a major salary increase, and a research post in the WU Social Science Institute, begun by Nicholas Demerath, then sociology chair. Located in what had been the WU president's house, I had the good fortune to meet my wife-to-be, Pat, there at a Sunday reception concluding a grant-sponsored conference. We saw each other again on campus when we attended a lecture by Justice William O. Douglas that week. She was a practicing attorney in the city, who studied at WU, before going to St. Louis University, where she earned her law degree and bachelors' before. We were married in April 1959, with family, friends, and colleagues from both universities there. Our son Peter was born in December 1960.

I continued to have ONR funds for my research and was able to resume it and to publish further on the IC model and on peer nominations. In an experiment manipulating *competence* and *length of time in a group*, I sought how these two key variables affected perceptions of a member as higher status (Hollander, 1961b). Subjects (151, about equal in number by gender) were given a brief description of a group member of their gender whom they were to imagine possessing two of these variable qualities, with each receiving only one of the eight combinations of "level of performance" and whether "in the group a long or short time." The form then asked: "Knowing this information, how willing would you be to have this person in a position of authority in the group?" Responses were made on a seven-point scale from "very willing" to "definitely not." Rising scores for accorded status were found to be significantly related to competence, and "new to group" was uniformly lower than "in group for some while" at each degree.

Subjects then provided an evaluation of the same person in terms of eight possible ways he or she might behave in the group, including "Interrupts to express comments," "Suggests changes from group plans," and "Discusses group concerns with outsiders." The first two are innovative behaviors that were more acceptable from a higher-status person, and the third was a breach of group trust, less acceptable for one of higher status. No gender effects were found. Results fit predictions from the IC model, and my paper was published in the *Journal of Abnormal and Social Psychology* (1961b).

## APA COMMITTEE ON PSYCHOLOGY IN NATIONAL AND INTERNATIONAL AFFAIRS

After the first year at WU, I was able to extend my interests in applying social psychology by accepting membership on the APA Working Group on Psychology in National and International Affairs, starting with the summer of 1959. The board established it at the behest of the then APA executive officer Roger Russell. Pat and I went to Washington for a couple of months that summer where I contributed to a study of what psychologists could do feasibly to make contributions in such areas as international tension reduction. Our Working Group filed a report based on interviews and other information from knowledgeable sources that led the following year to the creation of a follow-on, the APA Committee on Psychology in National and International Affairs. I was appointed to it for a three-year term, 1960–1963, under the chairmanship of Charles Osgood, a leading cognitive social psychologist at the University of Illinois, and eventually succeeded him in that post in 1962–1963.

Returning to WU in the fall of 1959, I continued to attend occasional meetings in Washington. In the course of these, I met the chairman of the Psychology Department at American University (AU) who told me about the new School of International Service (SIS) there and that the dean was interested in hiring a social psychologist to join with a sociologist and anthropologist in setting up and teaching a behavioral science curriculum for graduate and undergraduate students at SIS. The intent was to provide an alternative to usual area studies in traditional schools of diplomacy. The post was open starting in 1960–1961 and would carry a joint appointment as associate professor in psychology and probably sociology, if suitable. He asked me about my interest, or if someone I knew might be a candidate, and I agreed to consider it.

This was an interesting possibility that would bring me to Washington to do challenging things. I had hoped that the situation regarding the doctoral program in social would brighten at WU. The funding and territorial issues hampered progress, although a new social psychologist, Art Shulman, had been hired in psychology. I was not yet tenured and the prospect of my going to Washington, even for a year on leave, was clearly a deterrent to my getting it. Among others, I consulted with the psychology Chair, Marion Bunch, who had recruited me and seemed friendly and supportive. He spoke optimistically and wanted me to stay beyond the second year and work on certain issues. Others, like Nick Demerath, were encouraging, too, but I was not persuaded, and, with respect, felt otherwise.

## JOINING THE SCHOOL OF INTERNATIONAL SERVICE AT AMERICAN UNIVERSITY

In the Washington scene, the allure was becoming greater, however, with Osgood and several of my colleagues on the committee interested in my taking on a part-time role with it at APA's Central Office, then on 16th Street, just north of Massachusetts Avenue, if I decided to join the AU faculty. It was to be as interim executive secretary for the start up first year of the operation, 1960–1961.

When I visited AU to speak to colleagues there and the dean of SIS, Earnest Griffith, in late spring of 1960, he offered me the post of associate professor of social psychology, with joint appointments in psychology and sociology. With Pat's concurrence, I agreed to accept it starting with the fall semester, and we moved to Washington that summer. Pat was pregnant with our son, but stalwart during the move despite the lack of knowledge of our furniture's whereabouts for many days en route while we were set up in a motel outside Washington. (Later, it was explained that the truck driver had stopped for a visit on the way without properly notifying his firm.) Peter was born on December 7, 1960, in a snowstorm that coincided with what were many deflated celebrations, in advance of the Kennedy inauguration, after his election victory the previous month. I was allowed to sleep overnight on a cot in her room, with the baby in an adjoining alcove, at the Washington Hospital Center.

We had rented an apartment on upper Connecticut Avenue, near Nebraska Avenue, convenient to AU and APA, on or near major bus lines. Busy was the order of the day, with teaching and meetings on curriculum at AU. I greatly appreciated the opportunity to teach very able undergraduates at SIS and innovate a graduate course in international communication there. I also taught undergraduate social psychology in the usual departments and served on graduate committees for dissertations. One of them in psychology was for Ralph Rosnow, who became a lifelong friend and is a recent retiree from Temple University with a distinguished career in social psychology. I contributed a chapter (Hollander, 2006) to a book from his colleagues and friends that was dedicated to him.

Back in Washington in 1960, at APA we were getting activities under way to bring psychology to government policy, especially in such critical matters as international tension reduction. Indeed, the new administration taking office in early 1961 was ripe for attention to such ideas, given the Cold War with the Soviet Union. We gained access to the U.S. Senate, largely through Hubert Humphrey (D–Minnesota), to hold meetings with senators and staffers on these issues. His sister was high up at the new Arms Control and Disarmament Agency, to which he provided us access. Osgood was often featured as a presenter of his GRIT (Graduated Reciprocation in Tension-Reduction) Strategy, which was central to his later book, *An Alternative to War or Surrender* (1962). We had meetings too with the U.S. State Department and the related Information Agency, as well as the House of Representatives and the then U.S. Government Personnel Department, for whose directors Fred Fiedler and I conducted a half-day conference on current developments in the study of leadership.

We also made contact with the United Nations, about which I spoke and did an article published in the *IAAP Newsletter* (Hollander, 2005). A key episode was a meeting at the office of Ralph Bunche, then undersecretary-general, who was a friend of Otto Klineberg's, a member of our committee who was with us that day. It led to other meetings with UN officials and research that we undertook in its behalf. Subsequently, Larry Solomon, who became the full-time executive secretary of our committee in 1962–1964, with a grant we were able to get from the Marshall Foundation, arranged a conference through Brookings on making more effective UN public communications. It followed a study I had directed analyzing the coverage of UN activities in newspapers internationally. Such activities gained space and prominence mainly through conflict, as in a split of views and votes in the Security Council. However, many of the noteworthy UN activities are relatively nonconflictful, having to do with health, labor, and child welfare, as exemplified by the World Health Organization, International Labor Organization, and UN International Children's Emergency Fund, respectively. Therefore, I was not surprised to find that they received scant attention unless they had a conflict element in a story. A key question was how to get good works of the United Nations better known. Earlier I had gathered data for the U.S. portion of a study for UN Educational, Scientific, and Cultural Organization on attitudes of young people toward atomic power.

Given those commitments, I was pleased to cochair a subcommittee with Herbert Kelman to prepare a report anticipating how psychologists could aid in the UN International Cooperation Year (ICY) in 1965. We were joined by Urie Bronfenbrenner from the committee and Eugene Jacobson from APA's Committee on International Relations in Psychology (CIRP). Based on a two-day meeting of the four of us at Ann Arbor, Michigan, Kelman and I prepared a report published in the *American Psychologist* (AP) in 1964, and a committee report also in the AP in 1962.

All of these activities had been demanding, even with the sense of exhilaration from some successes. I was pleased at those inroads made and by the appointment of Larry Solomon as full-time executive secretary, which I had helped arrange. It also was gratifying to be elected Chair of the committee for 1962–1963, the third and last year of my term. Nevertheless, as much as I appreciated being involved with policy issues, and high-intensity activity, I lacked the time or circumstances to continue much scholarly work. However, there was a small beginning of something under way, a book of readings I had started to edit with Raymond Hunt, whom I met in the WU psychology department. He and his wife, Vi, had been among our closest friends there and had moved back to the University of Buffalo (UB) in 1961, where he had earned his doctorate in 1958. His dissertation there was on verbal learning under the text author and experimentalist Richard Bugelski, also a local person, who had earned a Yale Ph.D. and had studied with Clark Hull, the eminent learning theorist.

Ray was an extraordinarily broad-gauged social scientist, with creative interests in social psychology, among his other proclivities in clinical psychology, cultural anthropology, and linguistics, then organizational analysis, survey techniques, and management. At WU he and I planned a collection of readings in social psychology that would reflect a wider scope and have introductions to sections that we would prepare as coeditors, showing students the integrative nature of the field. That book emerged as *Current Perspectives in Social Psychology*, first published in 1963 by Oxford University Press, and in subsequent editions through the fourth in 1976. We also did a companion volume, *Classic Contributions to Social Psychology*, also from Oxford, in 1972. Both were widely adopted, with a third of the royalties to the American Psychological Foundation. While in contact to prepare the book, Ray told me that UB was to become part of the State University of New York by joining the system as its largest campus. It was set to occur in 1962. Long a fully developed private university, UB had major professional schools, in medicine since 1846, its year of founding, and law not much later. It also had schools of education, business, social work, and architecture, as well as other health sciences and undergraduate colleges, among the rest. New funds would make it possible to expand graduate study, including additional doctoral programs in psychology, to add to experimental and biopsychology, with clinical, and counseling psychology all in place. Developmental and community psychology were contemplated for the future.

Ray said that UB was to have an immediate search for a director of a social psychology doctoral program, with a role in adding more faculty, for which he wanted me to be a candidate. He presented it as an attractive alternative to my current post at AU. He was at WU as a friendly colleague to observe the contrast in those years. However, at that moment, in the spring of 1962, my initial thought was not to consider a move from Washington barely two years after arriving. Pat as well as those friends and colleagues at AU with whom I shared the possibility were mostly of the same view. On the other hand, although I was to become chair of the APA committee for a year, I would not have to be in Washington any longer on a regular basis. Several members including Charlie Osgood were favorable to my considering the substantial opportunity this would represent. It also would be resuming an academic career in my major field, after the significant diversion I had taken.

## GOING TO THE UNIVERSITY OF BUFFALO (UB) TO START A SOCIAL PSYCHOLOGY DOCTORAL PROGRAM, AS IT BECOMES SUNY AT BUFFALO

After our two-year interlude in Washington, we moved to Buffalo. UB was to become part of the State University of New York (SUNY) by joining the system as its largest campus in 1962, the year I became Director of the Social Psychology Doctoral Program and a Professor there. My father Victor still lived in Rochester, my birthplace, which I had left with my mother when I was about five. I now was about 65 miles away and glad to be able to see him and my sister, Maxine, from his second marriage. She had been an assistant in college to Urie Bronfenbrenner, who was my friend and colleague on the APA Committee in Washington. She and her husband have a daughter and were guests at our home in Buffalo as were we at theirs in Rochester. We would drive over there with our son, Peter, a few years older than his cousin, and visit with my father together, as well.

There was least one commitment that I joyfully undertook at the time of the August 1962 APA Convention in St. Louis. I was to convene and chair a conference on social influence research, under the auspices of ONR's group psychology branch, held at Washington University. It involved eight of us presenting and drawing inferences from our research, which was recorded for publication, after which I edited it. It came out the following year from UB as *A Convergence on Social Influence* (1963).

It was in our home across from the campus that we entertained colleagues and friends, and a stellar group of leading social psychologists who came to give speeches and seminars sponsored by our doctoral program, thanks to UB and grant funds. Solomon Asch, Leon Festinger, Irving Janis, Daniel Katz, and Muzafer Sherif were among those notables who came to visit in the first four years while we lived in that home, before we moved to suburban Amherst, where the new expansion campus was being built.

At UB we were able to create a fully equipped Small Groups Laboratory for experimental work on the third floor of its main building, Townsend Hall, which was extensively in use. The research done there included conformity experiments I did with Gordon Haaland, who was among the first Ph.D.s I directed at UB. We published one of those in the leading APA social psychology journal in 1965, with Jim Julian. Haaland went to a teaching position at the University of New Hampshire, where years later he became President. Eventually, he went to the presidency of Gettysburg College, from which he retired recently. Another early Ph.D. was S. K. Dani, who had a Master's degree from Cambridge, and returned to India, to be a professor, and then became principal of a college of psychology.

Jim Julian was a kindred thinker and my closest co-worker in leadership and conformity research at UB, with whom I had many productive years under contract support from the "Group Psychology Branch" of ONR, headed by Luigi Petrullo, a splendid person to have as a research monitor. Another person there for support was John Nagay, also highly esteemed, who provided funds in connection with my peer nominations research. Among our program's students who published with us were Rick Ryckman, Dick Sorrentino, Cal Regula, Rick Kimball, Steve Lewis, Charles Langan, Barry Fallon, Jan Yoder, Linda Neider, Jim Gleason, Jim Seaman, Orly Ben-Yoav, and Peter Carnevale. He joined the NYU faculty some years ago, and I was pleased to have him as a discussant at the New York Academy of Sciences.

Ray Hunt and I had been able to get a social psychology training grant from NIMH for doctoral study in social, with organizational psychology added later. We had been successful in recruiting many new faculty, including Jim Julian, Edgar Vinacke, Dean Pruitt, and Barbara Bunker, later joined by Brenda Major, Jim Blascovich, Bob Rice, Jenny Crocker, and Lynn Cooper. At UB, Vinacke and I started the Society of Experimental Social Psychology (SESP) in 1965 (see Hollander, 1968).

I had funding from ONR for a major effort in research on leadership at UB with Jim Julian, and we also wrote major analytic papers, including a coverage article, which appeared in the

*Psychological Bulletin* in 1969, on "Contemporary Trends in Leadership Processes," which appears here as Chapter 5. It received a good response and was reprinted in many places. We also did two chapters covering the research we had done that appeared in the series edited by Leonard Berkowitz on *Advances in Experimental Social Psychology* (1970, 1978).

Another study I did was with children, under a grant I had received from the National Institute of Child Health and Development (NICHD). Jim Marcia, a member of the UB clinical psychology faculty, was co-investigator, who shared an interest in parent and peer influence on youngsters, following the work of Urie Bronfenbrenner (1961a, b). Our collaboration was a reflection of the relatively free, cross-program interaction in the psychology department. It then had about 35 faculty members, with a remarkably congenial culture, and some like Marcia and myself who played tennis together.

The guiding hypothesis of our research was that children who perceive their parents' upbringing practices to be peer-oriented tend to be that way themselves. We also were interested in the leadership patterns among these 5th grade children (30 boys and 22 girls), who we interviewed and tested individually with situations we had developed, to see how the children responded. Sociometric ratings were also obtained in each class by having same-sex children rate each other on several scales, including those aimed at peer-orientation and self-orientation. A significant relationship was found between the reported parents' peer-orientation and the child's peer-orientation, as revealed by the interviews, questionnaire responses, and sociometric ratings (Hollander & Marcia, *Developmental Psychology*, 1970). Basically, children chosen by their peers as leaders were found more likely to be independent.

An experiment studying the effect of "failing" on group members' support of elected or appointed group leaders was done by two of our doctoral students, Barry Fallon and Myles Edwards, with me. As noted in Chapter 2, we found that a "rallying around" effect occurred, but in a "crisis" over time, followers were less willing to retain the elected leader than the appointed one (Hollander, Fallon, and Edwards, 1977). In line with the Hollander and Julian (1968; 1969, Chapter 5 here; 1970) view that personality and situational factors in leadership should be studied together, two of our doctoral students, Jim Gleason and Jim Seaman, did an experiment with me on task structure and Machiavellianism (Gleason, Seaman, and Hollander, 1978). As described in Chapter 8 here, sixteen four-man task groups were constructed composed of one Hi Mach, one Lo Mach, and two middle Machs, based on pretesting introductory psychology students with the Machiavellianism Scale. As expected, the Hi Machs were observed to show greater ascendance than the others, especially under the low structure condition. From the followers' perspective, as revealed by their post-interaction ratings of those preferred as future leaders of the group, the Middle Machs were significantly more desired for the leader role than either the Hi's or Lo's. Not knowing precisely why these others were different, followers clearly avoided those who scored at the extremes.

## LEARNING FROM EXPERIENCE: SOME LESSONS IN SELF-RENEWAL

My opportunities to go elsewhere, both physically and in terms of roles made possible rich learning experiences, as John Gardner (1963), had long advocated. I had the benefit of several years when I was on leave and away from my normal academic surroundings. Drawing upon those, I want to give prominence to some of the things that I learned and have helped shape my orientation toward Inclusive Leadership. This section is designed to capture some of the more important features of these experiences.

## A FULBRIGHT YEAR TEACHING AT ISTANBUL UNIVERSITY AND BEYOND

While at Carnegie Tech (CIT) my international interests led me to apply for a Fulbright Lectureship in Europe for the 1957-58 academic year. The limited number of social psychology teaching positions made for a constrained choice, so when I was offered such a post at Istanbul University I was glad to accept. It turned out to be a marvelous opportunity for exposure to another nation, including learning about Turkey, its people, culture, politics, and the Islamic religion. It also permitted me to travel for periodic lectures in seven countries. In the Summer of 1957, on returning from the Congress in Brussels and travel thereafter, I began studying the language with a Turkish student. I had received a year's leave from CIT and confirmation of the Fulbright Award, with an appointment as a Visiting Professor from Istanbul University. My splendid host was the Professor of Psychology and Chair, Mumtaz Turhan, who had earned his Ph.D. with Sir Frederick Bartlett at Cambridge, as well as having studied in Germany.

The University had been founded in 1492 as a mosque school and had become a major twentieth century institution in the Middle East, with a fully developed set of schools in the professions and the usual undergraduate arts and sciences college.

I lectured in English, which at least half the students understood, but had sequential translation into Turkish every paragraph or two. Two graduate assistants, Ms. Iffet Dinc and Mr. Yilmaz Ozakpinar, were marvelous young colleagues who very capably did the translating as well as aiding me with my research and other academic contacts and writing needs. Yilmaz did analyses with me for a study I had underway, and eventually earned his doctorate at Cambridge. Iffet helped translate a paper I wrote for a French journal, and came to the USA to earn a doctorate at Florida State University. The campus had many older but some newer buildings surrounded by greenery, and a familiar feel. The students wore distinctly modern, western attire. I taught a large undergraduate class in social psychology, another in research methods, and a graduate seminar in personality and social psychology.

I found the students earnest and motivated. Few spoke Turkish with me since what I'd learned was largely oriented to outside life, such as buying things in stores, or making other needs known. Mostly, the University folk were almost always multilingual and wanted to speak English with me, if not able to, then even my rusty high school French and college German often helped bridge the language gap.

I lived alone on a hillside on the Bhosporus, the central straits that separated Europe from Asia, in a two-room frame cottage that had a basic kitchen and a bathroom. Istanbul is on the same 42$^{nd}$ parallel as New York City, and can get cold, so heating with the kerosene heater that was provided, was essential, and there often were fuel shortages during the winter. I had a period of flu-like symptoms, and then my assistant Yilmaz made determined efforts to find the "gaz" (kerosene), and brought me food, especially soup, for which I was grateful. I did get to other parts of Turkey, including the capital city of Ankara, which is relatively modern and set in the central Anatolian plain, the Aegean Coast in the South, and Black Sea region in the North, from which Soviet naval ships and oil tankers came through these straits daily, that I could view from my cottage.

## GOING TO THE ROME INTERNATIONAL CONGRESS OF IAAP IN 1958 AND CONSIDERING WASHINGTON UNIVERSITY

The position at Washington University (WU) in St. Louis in social psychology was available the year I was to leave for the Fulbright Award in Turkey. I had been contacted about it and agreed to send my materials for consideration, possibly for the following year, on returning. In the Spring of 1958, while in Rome, at the International Congress of Applied Psychology I heard about the possible reopening of the WU position. I gave a paper at the Congress on peer nominations, and was able to visit the Vatican with other delegates, including my friend Edwin Fleishman, among others, in an audience with Pope Pius the XII. My paper was also solicited for, and published soon thereafter, in France in Revue de Psychologie Appliquee (Hollander, 1958b), thanks to Iffet Dinc's assistance with the translation. The interior of Vatican City and the papal quarters were stunningly beautiful. Beginning with the array of Swiss Guards, in the extraordinarily ornate Vatican, it was an impressive experience, even for non-Catholics, by any measure. The Pope spoke with us in his many languages, while walking around to extend greetings. Afterward, he delivered a paper about respecting the individual. He had been in office since 1939, and died within the year.

These remarkable days preceded my return, and consideration of going to WU, where I returned for another visit. I met with Marion Bunch the Psychology chair, and members of the faculty, to talk about the prospect they had in mind of an interdepartmental social psychology doctoral program. The quality of the faculty was superior, including Nick Demerath and Bob Hamblin in Sociology, Jules Henry in Cultural Anthropology, Dick DeCharms and Jack Glidewell in Education. The offer was for an Associate Professorship, at much more in salary. Though not yet with tenure, the prospects were said to be good, and doctoral courses were open for me with a lighter teaching load, and a place and staff support in a research institute that Demerath had organized and was directing.

At a Sunday reception in Winter at that Institute at the end of a conference, I met Pat, my wife-to-be. I had returned a day earlier than planned from giving a talk at a conference at Louisiana State University, organized by Bernard Bass and Luigi Petrullo from ONR. Had I returned on the original schedule, I would not have seen her because she had just come by to give a ride to her sister who was Assistant to Nicholas Demerath, the Director. In my first year at WU, in addition to meeting Pat, I taught both a graduate seminar and undergraduate course in social psychology. Both had some outstanding students, and one of the most memorable in the seminar was Peter Nathan, who became a distinguished psychologist, administrator, and life-long friend. He went on to earn his doctorate in clinical psychology at Harvard.

The hoped-for interdepartmental doctoral program in social psychology at WU was proving difficult to get underway. My role was essentially coordination, with no resources to allocate. Faculty relations and motivation were generally quite good, as I had expected. However, there were turf issues at the several departments involved that presented problems. Among those were credit for staffing, and funding for student stipends, if there was to be successful recruitment. The prospect of getting a training grant also proved remote at the time.

## SABBATICAL AT TAVISTOCK (1966–1967)

I had the benefit of a year's leave at the Tavistock Institute in London as an NIMH Senior Fellow for 1966–1967. It was a marvelous opportunity that occurred because I was due a leave, not having had one from academic duties for a dozen years, and Stanley Schneider at NIMH was the monitor for our social psychology training grant. A clinical psychologist, he most often oversaw grants in that field, but had taken an interest in our program as one of the first funded in social, starting in 1963. He was helpful with our renewals, and told me about the Senior Fellow Grant program. It was designed to provide additional study for professors who were involved in training doctoral students. I was interested in it primarily to become more conversant with organizational psychology as an area of study into which we would expand. The background I had was mainly from my days at Carnegie Tech with the Ford Foundation project that Herb Simon directed on decision-making in organizations. It was certainly relevant, but I wanted to gain breadth to help our social program extend in this direction. We achieved that in part by adding Barbara Bunker to our program faculty in

1970. She had recently received her Ph.D from Teachers College, Columbia, where Morton Deutsch was her mentor. Other faculty at the School of Management offered organizational courses that our students were able to take, and seemed glad to do so.

I was familiar with the Tavistock Institute in London and knew it was renowned for its unusual mix of research and practice. It spanned group dynamics, organizational analysis, leadership development, operations research, and psychotherapy, all involved in a multifaceted effort that occurred on and off-site. The Tavistock approach was a dynamic conception of human activity (M. Jones, 1953 on milieu therapy), with change as a major feature, and a "systems" view (Miller and Rice, 1967) of phenomena in reciprocal effects. I had made a brief visit there a Summer before and spoken to Harold Bridger, a principal member of the staff, to whom I was introduced by John Nagay from ONR. He was assigned to the ONR London Office, on leave from his permanent post at ONR Washington, where he had supported some of my research on peer nominations and critical incidents.

My fellowship at the Tavistock did fulfill my intentions to learn about the research work and other activities there. I had the opportunity to interact with many of the staff, attend meetings, and at times speak to matters about which I had some knowledge. My office was next to Fred Emery's, a brilliant organization researcher, who had a heavy schedule and a very fast delivery with an Australian accent, but he gave me time, which I enjoyed immensely. Another person was the esteemed A. K. Rice, whose name graces an institute for leadership training established by the Tavistock. A man of great competence and charm, he had the Fellows into his office on an occasional Friday afternoon for drinks and interesting chats. We learned in one of those that his education at Cambridge was in cultural anthropology and mathematics, a background he favored in his work, understandably. Among the Fellows that year was Alf Clarke from Australia and Eunice McCarthy from University College, Dublin, both of whom continued as friends. I spoke a couple of times to Eunice at the July, 2006 Applied Psychology Congress in Athens. With Pat, I had visited her and gave a talk at University College Dublin more than 25 years ago. Her significant activities internationally often have been on women's issues. Many Tavistock researchers had us to lunch for discussions, or into their meetings, including those in operations research, where learning could occur all around, and I acquired an appreciation of their approach.

In addition, I agreed to give some lectures at the London School of Economics when Hilde Himmelweit, the Professor and Chair of Social Psychology heard that I would be in London for a year. It was a marvelous opportunity to engage with an audience of mainly graduate students and faculty on my main topics of leadership-followership and conformity-independence. She was an extremely able, concerned researcher, who did a major book based on research she was involved in on the effects of TV on children (Himmelweit, 1958), at a time it was newly introduced in the UK.

I also had an opportunity to go to Paris to give lectures at the Institute of American Studies, and University of Paris. The memorable Director of the Institute, affiliated then with the SUNY system, was Simon Copans. An American who stayed in France after service as a soldier in WWII, he married a French woman and had an interesting academic life, but also was famously known for a jazz radio show in Paris, which was popular and more widely broadcast. He was close to Otto Klineberg, my mentor from Columbia, and friend thereafter. Klineberg was then retired from there, but doing race relations research at the University of Paris, in an institute he had established. He previously resided in Paris when a Director of Social Science research at UNESCO.

On one of my Paris trips, Copans arranged for me to speak on leadership, conformity, and independence to the equivalent of MBA students in the University's Ecole Superieur for Economics and Political Science. In an amphitheater seating perhaps 200, I spoke in English that they had to be able to understand, and at the end they pounded their feet in appreciation, which Copans who was there said was a great tribute. I considered it gratefully as a "peak experience" in Maslow's term.

## SABBATICAL AT HARVARD (1969–1970)

In the Summer of 1969, I had gone to Harvard to be a visitor on the faculty for a sabbatical year. I had many projects in the works, but mostly I observed and worked with Freed Bales, a colleague whose group dynamics laboratory in the Department of Social Relations had implications for my research on leadership. I also had opportunities to interact with valued colleagues including Robert Rosenthal, David McClelland, Leon Mann, Herbert Kelman, Ervin Staub, Tom Pettigrew, and Jerry Kagan. Especially important was contact, at times over lunch, with George Homans in Sociology, an intellectual predecessor of renown in social exchange theory, whose work I had frequently cited. We had met in 1967 when we both gave invited talks at an Annual Meeting of the British Psychological Society, while he was at the University of Kent and I at the Tavistock Institute. While a visitor at Harvard, I gave a number of seminar talks there, tutored a pair of undergraduate majors, and consulted on Ph.D. dissertations in my fields of interest. One of the latter was being done by Rick Boyatzis, a very able student of McClelland's, who has since gone on to do important work on leadership "competencies," about which he did a significant book, The Competent Manager (1982) that he inscribed to me, and I have near my desk to this day. My wife, Pat, took graduate work at the Law School, and our son Peter had a good 3rd grade at Peabody School in Cambridge, across the street from our faculty apartment.

Two events gave drama to the year, especially the Spring of 1970, when we had the "Kent State-Cambodia" unrest at Harvard, as happened elsewhere, which was disruptive only for a brief time. We were the tallest building on campus, William James Hall, and it had its elevators taken over by student protestors. They did give us a bit of time to take needed work and books from our offices. Mine was located in Social Relations, then chaired by Roger Brown. Also a social psychologist, I knew him from the 1953 APA Convention in Cleveland, the year following our Ph.D.s, when we were on the same panel on "Authoritarianism" reporting on our dissertation research, with Else Frenkel-Brunswik, a co-author of the famous book on the subject as Chair of the session and Discussant.

Brown and I had cordial relations, but he was particularly distracted by the other event of that year, the proposal to dissolve the Social Relations Department and distribute the faculty to psychology and elsewhere on campus. There were many meetings, often open to all, including students, mostly graduate, with a passionate expression of feelings, by such revered retirees as the noted sociologist Talcott Parsons. A founder of the department from the WW II era, he spoke eloquently about retaining it. However, it was a doomed cause, given what apparently was a prior administrative decision.

An interesting assignment came to me in a call from Donald Lindsley, a psycho-physiologist at UCLA, with a distinguished reputation. He asked me to join a NASA Panel on "Long-Duration Space Missions," which I readily did, and ultimately contributed to a report by that title. Not long after, I flew to Houston to meet with the others at the Johnson Space Center. There we met NASA project directors and astronauts, and had an opportunity to learn about the biohazards and physical stress issues of remaining in space for up to two-years, on what is still discussed about a "Mission to Mars." The chapter I co-wrote had to do with leadership, but also raised questions about the matters of cohesiveness, conformity, and communication that are important guideposts to my current emphasis on inclusive leadership. I very much enjoyed the opportunity to work with the others involved, such as Bob Helmreich, Bibb Latane, and Bill Haythorn, among others.

## SERVING AS PROVOST OF SOCIAL SCIENCES AT UB

Warren Bennis had been a psychology faculty member at the Sloan School at MIT and was brought to UB by President Martin Meyerson in 1967 to be the first Provost of Social Sciences and Administration. An enormous entity, it had a full-time faculty over 300 and more than 6000 students at all levels through the doctorate who were majors or minors in its disciplines and Schools of Business and Social Welfare.

In 1971, I became Provost, initially Acting, when Bennis's deputy, Ira Cohen, also from psychology, left the post after earlier succeeding Bennis who had been made VP for Academic Development by Meyerson. That was before Meyerson left for a year, arranging for an acting president Peter Regan, Executive Vice President, and professor of psychiatry, with Bennis as his No. 2 when unrest occurred at UB. Mostly it had to do with Vietnam War protests, in which buildings were occupied by the protestors. Force was seen to be required, so Buffalo Police were brought on campus, which offended a large share of students and faculty, as well as many in the community at large. Long after, strong feelings were associated with the events of that year, and especially the issue of police presence on campus.

The fact that I was on leave at Harvard that year made it possible later for me to be nominated in the Fall of 1971 first as Acting, then Provost, a year and a half after the events of 1970. I was not part of these events, and largely unaware of what occurred at UB that fateful year, but had the trust of many of my colleagues especially in the Social Sciences who supported my becoming their Provost. A new president had succeeded Meyerson in 1970, when he went to be president of the University of Pennsylvania. The new one was Robert Ketter, whom I knew when he was VP for Facilities at UB, and a professor of engineering with expertise in earthquakes.

Ketter's management style was decidedly un-inclusive, though he had a pose of geniality, as a gentleman from the South, his home state being West Virginia.

We provosts asked to have an informal dinner meeting with him to tell him about the communication problems we were persistently having, not least with his vice president who came from Mathematics, and would say regarding values issues, "Don't give me any arguments you can't back up with numbers." In a time of budget cuts, trying to arrive at reasoned judgments about such matters as inter-Faculty cooperation to share resources, we were discouraged, to say the least. When we did finally have the dinner meeting with Ketter, he announced early in the discussion that his concept of management was "to keep my people off balance." That statement alerted some of us to think about moving out of his administration, as we eventually did, and within another year I asked to return to faculty status.

As it happened, the directorship of the social psychology doctoral program, which I had previously occupied for two terms, totaling six years, had become open, and my colleagues urged me to take it again. In a smooth transition, in the Fall of 1973, I became director once more and resumed my earlier role teaching courses in the doctoral program and in undergraduate social psychology. I also got back to research and writing that had been harder by far to do when in the Provost role.

My request came at the end of a ten-week leave at Oxford University, which I had been promised earlier to catch up on my own scholarly work, especially writing. After returning to UB in June, having given prior notice, I completed pending business and in mid Summer of 1973 gave up my post as Provost to my Associate, Arthur Butler, an economist and fine colleague who was in charge during my leave.

The experience of serving as Provost with a large faculty and student body was highly positive, as I was able to put into action values I believed in, and that were seemingly effective, programmatically and practically. Those included having student and professional staff elected as representatives on all of the Social Sciences Faculty Committees, even promotion and budget ones. On the other hand, I saw the blunt reality of higher administration where one could have a big title, with a big office and staff, yet be relatively powerless, at least in the traditional sense. But persuasion still worked. Some bureaucratic battles were worth fighting on principal. I managed to arrange numerous faculty appointments above a firm salary scale to attract first-rate candidates who remained vital to our educational and scholarly mission, especially women and minorities. One example, among others, was an outstanding new Ph.D., who ultimately rose to a position of eminence in her field, and a deanship at UB. I learned a great deal by doing daily administrative duties, not least, that wisdom can come from good and bad experience, not just the latter.

## VISITING AT OXFORD, IN MICHAEL ARGYLE'S SOCIAL PSYCHOLOGY LABORATORY (SPRING 1973)

It was a joy to have two months leave, during my second year as Provost, to be visiting professor at Oxford, thanks to Michael Argyle. I gave seminar sessions on conformity and on leadership, and wrote a number of papers, one of which on "Conformity, Independence, and Civil Liberties" appears here as Chapter 18, with updated commentary. While at Oxford I was able to extend it from a talk I originally gave to the New York State Psychological Association (NYSPA). Later, I delivered it at university seminars, at Oxford, Reading, and Edinburgh, while I was in the UK, and then here at home. I also began preparing my book, *Leadership Dynamics (1978)*, during that "breather" from the Ketter administration's conflicts.

## THE NATIONAL ACADEMY OF SCIENCES/NATIONAL RESEARCH COUNCIL (1978–1980)

In the Fall of 1978, I was asked to meet with Wendell (Tex) Garner, a major experimental psychologist at Yale University. He invited me to New Haven where we dined at a favorite restaurant of his. He was Chair of an NAS/NRC Committee on Ability Testing In American Society, and asked me to consider taking over as Program Director for the Committee. I agreed to come to DC for a hearing of witnesses before the Committee held soon after. I met the staff and learned about the circumstances that led to the previous Director leaving. In that brief period of consultation I decided it would be an interesting and challenging assignment.

Among the many inter-disciplinary members were two psychologist colleagues I knew, Lee Cronbach and Janet Spence, who were encouraging of my taking on this role. Other members of the Committee were Alan Sloan and Burke Marshall, Harvard faculty members in Psychiatry and Law, respectively. The two main senior staffers were helpful, but as I learned later in discussions with them, and meetings, they had views which were set before my arrival at the end of 1978. I enjoyed reviewing what had been done, and became increasingly involved in the committee meetings that were set up every few months. However, I discovered that I was using more time on the preparation for these and less on the societal issues that confronted the Committee. The emphasis that seemed to be prevailing was more oriented to testing per se. Though I understood their importance, having studied psychometrics and assisted Robert Thorndike in his graduate course on the topic, I had hoped to have the report speak with more balance than it seemed likely to be doing. Indeed, the Chairman "Tex"Garner and I had been writing a chapter that included some of these societal issues, such as equity in the allocation of opportunity.

However, it was increasingly clear that a point of closure was needed so I could return to my academic pursuits. After more than a year, therefore, I asked to be relieved so that I could do so. Though I had contributed to the chapter that was largely altered in the report, and came out long after I had gone, it did not have my name associated with it, which was my preference. In speaking about my role to my director and colleague theres, I said it had become essentially administrative, though in taking it I thought it would be otherwise. That was as much an error of expectation on my part as any misinformation. With the passage of time, I look back upon the experience as instructive and worthwhile, especially in being able to cntribute to the NAS/NRC mission, and seeing at close hand how it operates.

## THE KELLOGG LEADERSHIP STUDIES PROJECT (KLSP)

John Gardner hosted a leadership meeting in January 1996 as part of the KLSP, funded by a Kellogg Foundation grant to the University of Maryland. It was held at Stanford, his alma mater, where he had received a B.A.(1935) and M. A. (1936) . His Ph.D. (1938) in psychology was earned at UC-Berkeley. He was then back at Stanford to teach leadership on the Business School faculty. I knew and admired him and was glad to be invited to participate in the meeting. Among several dozen leadership scholars and practitioners, I had my turn speaking about followership in a program guided by Gardner and the political scientists, James MacGregor Burns and Georgia Sorenson who were principals on the KLSP grant.

Jim Burns also was quite active in the International Society of Political Psychology (ISPP), and was then its President, when we met in the early '80s at an annual meeting in Washington. We conversed over the years at the meetings, and at one early in the '90s, he asked me to arrange a program on followership at the next meeting, at Harvard. I agreed, and we put on a panel discussion on "Dynamism in Leadership-Followership: How Followers Are Gained, Retained, and Lost" at the 1993 ISPP Meeting there. Subsequently, he called to see if I would like to set up a focus group on "Leadership-Followership" for the KLSP, which I was glad to do.

The first person I contacted about becoming part of the group was Lynn Offermann, a long-time colleague and friend at George Washington University (GWU), with whom I had written previously. The first of these, titled "Power and Leadership in Organizations: Relationships in Transition," appeared in *The American Psychologist* (1990) in a special issue on organizational psychology, and is reprinted here as Chapter 11. Also involved were Peter Vaill, former Dean of the GWU Business School, and Henry Sims of the University of Maryland at College Park Business School join us at our first meeting at the latter school in November of 1993. James McGregor Burns and Georgia Sorenson joined us to think about themes to be considered for further discussion.

Afterward, we were fortunate to fill out our group with David deVries and Ann Howard the next year. Others who took part at various times were Bobby Austin, Cynthia Cherrey, Barbara Kellerman, and Robert Kelley, alphabetically. We met twice a year for over three years and covered a large terrain. Chapter 15, written with Lynn Offermann, provides a survey of some of our KLSP group's activity. I was the first Convener, then phased down with Offermann as Co-Convener, and then she became Convener. In 1996, we presented a symposium on "Emerging Leadership Challenges in Organizations" at the APA Convention in Toronto, chaired by Lynn Offermann. In 1997, at the time of our group's publication, *The Balance of Leadership and Followership*, from the University of Maryland Burns Academy of Leadership. Our Introduction to this report which we co-edited is presented here in Chapter 15. She and I conducted a Roundtable at the Academy of Management in Boston on this topic, in 1997, with copies distributed to those in attendance, and to those interested in leadership and followership issues.

## EASTERN PSYCHOLOGICAL ASSOCATION

I had been active in the Eastern Psychological Association (EPA), the largest of the regionals in psychology, since my graduate student days at Columbia. In 1988–1989, after serving twice on its Board, I was elected to its presidency. A couple of years before, in April of 1986, I gave the Psi Chi honorary society talk at the EPA Annual Meeting in New York City. It was on leadership and attended by a number of colleagues and friends. One in particular, Sheldon Zalkind at Baruch College, was someone I had known from my Navy days at Pensacola when he came there on a consulting project.

We retained contact, and Pat and I would enjoy seeing him when in New York, and at professional meetings elsewhere. He had arranged to have me give a colloquium at Baruch in the 1970s, when it had a thriving Masters program. I enjoyed my visit, and eventually came to Baruch on a regular basis, to take part also in its I/O doctoral program. Zalkind's research was concerned with civil liberties issues, and he organized a symposium on it, published in the *Journal of Social Issues*, in connection with the 1976 Bicentennial Celebration. My paper on "Independence, Conformity, and Civil Liberties" was in it, and is Chapter 18 here.

## JOINING THE CITY UNIVERSITY OF NEW YORK (CUNY) (1988–)

In the mid-1980s, Sheldon Zalkind told me that a new City University doctoral program in organizational/industrial psychology was getting underway at Baruch. As noted, several faculty members from Baruch came to hear my EPA Psi Chi Address on leadership in New York, in the Spring of 1986, and the prospect of my visiting for a semester to teach in the graduate programs was raised. An invitation was extended thereafter, and I gladly agreed to teach in the Doctoral Program, with a seminar on leadership, and an organizational psychology course in the Masters Program for the Spring 1987 Semester.

A leave from UB was granted, and Pat and I sublet an apartment in Greenwich Village, for those four months. I also was able to take part in activities at the CUNY Graduate Center (GC), through which the doctoral program was administered. Florence Denmark, a long-time social psychology friend from SESP, APA, and EPA, was the Executive Officer for Psychology at the GC, and she and her husband Bob Wesner were hospitable. Otto Klineberg, a mentor and friend, was back from Paris and at the GC as a retiree. The experience overall was exhilarating, with good students and colleagues who were engaging. Our pleasure at being in New York was infectious.

Walter Reichman, Baruch's long-time Psychology Department Chairman, had become a respected friend. We explored the prospect of my coming back for academic year 1988–1989, after I returned to UB for the next academic year, as required under my leave arrangement. I readily agreed to do so, if at all possible. In the meantime, I had begun doing more research with doctoral students and in the Masters students' classes, gathering data using the "Critical Incidents" technique regarding follower perceptions of "good" and "bad" leadership. I knew that a permanent appointment at CUNY was in view when invited back for all of 1988-89, with the approval of Joel Lefkowitz, head of the I/O doctoral program, and its faculty. After becoming Emeritus in 1999, I continued to teach in the program for several years.

My doctoral research assistant was Dennis Kelly who had considerable experience at the Army Research Institute and elsewhere, and a Masters degree previously earned, though nominally a first-year student. He was my main associate, and we published a number of papers together, including one each presented at the EPA 1990, International Psychology

Congresses in Brussels 1992, and Montreal 1996, with several other doctoral students associated.

When I came back to New York for academic year 1988-89, I saw that prospects were coming into focus when I was taken to lunch by the Baruch Provost and Dean of Arts and Sciences (A&S), who asked about my research and interests, and other career matters. After lunch, there was talk of a CUNY Distinguished Professorship, the highest academic rank. Having looked over my vita, the Provost said he thought my qualifications merited pursuing it. He indicated it could be a long process, involving many recommendation letters, and scrutiny by other CUNY college presidents. If the Department and School of A&S were in favor of starting it, he was ready to go ahead. I was very pleased at this endorsement from him.

When I knew that a permanent appointment at CUNY was in view, I told my UB Dean and other colleagues there that I would probably not be returning, but instead asked to retire with Emeritus status. Suffice it to say, in June of 1989, I was taken to the CUNY Board of Trustees Meeting by the then President of Baruch, Joel Segall, and installed as a CUNY Distinguished Professor, with two others. In brief remarks, I introduced Pat and two colleagues from Baruch, Walter Reichman and Sheldon Zalkind, then expressed my thanks to the New York City schools, in particular for the benefits of the academic rigor I had encountered at Brooklyn Technical High School. Graduating from there was the starting point for this account, and brings me full circle, back to the beginning of my college years. I am grateful to be able to tell about much that is included here, and also for the reader's interest.

# APPENDIX

# Development of Inclusive Leadership Scale (ILS-16)

Research on the Inclusive Leadership (IL) Scale is being done collaboratively with my Baruch College colleague, Dr. Jaihyun Park. We have been encouraged by the results of a principal component factor analysis, with varimax rotation, performed for the 16 IL Scale items ($N = 267$). When the eigenvalue 1.00 criterion was used to determine the number of factors, the data yielded a three-factor solution. The initial eigen values for the three components were 6.28, 1.85, and 1.14 and they were changed to 3.22, 3.04, and 3.01, respectively, after rotation. The three components accounted for 58% of the total variance in the 16 items. The first factor loaded on items that are Communication-Action-Fairness (5 items); the second factor on Self-Interest-Disrespect (5 items); and the third on Support-Recognition (6 items). Complete lists of items for each factor are presented in Table A1, with factor loadings in Table A2. The results of the factor analysis indicate that this solution is viable and provides a framework to use the IL Scale in further research and practice.

**Table A1**
**Inclusive Leadership Scale Factors Items (ILS-16 items)***

**Support-Recognition (alpha. 83)**
Item #1: Asks for my ideas about my work
Item #7: Gives me recognition for my work contributions
Item #2: Encourages me to ask questions about my work
Item #8: Lets me make decisions about my work
Item #4: Listens to information from staff, even if bad news
Item #6: Shows interest in how I am doing my job

**Communication-Action-Fairness (alpha. 79)**
Item #19: Concerned with how things are, or are not, being done
Item #3: Provides clear goals to be achieved
Item #11: Applies rules consistently to all
Item #18: Takes needed action on problems identified by staff
Item #12: Shows concern with fairness

**Self-interest–Disrespect (alpha. 81)**
Item #16: Makes comments to put me down
Item #14: Blames me in front of others when things go wrong
Item #15: Rejects my ideas about my work
Item #9: Takes credit for work I did
Item #10: Thinks of his/her own interests only

*Copyright © 2007 by Edwin P. Hollander*
\* Four of the original 20 items were removed after pretesting.
Note that while many items in Factors I and II are similar to those in measures of "consideration" and "initiation of structure" (Fleishman, 1953a,b; 1989a,b), they were generated independently by using the words of respondents to critical incidents about leaders, suggesting the operation of convergent validity and the robustness of the concepts. Factor III appears to tap punitive behavior, not represented in other questionnaires.

**Table A2**
**Inclusive Leadership Scale With Factor Loadings (ILS-16 items)***

| Item | Support-Recognition | Communication-Action-Fairness | Self-Interest-Disrespect |
|---|---|---|---|
| Q1  | **.808** | .139  | .123 |
| Q7  | **.731** | .286  | .197 |
| Q2  | **.648** | .316  | .070 |
| Q8  | **.609** | −.001 | .416 |
| Q6  | **.544** | .536  | .070 |
| Q4  | **.489** | .408  | .164 |
| Q19 | .119 | **.736** | .157 |
| Q3  | .012 | **.710** | .196 |
| Q11 | .128 | **.655** | .037 |
| Q18 | .280 | **.653** | .284 |
| Q12 | .268 | **.630** | .336 |
| Q16 | .206 | .187 | **.836** |
| Q14 | .113 | .162 | **.816** |
| Q15 | .128 | .160 | **.768** |
| Q9  | .051 | .041 | **.569** |
| Q10 | .311 | .287 | **.501** |

* Four of the original 20 items were removed after pretesting.

# BIBLIOGRAPHY

Abelson, R. P., Aronson, E., McGuire, W. J., Newcomb, T. M., Rosenberg, M. J., & Tannenbaum, P. H. (Eds.). (1968). *Theories of cognitive consistency: A source book*. Chicago: Rand McNally.

Adams, B., & Webster, S. W. (1997). Foreword. In E. P. Hollander & L. R. Offermann (Eds.), *The balance of leadership and followership* (pp. i–iii). College Park: Burns Academy of Leadership, University of Maryland.

Adams, J. S. (1965). Inequity in social exchange. In L. Berkowitz (Ed.), *Advances in experimental social psychology*. Vol. 2. New York: Academic Press, pp. 267-299.

Adams, S. (1996). *The Dilbert Principle*. New York: HarperCollins.

Adler, A. (1925). *The practice and theory of individual psychology* (rev. ed). London: Routledge and Kegan Paul.

Adorno T. W., Frenkel-Brunswik, E., Levinson, D., & Sanford, N. (1950). *The authoritarian personality*. New York: Harper.

Allen, V. L. (1965). Situational factors in conformity. In L. Berkowitz (Ed.), *Advances in experimental social psychology*. Vol. 2. New York: Academic Press, pp. 133–175.

Allport, F. H. (1924). *Social psychology*. Boston: Houghton Mifflin.

Allport. F. H. (1934). The J-curve hypothesis of conforming behavior. *Journal of Social Psychology*, 5, pp. 141–183.

Allport, G. W. (1985). Historical background of social psychology. In G. Lindzey & E. Aronson (Eds.), *Handbook of social psychology* (3rd ed., pp. 1–46). New York: Random House.

Altman, I. (1975). *The environment and social behavior: Privacy, personal space, territory, and crowding*. Monterey, CA: Brooks/Cole.

Alvarez, R. (1968). Informal reactions to deviance in simulated work organizations: A laboratory experiment. *American Sociological Review*, 33, 895–912.

Anderson, L. R., & Fielder, F. E. (1964).The effect of participatory and supervisory leadership on group creativity. *Journal of Applied Psychology*, 48, 227–236.

Ansari, M. A., & Kapoor, A. (1987). Organizational context and upward influence tactics. *Organizational Behavior and Human Decision Processes*, 40, 39–49.

Ansbacher, H. L. (1951). The history of the leaderless group discussion technique. *Psychological Bulletin*, 48, 383–390.

Arenson, K. (2006, August 22). What organizations don't want to know can hurt. *New York Times*, p. D-1.

Argyle, M. (1957). Social pressure in public and private situations. *Journal of Abnormal and Social Psychology*, 54, 172–175.

Argyle, M. (1972). *The psychology of interpersonal behavior*, 2nd ed. Baltimore and Harmondsworth: Penguin Books.

Argyle, M. (1983). *The psychology of interpersonal behaviour*, 4th ed. Harmondsworth: Penguin.

Argyle, M. (1990). *The social psychology of work*. Harmondsworth: Penguin.

Argyle, M., & Henderson, M. (1985). *The anatomy of relationships*. London: Heinemann.

Argyris, C. (1968). On the effectiveness of research and development organizations. *American Scientist*, 56, 334–355.

Aries, E. (1976). Interaction patterns and themes of male, female, and mixed groups. *Small Group Behavior*, 7, 7–18.

Aronson, E., & Carlsmith, J. M. (1962). Performance expectancy as a determinant of actual performance. *Journal of Abnormal and Social Psychology*, 65, 178–182.

Asch, S. E. (1951). Effects of group pressure upon the modification and distortion of judgments. In H. Guetzkow (Ed.), *Groups, leadership and men* (pp. 177–190). Pittsburgh: Carnegie Press.

Asch, S. E. (1956). Studies of independence and conformity: A minority of one against a unanimous majority. *Psychological Monographs*, 70 (9, Whole No. 416).

Asch. S. E. (1959). A perspective on social psychology. In S. Koch (Ed.), *Psychology: A study of a science*. Vol. 3. New York: McGraw-Hill, pp. 363–384.

Asimov, I. (1973, September–October). Light verse. *Saturday Evening Post*, pp. 22–23.

Bair, J. T., & Hollander, E. P. (1953). Studies in motivation of student aviators at the Naval School of Aviation Medicine. *Journal of Aviation Medicine*, 24, 514–517, 522.

Baker, C. (1980). The Vroom-Yetton model of leadership-model: Theory or technique? *Omega, 8,* 9–10.
Baker, R. (1980, September 28). Perceiving the candidate. *New York Times Magazine,* p. 32.
Bales, R. F. (1950). *Interaction process analysis: A method for the study of small groups,* Reading, MA: Addison-Wesley.
Bales, R. F., & Slater, P. E. (1955). Role differentiation in small decision-making groups. In T. Parsons, et al. (Eds.), *Family, socialization, and interaction process* (pp. 259–306). Glencoe, IL: Free Press.
Banas, P. A. (1988). Employee involvement: A sustained labor/management initiative at the Ford Motor Company. In J. P. Campbell & R. J. Campbell (Eds.), *Productivity in organizations* (pp. 388–416). San Francisco: Jossey-Bass.
Bandura, A. (1977). *Social learning theory.* Englewood Cliffs, NJ: Prentice-Hall.
Bandura, A., & Walters, R. H. (1963). *Social learning and personality development.* New York: Holt, Rinehart & Winston.
Banta, T. J., & Nelson, C. (1964). Experimental analysis of resource location in problem-solving groups. *Sociometry, 2,* 488–501.
Barber, J. D. (1972). *The presidential character: Predicting performance in the White House.* Englewood Cliffs, NJ: Prentice-Hall.
Barnard, C. I. (1938). *The functions of the executive.* Cambridge, MA: Harvard University Press.
Barnard, C. I. (1952). A definition of authority. In R. K. Merton, A. P. Gray, B. Hockey, & H. C. Selvin, (Eds.), *Reader in bureaucracy* (pp. 180–185). Glencoe, IL: Free Press.
Barnes, L. B., & Kriger, M. P. (1986). The hidden side of organizational leadership. *Sloan Management Review, 28,* 15–25.
Barron, F. (1953). An ego-strength scale which predicts response to psychotherapy, *Journal of Consulting Psychology, 17,* 327–333.
Bartlett, F. C. (1932). *Remembering.* Cambridge: Cambridge University Press.
Bass, B. M. (1950). The leaderless group discussion technique. *Personnel Psychology, 3,* 17–32.
Bass, B. M. (1985). *Leadership and performance beyond expectations.* New York: Free Press.
Bass, B. M. (1997). Does the transactional-transformational leadership paradigm transcend organizational and national boundaries? *American Psychologist, 52*(2), 130–139.
Bass, B. M., & Riggio, R. E. (2006). *Transformational Leadership,* 2nd ed. Mahwah, NJ: Erlbaum.
Bavelas, A. (1960). Leadership: Man and function. *Administrative Science Quarterly, 4,* 491–498.
Bavelas, A., Hastorf, A. H., Gross, A. E., & Kite, W. R. (1965) Experiments on the alteration of group structure. *Journal of Experimental Social Psychology, 1,* 55–70.
Beloff, H. (1958). Two forms of social conformity: Acquiescence and conventionality. *Journal of Abnormal and Social Psychology, 56,* 99–104.
Benezet, L. T., Katz, J., & Magnusson, F.W. (1981). *Style and substance: Leadership and the college presidency.* Washington, DC: American Council on Education.
Bennis, W. G. (1990, December 31). Good followers make leaders look good. *New York Times,* p. A17.
Bennis, W. G. (1998). The end of leadership. In *Selected proceedings of the annual meeting of the Leaders/Scholars Association* (pp. 5–9). College Park, MD: Burns Academy of Leadership. University of Maryland.
Bennis, W. G. (2002, February 17). A corporate fear of too much truth. *New York Times,* pp. 4–11.
Bennis, W. G. (2007). The challenges of leadership in the modern world: Introduction to the special issue. *American Psychologist, 62,* 2–5.
Bennis, W. G., & Nanus, B. (1985). *Leaders.* New York: Harper and Row.
Bensimon, E. M. (1993). New presidents' initial actions: Transactional and transformational leadership. *Journal for Higher Education Management, 8*(2), 5–17.
Ben-Yoav, O., Hollander, E. P., & Carnevale, P. J. D. (1983). Leader legitimacy, leader-follower interaction, and followers' ratings of the leader. *Journal of Social Psychology, 121,* 111–115.
Berg, I. A. & Bass, B. M. (1961) (Eds.). *Conformity and deviation.* New York: Harper.
Berkowitz, L. (1956). Personality and group position. *Sociometry, 19,* 210–222.
Berkowitz, L. (1957). Liking for the group and the perceived merit of the group's behavior. *Journal of Abnormal and Social Psychology, 54,* 353–357.
Berkowitz, L. & Macauley, J. R. (1961). Some effects of differences in status level and status stability. *Human Relations, 14,* 135–148.
Beyer, J. M. (1999a). Taming and promoting charisma to change organizations. *Leadership Quarterly, 10*(2), 307–331.

Beyer, J. M. (1999b). Two approaches to studying charismatic leadership: Competing or complementary? *Leadership Quarterly, 10*(4), 575–589.
Bierstedt, R. (1950). An analysis of social power. *American Sociological Review,* 15, pp. 730–738.
Birnbaum, R. (1987). *The effects of presidential succession on institutional functioning in higher education.* New York: National Center for Postsecondary Governance and Finance, Teachers College, Columbia University.
Birnbaum, R. (1992). *How academic leadership works.* San Francisco: Josey-Bass.
Blake, R. R., Helson, H., & Mouton, J. S. (1956). The generality of conformity behavior as a function of factual anchorage, difficulty of task, and amount of social pressure. *Journal of Personality,* 25, 294–305.
Blake, R. R., & Mouton, J. S. (1961). Conformity, resistance and conversion. In I. A. Berg & B. M. Bass (Eds.), *Conformity and deviation.* New York: Harper, pp. 1–37.
Blau, P. M. (1964). *Exchange and power in social life.* New York: Wiley.
Bok, D. (1993). *The cost of talent.* New York: Free Press.
Bok, D. (2003). *Universities in the marketplace.* Princeton, NJ: Princeton University Press.
Bond, J. R., & Vinacke, W. E. (1961). Coalitions in mixed-sex triads. *Sociometry,* 24, 61–75.
Borgatta, E. F., & Stimson, J. (1963). Sex differences in interaction characteristics. *Journal of Social Psychology,* 60, 89–100.
Bower, M. (1997). *The will to lead.* Boston: Harvard Business School Press.
Boyatzis, R. (1982). *The competent manager: A model for effective performance.* New York: Wiley.
Boyd, N. K. (1972). Negotiation behavior by elected and appointed representatives serving as group leaders or as spokesmen under different cooperative group expectations. Doctoral dissertation. University of Maryland, Department of Psychology.
Brass, D. J. (1985). Men's and women's networks: A study of interaction patterns and influence in an organization. *Academy of Management Journal,* 28, 327–343.
Brewster, K. (1968). *Report to the Yale University Corporation.* New Haven, CT: Yale Corporation.
Bronfenbrenner, U. (1961). Some familial antecedents of responsibility and leadership in adolescents. In L. Petrullo & B. M. Bass (Eds.), *Leadership and interpersonal behavior* (pp. 239–271). New York: Holt, Rinehart, & Winston.
Bronfenbrenner, U. (1970). *Two worlds of childhood.* New York: Russell Sage Foundation.
Broverman, I., Vogel, S. R., Broverman, D. M., Clarkson, F. E., & Rosenkrantz, P. S. (1972). Sex-role stereotypes: A current appraisal. *Journal of Social Issues, 28*(2), 59–78.
Brown, J. F. (1936). *Psychology and the social order.* New York: McGraw-Hill.
Bunker, B. B., & Seashore, E. W. (1975). Breaking the sex role stereotypes. *Public Management,* 57, 5–11.
Burke, P. J. (1966). Authority relations and descriptive behavior in small discussion groups. *Sociometry,* 29, 237–250.
Burke, W. W. (1986). Leadership as empowering others. In S. Srivasta & Associates (Eds.), *Executive power: How executives influence people and organizations* (pp. 51–77). San Francisco: Jossey-Bass.
Burns, J. M. (1963). *The deadlock of democracy: Four-party politics in America.* Englewood Cliffs, NJ: Prentice-Hall.
Burns, J. M. (1965). *Presidential government: The crucible of leadership.* Boston: Houghton Mifflin.
Burns, J. M. (1978). *Leadership.* New York: Harper and Row.
Burns, J. M. (2007). Foreword. In R. A. Couto (Ed.), *Reflections on leadership* (pp. v–viii). New York: University Press of America.
Burton, R. (1963). Generality of honesty reconsidered. *Psychological Review,* 70, 481–499).
Byrne, J. A., Symonds, W. C., & Siler, J. F. (1991, April 1). CEO disease. *Business Week,* pp. 52–60.
Calder, B. J. (1977). An attribution theory of leadership. In B. M. Staw & G. R. Salancik (Eds.), *New directions in organizational behavior* (pp. 179–204). Chicago: St. Clair Press.
Campbell, A. (1976). Subjective measures of well-being. *American Psychologist,* 31, 117–124.
Campbell, A., Gurin, G., & Miller, W. E. (1954). *The voter decides.* New York: Harper and Row.
Cantril, H. (1958). Effective democratic leadership: a psychological interpretation. *Journal of Individual Psychology,* 14 128–138.
Cantril, H., Gaudet, H., & Herzog, H. (1940). *The invasion from Mars.* Princeton, NJ: Princeton University Press.
Carpenter, W. A., & Hollander, E. P. (1982). Overcoming hurdles to independence in groups. *Journal of Social Psychology,* 117, 237–241.

Carrieri, M., Manibay, M.E., & Hollander, E.P. (2000). Cross-Gender Perceptions of Leader Qualities. Paper at 28th Annual Hunter College Psychology Convention, May.
Carter, L. F., Haythorn, W., Meirowitz, B., & Lanzetta, J. (1951). The relation of categorizations and ratings in the observation of group behavior. *Human Relations*, 4, 239–253.
Carter, L. F., & Nixon, M. (1949). An investigation of the relationship between four criteria of leadership ability for three different tasks. *Journal of Psychology*, 27, 245–261.
Cartwright, D. (Ed.) (1959). *Studies in social power.* Ann Arbor: Research Center for Group Dynamics, University of Michigan.
Cartwright, D. C., & Zander, A. (Eds.) (1968). *Group dynamics: Research and theory.* (3rd ed.) New York: Harper & Row.
Catalyst. (2005). *Women "take care," men "take charge." Stereotyping of U.S. business leaders exposed.* New York: Catalyst Publication No. 062.
Cerulo, K. (2006). *Never Saw It Coming: Cultural Challenges to Envisioning the Worst.* Chicago: University of Chicago Press.
Chemers, M. M. (1993). An integrative theory of leadership. In M. M. Chemers & R. Ayman (Eds.), *Leadership theory and research: Perspectives and directions* (pp. 293–319). San Diego, CA: Academic Press.
Chemers, M. M. (1997). *An integrative theory of leadership.* Mahwah, NJ: Erlbaum.
Christie, R., & Geis, F. L. (1970). *Studies in Machiavellianism.* New York: Academic Press.
Ciulla, J. B. (1998). Leadership and the problem of bogus empowerment. In J. B. Ciulla (Ed.), *Ethics, the heart of leadership* (pp. 63–86). Westport, CT: Praeger.
Cleveland, J. N., Stockdale, J. N., & Murphy, K. R. (2000). *Sex and gender in organizations.* Mahwah, NJ: Erlbaum.
Clifford, C., & Cohen, T. S. (1964). The relationship between leadership and personality attributes perceived by followers. *Journal of Social Psychology*, 64, 57–64.
Cobb, A. T. (1984). An episodic model of power: Toward an integration of theory and research. *Academy of Management Review*, 1, 482–493.
Cohen, A. M., & Bennis, W. G. (1961). Continuity of leadership in communication networks. *Human Relations*, 14, 351–367.
Cohen, M. D., & March, J. G. (1974). *Leadership and ambiguity.* New York: McGraw-Hill.
Conger, J. A. (1990). The dark side of leadership. *Organizational Dynamics*, 19(2), 44–55.
Conger, J. A. (1991). Inspiring others: The language of leadership. *Academy of Management Executive*, 5(1), 31–45.
Conger, J. A. (1993). The brave new world of leadership training. *Organizational Dynamics*, 21(3), 46–58.
Conger, T. A., & Kanungo, R. N. (1988). *Charismatic leadership: The elusive factor in organizational effectiveness.* San Francisco: Jossey Bass.
Cooley, C. H. (1922). *Human nature and the social order.* New York: Scribner's.
Cooper, W. H., & Stone, T. H. (2006). Idiosyncrasy Credit Theory Revisited. *Proceedings of the Business History Division of the Administrative Sciences Association of Canada*, Banff, Alberta, June. 1
Corbett, S. (2007, March 18). The Women's War. *New York Times Magazine*, p. 41f.
Corry, J. (1995). *My times.* New York: Putnam.
Cowley, W. H. (1928). Three distinctions in the study of leaders. *Journal of Abnormal and Social Psychology*, 23, 144–157.
Cowley, W. H. (1980). *Presidents, professors, and trustees.* San Francisco: Jossey-Bass.
Crano, W. D. (2000). Milestones in the psychological analysis of social influence. In *Group dynamics: theory, research and practice* (4th ed., pp. 68–80).
Crano, W. D. (2004). Conformity. In G. R. Goethals, G. J. Sorenson, & J. M. Burns (Eds.), *Encyclopedia of leadership* (pp. 247–251). Thousand Oaks, CA: Sage.
Croner, M. D., & Willis, R. H. (1961). Perceived differences in task competence and asymmetry of dyadic influence. *Journal of Abnormal and Social Psychology*, 62, 705–708.
Crouch, A., & Yetton, P. (1987). Manager behavior, leadership style, and subordinate performance: An empirical extension of the Vroom-Yetton conflict rule. *Organizational Behavior and Human Decision Processes*, 39, 384–396.
Crowe, B. J., Bochner, S., & Clark, A. W. (1972). The effects of subordinates' behavior on managerial style. *Human Relations*, 25, 215–237.

Crutchfield, R. S. (1955). Conformity and character. *American Psychologist, 10*, 191–198.
Crutchfield, R. S. (1962). Conformity and creative thinking. In H. E. Gruber, G. Terrell, & M. Wertheimer (Eds.), *Contemporary approaches to creative thinking.* New York: Atherton, pp. 120–140.
Crutchfield, R. S. (1963). Independent thought in a conformist world. In S. M. Farber & R. H. L. Wilson (Eds.), *Conformity and conflict: Control of the mind.* (Part 2) New York: McGraw-Hill, pp. 208–228.
Crystal, G. (1991). *In search of excess: The overcompensation of American executives.* New York: W. W. Norton.
Curphy, G. J. (1993). An empirical investigation of the effects of transformational and transactional leadership on organizational climate, attrition, and performance. In K. E. Clark, M. B. Clark, & D. P. Campbell (Eds.), *Impact of leadership* (pp. 177–188). Greensboro, NC: Center for Creative Leadership.
Day, D. V., & Zaccaro, S. J. (2007). Leadership: A critical historical analyses of the influence of leadership traits. In Koppes, L. (Ed.), *Historical perspectives in industrial organizational psychology* (pp. 383–405). Mahwah, NJ: Erlbaum.
Deal, T. E., & Kennedy, A. A. (1982). *Corporate cultures: The rites and rituals of corporate life.* Reading, MA: Addison-Wesley.
Dean, J. (2003). *Worse than Watergate.* Boston: Houghton Mifflin.
Deaux, K. (1976). *The behavior of women and men.* Monterey, CA: Brooks/Cole.
deCharms, R. (1968). *Personal causation.* New York: Academic Press.
DeFrank, T. M. (1983, April 18). An overused 'weapon'? *Newsweek*, p. 23.
Demerath, N. J., Stephens, R. W., & Taylor, R. R. (1967). *Power, presidents, and professors.* New York: Basic Books.
Deming, W. E. (1992, February 1). Quoted in *The Economist*, p. 19.
Denmark, F. L. (1977). Styles of leadership. *Psychology of Women Quarterly, 2*(2), 99–113.
DePree, M. (1989). *Leadership is an art.* New York: Doubleday Dell.
DeSoto, C. B. (1961). The predilection for single orderings. *Journal of Abnormal and Social Psychology, 62*, 16-23.
Deutsch, M. (1975). Equity, equality, and need: What determines which value will be used as the basis of distributive justice? *Journal of Social Issues, 31*, 137–149.
DeVries, D. L. (1992). Executive selection: Advances but no progress. *Center for Creative Leadership: Issues and Observations, 12*, 1–5.
Dienesch, R. M., & Liden, R. C. (1986). Leader-member exchange model of leadership: A critique and further development. *Academy of Management Review, 11*, 618–634.
Dirks, K. T., & Ferrin, D. L. (2002). Trust in leadership: Meta-analysis findings and implications. *Journal of Applied Psychology, 87*, 611–621.
Dittes, J. E., & Kelley, H. H. (1956). Effects of different conditions of acceptance upon conformity to group norms. *Journal of Abnormal and Social Psychology, 53*, 100–107.
Drucker, P. F. (1985). *Innovation and entrepreneurship: Practice and principles.* New York: Harper and Row.
Drucker, P. F. (1988, January 6). Leadership: more doing than dash. *Wall Street Journal*, p. 14.
Drucker, P. F. (1993). *Post-capitalist society.* New York: HarperCollins.
Drucker, P. F. (1997). Toward a new organization. *Leader to Leader*, 1997, 6–8.
Dubno, P. (1965). Leadership, group effectiveness, and speed of decision. *Journal of Social Psychology, 65*, 351–360.
Eagly, A. H. (1978). Sex differences in influenceability. *Psychological Bulletin, 85*, 86–116.
Eagly, A. H., & Carli, L. L. (2007). *The truth about how women become leaders.* Boston: Harvard Business School Press.
Eagly, A. H., & Johannesen-Schmidt, M. C. (2001). The leadership style of women and men. *Journal of Social Issues, 57*, 781–797.
Eagly, A. H., & Johannesen-Schmidt, M. C., & van Engen, M. L. (2003). Transformational, transactional, and laissez-faire leadership styles: A meta-analysis comparing women and men. *Psychological Bulletin, 129*, 569–591.
Eagly, A. H., & Johnson, B. T. (1990). Gender and leadership style: A meta-analysis. *Psychological Bulletin, 108*, 233–256.
Edelman, M. (1977). *Political language: Words that succeed and policies that fail.* New York: Academic Press.

Ehrlich, S. B., Meindl, J. R., & Viellieu, B. (1990). The charismatic appeal of a transformational leader: An empirical case study of a small, high-technology contractor. *Leadership Quarterly, 14*, 229–248.

Elgie, D. M., Hollander, E. P., & Rice, R. W. (1988). Appointed and elected leader responses to favorableness of feedback and level of task activity from followers. *Journal of Applied Social Psychology, 16*, 1361–1370.

Emerson, R. M. (1962). Power-dependence relations. *American Sociological Review, 27*, 31–41.

Emler, N., & Hogan, R. (1991). Moral psychology and public policy. In W. M. Kurtines & J. L. Gewirtz (Eds.), *Handbook of moral behavior and development*, Vol. 3, *Applications* (pp. 69–93). Hillsdale, NJ: Erlbaum.

Erikson, E. H. (1975). *Life, history and the historical moment*. New York: W. W. Norton.

Eskilson, A., & Wiley, M. G. (1976). Sex composition and leadership in small groups. *Sociometry, 39*, 183–194.

Eskola, A. (1961). *Social influence and power in two-person groups*. Copenhagen: Munksgaard, 1961. (Doctoral dissertation, University of Helsinki; Vol. 6 of the *Transactions of the Westermarck Society*.)

Estrada, M., Brown, J., & Lee, F. (1995). Who gets the credit? Perceptions of idiosyncracy credit in work groups. *Small Group Research, 26*(1), 56–76.

Evan, W. M., & Zelditch, M. A. (1961). Laboratory experiment on bureaucratic authority. *American Sociological Review, 26*, 883–893.

Evans, M. G. (1970). The effects of supervisory behavior on the path-goal relationships. *Organizational Behavioral Human Performance, 5*, 277–298.

Evans, M. G. (1974). Extensions of a path-goal theory of motivation. *Journal of Applied Psychology, 59*, 172–178.

Eyde, L. D., & Quaintance, M. K. (1988). Ethical issues and cases in the practice of personnel psychology. *Professional Psychology, 19*, 148–154.

Fallon, B. J., & Hollander, E. P. (1976, August). *Sex-role stereotyping in leadership: A study of undergraduate discussion groups*. Paper presented at the Annual Convention of the American Psychological Association.

Fayol, H. (1916). Administration industrielle et générale. *Bulletin de la Societe de l'Industrie Minerale, 10*, pp. 5–162.

Fiedler, F. E. (1958). *Leader attitudes and group effectiveness*. Urbana: University of Illinois Press.

Fiedler, F. E. (1961). Leadership and leadership effectiveness traits. In L. Petrullo & B. M. Bass (Eds.), *Leadership and interpersonal behavior* (pp. 179–186). New York: Holt.

Fiedler, F. E. (1964). A contingency model of leadership effectiveness. In L. Berkowitz (Ed.), *Advances in experimental social psychology*, Vol. I. New York: Academic Press.

Fiedler, F. E. (1965). Engineer the job to fit the manager. *Harvard Business Review, 43*, 115–122.

Fiedler, F. E. (1965). The contingency model: A theory of leadership effectiveness. In H. Proshansky & B. Seidenberg (Eds.), *Basic studies in social psychology*. New York: Holt, Rinehart & Winston.

Fiedler, F. E. (1966). The effect of leadership and cultural heterogeneity on group performance: A test of a contingency model. *Journal of Experimental Social Psychology, 2*, 237–264.

Fiedler, F. E. (1967). *A theory of leadership effectiveness*. New York: McGraw-Hill.

Fiedler, F. E. (1972). Personality, motivational system, and the behavior of high and low LPC persons. *Human Relations, 25*, 391–412.

Fiedler, F. E. (1977). A rejoinder to Schriesheim and Kerr's premature obituary of the contingency model. In J. G. Hunt & L. L. Larson (Eds.), *Leadership: The cutting edge* (pp. 45–51). Carbondale: Southern Illinois University Press.

Fiedler, F. E. (1978). Recent developments in research on the contingency model. In L. Berkowitz (Ed.), *Group processes* (pp. 209–225). New York: Academic Press.

Fiedler, F. E., & Garcia, J. E. (1987). *New approaches to effective leadership*. New York: Wiley.

Fiedler, F. E., & House, R. J. (1988). Leadership theory and research: A report of progress. In C. L. Cooper & I. Robertson (Eds.), *International review of industrial and organizational psychology* (pp. 73–92). London: Wiley.

Fiedler, F. E., & Leister, A. F. (1977). Leader intelligence and task performance: A test of a multiple screen model. *Organizational Behavior and Human Performance, 20*, 1–14.

Fisher, J. L. (1984). *Power of the presidency*. New York: Macmillan and American Council on Education.

Fiske, S. T., & Taylor, S. E. (1991). *Social cognition*. New York: McGraw-Hill.

Flacks, R. (1967). The liberated generation: An exploration of the roots of student protest. *Journal of Social Issues, 23*(3), 52–75.

Flanagan, J. C. (1954). The critical incident technique. *Psychological Bulletin, 51,* 327–58.

Fleishman, E. A. (1953a). The description of supervisory behavior. *Journal of Applied Psychology, 37,* 1–6.

Fleishman, E. A. (1953b). Leadership climate, human relations, training, and supervisory behavior. *Journal of Applied Psychology, 37,* 205–222.

Fleishman, E. A. (1973). Twenty years of consideration and structure. In E. A. Fleishman & J. G. Hunt (Eds.), *Current developments in the study of leadership* (pp. 1–37). Carbondale: Southern Illinois University Press.

Fleishman, E. A. (1989a). Leadership Opinion Questionnaire (revised manual). Chicago, Ill: Vangent Human Capital Management.

Fleishman, E. A. (1989b). Supervisory Behavior Description (revised manual). Potomac, MD: Management Research Institute.

Fleishman, E. A. (1998). Patterns of leadership behavior related to employee grievances and turnover: Some post hoc reflections. *Personnel Psychology, 51,* 825–834.

Fleishman, E. A., & Harris, E. F. (1962). Patterns of leadership related to employee grievances and turnover. *Personnel Psychology, 15,* 43–56.

Fleishman, E. A., Harris, E. F., & Burtt, H. E. (1955). *Leadership and supervision in industry.* Columbus, OH: Bureau of Business Research, Ohio State University.

Fleishman, E. A., & Peters, D. R. (1962). Interpersonal values, leadership attitudes, and managerial "success." *Journal of Applied Psychology, 15,* 127–143.

Fleishman, E. A., & Salter, J. A. (1963). Relations between the leader's behavior and his empathy toward subordinates. *Journal of Industrial Psychology, 1*(3), 79–84.

Fleishman, E. A., & Zaccaro, S. J. (1992). Toward a taxonomy of team performance functions: Initial considerations, subsequent evaluations, and current formulations. In R. W. Swezey & E. Salas (Eds.), *Teams: Their training and performance* (pp. 31–55). Norwood, NJ: Ablex.

Fodor, E. M. (1974). Disparagement by a subordinate as an influence on the use of power. *Journal of Applied Psychology, 59,* 652–655.

Follett, M. (1949). The essentials of leadership. In L. Urwick (Ed.), *Freedom and coordination* (pp. 47–60). London: Management Publication Trust.

French, J. R. P., Jr. (1956). A formal theory of social power. *Psychological Review,* 181–194.

French, J. R. P., Jr. (1963). The social environment and mental health. *Journal of Social Issues, 19,* 39–56.

French, J. R. P., Jr., & Raven, B. H. (1959). The bases of social power. In D. Cartwright (Ed.), *Studies in social power.* Ann Arbor: University Michigan Press, (pp. 118–149).

Freud, S. (1921/1960). *Group psychology and the analysis of the ego.* New York: Bantam. [Originally published in German in 1921.]

Fromm, E. (1941). *Escape from freedom.* New York: Rinehart.

Fulbright, J. W. (1966). *The arrogance of power.* New York: Random House.

Gabriel, R., & Savage, P. (1978). *Crisis in command.* New York: Hill and Wang.

Galton, F. (1869). *Hereditary genius: An inquiry into its laws and consequences.* London: Macmillan. [Paperback edition by Meridian Books, New York, 1962.]

Gardner, J. W. (1961). *Excellence.* New York: Harper and Row.

Gardner, J. W. (1963). *Self-renewal: The individual and the innovative society.* New York: Harper and Row.

Gardner, J. W. (1987). Leaders and followers. *Liberal Education, 73*(2), 6–8.

Gardner, J. W. (1990). *On leadership.* New York: Free Press/Macmillan.

Geneen, H. (1984). *Managing.* New York: Doubleday.

Gerard, H. B. (1954). The anchorage of opinions in face-to-face groups. *Human Relations, 7,* 313–325.

Gerber, G. W. (2001). *Women and men police officers: Status, gender, and personality.* Westport, CT: Praeger.

Gibb, C. A. (1954). Leadership. In G. Lindzey (Ed.), *Handbook of social psychology* (pp. 877–920). Cambridge, MA: Addison-Wesley.

Gibb, C. A. (1968). Leadership. In G. Lindzey & E. Aronson (Eds.), *The handbook of social psychology* (2nd ed., pp. 205–282). Reading, MA: Addison-Wesley.

Gibb, C. A. (1947). The principles and traits of leadership. *Journal of Abnormal and Social Psychology, 42,* 267–284.

Gilbert, G. R., & Hyde, A. C. (1988). Followership and the federal worker. *Public Administration Review, 48,* 962–968.

Gilmer, B. V. H., & Karn, H. W. (1954). A basic psychology course for engineering students. *American Psychologist, 9,* 790–793.

Gioia, D., & Sims, H. P. (1986). *The thinking organization.* San Francisco: Jossey-Bass.

Gleason, J. M., Seaman, F. J., & Hollander, E. P. (1978). Emergent leadership processes as a function of task structure and Machiavellianism. *Social Behavior and Personality, 6,* 33–36.

Goldberg, S. C. (1954). Three situational determinants of conformity to social norms. *Journal of Abnormal and Social Psychology, 49,* 325–329.

Goldman, M., & Fraas, L. A. (1965). The effects of leader selection on group performance. *Sociometry, 28,* 82–88.

Goodman, P. S., Devadas, R., & Hughson, T. L. (1988). Groups and productivity: Analyzing the effectiveness of self-managing teams. In J. P. Campbell & R. J. Campbell (Eds.), *Productivity in organizations* (pp. 295–327). San Francisco: Jossey-Bass.

Gorden, R. L. (1952). Interaction between attitude and the definition of the situation in the expression of opinion. *American Sociological Review, 17,* 50–58.

Gordon, G. E., & Rosen, N. (1981). Critical factors in leadership succession. *Organizational Behavior and Human Performance, 27,* 227–254.

Gordon, L. V. & Medland, F. F. (1965). Leadership aspiration and leadership ability. *Psychological Reports, 17,* 388–390.

Gouldner, A. W. (Ed.). (1950). *Studies in leadership.* New York: Harper.

Gouldner, A. W. (1960). The norm of reciprocity: A preliminary statement. *American Sociological Review, 25,* 161–179.

Gouldner, A. W. (1964). Taking over. *Trans-action, 1*(3), 23–27.

Graen, G. (1975). Role making processes within complex organizations. In M. D. Dunnette (Ed.), *Handbook of industrial and organizational psychology* (pp. 1201–1245). Chicago: Rand-McNally.

Graen, G. B., & Scandura, T. A. (1987). Toward a psychology of dyadic organizing. In B. Staw & L. L. Cummings (Eds.), *Research in organizational behavior 9* (pp. 175–208). Greenwich, CT: JAI.

Graham, D. (1962). Experimental studies of social influence in simple judgment situations. *Journal of Social Psychology, 56,* 245–269.

Graham, P. (Ed.) (1995). *Mary Parker Follett: Prophet of management.* Boston: Harvard Business School Press.

Gray, J. H., & Densten, I. L. (2007). How leaders woo followers in the romance of leadership. *Applied Psychology: An International Review, 56*(4), 558–581.

Green, S. G., & Mitchell, T. R. (1979). Attributional processes of leaders in leader-member interactions. *Organizational Behavior and Human Performance, 23,* 429–458.

Green, S. G., Fairhurst, G. T., & Snavely, B. K. (1986). Chains of poor performance and supervisory control. *Organizational Behavior and Human Decision Processes, 38,* 7–27.

Greenleaf, R. K. (1977). *Servant leadership: A journey into the nature of legitimate power and greatness.* New York: Paulist Press.

Greenwald, A. (1985, June 20). *Totalitarian egos in the personalities of democratic leaders.* Symposium paper, presented at the Annual Meeting of the International Society of Political Psychology. Washington, DC.

Grusky, O. (1969). Succession with an ally. *Administrative Science Quarterly, 14,* 155–170.

Hackman, J. R. (1989). *Groups that work (and those that don't).* San Francisco: Jossey-Bass.

Hackman, J. R. (1998). Why teams don't work. In R. S Tindale, et al. (Eds.), *Theory and research on small groups* (pp. 245–267). New York: Plenum.

Hackman, J. R., & Wageman, R. (2007). Asking the right questions about leadership. *American Psychologist, 62,* 43–47.

Hamblin, R. L. (1958). Leadership and crises. *Sociometry, 21,* 322–335.

Handy, C. (1985). *Understanding organizations,* 2nd ed. London: Penguin.

Hare, A. P. (1976). *Handbook of small group research,* 2nd ed. New York: Free Press.

Harman, S. (2003). *Mind your own business.* New York: Doubleday Currency.

Haythorn, W., Couch, A., Haefner, D., Langham, P., & Carter, L. F. (1956). The effects of varying combinations of authoritarian and equalitarian leaders and followers. *Journal of Abnormal and Social Psychology, 53,* 210–219.

Hegarty, W. H. (1974). Using subordinate ratings to elicit behavioral changes in supervisors. *Journal of Applied Psychology, 59,* 764–766.
Heider, F. (1958). *The psychology of interpersonal relations.* New York: Wiley.
Heider. J. (1982). The leader who knows how to make things happen. *Journal of Humanistic Psychology, 27*(3), 33–39.
Heifetz, R. A. (1994). *Leadership without easy answers.* Cambridge: Belknap/Harvard University Press.
Heilbrun, A. R., Jr. (1968). Influence of observer and target sex judgments of sex-typed attributes. *Perceptual and Motor Skills, 27,* 1194.
Heine, P. J. (1971). *Personality in social theory.* Chicago: Aldine.
Heller, F. A., & Yukl, G. (1969). Participation, managerial decision making, and situational variables. *Organizational Behavior and Human Performance, 4,* 227–241.
Hemphill, J. K. (1949a). *Situational factors in leadership.* Columbus: Ohio State University, Personnel Research Board.
Hemphill, J. K. (1949b). The leader and his group. *Education Research Bulletin, 28,* 225–229, 245–246.
Hemphill, J. K. (1950). *Leader behavior description.* Columbus, OH: Personnel Research Board, Ohio State University.
Hemphill, J. K. (1961). Why people attempt to lead. In L. Petrullo & B. M. Bass (Eds.), *Leadership and interpersonal behavior.* New York: Holt, Rinehart & Winston.
Henry, J. (1963). *Culture against man.* New York: Random House.
Hevesi, D. (1992, March 20). United ways challenge method used to divide their donations. *New York Times,* p. B4.
Hicks, J. P. (1992, April 3). The steel man with kid gloves. *New York Times,* p. Dl.
Himmelweit, H. T., Oppenheim, A. N., & Vince, P. (1958). *Television and the child.* London: Oxford University Press.
Hirschhorn, L. (1997). *Reworking authority,* Cambridge: MIT Press.
Hodgkinson, C. (1983). *The philosophy of leadership.* Oxford, Eng.: Basil Blackwell.
Hoffman, L. R., Burke, R. J., & Maier, N. R. F. (1965). Participation, influence, and satisfaction among members of problem-solving groups. *Psychological Reports, 16,* 661–667.
Hofstede, G. (1980). *Culture's consequences: International differences in work-related values.* Beverly Hills, CA: Sage.
Hofstede, G. (1991). *Cultures and organizations: Software of the mind.* London: McGraw-Hill.
Hogan, R., Curphy, G. J., & Hogan, J. (1994). What we know about leadership: Effectiveness and personality. *American Psychologist, 49,* 493–504.
Hogan, R., & Hogan, J. (1995). *Hogan personality inventory manual,* 2nd ed. Tulsa, OK: Hogan Assessment Systems.
Hogan, R., & Kaiser, R. B. (2005). What we know about leadership. *Review of General Psychology, 9,* 169–180.
Hogan, R., Raskin, R., & Fazzini, D. (1990). The dark side of charisma. In K. E. Clark & M. B. Clark (Eds.), *Measures of leadership* (pp. 343–354). West Orange, NJ: Leadership Library of America.
Hollander, E. P. (1954a). Authoritarianism and leadership choice in a military setting. *Journal of Abnormal and Social Psychology, 49,* 365–370.
Hollander, E. P. (1954b). Peer nominations on leadership as a predictor of the pass-fail criterion in naval air training. *Journal of Applied Psychology, 38,* pp. 150–153.
Hollander, E. P. (1956). The use of popular literature in the undergraduate social psychology course. *American Psychologist, 11,* 95–96.
Hollander, E. P. (1958). Conformity, status, and idiosyncrasy credit. *Psychological Review, 65,* 117–127.
Hollander, E. P. (1958b). Sur les applications de la technique des nominations-entre-pairs. *Revue de Psychologie Applique* (France), 8, 189–198.
Hollander, E. P. (1959). Some points of reinterpretation regarding social conformity. *Sociological Review, 7,* 159–168.
Hollander, E. P. (1960a). Competence and conformity in the acceptance of influence. *Journal of Abnormal and Social Psychology, 61,* 361–365.
Hollander, E. P. (1960b). Reconsidering the issue of conformity in personality. In H. P. David & J. C. Brenglemann (Eds.), *Perspectives in personality research* (pp. 210–225). New York. Springer.
Hollander, E. P. (1961a). Emergent leadership and social influence. In L. Petrullo & B. M. Bass (Eds.), *Leadership and interpersonal behavior* (pp. 30–47). New York: Holt, Rinehart and Winston.

Hollander, E. P. (1961b). Some effects of perceived status on responses to innovative behavior. *Journal of Abnormal and Social Psychology, 49*, 247–250.
Hollander, E. P. (Ed). (1963). *A convergence on social influence.* Proceedings of the ONR Workshop of August, 1962. Buffalo: State University of New York at Buffalo.
Hollander, E. P. (1963). The "pull" of international issues in the 1962 election. In S. B. Withey (Chm.), Voter attitudes and the war-peace issue. Symposium presented at the American Psychological Association, Philadelphia, August 1963.
Hollander, E. P. (1964). *Leaders, groups, and influence.* New York: Oxford University Press.
Hollander, E. P. (1965). Validity of peer nominations in predicting a distant performance criterion. *Journal of Applied Psychology, 49*, 434–438.
Hollander, E. P. (1968). The society of experimental social psychology: An historical note. *Journal of Personality and Social Psychology, 9*, 280–282.
Hollander, E. P. (1971). Style, structure, and setting in organizational leadership. *Administrative Science Quarterly, 16*, 1–9.
Hollander, E. P. (1975). Independence, conformity and civil liberties: Some implications from social psychological research. *Journal of Social Issues, 31*(2), 55–67.
Hollander, E. P. (1978a). *Leadership dynamics: A practical guide to effective relationships.* New York: Free Press/Macmillan.
Hollander, E. P. (1978b). What is the crisis of leadership? *Humanitas, 14*, 285–296.
Hollander, E. P. (1979). The impact of Ralph M. Stogdill and the Ohio State Leadership Studies on a transactional approach to leadership. *Journal of Management, 5*(2), 157–165.
Hollander, E. P. (1980). Leadership and social exchange processes. In K. J. Gergen, M. S. Greenberg, & R. H. Willis (Eds.), *Social exchange: Advances in theory and research* (pp. 103–118). New York: Plenum.
Hollander, E. P. (1967/1981). *Principles and methods of social psychology,* 4th ed. New York and Oxford: Oxford University Press.
Hollander, E. P. (1983). Women and leadership. In H. H. Blumberg, A. P. Hare, V. Kent, & M. Davies (Eds.), *Small groups and social interaction* (vol. 1, pp. 187–195). London and New York: Wiley.
Hollander, E. P. (1985). Leadership and power. In G. Lindzey & E. Aronson (Eds.), *The handbook of social psychology* (3rd ed., pp. 485–537). New York: Random House.
Hollander, E. P. (1986). On the central role of leadership processes. *International Review of Applied Psychology, 35*, 39–52.
Hollander, E.P. (1987). *College and university leadership from a social psychological perspective: A transactional view.* Teachers College, Columbia University—National Center for Postsecondary Governance and Finance, Institutional Leadership Project Report Series.
Hollander, E. P. (1992a). The essential interdependence of leadership and followership. *Current Directions in Psychological Science, 1*, 71–75.
Hollander, E. P. (1992b). Leadership, followership, self, and others. *Leadership Quarterly, 3*(1), 43–54.
Hollander, E. P. (1993). Legitimacy, power, and influence: A perspective on relational features of leadership. In M. Chemers & R. Ayman (Eds.), *Leadership theory and research: Perspectives and directions* (pp. 29–47), San Diego, CA: Academic Press.
Hollander, E. P. (1995a). Ethical challenges in the leader-follower relationship. *Business Ethics Quarterly, 5*(1), 55–65.
Hollander, E. P. (1995b). Organizational leadership and followership: The role of interpersonal relations. In P. Collett & A. Furnham (Eds.), *Social psychology at work: Essays in honour of Michael Argyle* (pp. ). London and New York: Routledge.
Hollander, E. P. (1997). How and why active followers matter in leadership. In E. P. Hollander & L. R. Offermann (Eds.), *The balance of leadership and followership* (pp. 11–28). College Park: Kellogg Leadership Studies Project Report/Burns Academy of Leadership, University of Maryland.
Hollander, E. P. (2004). Upward Influence. In *The Encyclopedia of Leadership.* Gt. Barrington, MA: Berkshire/SAGE Publishing, (pp. 1605–1609).
Hollander, E. P. (2005). Applying psychology to policy issues at the UN and elsewhere: Then and now. *Newsletter of the International Association of Applied Psychology (IAAP), 17*(4), 5–8.
Hollander, E. P. (2006). Influence processes in leadership-followership: Inclusion and the idiosyncrasy credit model. In D. Hantula (Ed.), *Advances in social and organizational psychology* (pp. ). Mahwah: NJ, Erlbaum.

Hollander, E. P. (2007a). Raymond G. Hunt (1928–2006). *American Psychologist, 62*(4), 324.
Hollander, E. P. (2007b). Relating leadership to active followership. In R. A. Couto (Ed.), *Reflections on leadership* (pp. 57–66). Lanham, MD: University Press of America.
Hollander, E. P., & Bair, J. T. (1954). Attitudes toward authority-figures as correlates of motivation among naval aviation cadets. *Journal of Applied Psychology, 38*, 21–25.
Hollander, E. P., Fallon, B. J., & Edwards, M. T. (1977). Some aspects of influence and acceptability for appointed and elected group leaders. *Journal of Psychology, 95*, 289–296.
Hollander, E. P., & Hunt, R. G. (Eds.). (1963/1967, 1971, 1976). *Current perspectives in social psychology: Readings with commentary.* New York: Oxford University Press.
Hollander, E. P., & Hunt, R. G. (Eds.). (1972). *Classic contributions to social psychology: Readings with commentary.* New York: Oxford University Press.
Hollander, E. P., & Julian, J. W. (1968). Leadership. In E. F. Borgatta & W. W. Lambert (Eds.), *Handbook of personality theory and research* (pp. 890–899). Chicago: Rand McNally.
Hollander, E. P., & Julian, J. W. (1969). Contemporary trends in the analysis of leadership processes. *Psychological Bulletin, 71*, 387–397.
Hollander, E. P., & Julian, J. W. (1970). Studies in leader legitimacy, influence, and innovation. In L. Berkowitz (Ed.), *Advances in experimental social psychology* (5th edition, pp. 33–69). New York: Academic Press.
Hollander, E. P., & Julian, J. W. (1978). A further look at leader legitimacy, influence, and innovation. In L. Berkowitz (Ed.), *Group processes* (pp. 153–165). New York: Academic Press.
Hollander, E. P., Julian, J. W., & Haaland, G. A. (1965). Conformity process and prior group support. *Journal of Personality and Social Psychology, 2*, 852–858.
Hollander, E. P., Julian, J. W., & Sorrentino, R. M. (1969). *The leader's sense of constructive deviation.* ONR Technical Report No. 12, Buffalo: State University of New York (SUNY/Buffalo), Psychology Department. Reported in Hollander & Julian (1970).
Hollander, E. P., & Kelly, D. R. (1990, March 30). *Rewards from leaders as perceived by followers.* Paper presented at the meeting of the Eastern Psychological Association. Philadelphia.
Hollander, E. P., & Kelly, D. R. (1992, July 24). *Appraising relational qualities of leadership and followership.* Paper presented at the 25th International Congress of Psychology. Brussels, Belgium.
Hollander, E. P., & Kelly, D. R. (1990, March 30). *Rewards from leaders as perceived by followers: Further use of critical incidents and rating scales.* Annual Meeting of the Eastern Psychological Association. Philadelphia.
Hollander, E. P., & Marcia, J. E. (1970). Parental determinants of peer-orientation arid self-orientation among preadolescents. *Developmental Psychology, 2*, 292–302.
Hollander, E. P., & Offermann, L. (1990a). Power and leadership in organizations: Relationships in transition. *American Psychologist, 45*, 179–189.
Hollander, E. P., & Offermann, L. (1990b). Relational features of organizational leadership and followership. In K. E. Clark & M. B. Clark (Eds.), *Measures of leadership* (pp. 83–97). West Orange, NJ: Leadership Library of America.
Hollander, E. P., & Offermann, L. R. (Eds.). (1997). *The balance of leadership and followership.* College Park, MD: Kellogg Leadership Studies Project Report/Burns Academy of Leadership, University of Maryland.
Hollander, E. P., & Webb, W. B. (1955). Leadership, followership, and friendship: An analysis of peer nominations. *Journal of Abnormal and Social Psychology, 50*, 163–167.
Hollander, E. P., & Willis, R. H. (1964). Conformity, independence, and anticonformity as determinants of perceived influence and attraction. Chapter 19 in E. P. Hollander, *Leaders, groups, and influence.* New York: Oxford University Press, pp. 213–224.
Hollander, E. P., & Willis, R. H. (1967). Some current issues in the psychology of conformity and nonconformity. *Psychological Bulletin, 68*, 62–76.
Hollander, E. P., & Yoder, J. (1980). Some issues in comparing women and men as leaders. *Basic and Applied Social Psychology, 1*, 267–280.
Hollander, P. A. (1978). *Legal handbook for educators.* Boulder, CO: Westview.
Homans, G. C. (1950). *The human group.* New York: Harcourt Brace.
Homans, G. C. (1958). Social behavior as exchange. *American Journal of Sociology. 63*, 597–606.
Homans, G. C. (1961). *Social behavior: Its elementary forms.* New York: Harcourt, Brace and World.
Homans, G. C. (1962). *Sentiments and activities.* New York: Free Press.
Homans, G. C. (1974). *Social behavior: Its elementary forms,* rev. ed. New York: Harcourt Brace Jovanovich.

Hook, S. (1955). *The hero in history.* Boston: Beacon Press.
House, R. J. (1971). A path-goal theory of leader effectiveness. *Administrative Science Quarterly, 16,* 321–338.
House, R. J. (1977). A 1976 theory of charismatic leadership. In J. G. Hunt & L. L. Larson (Eds.), *Leadership: The cutting edge* (pp. 189–207). Carbondale: Southern Illinois University Press.
House, R. J., & Dessler, G. (1974). The path goal theory of leadership: Some post hoc and a priori tests. In J. G. Hunt & L. L. Larson (Eds.), *Contingency approaches to leadership* (pp. 29–55). Carbondale: Southern Illinois University Press.
House, R. J., Filley, A. C., & Kerr, S. (1971). Relation of leader consideration and initiating structure to R and D subordinates' satisfaction. *Administrative Science Quarterly, 16*(1), 19–32.
House, R. J., Hanges, P. J., Javidan, M., Dorfman, P. W. & Gupta, V. (2004). *Culture, leadership and organizations: The GLOBE study of 62 societies.* Thousand Oaks, CA: Sage.
House, R. J., Javidan, M., Hanges, P., & Dorfman, P. (2002). Understanding cultures and implicit leadership theories across the globe: An introduction to Project GLOBE. *Journal of World Business, 37*(1), 3–10.
House, R. J., & Mitchell, T. R. (1974). Path-goal theory of leadership. *Journal of Contemporary Business, 3*(4), 81–97.
House, R. J., & Shamir, B. (1993). Toward the integration of transformational, charismatic and visionary theories. In M. M. Chemers & R. Ayman (Eds.), *Leadership theory and research: perspectives and directions* (pp. 81–107). San Diego: Academic Press.
Hovland, C. I., Janis, I. L., & Kelley, H. H. (1953). *Communication and persuasion.* New Haven: Yale University Press.
Hovland, C. I., & Janis, I. L. (1959) (Eds.). *Personality and persuasibility.* New Haven: Yale University Press.
Howard, A. (1997). The empowering leader: Unrealized opportunities. In E. P. Hollander & L. R. Offermann (Eds.), *The balance of leadership and followership* (pp. 47–68). College Park: Kellogg Leadership Studies Project Report/Burns Academy of Leadership, University of Maryland.
Howard, A., & Bray, D. (1988). *Managerial lives in transition: Advancing age and changing times.* New York: Dorsey.
Howell, J. M., & Avolio, B. J. (1992). The ethics of charismatic leadership: submission or liberation? *Academy of Management Executive, 6*(2), 43–54.
Howell, J. M., & Shamir, B. (2005). The role of followers in the charismatic leadership process: Relationships and their consequences. *Academy of Management Review, 30*(1), 96–112.
Hunt, J. McV. (1965). Traditional personality theory in the light of recent evidence. *American Scientist, 53,* 60–96.
Iaccoca, L. (1984). *Iaccoca.* New York: Bantam.
Iaccoca, L. (2007). *Where have all the leaders gone?* New York: Simon & Schuster.
International Labor Office (ILO). (2007, March 7). *Global employment trends for women: Brief—2007.* Geneva: Author.
Jackson, J. M., & Saltzstein, H. D. (1958). The effect of person-group relationships on conformity processes. *Journal of Abnormal and Social Psychology, 57,* 17–24.
Jackson, P. W. (1961). *Life in classrooms.* New York: Holt, Rinehart and Winston.
Jacobs, T. O. (1970). *Leadership and exchange in formal organizations.* Alexandria, VA: Human Resources Research Organization.
Jacobs, T. O., & Jaques, E. (1987). Leadership in complex systems. In J. Zeidner (Ed.), *Human productivity enhancement* (pp. 7–65). New York: Praeger.
Jacobson, M. R., & Effertz, J. (1974). Sex roles and leadership perceptions of the leaders and the led. *Organizational Behavior and Human Performance, 12,* 383–396.
Jahoda, M. (1959). Conformity and independence. *Human Relations, 12,* 99–120.
Janda, K. F. (1960). Towards the explication of the concept of leadership in terms of the concept of power. *Human Relations, 13,* 345–363.
Janis, I. (1972). *Victims of groupthink: A psychological study of foreign policy decisions and fiascos.* Boston: Houghton Mifflin.
Janis, I. (1989). *Crucial decisions: Leadership in policymaking and crisis management.* New York: Free Press.
Janis, I. L., & Field, P. B. (1956). A behavioral assessment of persuasibility: Consistency of individual differences. *Sociometry, 19,* 241–259.

Janowitz, M. W. I. (1966). *Thomas on social organization and social personality.* Chicago: University of Chicago Press.
Jaques, E. (1961). *Equitable payment.* London: Wiley.
Jenness, A. (1932). The role of discussion in changing opinions regarding a matter of fact. *Journal of Abnormal and Social Psychology, 27,* 279–296.
Jenness, A. (1932a). Social influences in the change of opinion. *Journal of Abnormal and Social Psychology, 27,* 29–34.
Jennings, H. H. (1943). *Leadership and isolation.* New York: Longmans.
Jervis, R. (1976). *Perception and misperception in international politics.* Princeton, NJ: Princeton University Press.
Jones, E. E. (1964). *Ingratiation.* New York: Appleton-Century-Crofts.
Jones, E. E. (1965). Conformity as a tactic of ingratiation. *Science, 149,* 144–150.
Jones, E. E., & Nisbett, R. E. (1971). *The actor and the observer: Divergent perceptions of the causes of behavior.* New York: General Learning Press.
Jones, M. (1953). *The therapeutic community.* New York: Basic Books.
Julian, J. W., & Hollander, E. P. (1966). *A study of some role dimensions of leader-follower relations.* Technical Report No. 3, April 1966, State University of New York at Buffalo, Department of Psychology, Contract 4679, Office of Naval Research.
Julian, J. W., & Steiner, I. D. (1961). Perceived acceptance as a determinant of conformity behavior. *Journal of Social Psychology, 55,* 191–198.
Julian, J. W., Hollander, E. P., & Regula, C. R. (1969). Endorsement of the group spokesman as a function of his source of authority, competence, and success. *Journal of Personality and Social Psychology, 11,* 42–49.
Kaiser, R. (1983, July 10). Commentary on "All Things Considered." National Public Radio.
Kanter, R. M. (1977). *Men and women of the corporation.* New York: Basic Books.
Kanter, R. M. (1981). Power, leadership, and participatory management. *Theory Into Practice, 20,* 219–224.
Katz, D. (1964). The motivational basis of organizational behavior. *Behavioral Science, 9,* 131–146.
Katz, D., & Braly, K. W. (1935). Racial prejudice and stereotypes. *Journal of Abnormal Social Psychology, 30,* 175–193.
Katz, D., & Kahn, R. L. (1966). *The social psychology of organizations.* New York: Wiley.
Katz, D., & Kahn, R. L. (1978). *The social psychology of organizations,* 2nd ed. New York: Wiley.
Katz, D., Sarnoff, I., & McClintock, C. (1956). Ego-defense and attitude change. *Human Relations, 9,* 27–45.
Katzenbach, J. R., & Smith, O. K. (1993). *The wisdom of teams: Creating the high performance organization.* Cambridge, MA: Harvard Business School Press.
Kauffman, J. F. (1980). *At the pleasure of the board.* Washington, DC: American Council on Education.
Kearn, K. E. (1985). *Mentoring at work: Developmental relationships in organizational life.* Glenview, IL: Scott, Foresman.
Keeley, M. (2004). The trouble with transformational leadership. In J. B. Ciulla (Ed.), *Ethics, the heart of leadership* (pp. 111–144). Westport CT: Praeger.
Kellerman, B. (1984). *The political presidency: Practice of leadership.* New York: Oxford University Press.
Kellerman, B. (2004). *Bad leadership: What it is, how it happens, why it matters.* Boston: Harvard Business School Press.
Kellerman, B., & Rhode, D. L. (Eds.), (2007). *Women and leadership: The state of play and strategies for change.* New York: Wiley.
Kelley, R. E. (1988). In praise of followers. *Harvard Business Review, 88*(6), 1–8.
Kelley, R. L. (1992). *The power of followership.* Garden City, NY: Doubleday.
Kelly, D., Julien, T., & Hollander, E. P. (1992, April 4). *Further effects of good and bad leadership revealed by critical incidents and rating scales.* Paper presented at the Annual Meeting of the Eastern Psychological Association. Boston.
Kelman, H. C. (1950). Effects of success and failure on "suggestibility" in the autokinetic situation. *Journal of Abnormal and Social Psychology, 45,* 267–285.
Kelman, H. C. (1958). Compliance, identification, and internalization: Three processes of opinion change. *Journal of Conflict Resolution, 2,* 51–60.
Kelman, H. C. (1961). Processes of opinion change. *Public Opinion Quarterly, 25,* 57–78.
Kelman, H. C. (1966). Deception in social research. *Transaction, 3,* 20–24.

Kelman, H. C., & Hollander, E. P. (1964). International cooperation in psychological research. *American Psychologist, 19*, 779–782.

Kennedy, J. F. (1956). *Profiles in courage*. New York: Harper.

Kenny, D. A., & Zaccaro, S. J. (1983). An estimate of variance due to traits in leadership. *Journal of Applied Psychology, 68*, 678–685.

Kernell, S. (1978). Explaining presidential popularity. *American Political Science Review, 72*, 506–522.

Kerr, C., & Gade, M. L. (1986). *The many lives of academic presidents*. Washington, DC: Association of Governing Boards of University and Colleges.

Kerr, S. (1977). Substitutes for leadership: Some implications for organizational design. *Organization and Administrative Science, 8*, 135–146.

Kerr, S., & Jermier, J. (1978). Substitutes for leadership: Their meaning and measurement. *Organizational Behavior Human Performance, 22*, pp. 375–403.

Kershaw, D. N. (1972). A negative-income-tax experiment. *Scientific American, 227*, 19–25.

Kidd, J. S., & Campbell, D. T. (1955). Conformity to groups as a function of group success. *Journal of Abnormal and Social Psychology, 51*, 390–393.

Kiesler, C. A. (1969). Group pressures and conformity. In J. Mills (Ed.), *Advanced experimental social psychology*, pp. 235–306. New York: MacMillan.

Kiesler, C. A., & Kiesler, S. B. (1964). Role of forewarning in persuasive communications. *Journal of Abnormal and Social Psychology, 68*, 547–549.

Kiesler, C. A., & Kiesler, S. B. (1969). *Conformity*. Reading, MA: Addison-Wesley.

Kilmann, R. H., Saxton, M. J., Serpa, R., & Associates. (1985). *Gaining control of the corporate culture*. San Francisco: Jossey-Bass.

Kimball, R. K., & Hollander, E. P. (1974). Independence in the presence of experienced but deviate group member. *Journal of Social Psychology, 93*, 281–292.

Kinder, D. R. (1981). Presidents, prosperity, and public opinion. *Public Opinion Quarterly, 45*, 1–21.

Kipnis, D. (1976). *The powerholders*. Chicago: University of Chicago Press.

Kipnis, D., Schmidt, S., Swaffin-Smith, C., & Wilkinson, I. (1984). Patterns of managerial influence: Shotgun managers, tacticians, and bystanders. *Organizational Dynamics, 58–67*.

Kipnis, D., Schmidt, S., & Wilkinson, I. (1980). Intraorganizational influence tactics: Explorations in getting one's way. *Journal of Applied Psychology, 65*, 440–452.

Kirkhart, R. O. (1963). Minority group identification and group leadership. *Journal of Social Psychology, 59*, 111–117.

Kirkpatrick, S. A., & Locke, E. A. (1991). Leadership: do traits matter? *Academy of Management Executive, 5*(2), 48–60.

Klineberg, O. (1935). *Negro intelligence and selective migration*. New York: Columbia University Press.

Komaki, J. (2007). Daring to dream: Promoting social and economic justice at work. *Applied Psychology: An International Review, 56*, 624–662.

Koppes, L. (Ed.). (2007). *Historical perspectives in industrial organizational psychology*. Mahwah, NJ: Erlbaum.

Kotter, J. P. (1982). *The general managers*. New York: Free Press.

Kouzes, J. M., & Posner, B. Z. (1987). *The leadership challenge: How to get extraordinary things done in organizations*. San Francisco: Jossey-Bass.

Kraut, A. I., Pedigo, P. R., McKenna, D. D., & Dunnette, M. D. (1989). The role of the manager: What's really important in different management jobs? *Academy of Management Executive, 3*(4), 286–293.

Krech, D., Crutchfield, R. S., & Ballachey, E. (1962). *Individual in society*. New York: McGraw-Hill.

Lakoff, G. (2004). *Don't think of an elephant!* White River Junction, VT: Chelsea Green.

Lamm, H. (1973). Intragroup effects in intergroup negotiation. *European Journal of Social Psychology, 3*, pp, 179–192.

Laski, H. J. (1940). *The American presidency: An interpretation*. New York: Grosset and Dunlap.

Lasswell, H. D. (1948). *Power and personality*. New York: W. W. Norton.

Latane, B., & Darley, J. M. (1969). Bystander "apathy." *American Scientist, 57*, 244–268.

Leana, C. R. (1986). Predictors and consequences of delegation. *Academy of Management Journal, 29*, 754–774.

Leana, C. R. (1987). Power relinquishments versus powersharing: Theoretical clarification and empirical comparison of delegation and participation. *Journal of Applied Psychology, 72*, 228–233.

LeBon, G. (1897). *The crowd: A study of the popular mind,* 2nd ed. London: T. F. Unwin.
Ledford, G. E., Jr., Lawler, E. E., III, & Mohrman, S. A. (1988). The quality circle and its variations. In J. P. Campbell & R. J. Campbell (Eds.), *Productivity in organizations* (pp. 255–294). San Francisco: Jossey-Bass.
Levinson, H., & Rosenthal, S. (1984). *CEO: Corporate leadership in action.* New York: Basic Books.
Lewin, K. (1947). Frontiers in group dynamics: II. Channels of Group Life; social planning and action research. *Human Relations,* 1, pp. 143–153.
Lewin, K. (1947). Group decision and social change. In T. M. Newcomb & E. L. Hartley (Eds.), *Readings in social psychology* (pp. 330–344). New York: Holt.
Lewin, K., Lippitt, R., & White, R. K. (1939). Patterns of aggressive behavior in experimentally created "social climates." *Journal of Social Psychology,* 10, 271–299.
Lewis, S. A., Langan, C. J., & Hollander, E. P. (1972). Expectation of future interaction and the choice of less desirable alternatives in conformity. *Sociometry,* 35, 440–447.
Lewis-Beck, M. S., & Rice, T. W. (1982). Presidential popularity and presidential vote. *Public Opinion Quarterly,* 46, 534–537.
Liden, R. C., & Graen, G. (1980). Generalizability of the vertical dyad linkage model of leadership. *Academy of Management Journal,* 23, 451–465.
Likert, R. (1961). *New patterns of management.* New York: McGraw-Hill.
Lipman-Blumen, J. (2006). *The allure of toxic leaders: Why we follow destructive bosses and corrupt politicians—and how we can survive them.* New York: Oxford University Press.
Locke, E. A., & Schweiger, D. M. (1979). Participation in decision-making: One more look. In B. M. Staw (Ed.), *Research in organizational behavior* (1, pp. 265–339). Greenwich, CT: JAI.
Lockheed, M. E. (1977). Cognitive style effects on sex status in student work groups, *Journal of Educational Psychology,* 69, 158–165.
Lord, R. G., DeVader, C. L., & Alliger, G. M. (1986). A meta-analysis of the relation between personality traits and leadership perceptions: An application of validity generalization procedures. *Journal of Applied Psychology,* 71, 402–409.
Lord, R. G., & Maher, K. J. (1990). Leadership perceptions and leadership performance: Two distinct but interdependent processes. In J. Carroll (Ed.), *Advances in applied social psychology: Business settings* (4, pp. 129–154). Hillsdale, NJ: Erlbaum.
Lord, R. J., & Brown, D. J. (2004). *Leadership processes and follower self-identity.* Mahwah, NJ: Lawrence Earlbaum.
Luchins, A.S., & Luchins, E. H. (1961). On conformity with judgments of a majority or an authority. *Journal of Social Psychology,* 53, 303–316.
Maccoby, E. E., & Jacklin, C. N. (1974). *The psychology of sex differences.* Stanford, CA: Stanford University Press.
Maccoby, M. (1976). *The gamesman, the new corporate leaders.* New York: Simon and Schuster.
Maccoby, M. (1981). *The leader.* New York: Simon and Schuster.
Maccoby, M. (1989). Leadership for our time. In L. Atwater & R. Penn (Eds.), *Military leadership: Traditions and future trends* (pp. 41–46). Annapolis, MD: U.S. Naval Academy.
Maier, N. R., & Hoffman, L. R. (1965). Acceptance and quality of solutions a related to leader's attitudes toward disagreement in group problem solving. *Journal of Applied Behavioral Science,* 1, 373–386.
Mann, R. D. (1959). A review of the relationships between personality and performance in small groups. *Psychology Bulletin,* 56, 241–270.
Manz, C. C., & Sims, H. P., Jr. (1986). Beyond imitation: Complex behavioral and affective linkages resulting from exposure to leadership training models. *Journal of Applied Psychology,* 71, 571–578.
Manz, C. C., & Sims, H. P., Jr. (1987). Leading workers to lead themselves: The eternal leadership of self-managed work teams. *Administrative Science Quarterly,* 32, 106–128.
Manz, C. C., & Sims, H. P., Jr. (1989). *Super-leadership: Leading others to lead themselves.* New York: Prentice Hall.
Manz, C. C., & Sims, H. P., Jr. (1993). *Business without bosses: How self-managing teams are building high performing companies.* New York: Wiley.
Marak, G. E. (1964). The evolution of leadership structure. *Sociometry,* 27, 174–182.
March, J. G. (1981). How we talk and how we act: Administrative theory and administrative life. In T. J. Sergiovanni & J. E. Corbally (Eds.), *Leadership and organizational culture* (pp. 18–35). Champaign: University of Illinois Press.

March, J. G., & Simon, H.A. (1958). *Organizations.* New York: McGraw-Hill.

Marrow, A. J. (1969). *The practical theorist: The life and work of Kurl Lewin.* New York: Basic Books.

Marshall-Meis, J. C., Fleishman, E. A., Martin, J. A., Zaccaro, S. J., Baughman, W. A., & McGee, M. L. (2000). Development and evaluation of cognitive and meta-cognitive measures for predicting leadership potential. *Leadership Quarterly, 11,* 135–153.

Mausner, B. (1953). Studies in social interaction: III. Effect of variation in one partner's prestige on the interaction of observer pairs. *Journal of Applied Psychology, 37,* 391–393.

Mausner, B. (1954a). The effect of prior reinforcement on the interaction of observer pairs. *Journal of Abnormal and Social Psychology, 49,* 65–68.

Mausner, B. (1954b). The effect of one partner's success in a relevant task on the interaction of observer pairs. *Journal of Abnormal and Social Psychology, 49,* 557–560.

Mausner, B., & Block, B. L. (1957). A study of the additivity of variables affecting social interaction. *Journal of Abnormal and Social Psychology, 54,* 250–256.

Maynard, M. (2007, August 7). Once tainted, now handed Chrysler keys. *New York Times,* p. 1.

Mayo, E. (1933). *The human problems of an industrial civilization.* New York: Macmillan.

McCall, M. W., & Lombardo, M. M. (Eds.). (1977). *Leadership: Where else can we go?* Durham, NC: Duke University Press.

McCall, M. W., Lombardo, M. M., & Morrison, A. M. (1988). *The lessons of experience.* Ashland, MA: Lexington Books.

McClelland, D. (1975). *Power: The inner experience.* New York: Irvington.

McGrath, J. E., & Altman, I. (1966). *Small group research: A critique and synthesis of the field.* New York: Holt, Rinehart & Winston.

McGregor, D. (1960). *The human side of enterprise.* New York: McGraw-Hill.

McGregor, D. (1966). *Leadership and motivation.* (Essays edited by W. G. Bennis & E. H. Schein) Cambridge, Mass.: M.I.T. Press.

McGregor, D. (1967). *The professional manager.* New York: McGraw-Hill.

McGuire, W. (1964). Inducing resistance to persuasion. In L. Berkowitz (Ed.), *Advances in experimental social psychology.* Vol. 1. New York: Academic Press, 1964. pp. 191–229.

McGuire, W. J. (1968). *Immunization against persuasion.* New Haven: Yale University Press.

McGuire, W. J., & Millman, S. (1965). Anticipatory belief lowering following forewarning of a persuasive attack. *Journal of Personality and Social Psychology, 2,* 471–479.

McKee, J. P., & Sherriffs, A. C. (1957). The differential evaluation of males and females, *Journal of Personality, 25,* 356–371.

Mead, M. (1949). *Male and female.* New York: Morrow.

Megargee, E. I. (1969). Influence of sex roles on the manifestation of leadership. *Journal of Applied Psychology, 53,* 377–382.

Meindl, J. R., & Ehrlich, S. B. (1987). The romance of leadership and the evaluation of organizational performance. *Academy of Management Journal, 30,* 90–109.

Meindl, J. R., Ehrlich, S. B., & Dukerich, J. M. (1985). The romance of leadership. *Administrative Science Quarterly, 30,* 78–102.

Menzies, H. D. (1980). The ten toughest bosses. *Fortune, 101,* pp. 62–69.

Merei, F. (1949). Group leadership and institutionalization. *Human Relations, 2,* 23–39.

Meyer, H. H. (1982). Whither leadership and supervision? *Professional Psychology, 13,* 930.

Milgram, S. (1961). Nationality and conformity. *Scientific American,* 205(6), 45–51.

Milgram, S. (1965). Liberating effects of group pressure. *Journal of Personality and Social Psychology, 1,* 127–134.

Milgram, S. (1974). *Obedience to authority.* New York: Harper and Row.

Miller, E. J., & Rice, A. K. (1967). *Systems of organization.* London: Tavistock Publications.

Miller, G. A., Galanter, E., & Pribram, K. H. (1960). *Plans and the structure of behavior.* New York: Holt, Rinehart, and Winston.

Miller, K. I., & Monge, P. R. (1986). Participation, satisfaction, and productivity: A meta-analytic review. *Academy of Management Journal, 29,* 727–753.

Mintzberg, H. (1973). *The nature of managerial work.* New York: Harper and Row.

Mintzberg, H. (1983). *Power in and around organizations.* Englewood Cliffs, NJ: Prentice-Hall.

Mitchell, T. R., Green, S. G., & Wood, R. E. (1981). An attributional model of leadership and the poor-performing subordinate: Development and validation. In B. Shaw & L. Cummings (Eds.), *Research in organizational behavior* (3, pp. 197–234). Greenwich, CT: JAI.

Moede, W. (1920). *Experimentelle Massenpsychologie.* Leipzig: S. Hirzel.

Moreno, J. L. (1934). *Who shall survive?* New York: Beacon House.
Moreno, J. L. (Ed.). (1960). *The sociometry reader.* Glencoe, IL: Free Press.
Morrison, A., & Yon Glinow, M. A. (1990). Women and minorities in management. *American Psychologist, 45,* 200–208.
Morrison, A. M. (1992). *The new leaders.* San Francisco: Jossey-Bass.
Moscovici, S., Lage, E., & Naffrechoux, M. (1969). Influence of a consistent minority on the responses of a majority in a color perception task. *Sociometry, 32,* 365–380.
Mouton, J. S., Balke, R. R., & Olmstead, J. A. (1956). The relationship between frequency of yielding and the disclosure of personal identity. *Journal of Personality,* 24, 339–347.
Mowday, R. T. (1979). Leader characteristics, self-confidence, and methods of upward influence in organizational decision situations. *Academy of Management Journal, 22,* 709–725.
Mueller, J. E. (1970). Presidential popularity from Truman to Johnson. *American Political Science Review, 64,* 18–34.
Mulder, M. (1971). Power equalization through participation? *Administrative Science Quarterly, 16,* 31–38.
Mulder, M. (1981, July). *On the quantity and quality of power and the Q.W.L.* Paper presented at the International Conference on the Quality of Work Life, Toronto.
Munsterberg, H. (1914). *Psychology, general and applied.* New York: Appleton.
Murphy, G., Murphy, L. B., & Newcomb, T. M. (1937). *Experimental social psychology.* New York: Harper.
Murray, A. (2007). *Revolt in the boardroom: The new rules of power in corporate America.* New York: HarperCollins.
Nelson, P. D. (1964). Similarities and differences among leaders and followers. *Journal of Social Psychology, 63,* 161–167.
Nemeth, C., & Wachtler, J. (1983). Creative problem solving as a result of majority vs. minority influence. *European Journal of Social Psychology, 13,* 45–55.
Neustadt, R. (1960). *Presidential power: The politics of leadership.* New York: John Wiley.
Neustadt, R. (1990). *Presidential power and modern presidents,* rev. ed. New York: Free Press.
Newcomb, T. M. (1943). *Personality and social change.* New York: Dryden.
Newcomb, T. M., & Hartley, E. (Eds.). (1947). *Readings in social psychology.* New York: Holt.
Newport, F. (2007, January 20–21). Report on NPR of Gallup National Poll results on President Bush.
Ng, S. H. (1980). *The social psychology of power.* New York: Academic Press.
Nord, W. R. (1969). Social exchange theory: An integrative approach to social conformity. *Psychological Bulletin, 71,* 174–208.
Nord, W. R. (1994). Do mergers make acquired executives feel inferior? You bet! *Academy of Management Executive, 8*(2), 81–82.
Norris, F. (2007, October 12). Maybe it's time to restructure executive stock options. *New York Times,* p. C1.
O'Conner, K., & Yanus, A. B. (2004). Women and political leadership. In G. R. Goethals, G. J. Sorenson, & J. M. Burns (Eds.), *Encyclopedia of leadership* (pp. 1664–1671). Thousand Oaks, CA: Sage.
O'Leary, V. E. (1974). Some attitudinal barriers to occupational aspirations in women, *Psychological Bulletin, 81,* 809–826.
O'Leary, V. E. (1977). *Toward understanding women.* Monterey, CA: Brooks/Cole.
Offermann, L. R., & Kearney, C. T. (1988). Supervisor sex and subordinate influence strategies. *Personality and Social Psychology Bulletin, 14,* 360–367.
Offermann, L. R., & Kennedy, J. K., Jr. (1987, April). *Implicit theories of leadership: A look inside.* Paper presented at the meeting of the Society for Industrial and Organizational Psychology. Atlanta.
Offermann, L. R., & Malmaut, A. B. (2002). When leaders harass. The impact of target perceptions of organizational leaders and climate in harassment reporting and outcomes. *Journal of Applied Psychology, 87*(5), 885–893.
Offermann, L. R., & Matos, K. (2007). Best practices in leading diverse organizations. In J. A. Conger & R. E. Riggio (Eds.), *The practice of leadership: Developing the next generation of leaders* (pp. 277–299). San Francisco: Jossey-Bass.
Offermann, L. R., & Schrier, P. E. (1985). Social influence strategies: The impact of sex, role, and attitudes toward power. *Personality and Social Psychology Bulletin, 11,* 286–300.
Orne, M. T. (1962). On the social psychology of the psychological experiment: With particular reference to demand characteristics and their implications. *American Psychologist, 17,* 776–783.

Osborn, R. N., & Vicars, W. M. (1976). Sex stereotypes: An artifact in leader behavior and subordinate satisfaction analysis? *Academy of Management Journal, 19,* 439–449.

Osgood, C. E. (1962). *An alternative to war or surrender.* Illinois: University of Illinois Press.

Ottenad, T. (1977, December 25). Carter report card: The minuses pile up. *St. Louis Post-Dispatch,* p. C1.

Ouchi, W. G. (1981). *Theory Z: How American business can meet the Japanese challenge.* Reading, MA: Addison-Wesley.

Patten, T. H., Jr. (1981). *Organizational development through team building.* New York: Wiley.

Pence, E. C., Pendleton, W. C., Dobbins, G. H., & Sgro, J. A. (1982). Effects of causal explanations and sex variables on recommendations for corrective action following employee failure. *Organizational Behavior and Human Performance, 29,* 227–240.

Pepinsky, P.N. (1961). Social exceptions that prove the rule. In I. A. Berg & B. M. Bass (Eds.), *Conformity and deviation.* New York: Harper, 1961, pp. 424–434.

Pepinsky, P.N., Hemphill, J. N., & Shevitz, R. N. (1958). Attempts to lead, group productivity, and morale under conditions of acceptance and rejection. *Journal of Abnormal Social Psychology, 57,* 47–54.

Peters, T. J., & Waterman, R. H. (1983). *In search of excellence.* New York: Harper and Row.

Pfeffer, J. (1977). The ambiguity of leadership. In M. W. McCall, Jr. & M. M. Lombardo (Eds.), *Leadership: Where else can we go?* (pp. 13–34). Durham, NC: Duke University Press.

Pfeffer, J. (1981). *Power in organizations.* Marshfield, MA: Pitman.

Platt, J. (1973). Social traps. *American Psychologist, 28,* 641–651.

Podsakoff, P. M., & Schriesheim, C. A. (1985). Field studies of French and Raven's bases of power: Critique, reanalysis, and suggestions for future research. *Psychological Bulletin, 97,* 387–411.

Pondy, L. R. (1977). The other hand clapping: An information processing approach to organizational power. In T. H. Hammer, & S. B. Bacharach (Eds.), *Reward systems and power distributions.* Ithaca, NY: Cornell University Press.

Porter, L. W., Allen, R. W., & Angle, H. L. (1981). The politics of upward influence in organizations. In L. L. Cummings & B. M. Staw (Eds.), *Research in organizational behavior* (3, pp. 109–149). Greenwich, CT: JAI.

Porter, M. E. (1985). *Competitive advantage.* New York: Free Press.

Post, J. M. (1986). Narcissism and the charismatic leader-follower relationship. *Political Psychology, 7,* 675–688.

Potts, N. (1988, May 22). GE's management mission. *Washington Post,* pp. HI–H4.

Preston, M. G., & Heintz, R. K. (1949). Effects of participatory versus supervisory leadership on group judgment. *Journal of Abnormal and Social Psychology, 44,* 345–355.

Proshansky, H., Ittelson, W., & Rivulin, L. (Eds.). (1970). Freedom of choice and behavior in a physical setting. In *Environmental psychology: Man and his physical setting* (pp. 173–183). New York: Holt, Rinehart and Winston.

Pruitt, D. G. (1971). Choice shifts in group discussion: An introductory review. *Journal of Personality and Social Psychology, 20,* 339–360.

Pryer, M. W., Flint, A. W., & Bass, B. M. (1962). Group effectiveness and consistency of leadership. *Sociometry, 25,* 391–397.

Pugh, D. S., Hickson, D. J., Hinings, C. R., & Turner, C. (1968). Dimensions of organizational structure. *Administrative Science Quarterly, 13,* 65–105.

Quinn, R. J. (2006). Building an inclusive culture: The communicating managers program. In A. I. Kraut (Ed.), *Getting action from organizational surveys* (pp. 512–534). San Francisco: Jossey-Bass/Wiley.

Raven, B. (1965). Social influence and power. In I. D. Steiner & M. Fishbein (Eds.), *Current studies in social psychology.* New York: Holt, Rinehart & Winston.

Read, P. B. (1974). Source of authority and the legitimation of leadership in small groups. *Sociometry, 37,* 189–204.

Reedy, G. E. (1970). *The twilight of the presidency.* New York: World Publishing.

Reedy, G. E. (1973). *The presidency in flux.* New York: Columbia University Press.

Reeves, F. (1991, April 25). Pitt misled us, lawmaker asserts. *Pittsburgh Post-Gazette,* p. 1.

Reich, R. B. (1987). Entrepreneurship reconsidered: The team as hero. *Harvard Business Review, 65*(3), 77–83.

Rice, A. K. (1970). *The modern university.* London: Tavistock.

Rice, R. W., Bender, L. R., & Vitters, A. G. (1980). Leader sex, follower attitudes toward women, and leadership effectiveness: A laboratory experiment. *Organizational Behavior and Human Performance, 25,* 46–78.

Rice, R. W., & Kastenbaum, D. R. (1983). The contingency model of leadership: Some current issues. *Basic and Applied Social Psychology, 4,* 373–392.

Ricks, T. E. (2006). *Fiasco.* New York: Penguin.

Ridgeway, C. L. (1981). Nonconformity, competence, and influence in groups: A test of two theories. *American Sociological Review, 46,* 333–347.

Riecken, H. W. (1958). The effect of talkativeness on ability to influence group solutions to problems. *Sociometry, 21,* 309–321.

Riesman, D., Glazer, N., & Denney, R. (1950). *The lonely crowd: A study of the changing American character.* New Haven: Yale University Press.

Rimer, S. (2007, February 12). Coming of age in a changed world: Catherine Drew Gilpin Faust. *New York Times,* p. A18.

Roethlisberger, F. J., & Dickson, W. J. (1939). *Management and the worker.* Cambridge, MA: Harvard University Press.

Rokeach, M. (1960). *The open and closed mind.* New York: Basic Books.

Rosen, S., Levinger, G., & Lippitt, R. (1961). Perceived sources of social power. *Journal of Abnormal and Social Psychology, 62,* 439–441.

Rosenblatt, R. (1997). *Coming apart.* Boston: Little, Brown.

Rosovsky, H. (2003). *The university. A user's guide.* Cambridge: Harvard University Press.

Rossiter, C. (1956). *The American presidency.* New York: Harcourt, Brace and World.

Rost, J. C. (1991). *Leadership for the twenty-first century.* Westport, CT: Praeger.

Rudraswamy, V. (1964). An investigation of the relationship between perceptions of status and leadership attempts. *Journal of the Indian Academy of Applied Psychology, 1,* 12–19.

Rush, M. C., Thomas, J. C., & Lord, R. G. (1977). Implicit leadership theory: A potential threat to the internal validity of leader behavior questionnaires. *Organizational Behavior and Human Performance, 20,* 93–110.

Sabath, G. (1964). The effect of disruption and individual status on person perception and group attraction. *Journal of Social Psychology, 64,* 119–130.

Salamone, F. (2004). Margaret Mead. In G. R. Goethals, G. J. Sorenson, & J. M. Burns (Eds.), *Encyclopedia of leadership* (p. 987). Thousand Oaks, CA: Sage.

Salas, E., DeRouin, R. E., & Gade, P. A. (2007). The military's contribution to our science and practice: People, places and findings. In L. L Koppes (Ed.), *Historical perspectives and industrial and organizational psychology* (pp. 169–189).

Samuelson, R. (1993, May 10). The death of management. *Newsweek,* p. 55.

Sanford, F. (1950). *Authoritarianism and leadership.* Philadelphia: Institute for Research in Human Relations.

Sashkin, M. (1984). Participative management is an ethical imperative. *Organizational Dynamics, 12,* 4–22.

Schachter, S. (1951). Deviation, rejection, and communication. *Journal of Abnormal and Social Psychology, 46,* 190–207.

Schein, E. (1985). *Organizational culture and leadership.* San Francisco: Jossey-Bass.

Schein, V. E. (1973). Relationship between sex role stereotypes and requisite management characteristics. *Journal of Applied Psychology, 57,* 95–100.

Schein, V. E. (1985). *Organizational culture and leadership: A dynamic view.* San Francisco: Jossey-Bass.

Schein, V. E. (1990). Organizational culture. *American Psychologist, 45,* 109–119.

Schemo, A. (2006, October 31). At college for deaf, trustees drop new leader. *New York Times,* p. A17.

Schlesinger, A. M. (1973). *The imperial presidency.* Boston: Houghton Mifflin.

Schmidt, K. O. (1975). *Tao Te Ching.* Lakemont, GA: CSA Press.

Schonbar, R. A. (1945). The interaction of observer-pairs in judging visual extent and movement: The formation of social norms in "structured" situations. *Archives of Psychology, 41,* No. 299.

Schriesheim, C. A., & Kerr, S. (1977). R.I.P. LPC: A response to Fiedler. In J. G. Hunt & L. L. Larson (Eds.), *Leadership: The cutting edge* (pp. 51–56). Carbondale: Southern Illinois University Press.

Schulman, G. L. (1967). Asch conformity studies: Conformity to the experimenter and/or to the group? *Sociometry, 30,* 26–40.

Schwager, E. H., Kelly, D. R., Julien, T., & Hollander, E. P. (1993, April 19). *What women and men perceive as good and bad leadership.* Presented at the Annual Meeting of the Eastern Psychological Association. Arlington, VA.

Schwartz, N. D. (2007, November 10). C.E.O evolution phase 3: After empire builders and repair experts, the team captain. *New York Times,* p.C1.

Schwartzkopf, N. H. (1993). *It doesn't take a hero.* New York: Bantam Books.

Schweiger, D. M., & Leana, C. R. (1986). Participation in decision making. In E. A. Locke (Ed.), *Generalizing from laboratory to field settings* (pp. 147–166). Lexington, MA: Heath.

Scodell, A., & Mussen, P. (1953). Social perception of authoritarians and nonauthoritarians. *Journal of Abnormal and Social Psychology,* 48, 181–184.

Sears, R. R. (1960). The 1958 Summer research project on identification. *Journal of Nursery Education,* 16, (2) page # ?.

Secord, P. F., & Backman, C. W. (1961). Personality theory and the problem of stability and change in individual behavior: An interpersonal approach. *Psychological Review,* 68, 21–33.

Selznick, P. (1984). *Leadership in administration.* Berkeley: University of California Press.

Shartle, C. L., Stogdill, R. M., & Campbell, D. T. (1949). *Studies in naval leadership.* Columbus: Personnel Research Board, Ohio State University.

Shaw, M. E. (1955). A comparison of two types of leadership in various communication nets. *Journal of Abnormal and Social Psychology,* 50, 127–134.

Shaw, M. E., & Blum, J. M. (1966). Effects of leadership style upon group performance as a function of task structure. *Journal of Personality and Social Psychology,,* 3, 238–242.

Sherif, M. (1935). A study of some social factors in perception. *Archives of Psychology,* 27, 187.

Sherif, M., & Sherif, C. W. (1953). *Groups in harmony and tension: An integration of studies on intergroup relations.* New York: Harper.

Sidey, H. (1983, August 22). The presidency. How to do nothing well. *Time,* p. 12.

Sigelman, L. (1979). The dynamics of presidential support: An overview of research findings. *Presidential Studies Quarterly,* 9, 206–216.

Simon, H. (1947). *Administrative behavior.* New York: Free Press.

Simon, H. (1957). *Models of man: Social and rational.* New York: Wiley.

Simon, H. (1991). *Models of my life.* New York: Basic Books.

Slater, P. E., & Bennis, W. G. Democracy is inevitable. *Harvard Business Review,* 42(2), 51–59.

Smith, H. (1978, January 8). Problems of a problem solver. *New York Times Magazine,* pp. 30–32.

Smith, J. E., Carson, K. P., & Alexander, R. A. (1984). Leadership: It can make a difference. *Academy of Management Journal,* 27, 765–776.

Smith, K. H. (1961). Ego strength and perceived competence as conformity variables. *Journal of Abnormal and Social Psychology,* 62, 169–171.

Snyder, R. C., Bruck, H. W., & Sapin, B. (1962). *Foreign policy decision-making: An approach to the study of international politics.* New York: Free Press.

Sommer, R. (1969). *Personal space: The behavioral basis of design.* Englewood Cliffs, NJ: Prentice-Hall.

Sorenson, T. C. (1963). *Decision-making in the White House.* New York: Columbia University Press.

Sorrentino, R. M., & Boutillier, R. G. (1975). The effect of quantity and quality of verbal interaction on ratings of leadership ability. *Journal of Experimental Social Psychology,* 11, 403–411.

Spence, J. T., & Helmreich, R. (1972). The attitudes toward women scale: An objective instrument to measure attitudes toward the rights and roles of women in contemporary society, *Journal Supplement Abstract Service,* 2, 66.

Spiller, G. (1929). The dynamics of greatness. *Sociological Review,* 21, 218–232.

*Statistical abstract of the United States.* (1979). Washington, DC: Government Printing Office.

Steinem, G. (2008, January 8). Women are never front runners. *New York Times,* p. A23.

Steiner, I. (1964). Group dynamics. *Annual Review of Psychology,* 15, 421–446.

Sternberg, R. J. (2007). A systems model of leadership: WICS. *American Psychologist,* 62, 34–42.

Stewart, R. (1982). *Choices for the manager.* Englewood Cliffs, NJ: Prentice-Hall.

Stogdill, R. M. (1948). Personal factors associated with leadership. *Journal of Psychology,* 25, 35–71.

Stogdill, R. M. (1959). *Individual behavior and group achievement.* New York: Oxford University Press.

Stogdill, R. M. (1974). *Handbook of leadership.* New York. Free Press.

Stogdill, R. M., & Shartle, C. L. (1948). Methods for determining patterns of leadership behavior in relation to organization structure and objectives. *Journal of Applied Psychology,* 32, 286–291.

Stokes, H. (1987). Quoated in E. P. Hollander, *College and university leadership from a social psychological perspective: A transactional view* (p. 20). New York: National Center for Postsecondary Governance and Finance, Teachers College, Columbia University.

Stone, T. H., & Cooper, W. H. (2008). Emerging credits. *Leadership Quarterly*, in press.

Strodtbeck, F. L., & Mann, R. D. (1956). Sex role differentiation in jury deliberations. *Sociometry, 19*, 3–11.

Suedfeld, P., & Tetlock, P. E. (1977). Integrative complexity of communication in international crises. *Journal of Conflict Resolution, 21*, 169–184.

Sundstrom, E., DeMeuse, K. P., & Futrell, D. (1990). Work teams: Applications and effectiveness. *American Psychologist, 45*(2), 120–133.

Sussman, M., & Vecchio, R. (1982). A social influence interpretation of worker motivation. *Academy of Management Review, 7*, 177–186.

Synder, M. (1979). Self-monitoring processes. In L. Berkowitz (Ed.), *Advances in experimental social psychology* (12, pp. 86–128). New York: Academic Press.

Tajfel, H., & Turner, J. (1979). An integrative theory of intergroup conflict. In W. G. Austin & S. Worchel (Eds.), *The social psychology of intergroup relations* (pp. 56–65). Monterey, CA: Brooks/Cole.

Tannenbaum, R. (1968). *Control in organizations.* New York: McGraw-Hill.

Tannenbaum, R., & Schmidt, W. H. (1958). How to choose a leadership pattern. *Harvard Business Review, 36*, 95–101.

Tarde, G. (1903). *The laws of imitation* [translated from 2nd French edition by E. C. Parsons; original, 1890]. New York: Holt.

Tavris, C., & Offir, C. (1977). *The longest war: Sex differences in perspective.* New York: Harcourt.

Tetlock, P. E. (1983). Cognitive style and political ideology. *Journal of Personality and Social Psychology, 45*, 118–126.

*The Washington Post.* (1978, February 15). p. A22.

Thibaut, J. W., & Kelley, H. H. (1959). *The social psychology of groups.* New York: Wiley.

Thibaut, J. W., & Riecken, H. W. (1955). Some determinants and consequences of the perception of social causality. *Journal of Personality, 24*, 113–133.

Thibaut, J. W., & Strickland, L. H. (1956). Psychological set and social conformity. *Journal of Personality, 25*, 115–129.

Thomas, L., & Anderson, J. (2007, October 29). A risk-taker's reign at Merrill ends with a swift, messy fall. *New York Times,* p. 1.

Thorndike, R. L. (1949). *Personnel Selection.* New York: Wiley.

Thornton, G. C., & Byham, C. C., III (1982). *Assessment centers and managerial performance.* New York: Academic Press.

Thornton, G. C., & Cleveland, J. N. (1990). Developing managerial talent through simulation. *American Psychologist, 45*, 190–199.

Thrasher, F. M. (1927). *The gang.* Chicago: University of Chicago Press.

Titus, H., & Hollander, E. P. (1957). The California F scale in psychological research: 1950–1955. *Psychological Bulletin, 54*, 47–65.

Torrance, E. P. (1955). Some consequences of power differences in permanent and temporary three-man groups. In P. Hare, E. F. Borgatta, & R. F. Bales (Eds.), *Small groups* (pp. 482–492). New York: Knopf.

Trempe, J., Rigny, A., & Haccoun, R. (1985). Subordinate satisfaction with male and female managers: Role of perceived supervisory influence. *Journal of Applied Psychology, 70*, 44–47.

Tuchman, B. (1984). *The march of folly: From Troy to Vietnam.* New York: Ballantine Books.

Tucker, R. C. (1981). *Politics as leadership.* Columbia: University of Missouri Press.

Tuddenham, R. D. (1959). Correlates of yielding to a distorted group norm. *Journal of Personality, 27*, 272–284.

Turner, R. H. (1969). The public perception of protest. *American Sociological Review, 34*, 815–831.

Turner, R. H. (1973). Unresponsiveness as a social sanction. *Sociometry, 36*, 1–19.

Vaill, P. B. (1982). The purposing of high-performing systems. *Organizational Dynamics, 11*(2), 23–39.

Vaill, P. B. (1989). *Managing as a performing art.* San Francisco: Jossey-Bass.

Vaill, P. (1996). *Learning as a way of being.* San Francisco: Jossey-Bass.

Vaill, P. (1997). The learning challenges of leadership. In E. P. Hollander & L. R. Offermann (Eds.), *The balance of leadership and followership* (pp. 71–84). College Park: Kellogg Leadership Studies Project Report/Burns Academy of Leadership, University of Maryland.

Valenti, J. (2007). *This time, this place.* New York: Harmony Books.

Vandaveer, V. V., & Varca, P. E. (1988). *Managing performance: Development of a new performance appraisal system for managers* (Tech. Rep.). St. Louis, MO: Southwestern Bell Telephone Company.

Vanderslice, V. J. (1988). Separating leadership from leaders: an assessment of the effect of leader and follower roles in organizations. *Human Relations, 41,* 677–696.

Vaughn, G.M. (1694). The trans-situational aspect of conformity behavior. *Journal of Personality, 32,* 335–354.

Vaughn, G. M., & Mangan, G. L. (1963). Conformity to group pressure in relation to the value of the task material. *Journal of Abnormal and Social Psychology, 66,* 179–183.

Veblen, T. (1918). *The higher learning in America: A memorandum on the conduct of universities by business men.* New York: B. W. Huebsch.

Verba, S. (1961). *Small groups and political behavior: A study of leadership.* Princeton, NJ: Princeton University Press.

Viorst, J. (1998). *Imperfect control: Our lifelong struggle with power and surrender.* New York: Simon and Schuster.

Vroom, V. H. (1964). *Work and motivation.* New York: Wiley.

Vroom, V. H., & Jago, A. G. (1988). *The new leadership: Managing participation in organizations.* Englewood Cliffs, NJ: Prentice-Hall.

Vroom, V. H., & Jago, A. G. (2007). The role of the situation in leadership. *American Psychologist, 62,* 17–24.

Vroom, V. H., & Yetton, P. W. (1973). *Leadership and decision-making.* Pittsburgh: University of Pittsburgh Press.

Wagner, J. A., III, & Gooding, R. Z. (1987). Shared influence and organizational behavior: A meta-analysis of situational variables expected to moderate participation-outcome relationships. *Academy of Management Journal, 30,* 524–541.

Wahrman, R., & Pugh, M. (1974). Sex, nonconformity and influence. *Sociometry, 37,* 137–147.

Waldera, L. (1988). *The effects of influence strategy, influence objective, and leader-member exchange on upward influence.* Unpublished doctoral dissertation, George Washington University.

Walker, E. L., & Heyns, R. W. (1962). *Anatomy for conformity.* Englewood Cliffs, N. J.: Prentice-Hall.

Wallace, J. L. (1996). *An examination of comparable behavioral and motivational features of transactional and transformational leadership as regards effectiveness and follower satisfaction.* Unpublished doctoral dissertation, Baruch College and Graduate Center, City University of New York.

Webb, W. B., & Hollander, E. P. (1956). Comparison of three morale measures: A survey, pooled group judgments, and self-evaluations. *Journal of Applied Psychology, 40,* 17–20.

Weber, M. (1946). The sociology of charismatic authority. In H. H. Gerth & C. W. Mills (Eds. and Trans.), *From Max Weber: Essays in sociology* (pp. 245–252). New York: Oxford University Press. [Original work published in German, 1921.]

Weber, M. (1947). *The theory of social and economic organization.* (Trans. and ed. by T. Parsons & A. M. Henderson.) New York: Oxford University Press.

Weick, K. E. (1969). Laboratory organizations and unnoticed causes. *Administrative Science Quarterly, 14,* 294–303.

Weiner, H., & McGinnies, E. (1961). Authoritarianism, conformity, and confidence in a perceptual judgment situation. *Journal of Social Psychology, 55,* 77–84.

Westerlund, G. (1952). *Group leadership: A field experiment.* Stockholm: Nordisk Rotogravyr.

Westerlund, G. (1971, July 25). Welcoming address to the XVIIth International Congress of Psychology. Liege, Belgium.

Westphal, J. D., & Khanna, P. (2003). Keeping directors in line: Social distancing as a control mechanism in the corporate elite. *Administrative Science Quarterly, 48,* 361–398.

Wheatley, M. (2007). A new paradigm for a new leadership. In R. A. Couto (Ed.), *Reflections on leadership* (pp. 104–115). Lanham, MD: University Press of America.

Wheatley, M. J. (1992). *Leadership and the new science: Learning about organizations from an orderly universe.* San Francisco: Berrett-Koehler.

Whiteside, D. E. (1985). *Command excellence: What it takes to be the best!* Washington, DC: Department of the Navy, Leadership Division, Naval Military Personnel Command.
Whyte, W. H. (1956). *The organization man.* New York: Simon and Schuster.
Wiggins, J. A., Dill, F., & Schwartz, R. D. (1965). On "status-liability-" *Sociometry,* 28, 197–209.
Will, G. (1991, September 2). Corporate raiders. *Boston Globe,* p. 15.
Willis, R. H. (1961). Social influence and conformity— Some research perspectives. *Acta Sociologica,* 5, 100–114.
Willis, R. H. (1963). Two dimensions of conformity-nonconformity. *Sociometry,* 26, 499–523.
Willis, R. H. (1964). Descriptive models of social response. Technical report, November 1964, Washington University, Nonr 816(12), Office of Naval Research.
Willis, R. H. (1965). Conformity, independence, and anti-conformity. *Humanitas,* 18, 373–388.
Willis, R. H. (1965b). The phenomenology of shifting agreement and disagreement in dyads. *Journal of Personality,* 33, 188–199.
Willis, R. H. (1965c). Social influence, information processing, and net conformity in dyads. *Psychological Reports,* 17, 147–156.
Willis, R. H. (1966). Shifting agreement and disagreement in dyads under conditions of perceived differences in task competence. Technical report, August 1966, Washington University, Nonr 816(12), Office of Naval Research.
Willis, R. H., & Hollander, E. P. (1964a). An experimental study of three response modes in social influence situations. *Journal of Abnormal and Social Psychology,* 69, 150–156.
Willis, R. H., & Hollander, E. P. (1964b). Supplementary note: Modes of responding in social influence situations. *Journal of Abnormal and Social Psychology,* 69, 157.
Wills, G. (1994). *Certain trumpets.* New York: Simon and Schuster.
Wills, G. (2007, January 27). At ease, Mr. President. *New York Times,* p. A23.
Wilson, R. S. (1960). Personality patterns, source attractiveness, and conformity. *Journal of Personality,* 28, 186–199.
Winter, D. G. (1973). *The power motive.* New York: Free Press.
Wolf, I. S. (1959). Social influence: Self confidence and prestige determinants. *Psychological Record,* 9, 71–79.
Wood, M. T. (1973). Power relationships and group decision making in organizations. *Psychological Bulletin,* 79, 280–293.
Yamarrino, F. J. (2000). Leadership skills: Introduction and overview. *Leadership Quarterly,* 11, 305–306.
Yammarino, F. J., & Bass, B. M. (1990). Long-term forecasting of transformational leadership and its effects among Naval Officers: Some preliminary findings. In K. E. Clark & M. B. Clark (Eds.), *Measures of leadership* (pp. 151–169). West Orange, NJ: Leadership Library of America.
Yoder, J. (2001). Making leadership work more effectively for women. *Journal of Social Issues,* 57, 815–828.
Young, K. (1956). *Social psychology.* (3rd ed.) New York: Appleton-Century-Crofts.
Yukl, G. (1981). *Leadership in organizations,* 2nd ed. Englewood Cliffs, NJ: Prentice-Hall.
Yukl, G. (1999). An evaluation of conceptual weakness in transformational and charismatic leadership theories. *Leadership Quarterly,* 10(2), 285–305.
Zaccaro, S. J. (2007). Trait-based leadership. *American Psychologist,* 62, 6–16.
Zaccaro, S. J., Foti, R. J., & Kenny, D. A. (1991). Self-monitoring and trait-based variance in leadership: An investigation across multiple group situations. *Journal of Applied Psychology,* 76, 308–315.
Zaleznik, A. (1977). Managers and leaders: Are they different? *Harvard Business Review,* 55, 67–78.
Zaleznik, A., & Kets deVries, M. F. R. (1975). *Power and the corporate mind.* Boston: Houghton Mifflin.
Zdep, S. M., & Oakes, W. I. (1967). Reinforcement of leadership behavior in group discussion. *Journal of Experimental Social Psychology,* 3, 310–320.
Zetterberg, H. L. (1957). H. L. Compliant actions. *Acta Sociologica,* 8, 179–190.
Zimbardo, P. G. (1977). *Shyness.* Reading, MA: Addison-Wesley.
Zimbardo, P. G., Banks, W. C., Hanev, C., & Jaffe, D. (1973, April 8). A Pirandellian prison. *New York Times Magazine,* pp. 38ff.

# NAME INDEX

## A

Adams, B., 157
Adams, J. S., 181
Adams, S., 22
Adler, A., 29
Adorno T. W., 165
Alexander, R. A., 127
Allen, R. W., 125
Allen, V. L., 172
Alliger, G. M., 81, 84, 118, 140, 146
Allport, F. H., 131, 151, 173, 175, 177, 187
Alvarez, R., 15, 34, 38, 87, 143
Anderson, J., 11
Anderson, L. R., 62, 63
Angle, H. L., 125
Ansari, M. A., 125
Ansbacher, H. L., 133
Argyle, M., 13, 129, 135, 178, 217
Aries, E., 77
Aronson, E., 24, 103, 176, 185
Arpey, G. J., 11
Asch, S. E., 171, 173, 175, 177, 178, 181, 187, 189, 210
Asimov, I., 186
Austin, B., 157, 218
Avolio, B. J., 18, 136, 151
Ayman, R., 139, 140

## B

Backman, C. W., 61
Bair, J. T., 132, 202
Bales, R. F., 76, 77, 215
Ballachey, E., 176
Banas, P. A., 123
Bandura, A., 29, 64, 82
Banta, T. J., 60
Barber, J. D., 104, 105, 112
Barnard, C. I., 12, 13, 22, 52, 130, 152
Barnes, L. B., 68, 130
Barron, F., 179
Bartlett, F. C., 212
Bass, B. M., 9, 10, 18, 30, 38, 56, 60, 71, 81, 88, 120, 133, 135, 136, 155, 172, 213
Bavelas, A., 5, 60, 61
Beloff, H., 174, 183
Ben-Yoav, O., 28, 85, 119, 126, 145, 210

Bender, L. R., 78, 165
Benezet, L. T., 96, 100
Bennis, W. G., 3, 11, 12, 30, 59, 62, 71, 88, 100, 216
Bensimon, E. M., 9, 56, 99
Berg, I. A., 172
Berkowitz, L., 178, 182, 211
Beyer, J. M., 9
Bierstedt, R., 29
Birnbaum, R., 91, 99, 101
Bishop, E. G., 201
Blake, F., 10
Blake, R. R., 178
Blascovich, J., 210
Blau, P. M., 58, 181
Block, B. L., 178
Blum, J. M., 64
Blumberg, H., 75
Bochner, S., 70
Bok, D., 95, 98, 152, 154
Bond, J. R., 76, 113
Borgatta, E. F., 75
Boutillier, R. G., 34, 86, 143
Bower, M., 11, 22, 39, 47, 195
Boyatzis, R., 100, 120, 126, 215
Boyd, N. K., 35
Brass, D. J., 125
Bray, D., 82, 127, 133
Brewster, K., 92, 101
Bridger, H., 214
Bronfenbrenner, U., 192, 209, 210, 211
Broverman, D. M., 76
Broverman, I., 76
Brown, D. J., 13, 25
Brown, J., 15
Brown, J. F., 62
Brown, R., 215
Bruck, H. W., 141
Bruner, J., 165
Bugelski, R., 209
Bunch, M., 207, 213
Bunker, B. B., 78, 210, 213
Burke, P. J., 59
Burke, R. J., 122
Burke, W. W., 117, 121
Burns, J. M., 5, 9, 17, 18, 30, 38, 55, 56, 71, 81, 88, 103, 106, 109, 120, 135, 136, 152, 157, 218
Burtt, H. E., 55
Bush, G. H. W., 109, 114

Bush, G. W., 103, 104, 109, 113
Butler, A., 216
Byrne, J. A., 3, 87, 133, 135, 153

## C

Calder, B. J., 30, 57, 84, 93, 146, 195
Campbell, A., 110
Campbell, D. T., 132, 177
Campeau, R., 18, 136, 151
Cantril, H., 84, 134, 153
Carli, L. L., 73
Carlsmith, J. M., 176
Carnevale, P. J. D., 28, 85, 119, 126, 145, 210
Carrieri, M., 74
Carson, K. P., 127
Carter, J., 16, 48, 53, 104, 109, 112, 113, 114, 115
Carter, L. F., 62
Carter, R., 114
Cartwright, D. C., 29, 58, 179
Cerulo, K., 11
Charcot, J. M., 151
Chemers, M. M., 56, 136, 139, 140
Cherrey, C., 157, 218
Christie, R., 82
Churchill, W., 115
Ciulla, J. B., 6, 149
Clark, A. W., 70
Clark, B., 202
Clarke, A., 214
Clarkson, F. E., 76
Cleveland, J. N., 75, 127
Clifford, C., 61
Clinton, W. J., 15, 48, 196
Cobb, A. T., 127
Cohen, A. M., 62
Cohen, I., 216
Cohen, M. D., 92, 98, 100
Cohen, T. S., 61
Collett, P., 129
Conger, J. A., 37, 82, 87, 141
Cooley, C. H., 172
Cooper, L., 210
Cooper, W. H., 19
Copans, S., 214, 215
Corbett, S., 75
Corry, J., 17
Cowley, W. H., 4, 24, 52, 85, 118
Crano, W. D., 172
Crocker, J., 210
Cronbach, L., 217
Croner, M. D., 177, 179
Cronholm, L., 197

Crouch, A., 122
Crowe, B. J., 70
Crutchfield, R. S., 176, 177, 179, 180, 183, 187
Crystal, G., 135, 153
Cunningham, R., 201
Curphy, G. J., 56, 131, 136

## D

Dani, S. K., 210
Darley, J. M., 191
Davies, M., 75
Deal, T. E., 120
Dean, J., 103
Deaux, K., 75, 76
DeCharms, R., 29, 213
DeLorean, J., 18, 82, 136, 151
Demerath, N. J., 100, 206, 207, 213
DeMeuse, K. P., 130
Deming, W. E., 134, 153
Denmark, F. L., 78, 219
Denney, R., 180, 188
Densten, I. L., 5, 16, 39
DePree, M., 3, 135, 150
DeRouin, R. E., 10
DeSoto, C. B., 175
Deutsch, M., 152, 166, 214
Devadas, R., 121, 123
DeVader, C. L., 81, 84, 118, 140, 146
DeVries, D. L., 13, 135, 150, 157, 218
Dickson, W. J., 131
Dienesch, R. M., 32, 69, 100, 119, 132, 142, 146
Dill, F., 182
Dinc, I., 212, 213
Dittes, J. E., 61, 164, 166
Dobbins, G. H., 120
Dorfman, P., 7
Douglas, W. O., 206
Drucker, P. F., 7, 13, 22, 88, 135, 149, 150, 154
Dubno, P., 61
Dukerich, J. M., 127, 135
Dunnette, M. D., 82

## E

Eagly, A. H., 56, 73, 76
Edelman, M., 115
Edwards, M. T., 28, 144, 211
Effertz, J., 77
Ehrlich, S. B., 16, 18, 21, 56, 57, 69, 127, 135, 136
Eisenhower, D. D., 82, 107, 110

Elgie, D. M., 71, 85, 126, 145
Emerson, R. M., 29, 58, 133, 152
Emery, F., 214
Emler, N., 22, 135, 149, 155
Erikson, E. H., 85, 134, 151
Eskilson, A., 77
Estrada, M., 15
Evan, W. M., 61
Eyde, L. D., 127

## F

Fairhurst, G. T., 123, 127
Fallon, B. J., 28, 77, 144, 210, 211
Faust, C. D. G., 74, 93
Fayol, H., 13, 57
Fazzini, D., 13, 71, 88, 120, 135, 150
Festinger, L., 166, 210
Fiedler, F. E., 25, 27, 31, 56, 58, 59, 62, 63, 70, 88, 92, 118, 127, 132, 139, 145, 208
Fiorina, C., 74
Fiske, S. T., 171
Flacks, R., 192
Flanagan, J. C., 132, 202
Fleishman, E. A., 5, 26, 31, 32, 37, 41, 55, 67, 81, 132, 201, 213, 221
Flint, A. W., 60
Flowerman, S., 203
Follett, M. P., 13, 130, 140, 198
Ford, G., 104, 109, 113
Foti, R. J., 87
Fraas, L. A., 27, 62, 144
French, J. R. P., Jr., 29, 173, 179
Frenkel-Brunswik, E., 165, 215
Freud, S., 4, 64, 84, 118, 134, 151, 153
Fromm, E., 84, 134, 151, 188
Fulbright, W., 103
Furnham, A., 129
Futrell, D., 130

## G

Gabriel, R., 134, 153
Gade, M. L., 100
Gade, P. A., 10
Galanter, E., 189
Galton, F., 24, 49
Garcia, J. E., 31, 70, 92, 118
Gardner, J. W., 3, 4, 15, 35, 150, 151, 186, 211, 218
Garner, W., 217
Geis, F. L., 82
Geneen, H., 31

Gerard, H. B., 155, 177
Gerber, G. W., 75
Gibb, C. A., 25, 82
Gilmer, H., 204
Gioia, D., 118
Giuliani, R., 105
Glazer, N., 180, 188
Gleason, J. M., 82, 210, 211
Glidewell, J., 213
Goldberg, S. C., 178
Goldman, M., 27, 62, 144
Goldstein, M., 197
Gooding, R. Z., 122
Goodman, P. S., 121, 123
Gorden, R. L., 178
Gordon, G. E., 127
Gordon, L. V., 60
Gore, A., 103
Gouldner, A. W., 5, 27, 132, 180, 181, 201
Gowing, M., 13
Graen, G., 32, 69, 100, 119, 121, 132, 142, 146
Graham, D., 172
Graham, P., 13
Gray, J. H., 5, 16, 39
Graybiel, A., 202
Green, S. G., 67, 85, 119, 120, 123, 127
Greenleaf, R. K., 159
Greenwald, A., 87, 134, 152
Griffith, E., 208
Grinsted, A., 202
Gross, A. E., 60
Guetzkow, H., 205
Gurin, G., 110

## H

Haaland, G. A., 177, 210
Haccoun, R., 125
Hackman, J. R., 6, 38, 55, 130, 150, 198
Hall, C., 199
Hamblin, R. L., 144, 213
Hanges, P., 7
Hare, A. P., 75
Harman, S., 3
Harris, E. F., 26, 41, 55
Hartley, E., 201
Hastorf, A. H., 60, 165
Haythorn, W., 62, 215
Hegel, M., 151
Heider, F., 27, 29, 86, 119, 142, 182
Heider, J., 12
Heifetz, R. A., 15
Heilbrun, A. R., Jr., 75
Heine, P. J., 75

Heintz, R. K., 62, 63
Heller, F. A., 122
Helmreich, B., 215
Helson, H., 178
Hemphill, J. K., 5, 27, 58, 59, 60, 132, 201
Henderson, M., 13, 129, 135
Henry, J., 191, 213
Henry, P., 103, 104
Hevesi, D., 154
Heyns, R. W., 174, 175, 178
Hicks, J. P., 134, 153
Himmelweit, H., 214
Hirschhorn, L., 47
Hockfield, S., 74
Hodgkinson, C., 150, 151
Hoffman, L. R., 59, 122, 190
Hofstede, G., 158
Hogan, J., 81, 131
Hogan, R., 13, 22, 71, 81, 88, 120, 131, 135, 149, 150, 155
Hollander, E. P., 3, 4, 5, 6, 13, 14, 16, 17, 23, 24, 26, 28, 32, 33, 34, 35, 38, 55, 56, 57, 58, 59, 60, 61, 62, 64, 67, 68, 71, 74, 76, 77, 78, 79, 82, 83, 84, 85, 86, 87, 88, 101, 106, 117, 118, 119, 121, 126, 127, 129, 130, 131, 132, 133, 134, 135, 140, 141, 142, 143, 144, 145, 146, 147, 149, 150, 151, 152, 153, 154, 155, 157, 164, 167, 169, 171, 172, 174, 175, 176, 177, 180, 181, 182, 186, 187, 188, 189, 192, 202, 203, 204, 205, 206, 208, 210, 211, 213, 221
Hollander, P. A., 92
Homans, G. C., 5, 18, 28, 32, 33, 40, 55, 60, 68, 86, 106, 118, 119, 130, 132, 136, 141, 142, 164, 181, 182, 188, 201, 215
Hook, S., 24
Horner, M., 4
House, R. J., 7, 18, 30, 88, 127, 132, 136, 151
Hovland, C. I., 179
Howard, A., 67, 82, 117, 127, 133, 157, 198, 218
Howell, J. M., 3, 18, 136, 151
Hughson, T. L., 121, 123
Hull, C., 209
Humphrey, H., 208
Hunt, J. McV., 61, 179, 180
Hunt, R. G., 129, 171, 209, 210

## I

Iaccoca, L., 31

## J

Jacklin, C. N., 77
Jackson, J. M., 166, 176
Jacobs, T. O., 16, 18, 28, 35, 39, 106, 126, 144
Jacobson, E., 209
Jacobson, M. R., 77
Jago, A. G., 6, 27, 37, 43, 100, 124
Jahoda, M., 175, 178
Janda, K. F., 58
Janis, I. L., 21, 43, 114, 141, 142, 179, 188, 189, 210
Janowitz, M. W. I., 110
Jaques, E., 28, 126
Javidan, M., 7
Jefferson, T., 51
Jenness, A., 177, 187
Jennings, H. H., 5, 201
Jermier, J., 57, 195
Jervis, R., 141
Johannesen-Schmidt, M. C., 56, 73
Johnson, L. B., 48, 103, 104, 106, 109, 113, 114, 115, 196
Johnson, S., 104
Jones, E. E., 30, 33, 93, 181, 188
Jones, M., 214
Julian, J. W., 14, 16, 23, 28, 33, 35, 55, 57, 58, 62, 82, 85, 86, 87, 106, 119, 132, 133, 141, 142, 144, 145, 177, 180, 182, 210, 211

## K

Kagan, J., 215
Kahn, R. L., 15, 16, 35, 58, 63, 85, 119, 130, 139, 144
Kaiser, R., 112
Kanter, R. M., 76, 117, 121
Kapoor, A., 125
Katz, D., 15, 16, 35, 58, 63, 85, 119, 130, 139, 144, 173, 186, 210
Katz, J., 96, 100
Katzenbach, J. R., 39, 130, 150, 198
Kauffman, J. F., 100
Kearney, C. T., 126
Keeley, M., 22
Kellerman, B., 47, 75, 84, 157, 218
Kelley, H. H., 29, 33, 61, 164, 166, 181
Kelley, R. E., 130, 140, 151, 157, 218
Kelley, R. L., 12
Kelly, D. R., 69, 83, 146, 155, 219
Kelman, H. C., 64, 173, 177, 178, 188, 209, 215
Kennedy, A. A., 120
Kennedy, E., 109
Kennedy, J. F., 5, 106, 107, 108, 109, 111, 190

Kennedy, J. K., Jr., 127
Kenny, D. A., 81, 87
Kent, V., 75
Kernell, S., 110
Kerr, C., 100
Kerr, S., 57, 195
Kets deVries, M. F. R., 118
Ketter, R., 216, 217
Kidd, J. S., 177
Kiesler, C. A., 178, 188
Kiesler, S. B., 178, 188
Kilmann, R. H., 31, 101, 120
Kimball, R. K., 189, 210
Kinder, D. R., 110
King, L., 105
Kipnis, D., 64, 85, 87, 118, 119, 121, 125, 126, 133, 152
Kirkhart, R. O., 62
Kirkpatrick, S. A., 68, 81, 131
Kite, W. R., 60
Klineberg, O., 201, 203, 208, 214, 219
Komaki, J., 37
Kotter, J. P., 126
Kouzes, J. M., 68, 69, 83, 118, 127, 130, 141, 146, 155
Kraut, A. I., 82
Krech, D., 176
Kriger, M. P., 68, 130

## L

Lage, E., 189, 205
Lakoff, G., 115
Lamm, H., 35
Lance, B., 53
Langan, C. J., 188, 189, 210
Lanzetta, J., 62
Lao Tzu, 12, 21, 151
Laski, H. J., 105
Lasswell, H. D., 115
Latane, B., 191, 215
Lawler, E. E., III, 121, 122
Lay, K., 185
Leana, C. R., 6, 122, 123
LeBon, G., 151
Ledford, G. E., Jr., 121, 122
Lee, F., 15
Lefkowitz, J., 219
Leister, A. F., 25, 31, 118
Levinger, G., 62
Levinson, D., 165, 199, 201, 203
Levinson, H., 126
Lewin, K., 5, 62, 131, 201, 202
Lewis, S. A., 188, 189, 210
Liden, R. C., 32, 69, 100, 119, 132, 142, 146
Likert, R., 31, 117, 120, 131, 139, 201

Lindsay, J., 17
Lindsley, D., 215
Lindzey, G., 24, 103
Lipman-Blumen, J., 47
Lippitt, R., 62, 131
Locke, E. A., 6, 68, 81, 121, 123, 131
Lockheed, M. E., 79
Lombardo, M. M., 26, 69, 83, 125, 146, 155
Lord, R. G., 13, 25, 30, 57, 68, 81, 83, 84, 118, 130, 135, 140, 146, 155
Lorge, I., 201
Luchins, A. S., 177
Luchins, E. H., 177
Lynd, R., 202

## M

MacArthur, D. A., 82
Macauley, J. R., 182
McCall, M. W., 26, 69, 83, 125, 146, 155
McCarthy, E., 214
McClelland, D., 4, 28, 29, 82, 87, 105, 118, 215
McClintock, C., 173
Maccoby, E. E., 77
Maccoby, M., 31, 82, 118
McGinnies, E., 179
McGovern, G., 111
McGregor, D., 8, 31, 59, 79, 117, 131
McGuire, W. J., 178
Machiavelli, 21
McKee, J. P., 75
McKenna, D. D., 82
McKinnell, H., 10
Magnusson, F.W., 96, 100
Maher, K. J., 13, 68, 83, 84, 118, 130, 135, 140, 146, 155
Maier, N. R. F., 59, 122, 190
Major, B., 210
Malmaut, A. B., 74
Mangan, G. L., 178
Manibay, M. E., 74
Mann, L., 215
Mann, R. D., 25, 61, 76, 77, 172
Manz, C. C., 123, 124, 125, 130, 151, 198
Marak, G. E., 61
March, J. G., 31, 32, 92, 98, 100, 205
Marcia, J. E., 192, 211
Marrow, A. J., 131
Marshall, B., 217
Marshall, G. C., 82
Maslow, A., 215
Matos, K., 75
Mausner, B., 177, 178
Mayo, E., 131
Mead, M., 76, 201
Meanor, B., 205

Medland, F. F., 60
Megargee, E. I., 77
Meindl, J. R., 16, 18, 21, 56, 57, 69, 127, 135, 136
Meirowitz, B., 62
Menzies, H. D., 84, 133, 150
Merei, F., 182
Merton, R., 202
Meyer, H. H., 68
Meyerson, M., 216
Milgram, S., 21, 178, 180, 189
Milken, M., 18, 136, 151
Miller, E. J., 99, 214
Miller, G. A., 189
Miller, K. I., 122
Miller, M., 205
Miller, W. E., 110
Millman, S., 178
Mintzberg, H., 22, 100, 121
Mitchell, T. R., 67, 85, 119, 120
Modigliani, F., 205
Moede, W., 187
Mohrman, S. A., 121, 122
Monge, P. R., 122
Montaigne, 21
Moreno, J. L., 5, 132, 201
Morrison, A. M., 26, 69, 75, 83, 125, 127, 146, 155, 158
Moscovici, S., 189, 205
Mouton, J. S., 178
Mowday, R. T., 125
Mulally, A., 38
Mulder, M., 6, 10, 29, 57, 122, 124, 133, 149, 152, 159
Münsterberg, H., 131, 187
Murphy, K. R., 75
Murray, A., 11

## N

Naffrechoux, M., 189, 205
Nagay, J., 210, 214
Nanus, B., 3, 11, 30, 71, 88, 100
Nardelli, R., 10
Nathan, P., 213
Neider, L., 210
Nelson, C., 60
Nelson, P. D., 62
Nemeth, C., 143
Neustadt, R., 13, 104
Newcomb, T. M., 165, 201
Newell, A., 205
Newport, F., 103
Ng, S. H., 29

Nisbett, R. E., 30, 93
Nixon, R., 48, 104, 105, 111, 112, 114, 196
Nord, W. R., 33

## O

Oakes, W. I., 60
O'Conner, K., 74
Offermann, L. R., 6, 14, 68, 74, 75, 82, 83, 84, 86, 88, 117, 125, 126, 127, 132, 140, 147, 151, 157, 158, 218
Offir, C., 76
O'Leary, V. E., 75, 77, 78
Olmstead, J. A., 178
O'Neal, S., 3, 11
Orne, M. T., 178
Osborn, R. N., 79
Osgood, C., 207, 209
Ottenad, T., 53
Ouchi, W. G., 31, 117, 131
Ozakpinar, Y., 212

## P

Park, J., 221
Parsons, T., 215
Patten, T. H., Jr., 125
Pedigo, P. R., 82
Pelosi, N., 74
Pence, E. C., 120
Pendleton, W. C., 120
Pepinsky, P. N., 60, 182
Peters, T. J., 31, 101
Petrullo, L., 210, 213
Pettigrew, T., 215
Pfeffer, J., 16, 29, 30, 57, 69, 84, 99, 121, 124, 154
Pius XII, Pope, 213
Plato, 21
Podsakoff, P. M., 126
Pondy, L. R., 29
Porter, L. W., 125
Porter, M. E., 87
Posner, B. Z., 68, 69, 83, 118, 127, 130, 141, 146, 155
Post, J. M., 12, 18, 88, 134, 136, 152, 158
Potts, N., 125
Preston, M. G., 62, 63
Pribram, K. H., 189
Prince, C., 3, 151
Pruitt, D. G., 28, 191, 210
Pryer, M. W., 60
Pugh, M., 15, 74, 143

## Q

Quaintance, M. K., 127
Quinn, R. J., 4

## R

Raskin, R., 13, 71, 88, 120, 135, 150
Raven, B. H., 29, 58, 173
Read, P. B., 34, 140
Reagan, R., 16, 104, 105, 109, 110, 112, 113, 114
Reedy, G. E., 104, 113, 114
Reeves, F., 154
Regan, P., 216
Regula, C. R., 62, 210
Reich, R. B., 12, 198
Reichman, W., 219, 220
Rhode, D. L., 75
Rice, A. K., 99, 214
Rice, R. W., 71, 78, 85, 126, 145, 210
Ricks, T. E., 103
Ridgeway, C. L., 34, 86, 143
Riecken, H. W., 60, 182
Riesman, D., 180, 188
Riggio, R. E., 9
Rigny, A., 125
Rimer, S., 74, 93
Roethlisberger, F. J., 131
Rokeach, M., 31, 100, 165
Roosevelt, F. D., 105
Rosen, N., 127
Rosen, S., 62
Rosenblatt, R., 97
Rosenkrantz, P. S., 76
Rosenthal, R., 215
Rosenthal, S., 126
Rosnow, R., 208
Rossiter, C., 104, 108
Rost, J. C., 6, 149, 150
Rudraswamy, V., 60
Rush, M. C., 30, 57, 84, 146
Russell, M., 104
Russell, R., 207
Ryckman, R., 210

## S

Sabath, G., 182
Salas, E., 10
Saltzstein, H. D., 166, 176
Samuelson, R., 150
Sanford, F., 5, 23, 27, 84, 130, 132, 140, 201
Sanford, N., 165

Sapin, B., 141
Sarnoff, I., 173
Sartre, J. P., 11, 106, 155
Sashkin, M., 122
Savage, P., 103, 134, 153
Saxton, M. J., 31, 101, 120
Scandura, T. A., 121, 142
Scarr, S., 67
Schachter, S., 167, 188
Schein, V. E., 31, 77, 101, 120
Schemo, A., 97
Schlesinger, A. M., 103, 113
Schmidt, K. O., 151
Schmidt, S., 125, 126
Schmidt, W. H., 122
Schneider, S., 213
Schonbar, R. A., 177
Schrier, P. E., 75, 125
Schriesheim, C. A., 126
Schulman, G. L., 187
Schwartz, N. D., 3
Schwartz, R. D., 182
Schweiger, D. M., 6, 121, 122, 123
Seaman, F. J., 82, 210, 211
Sears, R. R., 64
Seashore, E. W., 78
Secord, P. F., 61
Segall, J., 197, 220
Selznick, P., 63, 101
Serpa, R., 31, 101, 120
Sgro, J. A., 120
Shamir, B., 3, 18, 136, 151
Shartle, C. L., 132, 201
Shaw, M. E., 64
Sherif, C. W., 43
Sherif, M., 43, 171, 177, 181, 187, 191, 210
Sherriffs, A. C., 75
Shevitz, R. N., 60
Shoben, J., 203
Sigelman, L., 110
Siler, J. F., 3, 87, 133, 135, 153
Simon, H. A., 2, 3, 4, 5, 149, 205, 213
Sims, H. P., Jr., 118, 123, 124, 125, 130, 151, 157, 198, 218
Slater, P. E., 59, 76
Sloan, A., 217
Smith, J. E., 127
Smith, K. H., 179
Smith, O. K., 39, 130, 150, 198
Smith, R., 135, 150
Snavely, B. K., 123, 127
Snyder, M., 82, 87
Snyder, R. C., 141
Solomon, L., 208, 209
Sorenson, G., 157, 218
Sorenson, T. C., 106

Sorrentino, R. M., 34, 86, 143, 144, 145, 210
Spence, J., 217
Spiller, G., 24
Staub, E., 215
Steiner, I. D., 58, 165, 182
Stephens, R. W., 100
Sternberg, R. J., 55
Stevenson, A., 107, 110
Stewart, R., 67, 83, 101, 118, 130, 140
Stimson, J., 75
Stockdale, J. N., 75
Stogdill, R. M., 5, 25, 61, 63, 87, 131, 132, 201
Stokes, H., 101
Stone, T. H., 19
Strickland, L. H., 166, 178
Strodtbeck, F. L., 76, 77
Suedfeld, P., 31, 118
Summers, L., 74, 93
Sundstrom, E., 130
Sussman, M., 125
Swaffin-Smith, C., 125, 126
Symonds, W. C., 3, 87, 133, 135, 153

## T

Taft, R., 200
Tajfel, H., 171
Tannenbaum, R., 122, 123
Tarde, G., 151
Tavris, C., 76
Taylor, R. R., 100
Taylor, S. E., 171
Tetlock, P. E., 31, 118
Thibaut, J. W., 29, 33, 166, 178, 181, 182
Thomas, J. C., 30, 57, 84, 146
Thomas, L., 11
Thomas, W. I., 110
Thoreau, H. D., 172
Thorndike, R. L., 201, 203, 204, 217
Thornton, G. C., 127
Thrasher, F. M., 24
Titus, E., 203
Titus, H., 203
Torrance, E. P., 143
Trempe, J., 125
Tuchman, B., 42
Tucker, R. C., 106
Tuddenham, R. D., 179
Turhan, M., 212
Turner, J., 171
Turner, R. H., 115, 191

## U

Usher, T., 134, 153

## V

Vaill, P. B., 4, 11, 37, 47, 97, 117, 157, 158, 185, 218
Valenti, J., 103
Van Engen, M. L., 73
Vandaveer, V. V., 124
Vanderslice, V. J., 67, 68, 71, 130, 151
Varca, P. E., 124
Vaughn, G. M., 178, 179
Veblen, T., 95
Vecchio, R., 125
Verba, S., 15
Vicars, W. M., 79
Viellieu, B., 18, 56, 136
Vinacke, W. E., 76, 210
Viorst, J., 4
Vitters, A., 78
Vogel, S. R., 76
Von Glinow, M. A., 127
Vroom, V. H., 6, 27, 37, 43, 100, 122, 124, 132

## W

Wachtler, J., 143
Wageman, R., 6, 55
Wagner, J. A., III, 122
Wahrman, R., 15, 74, 143
Waldera, L., 125
Walker, E. L., 174, 175, 178
Wallace, J. L., 9, 56, 99
Walters, R. H., 64
Wanner, E., 11
Washington, G., 103
Waterman, R. H., 31, 101
Watkins, S., 185
Watson, G., 201, 203
Webb, W. B., 5, 68, 83, 118, 130, 132, 141, 204
Webber, C., 201
Weber, M., 12, 17, 18, 29, 30, 56, 61, 64, 88, 135, 151, 152
Webster, S. W., 157
Weiner, H., 179
Welch, J. F., Jr., 125
Wesner, B., 219
Westerlund, G., 131
Wheatley, M. J., 6, 81
White, R. K., 62, 131
Whiteside, D. E., 130
Whyte, W. H., 180, 188
Wiggins, J. A., 182
Wiley, M. G., 77
Wilkinson, I., 125, 126
Willis, R. H., 171, 172, 174, 175, 176, 177, 179, 185, 187, 188

Wills, G., 5, 103, 104, 154
Wilson, R. S., 74, 179
Winter, D. G., 29, 105
Wolf, I. S., 177
Wood, M. T., 29
Wood, R. E., 85, 120

## Y

Yammarino, F. J., 32, 71, 88
Yanus, A. B., 74
Yetton, P. W., 27, 100, 122, 124, 132
Yoder, J., 74, 76, 78, 210
Young, K., 174
Yukl, G., 9, 18, 56, 81, 122

## Z

Zaccaro, S. J., 32, 37, 55, 81, 87
Zaleznik, A., 118, 127, 186
Zalkind, S., 219, 220
Zander, A., 58
Zdep, S. M., 60
Zelditch, M. A., 61
Zetterberg, H. L., 179

# SUBJECT INDEX

## A

Acceptance capital, 15
Acceptance theory of authority, 12–13, 130
Accountability, 3, 52–53, 149
Acquiescence, 174
Appointment-election, 27–28, 34–35
Army Research Institute (ARI), 32
Attribution approaches, 21, 68–69, 84, 118, 121
    leader qualities and performance, 146
Authentic leader, 10
Authority, 28, 41, 51–52, 58, 143
    acceptance theory of, 12–13, 130
    legitimacy as basis of, 85
    source and nature of, 62–63
Autocratic leadership, 4, 27, 131, 159
Automaton conformity, 188

## B

Barriers to empowerment, 123–124
Barron's Ego-Strength Scale, 179
Brainstorming, 43

## C

Carter administration, 53
Character. see Trait approaches
Charisma, 3, 17, 158
    effects of, 151–152
Charismatic leaders, 10, 12, 17, 30, 56, 64, 88
    poor outcomes and, 142
    power and, 134
    transactional (TA) leadership and, 135–136
    transformational (TF) leadership and, 18, 71, 88, 120, 135–136
Chief executive officer (CEO) compensation, 10, 154, 159
Chief executive officer (CEO) disease, 3
Choice shift phenomenon, 191
Civil liberties, 185–186, 191–192
Coaching, 72
Coenotrophic behavior, 174
Coercive power, 29
Cohesiveness, 55
College and university leadership, 91–101
    commercialization problem, 95
    conveying structure and style, 99–100
    decision processes and fund raising, 94–95, 197
    defining success, 98–99
    department chair as leader, 93–94
    expectations and perceptions, 92–93
    implications and conclusions, 101
    inclusive leadership, 91–92, 95
    interpersonal relations, 96
    management and, 100–101
    presidential role/roles, 92
    selection of administrators, 96
    student leadership, 96–98
Commercialization problem, 95
Communication
    information flow, 12
    as open and honest, 38
    two-way communication, 5, 190
Company man, 31
Competition, 3
Compliance, 188
Conflict resolution, 42–43, 59
    problem subordinates, 59
Conforming society, 180
Conformity, 33, 163–164, 185
    automaton conformity, 188
    conceptual/psychological definition of, 174
    descriptive criteria, 174
    experiments on, historical context of, 187
    group norms, 142
    independence vs., 187–188
    leadership and, 8, 51
    movement conformity, 177–178
    operational definitions of, 173
    perceptual element in, 168
    personality and, 179–181
    as process, 169
    psychology of, 171–172
    questions on, 164–165
    research on, 172–173, 182–183
    situation and, 178–179
    social conformity, 167–168
    social exchange and, 181–182
    social response and, 175–176
    social uses of, 188–189
    status and, 164, 168–169, 182
Conformity research, 173
Consensus, 93–94
Consent of the governed, 3

## SUBJECT INDEX

Consultative style, 27
Content analyses, 42
Contingency models, 27–28, 49, 63
Conventionality, 174
Cooperation/cooperative action, 3, 22
Counter-power, 29
Craftsman managerial type, 31
Credibility, 52–53
Credibility gap, 52, 106
Credit, 13–14, 15, 18, 70, 86
    derivative credit, 86, 143
    idiosyncrasy credit, 14–16, 51, 86–87, 143, 166–168, 188
Crisis of leadership, 152
Critical incidents research, 17, 42, 132

### D

Decision making, 3, 6
    educational leadership, 94–95
    leader styles in, 27
    participation in (PDM), 121–121
    shared decision making, 12
Definition of the situation, 171
Democracy, 196
Democratic leadership, 4, 131
Department chairperson, as leader, 93–94
    building consensus, 93–94
    common mission, 93–94
    management functions, 94
    motivating scholarship/educational environment, 94
    promoting cooperative relations, 94
    securing resources, 94
Dependability, as social requirements, 186–189
Dependence-independence, 175
Derailment of leaders, 83, 155
Derivative credit, 86, 143
Diversity issues, 158
Dysfunctional leadership, 47

### E

Ego-ideal, 84, 134, 151, 153
Ego trips, 87
Employee give-backs, 11
Empowerment, 47, 117
    barriers to, 123–124
    modeling/mentoring, 124–125
Equity/equity issues, 40, 47, 50, 149
Ethical issues
    charisma and its effects, 151–152
    historical context of, 151
    joining or distancing followers, 153–154
    leader-follower relationship, 149–150
    leader performance, 154–155
    morality and, 6–7
    mutual identification, 153
    power and identification, 152
    self-serving biases, 152–153
Ethical leaders, 18, 136
Expert power, 29

### F

Facilitation, 72
Fair exchange, 39–41, 47
    equity, 40
    leadership as transaction, 50, 106
    system progress, 40
Fairness, 3, 37, 38, 50, 149, 197
    fair exchange, 39–41, 47
Feedback, 38, 39, 77, 133, 152
Follower(s); see also Leader-follower relationship
    attributions about leaders, 84
    consent of the governed, 3
    diversity issues and, 158
    expectations of, 83
    leader responses to, 70–71
    leaders role with, 39
    leadership and, 3–4, 130, 140–142
    passivity, compliance, and independence, 4
    perceptions of leader's qualities, 5, 27, 81, 83–84, 110
    respect for, 41
    responsiveness of, 34–35
Formal leaders, 12
Forward-looking approach, 38
4 R's (Respect, Recognition, Responsiveness and Responsibility), 3, 5, 40, 195
Free society, 186
Free speech, 186
Fund raising activities, 94–95
Fundamental attribution error, 30, 57

### G

Gamesman managerial type, 31
Gender differences, in social behavior, 75–76
Globe Research Program, 7
Goal setting, 38, 124
Golden parachutes, 149
"Great Man" theory, 12, 24, 49
Group(s)
    identification with leader, 64–65
    interpersonal and group processes, 131
    leader legitimacy and, 143

leader's authority, 62–63
leader's effectiveness in, 59
motivation to belong, 166
perceptions of leadership functions in, 61–62
Group conformity, 177–178
Group expectancies, 165–166
Group performance, 31
Group style, 27
Groupthink phenomenon, 21, 114, 141, 172

## H

Hawthorne studies, 131
Headship, 4, 52, 85, 118
Heroic leader bias, 9
Hollander, E. P., biography of, 199–220
    APA Committee, 207
    at American University, 207–209
    Argyle's social psychology laboratory, 217
    at Carnegie Tech, 204–205
    at City University of New York (CUNY), 219–220
    college and military service, 199–200
    at Columbia University, 200–202
    early career as writer, 200–201
    Eastern Psychology Association (EAP), 219
    Ford Foundation project, 205
    Fulbright at Istanbul University, 212
    Harvard sabbatical, 215
    Idiosyncrasy Credit Model, 206–207
    Kellogg Leadership Studies Project (KLSP), 157, 218
    National Academy of Sciences/National Research Council, 217–218
    Ph.D. studies, 202–203
    as provost at UB, 216–217
    research as naval aviation psychologist, 202
    Rome International Congress of IAAP, 212–213
    Tavistock sabbatical, 213–214
    at University of Buffalo (UB)/SUNY, 210–211
    at Washington University, 206–207
Honesty, 69
Human relations approach, 31, 117

## I

Identification processes, 64, 84–85
    in leader-follower relationship, 133–135
    mutual identification, 153
    power vs., 152
    presidential leadership and, 110–111

Idiosyncrasy credit, 14–16, 51, 86–87, 143, 166–168, 188
Idiosyncrasy credit (IC) model, 14–16, 32–33, 50–51, 60, 70, 86–87, 133, 142–143, 163–164, 166–167
    conformity-nonconformity and, 181–182
    critique of, 19
    inclusive leadership and, 38
    leader legitimacy and, 144
    presidential leadership, 106
Implicit leadership theories (ILTs), 13, 30, 57, 84–85, 146
Impression management, 112
Inclusive culture, 3–4
Inclusive leadership (IL), 139, 195–198; see also Leader-follower relationship
    applications and implications of, 37
    conflict resolution and, 42–43
    context/concepts of, 7–8
    cooperative action and, 22
    decision making and power sharing, 6
    ethics and morality, 6–7
    foundations of, 5–6
    four Rs of, 3, 40
    higher education, challenges of, 91–92, 95
    learning skills of, 37–38
    legitimacy and credit, 13–16
    listening in, 4–5
    measurement of, 42
    overview of, 3–4
    performance over time, 38–39
    power distance, 10–12
    presidential leadership and, 106
    TF leadership and IC model, 38
Inclusive Leadership Scale (ILS), 42, 43, 221–222
Independence, 175, 185
    anticonformity and, 185
    conformity vs., 187–188
    disapproval and, 190
    fear of disruptions, 190
    impediments to, 189–190
    independent position, effects of, 189
    lack of perceived alternatives, 190
    personal detachment and, 190–191
    pluralistic ignorance concept, 190
    sense of impotence and, 191
    as social requirements, 186–187
    social uses of, 188–189
Influence, 28–29, 33, 58, 60, 130, 134, 182
    informal influence, 125–126
    power vs., 29, 141
    resistance to, 178
    upward influence, 3, 67, 125
Informal influence, 125–126
Informal leaders, 12, 169
Information, 141

## SUBJECT INDEX

Innovation potential, 33
Inspirational leadership, 69
Insularity, 3
International Labor Organization (ILO), 73
Interpersonal evaluation, 37
Interpersonal influence processes, 163
Interpersonal skills, 26, 55, 57, 73
    college and university leadership, 96
    early research on, 131
    group processes and, 131
    inclusive leadership skills, 37–38
    seven guiding IL practices, 38
Iron Law of Oligarchy, 198

### J

J curve hypothesis (Allport), 173, 175
Japanese management practices, 117, 131
Jungle fighter managerial type, 31

### K

Kellogg Leadership Studies Project (KLSP), 157, 218

### L

Labor-management relations, 196
Laissez-faire leadership, 131, 159
Leader
    awareness of followers needs, 196
    as cultural learner, 158
    derailment of, 83, 155
    effectiveness of, 63–64
    goal-setting activity of, 59
    idealized images of leadership, 16
    identification with, 64–65, 84–85
    legitimacy of, 55, 143–146
    personality characteristics, 58, 146
    qualities by stages, 82–83
    responses to followers, 70–71
    self-concept of, 84–85, 87, 155
    self-serving biases, 87–88
    women as, 77–78
Leader-centric model/leader centrism, 3, 11, 12, 149
Leader-follower relationship, 4, 58, 83–84, 140–142
    active follower, 70
    awareness of needs, 196
    balance of, 157–159
    centrality of, 150–151
    critical incidents research, 17
    decision making in, 6
    dominance and submission in, 81
    ethical challenges in, 149–155
    ethics and morality, 6–7
    fair-exchange and, 39–41
    formal vs. informal leaders, 12
    4 R's in, 3, 5
    identification in, 133–135
    inequities in organizations, 10–11
    interdependence of, 67
    joining or distancing followers, 153–154
    leader's self-concept and, 7
    legitimacy and credit, 13–14, 27–28, 58
    listening in, 4–5
    in organizational setting, 118–119
    power sharing in, 6, 133–135
    psychological contract, 40–41
    role-making between, 32
    seven guiding IL practices, 38
    shared decision making, 12
    social exchange between, 55–56
    transactional (TA) leadership and, 9–10, 56, 70, 142
    transforming (TF) leadership and, 9–10
    unity of, 68, 72
Leader legitimacy, 13–14, 16
Leader-Member Exchange (LMX), 32, 70, 100, 119, 142
Leader styles, 27, 100, 120
Leaderless group discussion (LGD), 133
Leader's self-concept, 7
Leadership; see also College and university leadership; Inclusive leadership (IL); Organizational leadership; Presidential leadership; Transactional (TA) leadership; Transformational (TF) leadership
    authority relationships, 58, 62–63
    cognitive component of, 31
    conformity and, 8
    credibility and accountability, 52–53
    crisis of, 47–49
    defined, 55
    dynamic realities of, 26
    effectiveness of, 58
    elected vs. appointed leaders, 27–28, 34–35
    flexibility in style of, 9
    followers and, 3–4, 130
    gender and, 69
    headship vs., 4, 52
    historical overview of, 49–50
    idiosyncrasy credit (IC) model of, 14–16
    influence relationship of, 58
    leader-centric conceptions of, 3
    as learning process, 47
    legitimacy and authority, 51–52, 60–61
    management and, 100–101
    new vs. old view on, 22–24

SUBJECT INDEX | 261

in organizations, 117–118
perception within groups, 61–62
power and, 3, 58
relational features of, 139–142
relational qualities of, 69–70
student leadership, 96–98
substitutes for, 195
tangible/intangible rewards in, 13
as transaction, 50–51
women and, 73–79
Leadership organization, 47, 195
Leadership processes, 59
contemporary analysis of, 55–57
situational view of, 58–59
Leadership qualities, 3
becoming vs. performing, 21
qualities by stages, 82–83
Leadership research
challenges to, 126–127
contingency models, 27–28, 49
historical background of, 21–22, 49–50
individual and the situation, 25–28, 49
new vs. old views, 22–24
perceptions of performance, 30
perceptual attributional conceptions, 21
power and influence, 28–29
situational approach, 21, 26–27, 49
style and substance, 30–32
trait approaches, 21, 24–25, 49
transactional and social exchange models, 32–33, 49
Legitimacy, 18, 27, 34, 51–52, 139
as basis of authority, 85
features and effect of, 143–146
leader legitimacy, 13–14, 16
legitimate power, 29
social exchange in leadership, 60–61
as source for leading, 37, 119
Locus of leadership, 23
Loyalty, 5, 38, 130, 149

## M

Machiavellianism, 82–83
Management, 100–101
Managerial types, 31
Meaning makers, 141
Mentoring, 124–125
Milgram's obedience to authority study, 21, 178, 180
Misleaders, 13, 22, 150
Modeling, 124–125
Moral values, 6–7, 158
Motivation, 165–166
Movement conformity, 177–178

Mutual dependency, 96
Mutual identification, 153

## N

Nonconformity
defined, 174
psychology of, 171–172
research on, 172–173, 182–183, 187
situational bases for, 179
social exchange and, 181–182
social response and, 175–176
Noninclusion, 195–197
Norms, 165–166

## O

Organizational culture, 31, 120
leader style and, 120
Organizational leadership
barriers to empowerment, 123–124
career development and, 124–125
culture and leader style, 120
importance of, 130
informal influence, 125–126
interpersonal and group processes, 131
interpersonal relations, 129–131
leader-follower roles, 118–119, 133–135
leader's legitimacy of, 119
modeling and mentoring, 124–125
newer developments/orientations, 120–121
power, role of, 121–123
research challenges, 126–127
situational approach, 131–133
transactional approaches, 119–120

## P

Participation in decision making (PDM), 121–122
Participative leadership, 3, 117, 126
Passivity of followers, 4
Pay gap, 73
Perceptiveness, 87
Perceptual attributional conceptions, 21
Performance
images vs., 115
leader performance, 154–155
perceptions of, 30
performance indicators, 57
performance over time, 38–39
Personality traits, 61, 105
conformity and, 179–181
Pluralistic ignorance, 190

Political leadership, 64, 158
Power, 3, 14, 28–29, 130, 139
    corrupting influences of, 133, 152
    distributing power, 122–123
    ethical issues in leadership, 149–151
    identification and, 152
    influence vs., 29, 141
    in leader-follower relationship, 133–135
    metamorphoses of power, 119, 133, 152
    mutual dependency and, 96
    in organization, 118, 121–123, 127
Power distance, 10–12, 29, 149, 152
Power over people, 198
Power sharing, 6, 117, 121–122
Presidential leadership, 103–116
    as commander-in-chief, 103
    economic issues, 108
    identification, perception, voting behavior, 110–111
    idiosyncrasy credit concept, 106
    images vs. performance, 115–116
    impression management, 112
    inclusive leadership and, 106
    international issues, 107–108
    the mandate, 113–114
    multiple roles of, 104–105
    party loyalty, 108–110
    party, popularity, promise, performance, 104–105
    policy making, 114
    popularity, 112
    post-election surveys, 107–110
    promise and performance, 112–113
    social exchange, 106
    social psychological perspective, 105–106
    transactional view of, 106
Presidential partisanship, 108
Psychological contract, 40–41

## Q

Quality circles, 121

## R

Recognition, 3, 5, 38, 195
Reference group, 171
Referent power, 29
Respect, 3, 5, 38, 41, 158, 195
Responsibility, 3, 5, 11, 28, 38, 149, 190–191, 195
Responsiveness to followers, 3, 5, 34–35, 57, 195
Reward power, 29, 57, 73, 144
Roles/role conflict, 100, 165–166
"Romance of Leadership," 16, 57

## S

Self-fulfilling prophecy, 171
Self-identity, 13, 84–85
Self-monitoring, 87
Self-serving biases, 87–88, 152–153
Seniority, 143
Sex differences. see Women
Situational approaches, 21, 24, 26–27, 49, 58–59
    conformity and, 178–179
    organizational leadership, 131–133
Social conformity, 167–168
Social contract, 11
Social exchange, 32, 37, 55–57
    conformity-nonconformity and, 173, 181–182, 188–189
    fair exchange, 39–41
    gender differences in, 75–76
    independence and, 188–189
    leadership as transaction, 50–51
    legitimacy and, 60–61
    non-normativity and, 33
    organizational leadership, 119
    presidential leadership and, 106
Social identity, 171
Social reality, 171
Social response, 174
    pure anticonformity, 176
    pure conformity, 175–176
    pure independence, 176
    two-dimensional approach to, 175–177
    unidimensional approaches, 174–175
    variability/self anticonformity, 176
Social self, 87
Social stimulus values, 176
Spence-Helmreich Attitudes Toward Women Scale, 78
Status, 33–34, 60, 61, 163–164, 166
    conformity and, 164, 168–169, 182
Stereotypes, 75
Stewardship, 150
Student leadership, 96–98
Student protest movements, 97
Succession, 60–61
System progress, 40

## T

Teams, 3, 11, 31, 81, 129–130, 149, 150, 159; see also Groups
    self-managed teams, 123
    social structure/context of, 55
Theory Z, 131

Total Quality Management (TQM), 134, 153
Trait approaches, 21, 24–25, 49, 61, 118
    leader traits/follower attributions, 68–69, 118
Trait-in-situation model, 24
Transactional (TA) leadership, 9–10, 18, 30, 32, 49–51, 56, 81, 85–86, 142
    active follower and, 70
    charisma and, 135–136
    higher education setting, 99
    in organizational setting, 119–120
    presidential leadership, 106
    women and, 73
Transformational (TF) leadership, 9–10, 18, 30, 56, 81, 152
    charisma and, 18, 71, 88, 120, 135–136
    higher education setting, 99
    inclusive leadership and, 38
    women and, 73
Trust, 5, 38, 149

## U

Upward influence, 3, 67, 125

## V

Vertical dyadic linkage (VDL) model, 32
Vision, 71, 141, 156, 159

## W

Women
    in elected office, 74
    leadership/leader role and, 73–79
    performance as leader, 78–79
    social behavior and, 75–76
    transactional (TA) practice, 73
    transforming (TF) leadership and, 73